Conte...

First published in
2006 by Philip's a
division of Octopus
Publishing Group Ltd
2–4 Heron Quays
London E14 4JP
www.philips-maps.co.uk

First edition 2006
First impression 2006

Cartography by Philip's
Copyright © 2006 Philip's

Ordnance Survey®

This product includes mapping data licensed
from Ordnance Survey®, with the permission of the
Controller of Her Majesty's Stationery Office.
© Crown copyright 2006. All rights reserved.
Licence number 100011710

Data for the speed cameras provided by PocketGPSWorld.com Ltd.

Information for Tourist Attractions in England supplied by the British Tourist Authority / English Tourist Board.
Information for National Parks, Areas of Outstanding Natural Beauty, National Trails and Country Parks in
Wales supplied by the Countryside Council for Wales. Information for National Parks, Areas of Outstanding
Natural Beauty, National Trails and Country Parks in England supplied by the Countryside Agency. Data for Regional
Parks, Long Distance Footpaths and Country Parks in Scotland provided by Scottish Natural Heritage.

Gaelic name forms used in the Western Isles provided by Comhairle nan Eilean.

Data for the National Nature Reserves in England provided by English Nature. Data for the National Nature Reserves in Wales provided
by Countryside Council for Wales. Darparwyd data'n ymwneud â Gwarchodfeydd Natur Cenedlaethol Cymru gan Gyngor Cefn Gwlad Cymru.

Information on the location of National Nature Reserves in Scotland was provided by Scottish Natural Heritage.

Data for National Scenic Areas in Scotland provided by the Scottish Executive Office. Crown copyright material is reproduced with the
permission of the Controller of HMSO and the Queen's Printer for Scotland. Licence number C02W0003960.

Printed in Great Britain by Scotprint

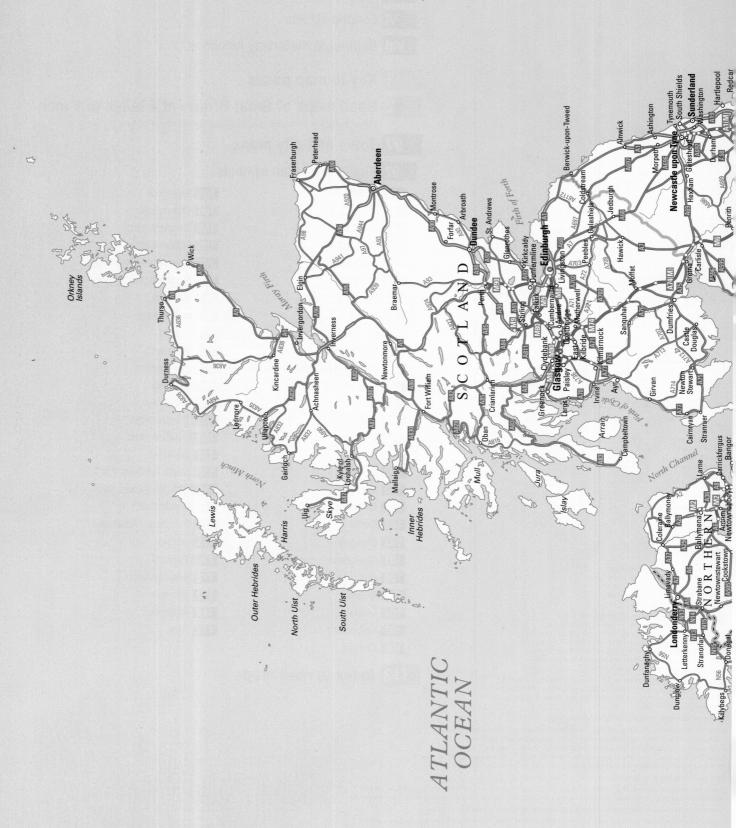

Road map symbols

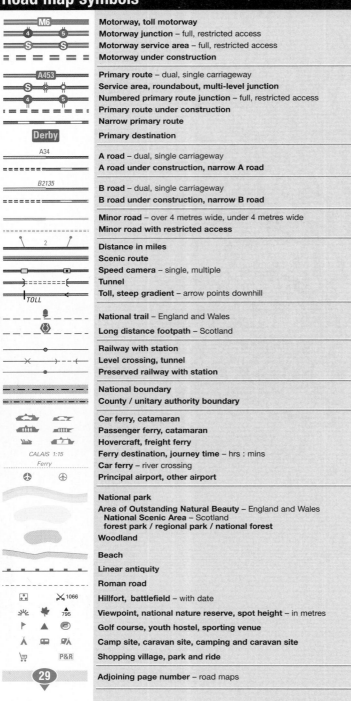

M6
Motorway, toll motorway
Motorway junction – full, restricted access
Motorway service area – full, restricted access
Motorway under construction

A453
Primary route – dual, single carriageway
Service area, roundabout, multi-level junction
Numbered primary route junction – full, restricted access
Primary route under construction
Narrow primary route

Derby
Primary destination

A34
A road – dual, single carriageway
A road under construction, narrow A road

B2135
B road – dual, single carriageway
B road under construction, narrow B road

Minor road – over 4 metres wide, under 4 metres wide
Minor road with restricted access

Distance in miles
Scenic route
Speed camera – single, multiple
Tunnel
Toll, steep gradient – arrow points downhill

National trail – England and Wales
Long distance footpath – Scotland

Railway with station
Level crossing, tunnel
Preserved railway with station

National boundary
County / unitary authority boundary

Car ferry, catamaran
Passenger ferry, catamaran
Hovercraft, freight ferry
Ferry destination, journey time – hrs : mins
CALAIS 1:15
Ferry
Car ferry – river crossing
Principal airport, other airport

National park
Area of Outstanding Natural Beauty – England and Wales
 National Scenic Area – Scotland
 forest park / regional park / national forest
Woodland

Beach
Linear antiquity
Roman road

Hillfort, battlefield – with date
Viewpoint, national nature reserve, spot height – in metres
Golf course, youth hostel, sporting venue
Camp site, caravan site, camping and caravan site
Shopping village, park and ride

29
Adjoining page number – road maps

Tourist information

† Abbey / cathedral / priory	⚓ Historic ship	ℹ Tourist information centre – open all year
🏛 Ancient monument	🏠 House	ℹ Tourist information centre – open seasonally
🐠 Aquarium	🏡 House and garden	
🏛 Art gallery	🏁 Motor racing circuit	🦁 Zoo
🦅 Bird collection / aviary	🏛 Museum	✦ Other place of interest
🏰 Castle	Ⓟ Picnic area	
⛪ Church	🚂 Preserved railway	
🌳 Country park – England and Wales	🏇 Race course	**Relief**
🐾 Country park – Scotland	🏛 Roman antiquity	
🐎 Farm park	⛲ Safari park	
🌸 Garden	🎡 Theme park	

Relief

	Feet	metres
	3000	914
	2600	792
	2200	671
	1800	549
	1400	427
	1000	305
	0	0

Road map scale: 1: 265 320, 4·2 miles to 1 inch

0 1 2 3 4 5 6 7 8 9 miles

0 1 2 3 4 5 6 7 8 9 10 11 12 13 14 15 km

Route-finding system

Town names printed in yellow on a green background are those used on Britain's signposts to indicate primary destinations. To find your route quickly and easily, simply follow the signs to the primary destination immediately beyond the place you require.

Below Driving from St Ives to Camborne, follow the signs to Redruth, the first primary destination beyond Camborne. These will indicate the most direct main route to the side turning for Camborne.

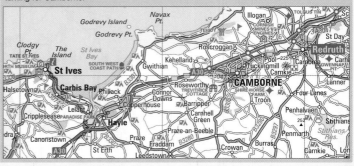

Speed Cameras

Fixed camera locations are shown using the ☐ symbol.

In congested areas the ▣ symbol is used to show that there are two or more cameras on the road indicated.

Due to the restrictions of scale the camera locations are only approximate and cannot indicate the operating direction of the camera. Mobile camera sites, and cameras located on roads not included on the mapping are not shown. Where two or more cameras are shown on the same road, drivers are warned that this may indicate that a SPEC system is in operation. These cameras use the time taken to drive between the two camera positions to calculate the speed of the vehicle.

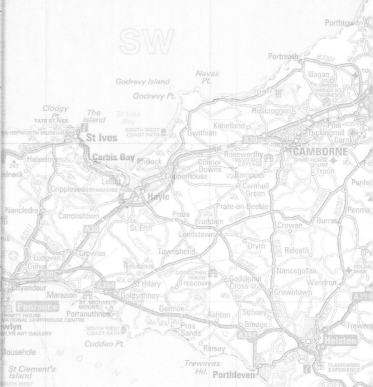

Distance table

How to use this table

Distances are shown in miles and, in *italics*, kilometres.
For example, the distance between Aberdeen and Bournemouth is 564 miles or *908* kilometres.

	London	Aberdeen	Aberystwyth	Ayr	Berwick-upon-Tweed	Birmingham	Blackpool	Bournemouth	Braemar	Brighton	Bristol	Cambridge	Cardiff	Carlisle	Doncaster	Dover	Dundee	Edinburgh	Exeter	Fishguard	Fort William	Glasgow	Gloucester	Great Yarmouth	Harwich	Holyhead	Inverness	John o' Groats	Kingston upon Hull	Kyle of Lochalsh	Land's End	Leeds	Leicester	Lincoln	Liverpool	Manchester	Newcastle upon Tyne	Norwich	Nottingham	Oban	Oxford	Plymouth	Portsmouth	Sheffield	Shrewsbury	Southampton	Stranraer	Swansea
Aberdeen	517 / *832*																																														
Aberystwyth	211 / *340*	445 / *716*																																													
Ayr	394 / *634*	183 / *295*	317 / *510*																																												
Berwick-upon-Tweed	352 / *567*	182 / *293*	311 / *501*	134 / *216*																																											
Birmingham	117 / *188*	420 / *676*	114 / *183*	289 / *465*	274 / *441*																																										
Blackpool	226 / *364*	308 / *496*	153 / *246*	180 / *290*	181 / *291*	123 / *198*																																									
Bournemouth	107 / *172*	564 / *908*	207 / *333*	436 / *702*	412 / *663*	147 / *237*	270 / *435*																																								
Braemar	482 / *776*	59 / *95*	405 / *652*	143 / *230*	148 / *238*	385 / *620*	281 / *452*	524 / *843*																																							
Brighton	52 / *84*	573 / *922*	253 / *407*	446 / *718*	409 / *658*	163 / *262*	286 / *460*	92 / *148*	534 / *859*																																						
Bristol	122 / *196*	493 / *793*	125 / *201*	370 / *595*	362 / *583*	81 / *130*	204 / *328*	82 / *132*	477 / *768*	147 / *237*																																					
Cambridge	54 / *87*	471 / *758*	214 / *344*	357 / *575*	306 / *493*	100 / *161*	208 / *335*	154 / *248*	438 / *705*	116 / *187*	169 / *272*																																				
Cardiff	157 / *253*	505 / *813*	105 / *169*	382 / *615*	368 / *592*	103 / *166*	209 / *336*	117 / *188*	483 / *778*	182 / *293*	45 / *72*	190 / *306*																																			
Carlisle	301 / *484*	221 / *356*	224 / *360*	93 / *150*	87 / *140*	196 / *315*	87 / *140*	343 / *552*	196 / *316*	370 / *596*	277 / *446*	264 / *425*	289 / *465*																																		
Doncaster	171 / *275*	344 / *554*	176 / *283*	235 / *378*	184 / *296*	94 / *151*	94 / *151*	235 / *378*	310 / *499*	236 / *380*	175 / *282*	116 / *187*	209 / *336*	142 / *229*																																	
Dover	71 / *114*	588 / *947*	297 / *478*	478 / *769*	424 / *683*	194 / *312*	312 / *502*	174 / *280*	553 / *890*	82 / *132*	202 / *325*	125 / *201*	238 / *383*	389 / *626*	242 / *390*																																
Dundee	448 / *721*	67 / *108*	376 / *605*	117 / *188*	113 / *182*	349 / *562*	239 / *385*	495 / *797*	52 / *84*	517 / *832*	430 / *692*	406 / *654*	441 / *710*	152 / *245*	275 / *443*	523 / *842*																															
Edinburgh	390 / *628*	125 / *201*	320 / *515*	73 / *117*	57 / *92*	292 / *470*	183 / *295*	439 / *707*	91 / *146*	456 / *734*	373 / *600*	345 / *555*	385 / *620*	96 / *154*	219 / *352*	462 / *744*	56 / *90*																														
Exeter	181 / *291*	569 / *916*	201 / *323*	446 / *718*	428 / *689*	157 / *253*	282 / *454*	82 / *132*	550 / *885*	184 / *296*	76 / *122*	249 / *401*	121 / *195*	353 / *568*	251 / *404*	248 / *399*	518 / *834*	450 / *724*																													
Fishguard	260 / *418*	504 / *811*	56 / *90*	373 / *600*	371 / *597*	170 / *274*	209 / *336*	222 / *357*	493 / *794*	291 / *468*	154 / *248*	270 / *435*	112 / *180*	297 / *478*	247 / *398*	331 / *533*	460 / *740*	399 / *642*	230 / *370*																												
Fort William	510 / *821*	149 / *240*	430 / *692*	133 / *214*	190 / *306*	392 / *631*	296 / *476*	539 / *867*	125 / *201*	575 / *926*	486 / *782*	479 / *771*	485 / *781*	206 / *332*	357 / *575*	596 / *959*	127 / *204*	144 / *232*	560 / *901*	486 / *782*																											
Glasgow	397 / *639*	145 / *233*	320 / *515*	33 / *53*	101 / *163*	292 / *470*	183 / *295*	439 / *707*	110 / *177*	468 / *753*	373 / *600*	372 / *599*	385 / *620*	96 / *154*	249 / *401*	488 / *786*	83 / *134*	44 / *71*	449 / *723*	376 / *605*	101 / *163*																										
Gloucester	109 / *175*	468 / *753*	102 / *164*	330 / *531*	318 / *512*	56 / *90*	174 / *280*	99 / *159*	443 / *713*	159 / *256*	35 / *56*	123 / *198*	56 / *90*	247 / *398*	150 / *241*	191 / *307*	410 / *660*	349 / *562*	111 / *179*	153 / *246*	454 / *731*	346 / *557*																									
Great Yarmouth	128 / *206*	517 / *832*	294 / *473*	402 / *647*	345 / *555*	180 / *290*	252 / *406*	240 / *386*	477 / *768*	180 / *290*	275 / *443*	82 / *132*	284 / *457*	320 / *515*	167 / *269*	185 / *298*	484 / *779*	386 / *621*	335 / *539*	366 / *589*	527 / *848*	419 / *674*	225 / *362*																								
Harwich	76 / *122*	535 / *861*	281 / *452*	425 / *684*	372 / *599*	167 / *269*	275 / *443*	187 / *301*	504 / *811*	128 / *206*	217 / *349*	67 / *108*	246 / *396*	336 / *541*	194 / *312*	125 / *201*	469 / *755*	413 / *665*	279 / *449*	337 / *542*	543 / *874*	432 / *695*	196 / *316*	82 / *132*																							
Holyhead	269 / *433*	439 / *707*	111 / *179*	305 / *491*	311 / *501*	148 / *238*	141 / *227*	288 / *463*	426 / *686*	334 / *538*	206 / *332*	270 / *435*	216 / *348*	231 / *372*	181 / *291*	360 / *580*	394 / *634*	333 / *536*	282 / *454*	167 / *269*	438 / *705*	330 / *531*	191 / *307*	334 / *538*	349 / *562*																						
Inverness	550 / *885*	105 / *169*	486 / *782*	199 / *320*	215 / *346*	458 / *737*	348 / *560*	597 / *961*	75 / *121*	617 / *993*	539 / *867*	505 / *813*	549 / *884*	262 / *422*	383 / *617*	622 / *1001*	132 / *212*	158 / *254*	618 / *995*	542 / *872*	66 / *106*	166 / *267*	504 / *811*	553 / *890*	569 / *916*	474 / *763*																					
John o' Groats	663 / *1067*	232 / *373*	601 / *967*	328 / *528*	342 / *550*	574 / *924*	478 / *769*	724 / *1165*	202 / *325*	741 / *1193*	668 / *1075*	630 / *1014*	680 / *1094*	391 / *629*	507 / *816*	746 / *1201*	259 / *417*	285 / *459*	744 / *1197*	671 / *1080*	195 / *314*	295 / *475*	628 / *1011*	677 / *1090*	693 / *1116*	603 / *970*	129 / *208*																				
Kingston upon Hull	184 / *296*	364 / *586*	223 / *359*	251 / *404*	185 / *298*	134 / *216*	127 / *204*	264 / *425*	327 / *526*	245 / *394*	233 / *375*	139 / *224*	244 / *393*	158 / *254*	47 / *76*	256 / *412*	295 / *475*	234 / *377*	309 / *497*	280 / *451*	369 / *594*	254 / *409*	169 / *272*	207 / *333*	196 / *316*	231 / *372*	394 / *634*	518 / *834*																			
Kyle of Lochalsh	586 / *943*	189 / *304*	499 / *803*	212 / *341*	263 / *423*	471 / *758*	372 / *599*	618 / *995*	159 / *256*	651 / *1048*	552 / *888*	555 / *893*	564 / *908*	275 / *443*	432 / *695*	671 / *1080*	186 / *299*	216 / *348*	628 / *1011*	567 / *913*	79 / *127*	179 / *288*	528 / *850*	602 / *969*	611 / *983*	514 / *827*	84 / *135*	189 / *304*	445 / *716*																		
Land's End	297 / *478*	692 / *1114*	313 / *504*	570 / *917*	552 / *888*	281 / *452*	405 / *652*	205 / *330*	665 / *1070*	308 / *496*	200 / *322*	374 / *602*	245 / *394*	477 / *768*	374 / *602*	381 / *613*	642 / *1033*	574 / *924*	123 / *198*	353 / *568*	686 / *1104*	573 / *922*	235 / *378*	446 / *718*	390 / *628*	405 / *652*	741 / *1193*	868 / *1397*	421 / *678*	763 / *1228*																	
Leeds	189 / *304*	327 / *526*	169 / *272*	212 / *341*	156 / *251*	113 / *182*	72 / *116*	255 / *410*	293 / *472*	260 / *419*	194 / *312*	145 / *233*	232 / *373*	119 / *192*	29 / *47*	260 / *418*	258 / *415*	202 / *325*	270 / *435*	237 / *381*	329 / *530*	215 / *346*	174 / *280*	196 / *315*	223 / *359*	176 / *283*	360 / *579*	487 / *784*	55 / *89*	394 / *634*	405 / *652*																
Leicester	97 / *156*	414 / *666*	153 / *246*	299 / *481*	252 / *406*	39 / *63*	140 / *225*	158 / *254*	389 / *626*	166 / *267*	120 / *193*	68 / *109*	154 / *248*	206 / *332*	74 / *119*	185 / *298*	349 / *562*	296 / *476*	196 / *315*	209 / *336*	422 / *679*	314 / *505*	85 / *137*	140 / *225*	147 / *237*	190 / *306*	461 / *742*	588 / *947*	102 / *164*	500 / *805*	320 / *515*	95 / *153*															
Lincoln	131 / *211*	383 / *616*	199 / *320*	274 / *441*	224 / *360*	90 / *145*	128 / *206*	209 / *336*	357 / *575*	197 / *317*	183 / *295*	85 / *137*	208 / *335*	191 / *307*	39 / *63*	202 / *325*	314 / *505*	258 / *415*	247 / *398*	272 / *438*	399 / *642*	291 / *468*	159 / *256*	128 / *206*	155 / *249*	216 / *348*	427 / *687*	554 / *892*	44 / *71*	476 / *766*	371 / *597*	68 / *109*	51 / *82*														
Liverpool	202 / *325*	341 / *549*	104 / *167*	213 / *343*	219 / *352*	93 / *150*	49 / *79*	234 / *377*	318 / *512*	272 / *438*	161 / *259*	194 / *312*	169 / *272*	120 / *193*	86 / *138*	299 / *481*	286 / *460*	216 / *348*	237 / *381*	160 / *257*	329 / *530*	216 / *348*	140 / *225*	240 / *386*	265 / *427*	102 / *164*	382 / *615*	511 / *822*	130 / *209*	407 / *655*	361 / *581*	75 / *121*	130 / *209*	129 / *208*													
Manchester	185 / *298*	340 / *547*	129 / *208*	212 / *341*	196 / *315*	80 / *129*	48 / *77*	227 / *365*	318 / *512*	257 / *414*	161 / *259*	165 / *266*	183 / *295*	119 / *192*	61 / *98*	276 / *444*	285 / *459*	215 / *346*	236 / *380*	197 / *317*	329 / *530*	215 / *346*	126 / *203*	212 / *341*	228 / *367*	124 / *200*	373 / *600*	500 / *805*	95 / *153*	406 / *654*	361 / *581*	40 / *64*	92 / *148*	84 / *135*	35 / *56*												
Newcastle upon Tyne	286 / *460*	235 / *378*	257 / *414*	149 / *240*	64 / *103*	207 / *333*	129 / *208*	347 / *558*	201 / *323*	352 / *567*	299 / *481*	241 / *388*	325 / *523*	57 / *92*	114 / *183*	358 / *576*	166 / *267*	110 / *177*	364 / *586*	329 / *529*	253 / *407*	148 / *238*	266 / *428*	281 / *452*	308 / *496*	272 / *438*	268 / *431*	395 / *636*	132 / *212*	318 / *512*	498 / *802*	92 / *148*	187 / *301*	159 / *256*	168 / *270*	132 / *212*											
Norwich	114 / *183*	496 / *798*	276 / *444*	382 / *615*	328 / *528*	166 / *267*	232 / *373*	214 / *344*	457 / *735*	175 / *282*	252 / *406*	62 / *100*	262 / *422*	289 / *465*	147 / *237*	174 / *280*	422 / *679*	366 / *589*	308 / *496*	343 / *552*	504 / *811*	385 / *620*	204 / *328*	20 / *32*	73 / *117*	311 / *501*	529 / *852*	654 / *1053*	149 / *240*	582 / *937*	421 / *678*	176 / *283*	119 / *192*	105 / *169*	220 / *354*	185 / *298*	264 / *425*										
Nottingham	122 / *196*	393 / *633*	164 / *264*	274 / *441*	221 / *356*	50 / *80*	111 / *179*	183 / *295*	353 / *568*	193 / *311*	145 / *233*	83 / *134*	172 / *277*	194 / *312*	43 / *69*	205 / *330*	328 / *528*	262 / *422*	221 / *356*	220 / *354*	401 / *646*	293 / *472*	110 / *177*	153 / *246*	150 / *241*	185 / *298*	430 / *692*	557 / *896*	90 / *145*	479 / *771*	345 / *555*	70 / *113*	25 / *40*	35 / *56*	98 / *158*	73 / *118*	157 / *253*	130 / *209*									
Oban	499 / *803*	178 / *286*	412 / *663*	94 / *151*	180 / *290*	384 / *618*	285 / *459*	530 / *853*	141 / *227*	565 / *910*	465 / *748*	468 / *753*	477 / *768*	188 / *303*	346 / *557*	585 / *942*	117 / *188*	123 / *198*	549 / *884*	481 / *774*	49 / *79*	92 / *148*	441 / *710*	515 / *829*	524 / *843*	427 / *687*	117 / *188*	244 / *393*	346 / *557*	128 / *206*	665 / *1070*	307 / *494*	419 / *674*	387 / *623*	308 / *496*	307 / *494*	233 / *375*	492 / *792*	390 / *628*								
Oxford	57 / *92*	483 / *777*	154 / *248*	353 / *568*	324 / *521*	64 / *103*	187 / *301*	90 / *145*	465 / *749*	108 / *174*	74 / *119*	83 / *134*	108 / *174*	260 / *418*	145 / *233*	141 / *227*	433 / *697*	372 / *599*	156 / *251*	205 / *330*	472 / *760*	356 / *573*	52 / *84*	200 / *322*	145 / *233*	238 / *383*	532 / *856*	656 / *1056*	192 / *309*	550 / *885*	274 / *441*	168 / *270*	73 / *117*	137 / *221*	172 / *277*	144 / *232*	260 / *418*	145 / *233*	109 / *175*	462 / *744*							
Plymouth	218 / *351*	615 / *990*	237 / *382*	492 / *792*	474 / *763*	203 / *327*	328 / *528*	128 / *206*	587 / *945*	224 / *361*	122 / *196*	293 / *472*	167 / *269*	399 / *642*	297 / *478*	300 / *483*	552 / *888*	496 / *798*	46 / *74*	264 / *425*	595 / *958*	495 / *797*	157 / *253*	365 / *588*	309 / *497*	328 / *528*	664 / *1069*	790 / *1271*	355 / *571*	674 / *1085*	89 / *143*	316 / *509*	242 / *389*	293 / *472*	283 / *455*	283 / *455*	410 / *660*	343 / *552*	267 / *430*	587 / *945*	199 / *320*						
Portsmouth	70 / *113*	560 / *901*	222 / *357*	430 / *692*	401 / *645*	141 / *227*	264 / *425*	52 / *84*	547 / *881*	48 / *77*	97 / *156*	144 / *232*	142 / *229*	348 / *560*	234 / *377*	130 / *209*	514 / *827*	453 / *729*	135 / *217*	251 / *404*	555 / *893*	448 / *721*	119 / *192*	221 / *356*	166 / *267*	311 / *501*	613 / *987*	737 / *1186*	269 / *433*	633 / *1019*	259 / *417*	257 / *414*	162 / *261*	201 / *323*	254 / *409*	236 / *380*	337 / *542*	207 / *333*	191 / *307*	545 / *877*	77 / *124*	176 / *283*					
Sheffield	159 / *256*	360 / *579*	159 / *256*	245 / *394*	190 / *306*	76 / *122*	86 / *138*	216 / *348*	320 / *515*	226 / *364*	161 / *259*	120 / *193*	194 / *312*	152 / *245*	18 / *29*	245 / *394*	291 / *468*	235 / *378*	237 / *381*	215 / *346*	348 / *560*	248 / *399*	126 / *203*	166 / *267*	187 / *301*	168 / *270*	393 / *632*	520 / *837*	65 / *105*	427 / *687*	361 / *581*	33 / *53*	62 / *100*	46 / *74*	72 / *116*	38 / *61*	125 / *201*	146 / *235*	37 / *60*	339 / *546*	135 / *217*	283 / *455*	230 / *370*				
Shrewsbury	160 / *258*	399 / *642*	77 / *124*	269 / *433*	265 / *426*	45 / *72*	98 / *158*	185 / *298*	371 / *597*	226 / *364*	103 / *166*	159 / *256*	111 / *179*	176 / *283*	109 / *175*	251 / *404*	330 / *531*	274 / *441*	179 / *288*	145 / *233*	382 / *615*	272 / *438*	77 / *124*	225 / *362*	240 / *386*	113 / *182*	438 / *705*	567 / *912*	169 / *272*	451 / *726*	303 / *488*	109 / *175*	84 / *135*	133 / *214*	58 / *93*	69 / *111*	201 / *323*	205 / *330*	93 / *150*	364 / *586*	106 / *171*	225 / *362*	207 / *333*	82 / *132*			
Southampton	77 / *124*	547 / *880*	201 / *323*	417 / *671*	388 / *624*	128 / *206*	251 / *404*	31 / *50*	532 / *856*	61 / *98*	76 / *122*	148 / *238*	121 / *195*	324 / *521*	209 / *336*	143 / *230*	500 / *805*	438 / *705*	105 / *169*	233 / *375*	541 / *871*	433 / *697*	105 / *169*	220 / *354*	164 / *264*	293 / *472*	598 / *963*	723 / *1164*	256 / *412*	618 / *995*	228 / *367*	232 / *373*	137 / *220*	204 / *328*	239 / *385*	221 / *356*	324 / *521*	206 / *332*	176 / *283*	530 / *853*	64 / *103*	151 / *243*	21 / *34*	199 / *320*	185 / *298*		
Stranraer	402 / *647*	228 / *367*	325 / *523*	51 / *82*	170 / *274*	297 / *478*	188 / *303*	444 / *715*	194 / *312*	475 / *765*	378 / *608*	379 / *610*	390 / *628*	101 / *163*	257 / *414*	496 / *798*	167 / *269*	124 / *200*	454 / *731*	392 / *631*	195 / *314*	84 / *135*	343 / *552*	426 / *686*	410 / *660*	338 / *544*	262 / *422*	379 / *610*	259 / *417*	263 / *423*	585 / *942*	220 / *354*	330 / *531*	298 / *480*	221 / *356*	220 / *354*	158 / *254*	403 / *649*	290 / *467*	148 / *238*	379 / *610*	500 / *805*	461 / *742*	263 / *423*	277 / *446*	445 / *716*	
Swansea	194 / *312*	507 / *816*	73 / *117*	379 / *610*	383 / *616*	119 / *192*	216 / *348*	167 / *269*	505 / *813*	222 / *357*	85 / *137*	227 / *365*	41 / *66*	309 / *497*	232 / *373*	274 / *441*	473 / *761*	412 / *663*	161 / *259*	67 / *108*	496 / *798*	409 / *658*	89 / *143*	329 / *530*	267 / *430*	184 / *296*	572 / *921*	696 / *1120*	264 / *425*	594 / *956*	285 / *459*	248 / *399*	177 / *285*	233 / *375*	195 / *314*	187 / *301*	347 / *559*	301 / *485*	192 / *309*	506 / *815*	141 / *227*	206 / *332*	182 / *293*	217 / *349*	118 / *190*	161 / *259*	417 / *671*	
York	207 / *333*	319 / *513*	195 / *314*	214 / *344*	148 / *238*	130 / *209*	96 / *154*	269 / *433*	285 / *459*	275 / *443*	222 / *357*	165 / *266*	244 / *393*	121 / *195*	34 / *55*	282 / *454*	250 / *402*	194 / *312*	287 / *462*	261 / *420*	330 / *531*	217 / *349*	189 / *304*	201 / *323*	228 / *367*	204 / *328*	352 / *566*	479 / *771*	37 / *60*	407 / *655*	411 / *661*	24 / *39*	108 / *174*	75 / *121*	99 / *159*	64 / *103*	84 / *135*	181 / *291*	77 / *124*	309 / *497*	181 / *291*	333 / *536*	278 / *448*	52 / *84*	133 / *214*	258 / *415*	222 / *357*	272 / *438*

Restricted motorway junctions

M1	Northbound	Southbound
2	No exit	No access
4	No exit	No access
6a	No exit	No access
	Access from M25 only	Exit to M25 only
7	No exit	No access
	Access from M10 only	Exit to M10 only
17	No access	No exit
	Exit to M45 only	Access from M45 only
19	No exit to A14	No access from A14
21a	No access	
23a	Exit to A42 only	
24a	No exit	No access
35a	No access	No exit
43	No exit to M621 northbound	
48	No exit to A1 southbound	

M2	Eastbound	Westbound
1	Access from A2 eastbound only	Exit to A2 westbound only

M3	Eastbound	Westbound
8	No exit	No access
10	No access	No exit
13	No access to M27 eastbound	
14	No exit	No access

M4	Eastbound	Westbound
1	Exit to A4 eastbound only	Access from A4 westbound only
2	Access to A4 eastbound only	Access to A4 westbound only
21	No exit	No access
23	No access	No exit
25	No exit	No access
25a	No exit	No access
29	No exit	No access
38		No access
39	No exit or access	No exit
41	No access	No exit
41a	No exit	No access
42	Exit to A483 only	Access from A483 only
42	Access from A483 only	No access

M5	Northbound	Southbound
10	No exit	No access
11a	No access from A417 eastbound	No exit to A417 westbound

M6	Northbound	Southbound
3a	No access	No exit
	Exit to M42 northbound only	Access from M6 eastbound only
4a	No exit	No access
	Access from M42 southbnd only	Exit to M42 only
5	No access	No exit
10a	No access	No exit
	Exit to M54 only	Access from M54 only
11a	No exit / access	No access / exit
	No access M6 TOLL	
20	No exit to M56 eastbound	No access from M56 westbound
24	No exit	No access
25	No access	No exit
30	No exit	No access
	Access from M61 northbound only	Exit to M61 southbound
31a	No access	No exit

M6 Toll	Northbound	Southbound
T1		No exit
T2	No exit / access	No access
T5	No exit	No access
T7	No access	No exit
T8	No access	No exit

M8	Eastbound	Westbound
8	No exit to M73 northbound	No access from M73 southbound
9	No access	No exit
13	No exit southbound	No access
14	No access	No exit
16	No exit	No access
17	No exit	No access
18		No access
19	No exit to A814 eastbound	No access from A814 westbound
20	No exit	No access
21	No access	No exit
22	No exit	No access
	Access from M77 only	Exit to M77 only
23	No exit	No access
25	Exit to A739 northbound only	Exit to A739 northbound only
	Access from A739 southbound only	Access from A739 southbound only
25a	No exit	No access
28	No exit	No access
28a	No exit	No access

M9	Eastbound	Westbound
1a	No exit	No access
2	No access	No exit
3	No exit	No access
6	No access	No exit
8	No exit	No access

M11	Northbound	Southbound
4	No exit	No access
5	No access	No exit
9	No access	No exit
13	No access	No exit
14	No exit to A428 westbound	Access from A14 westbound only

M20	Eastbound	Westbound
2	No access	No exit
3	No exit	No access
	Access from M26 eastbound only	Exit to M26 westbound only
11a	No access	No exit

M23	Northbound	Southbound
7	No exit to A23 southbound	No access from A23 northbound
10a	No exit	No access

M25	Clockwise	Anticlockwise
5	No exit to M26 eastbound	No access from M26 westbound
19	No access	No exit
21	No exit to M1 southbound	No exit to M1 southbound
	Access from M1 southbound only	Access from M1 southbound only
31	No exit	No access

M27	Eastbound	Westbound
10	No exit	No access
12	No access	No exit

M40	Eastbound	Westbound
3	No exit	No access
7	No exit	No access
8	No exit	No access
13	No exit	No access
14	No access	No exit
16	No access	No exit

M42	Northbound	Southbound
1	No exit	No access
7	No access	No exit
	Exit to M6 northbound only	Access from M6 northbound only
7a	No access	No exit
	Exit to M6 only	Access from M6 northbound only
8	No exit	Exit to M6 northbound
	Access from M6 southbound only	Access from M6 southbound only

M45	Eastbound	Westbound
M1 junc 17	Access to M1 southbound only	No access from M1 southbound
With A45 (Dunchurch)	No access	No exit

M48	Eastbound	Westbound
M4 junc 21	No exit to M4 westbound	No access from M4 eastbound
M4 junc 23	No access from M4 westbound	No exit to M4 eastbound

M49		Southbound
18a		No exit to M5 northbound

M53	Northbound	Southbound
11	Exit to M56 eastbound only	Exit to M56 eastbnd only
	Access from M56 westbound only	Access from M56 westbound only

M56	Eastbound	Westbound
2	No exit	No access
4	No exit	No access
7		No access
8	No exit or access	No exit
9	No access from M6 northbound	No access to M6 southbound
15	No exit to M53	No access from M53 northbound

M57	Northbound	Southbound
3	No exit	No access
5	No exit	No access

M58	Eastbound	Westbound
1	No exit	No access

M60	Clockwise	Anticlockwise
2	No exit	No access
3	No exit to A34 northbound	No exit to A34 northbound
4	No access to M56	No exit to M56
5	No exit to A5103 southbound	No exit to A5103 northbound
14	No exit to A580	No access from A580
16	No exit	No access
20	No access	No exit
22		No access
25	No access	
26		No exit or access
27	No exit	No access

M61	Northbound	Southbound
2	No access from A580 eastbound	No exit to A580 westbound
3	No access from A580 eastbound	No exit to A580 westbound
	No access from A666 southbound only	
M6 junc 30	No exit to M6 southbound	No access from M6 northbound

M62	Eastbound	Westbound
23	No access	No exit

M65	Eastbound	Westbound
9	No access	No exit
11	No exit	No access

M66	Northbound	Southbound
1	No access	No exit

M67	Eastbound	Westnd
1a	No access	No exit
2	No exit	No access

M69	Northbound	Southbound
2	No exit	No access

M73	Northbound	Southbound
2	No access from M8 or A89 eastbound	No exit to M8 or A89 westbound
	No exit to A89	No access to A89
3	Exit to A80 northbound only	Access from A80 southbound only

M74	Northbound	Southbound
2	No access	No exit
3	No exit	No access
7	No exit	No access
9	No exit or access	No access
10		No access
11	No exit	No access
12	No access	No exit

M77	Northbound	Southbound
4	No exit	No access
M8 junc 22	Exit to M8 eastbound only	Access from M8 westbound only
6	No exit	No access
7	No exit or access	
8	No access	No access

M80	Northbound	Southbound
3	No access	No exit
5	No access from M876	No exit to M876

M90	Northbound	Southbound
2a	No access	No exit
7	No exit	No access
8	No access	No exit
10	No access from A912	No exit to A912

M180	Northbound	Southbound
1	No access	No exit

M621	Eastbound	Westbound
4	No exit or access	
5	No exit	No access
6	No access	No exit

M876	Northbound	Southbound
2	No access	No exit

A1(M)	Northbound	Southbound
2	No access	No exit
3		No access
5	No exit	No access
40	No access	No exit
44	No exit, access from M1 only	Exit to M1 only
57	No access	No exit
65	No access	No exit

A3(M)	Northbound	Southbound
1		No access
4	No access	No exit

A38(M)	Northbound	Southbound
With Victoria Road (Park Circus) Birmingham	No exit	No access

A48(M)	Northbound	Southbound
M4 Junc 29	Exit to M4 eastbound only	Access from M4 westbound only
29a	Access from A48 eastbound only	Exit to A48 westbound only

A57(M)	Eastbound	Westbound
With A5103	No access	No exit
With A34	No access	No access

A58(M)		Southbound
With Park Lane and Westgate, Leeds		No access

A64(M)	Eastbound	Westbound
With A58 Clay Pit Lane, Leeds	No access	No exit
With Regent Street, Leeds	No access	No access

A74(M)	Northbound	Southbound
18	No access	No exit
22	No access	No exit

A167(M)	Northbound	Southbound
With Camden St, Newcastle	No exit	No exit or access

A194(M)	Northbound	Southbound
A1(M) junc 65 Gateshead Western Bypass	Access from A1(M) northbound only	Exit to A1(M) southbound only

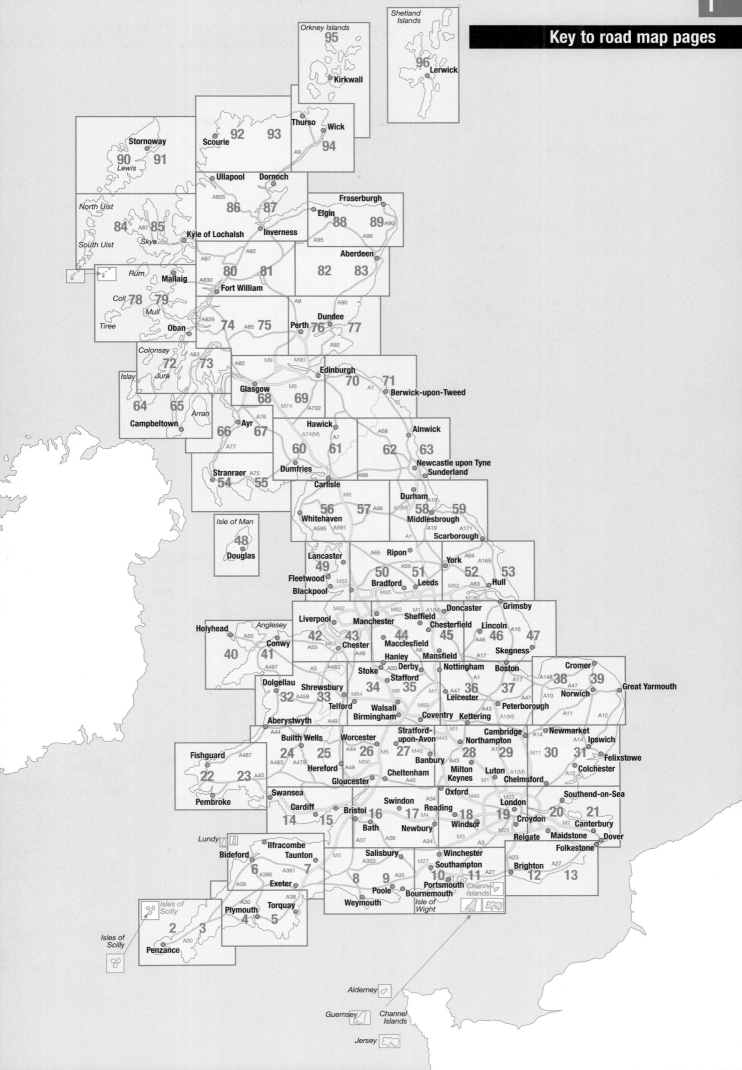

2

Isles of Scilly

SV

North West Passage

St Helens
KING CHARLES CASTLE
White Island
Bryher
St Martin's
CROMWELL'S CASTLE
New Grimsby
Higher Town
Bryher
Tresco
TRESCO ABBEY GARDENS
Crow Sound
Eastern Isles
Samson
The Road
BANT'S CARN
Newford
51
INNISIDGEN CAIRNS
Maypole
LONGSTONE HERITAGE CEN.
St Mary's
Crim Rocks
Broad Sound
Hugh Town
ST. MARY'S
GARRISON WALLS
Old Town
Annet
Smith Sound
St Mary's Sound
PENZANCE 2:40 (Apr-Nov)
St Agnes
Gugh
St Agnes
Bishop Rock

SW

CORNWALL

St Agnes Hd.
PERRANPORTH
SOUTH WEST COAST PATH
St Agnes
Trevellas
Mithia
Goont
Porthtowan
Mount Hawke
Three Burrows
Blackwater
Mawla
Portreath
Illogan
Scorrier
St Day
Roscroggan
Redruth
Godrevy Island
Navax Pt.
Kehelland
Pool
CORNISH MINES 'N ENGINES
Tuckingmill
Camborne
Gwennap
Carharrack
Gwenn
The Carracks
Clodgy Pt.
The Island
St Ives Bay
Gwithian
TATE ST IVES
SOUTH WEST COAST PATH
CAMBORNE
Lanner
Connor Downs
Roseworthy
TREVITHICK COTTAGE
SHIRE HORSE FARM
Four Lanes
The Island
Phillack
Copperhouse
Barripper
Penhalvaen
BARBARA HEPWORTH MUSEUM
St Ives
Carbis Bay
Lelant
PARADISE PARK
Carnhell Green
Stithians
Stithians Res.
Gurnard's Head
Zennor
Halsetown
Hayle
Praze
Leedstown
Crowan
Burras
Carnkie
Longdow
Porthmeor
Towednack
247
WAYSIDE FOLK MUSEUM
Nancledra
Canonstown
St Erth
Relubbus
Drym
Releath
Porkellis
Rame
Morvah
Bojewyan
CHYSAUSTER ANCIENT VILLAGE
Newmill
Townshend
GODOLPHIN HOUSE
SOUTH WEST COAST PATH
252
Higher Boscaswell
Pendeen
PENZANCE HELIPORT
Ludgvan
Crowlas
Godolphin Cross
Nancegollan
Wendron
GEEVOR TIN MINE MUSEUM
Trewellard
Madron
TRENGWAINTON
Gulval
Crowntown
A394
Botallack
Carnyorth
A3071
Heamoor PENZANCE
Chyandour
Marazion
Goldsithney
Sithney
Trewennack
Cape Cornwall
St Just
Newbridge
ST. MICHAEL'S MOUNT
Germoe
Ashton
Breage
Helston
The Bisons
BALLOWALL BARROW
LAND'S END
Bosavern
TRINITY HOUSE NATIONAL LIGHTHOUSE CENTRE
Penzance
Perranuthnoe
Praa Sands
Gweek
NATIONAL SEAL SANCTUARY
Kelynack
224
Sancreed
Res.
Tredavoe
Newlyn
Cudden Pt.
Rinsey
FLAMBARDS EXPERIENCE
Mawgan
Brane
CARN EUNY VILLAGE
Lower Drift
NEWLYN ART GALLERY
Trewavas Hd.
Garras
St Marti
Sennen Cove
Crows-an-wra
Catchall
Paul
Mousehole
Porthleven
TRELOWA
FOGU
Newtown
Sennen
St Buryan
Kerris
St Clement's Island
Porthleven Sands
The Loe
Gunwalloe
LAND'S END
Trewoofe
SOUTH WEST COAST PATH
Cury
Cross Lanes
Trat
Polgigga
Boskenna
Lamorna
MOUNT'S BAY
GOONHILLY SATELLITE EARTH STATION
Porthcurno
Treen
TREGIFFIAN BURIAL CHAMBER
Lamorna Cove
Mullion
Goonhilly Dow
St Levan
MINACK OPEN AIR THEATRE
Penhale
Trela
Gwennap Hd.
Runnel Stone
Mullion Cove
Gwen
Kuggar
Mullion Island
Mullion Cove
Predannack Wollas
St Ruan
Gwen
Longships
Whitesand Bay
Vellan Hd.
Ruan Min
Kynance Cove
Grade
Cadgwith
Llandewednock
Lizard
Hot Pt.
LIZARD POINT
Lizard

ISLES OF SCILLY 2:40 (Apr-Nov)

0 1 2 3 4 5 6 miles
0 1 2 3 4 5 6 7 8 9 10km

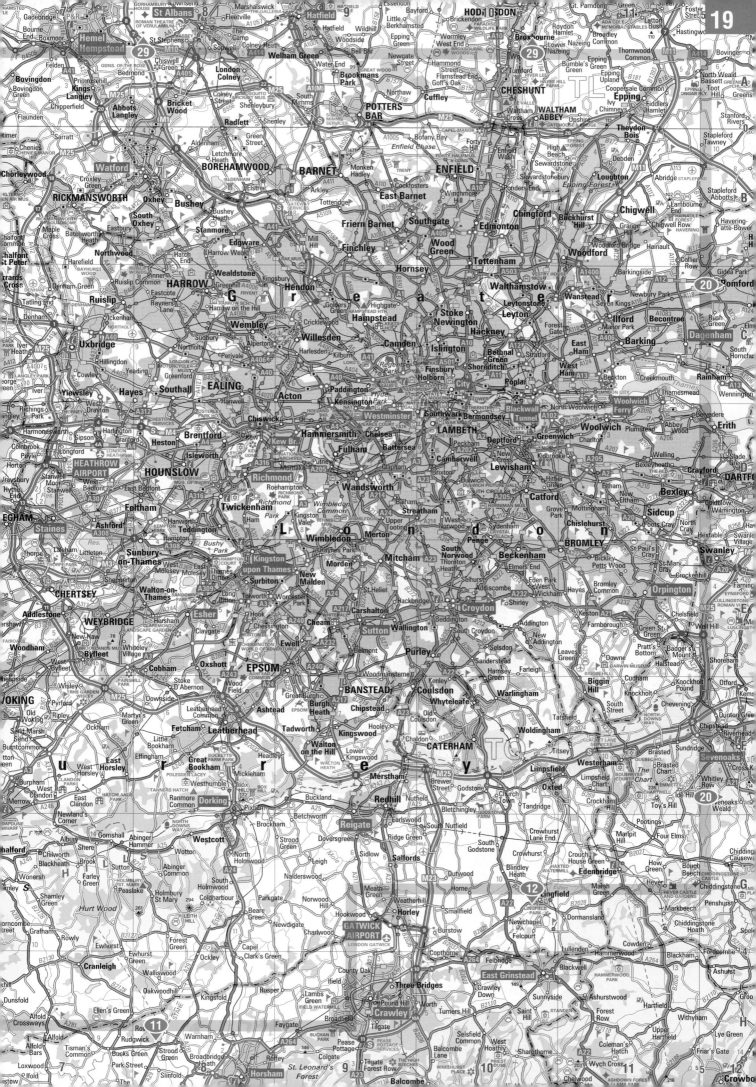

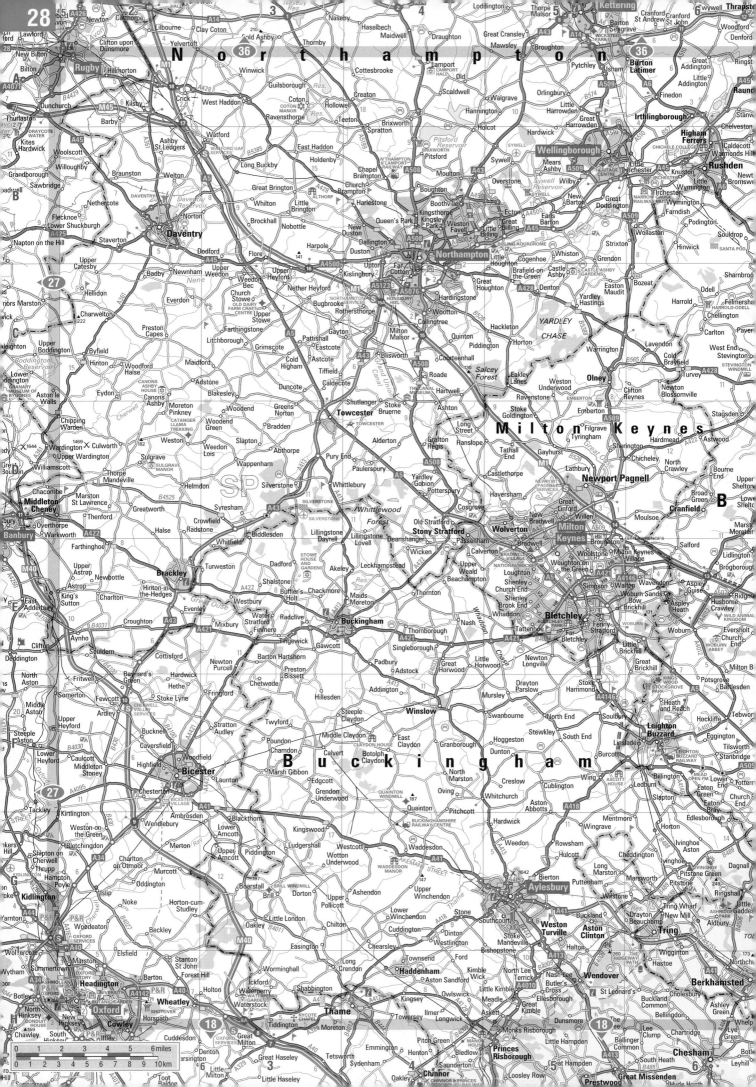

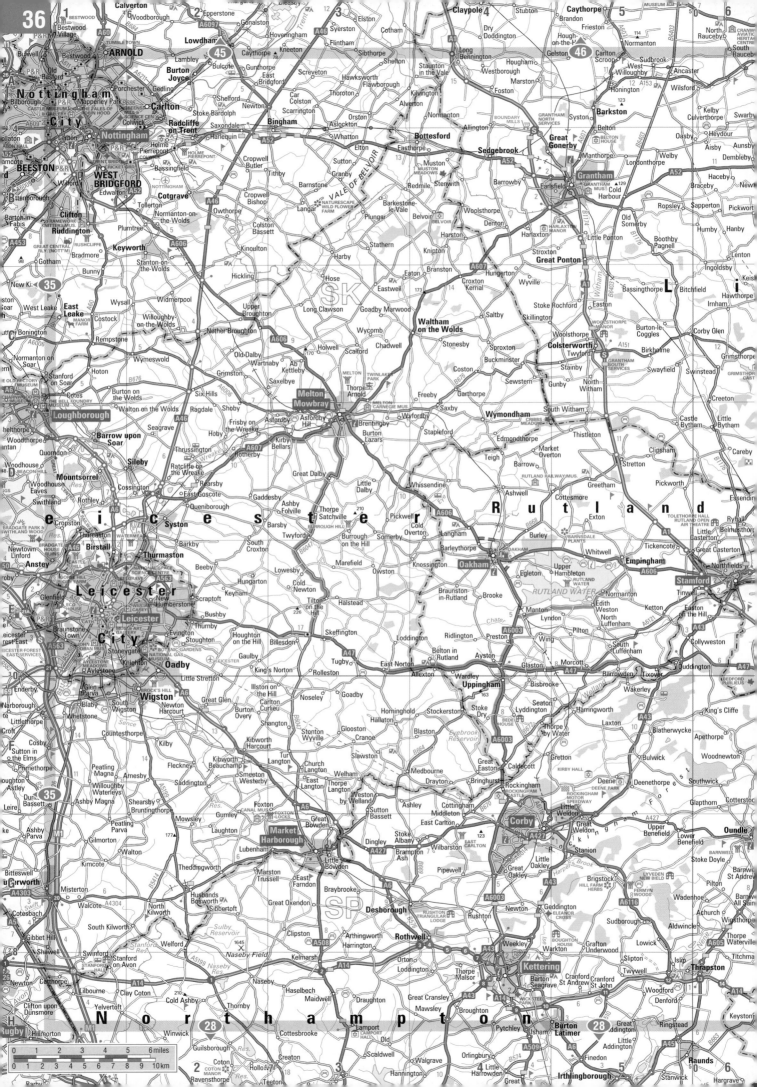

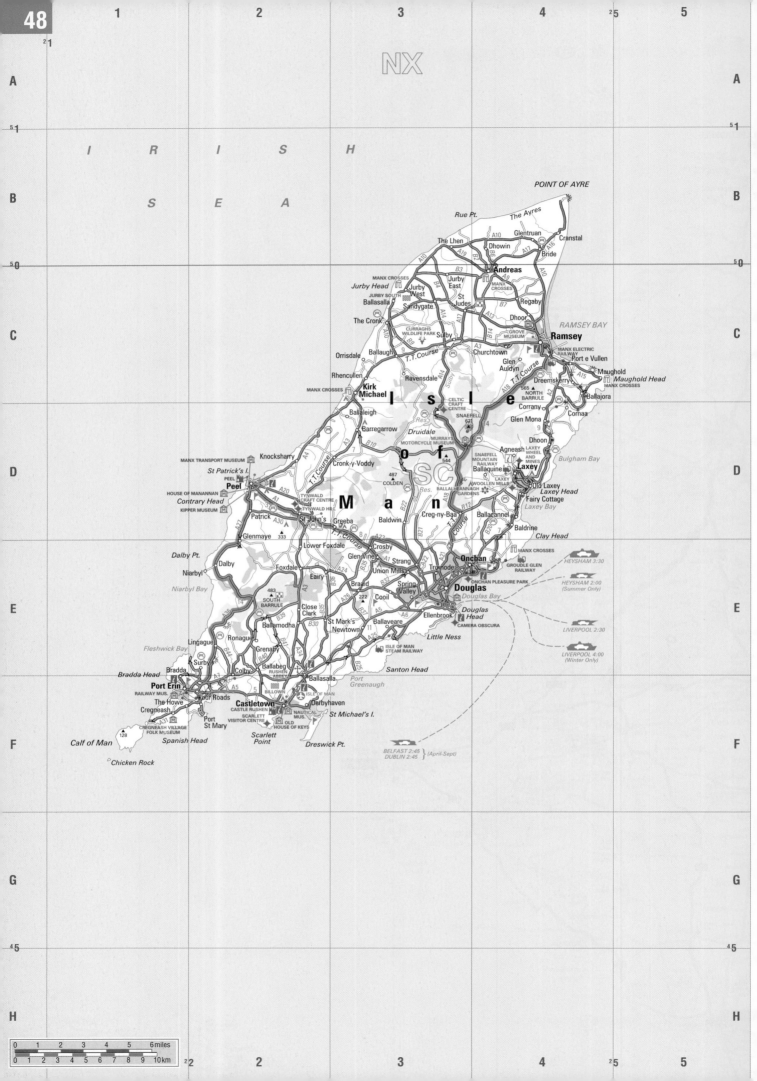

NX

IRISH

SEA

POINT OF AYRE

Rue Pt.   The Ayres

The Lhen   Glentruan   Cranstal
          Dhowin   Bride
Jurby Head   Jurby   Andreas
MANX CROSSES   East   St   Regaby
Jurby   Jurby   Judes
West   Sandygate
Ballasalla   MANX CROSSES
The Cronk   Dhoor
          CURRAGHS   RAMSEY BAY
          WILDLIFE PARK   GROVE
Orrisdale   Ballaugh   Suby   MUSEUM   Ramsey   MANX ELECTRIC
          Churchtown   RAILWAY
          T.T.Course   Glen   Port e Vullen
Rhencullen   Auldyn   Maughold
          Ravensdale   Dreemskerry   Maughold Head
MANX CROSSES   Kirk   NORTH   MANX CROSSES
          Michael   CELTIC   565   BARRULE   Ballajora
          CRAFT   Corrany
          Ballaleigh   CENTRE   Snaefell   Cornaa
          621   Glen Mona
          Barregarrow   Druidale
          MURRAYS   Dhoon
          MOTORCYCLE MUSEUM   Agneash   LAXEY
Knocksharry   SNAEFELL   WHEEL
MANX TRANSPORT MUSEUM   Cronk-y-Voddy   MOUNTAIN   AND MINES   Bulgham Bay
St Patrick's I.   544   RAILWAY   Laxey
PEEL   Ballaquine   Old Laxey
HOUSE OF MANANNAN   Peel   487   LAXEY   Laxey Head
          COLDEN   BALLAHEANNAGH   WOOLLEN MILLS   Fairy Cottage
Contrary Head   GARDENS   Laxey Bay
KIPPER MUSEUM   TYNWALD   Man
          CRAFT CENTRE   Ballacannel
          Patrick   TYNWALD HILL   Greeba   Baldrine
          St John's   Baldwin   Creg-ny-Baa   Clay Head
          Glenmaye   333   Crosby   MANX CROSSES
          Lower Foxdale   GlenVine   GROUDLE GLEN
Dalby Pt.   Dalby   Strang   Onchan   RAILWAY   HEYSHAM 3:30
          Foxdale   Union Mills   Tromode   ONCHAN PLEASURE PARK   HEYSHAM 2:00
Niarbyl   Eairy   Braaid   Spring   Douglas   (Summer Only)
Niarbyl Bay   483   222   Valley   Douglas Bay   LIVERPOOL 2:30
          SOUTH   Cooil   Ellenbrook   Douglas
          BARRULE   Close   St Mark's   Ballaveare   Head   LIVERPOOL 4:00
          Clark   Newtown   Little Ness   CAMERA OBSCURA   (Winter Only)
Fleshwick Bay   Ballamodha   ISLE OF MAN
          Lingague   Ronague   Grenaby   STEAM RAILWAY
Bradda Head   Surby   Colby   Ballabeg   Santon Head
          Bradda   RUSHEN   Ballasalla   Port
Port Erin   Four Roads   ABBEY   Greenaugh
RAILWAY MUS.   BILLOWN   ISLE OF
The Howe   Cregneash   Castletown   MAN
          Port   CASTLE RUSHEN   NAUTICAL   Derbyhaven
CREGNEASH VILLAGE   St Mary   SCARLETT   MUS.   St Michael's I.
FOLK MUSEUM   128   VISITOR CENTRE   OLD
Calf of Man   Scarlett   HOUSE OF KEYS
          Spanish Head   Point   Dreswick Pt.
Chicken Rock   BELFAST 2:45   (April-Sept)
          DUBLIN 2:45

0 1 2 3 4 5 6miles
0 1 2 3 4 5 6 7 8 9 10km

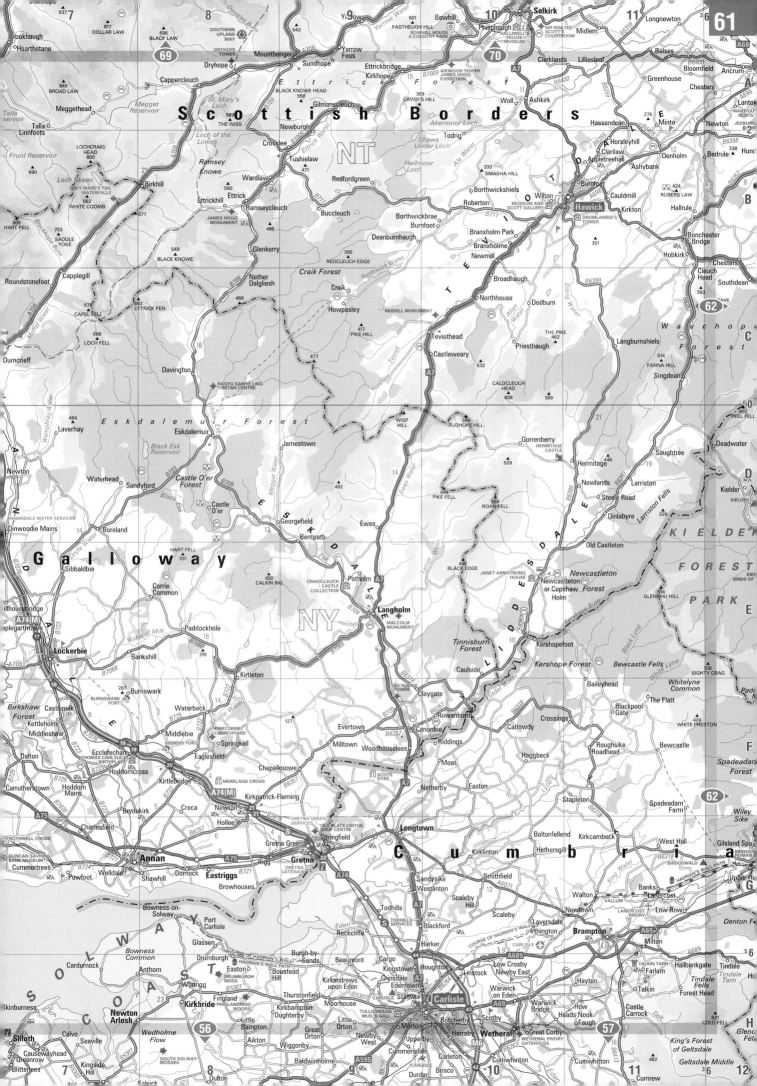

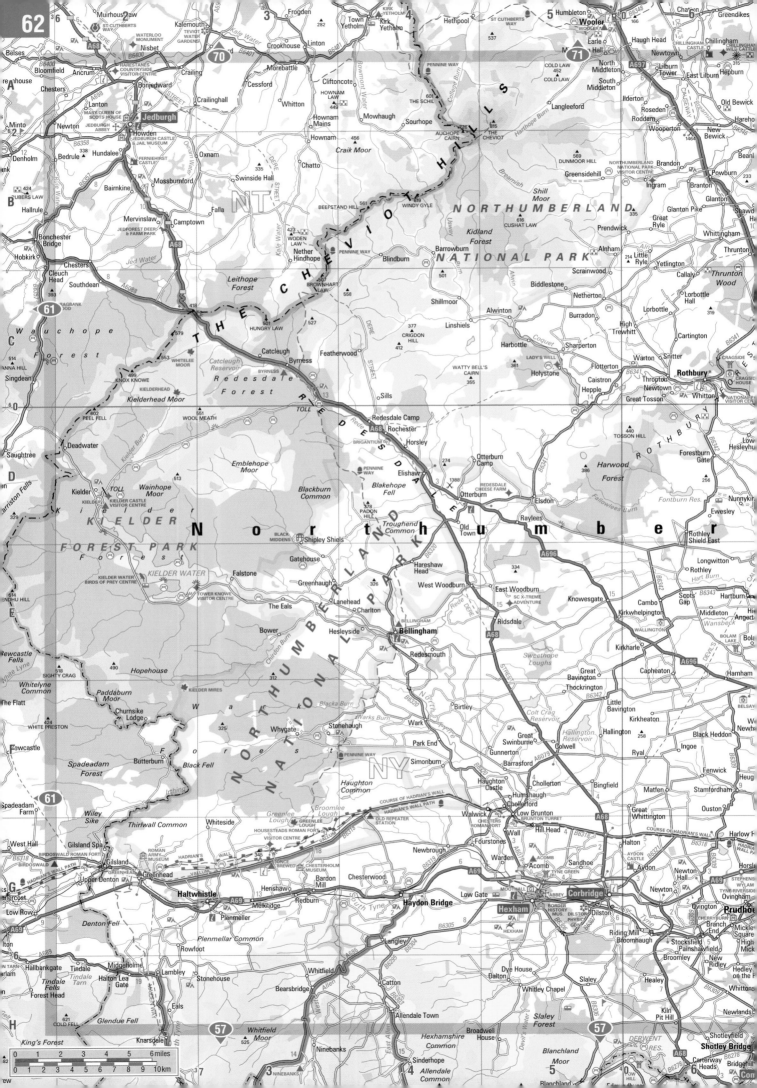

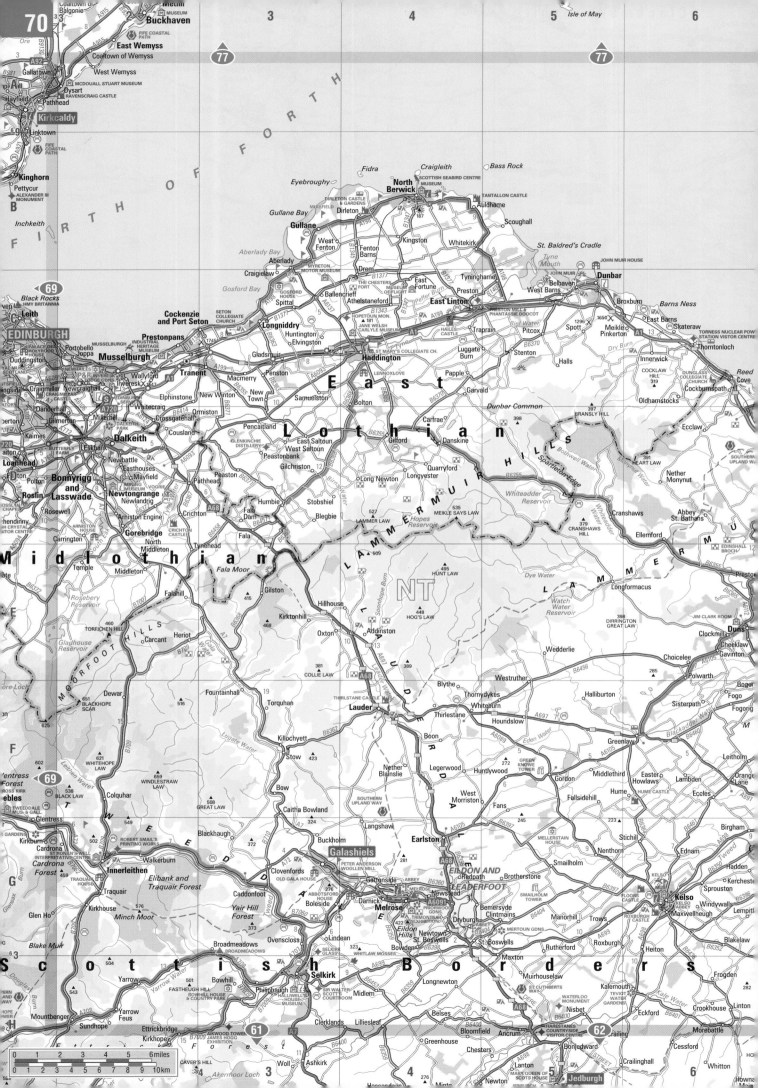

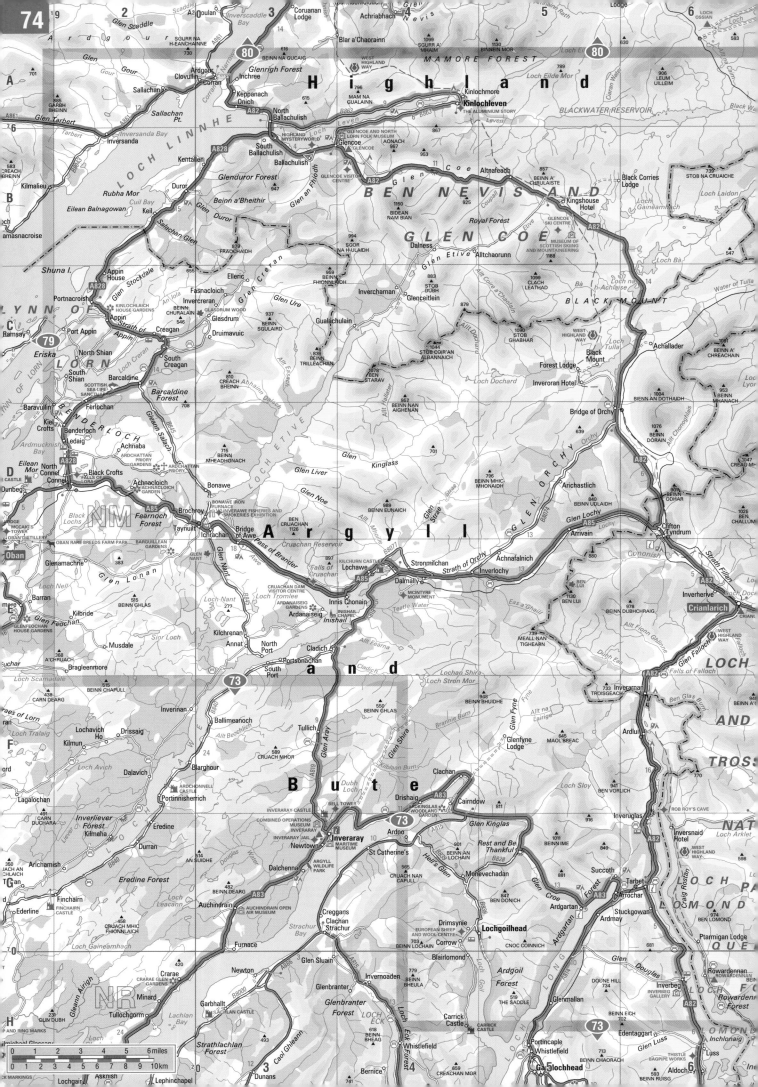

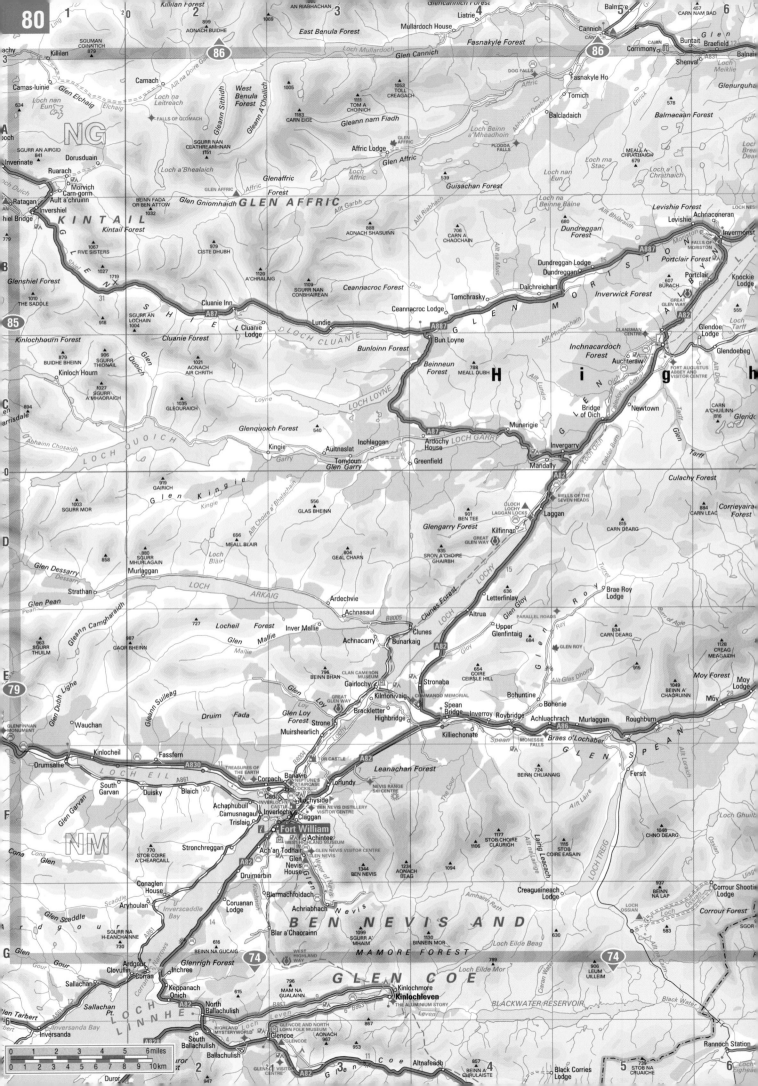

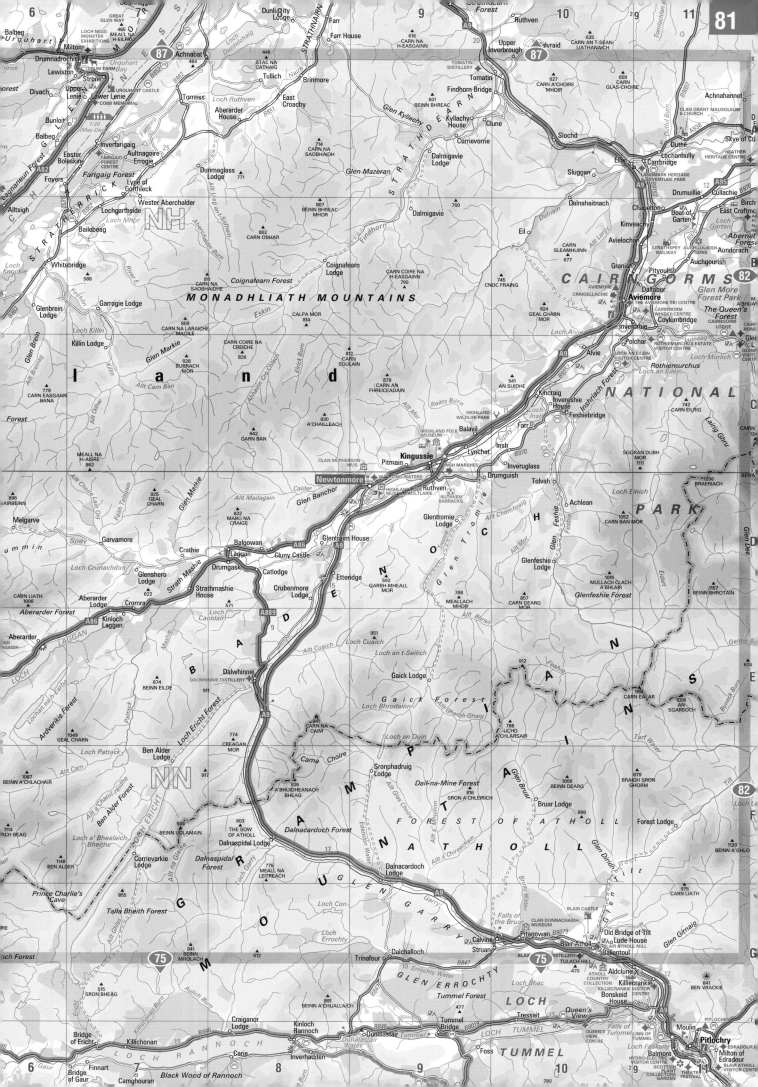

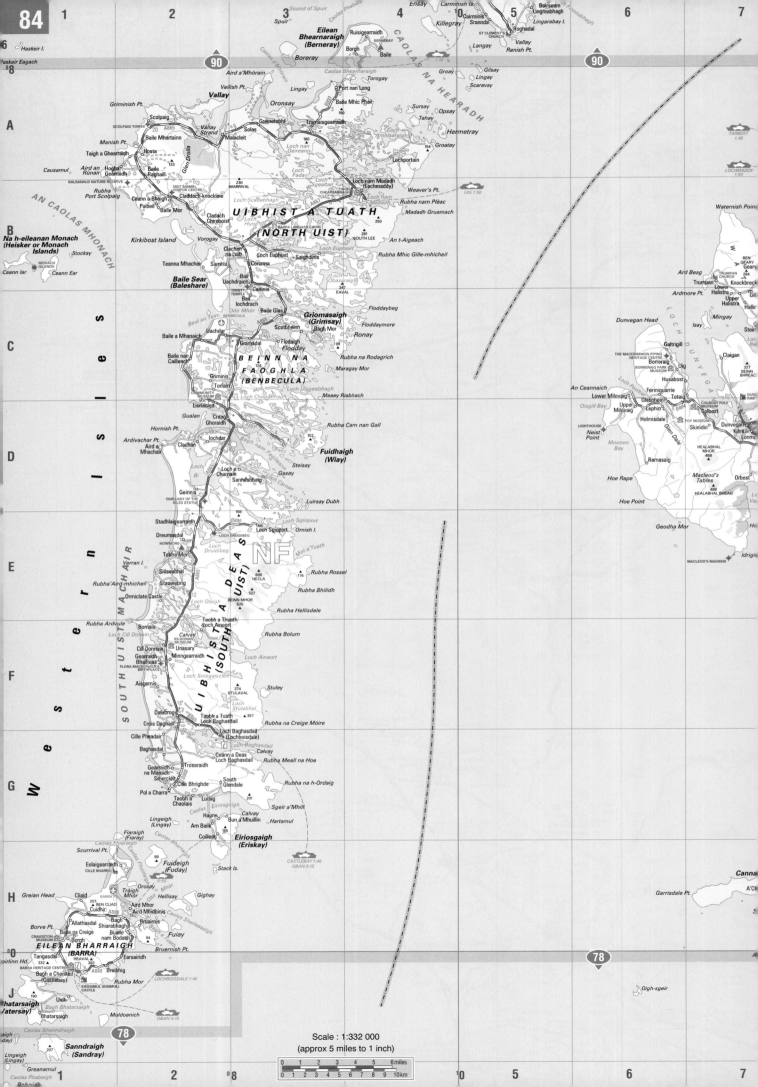

Scale : 1:332 000
(approx 5 miles to 1 inch)

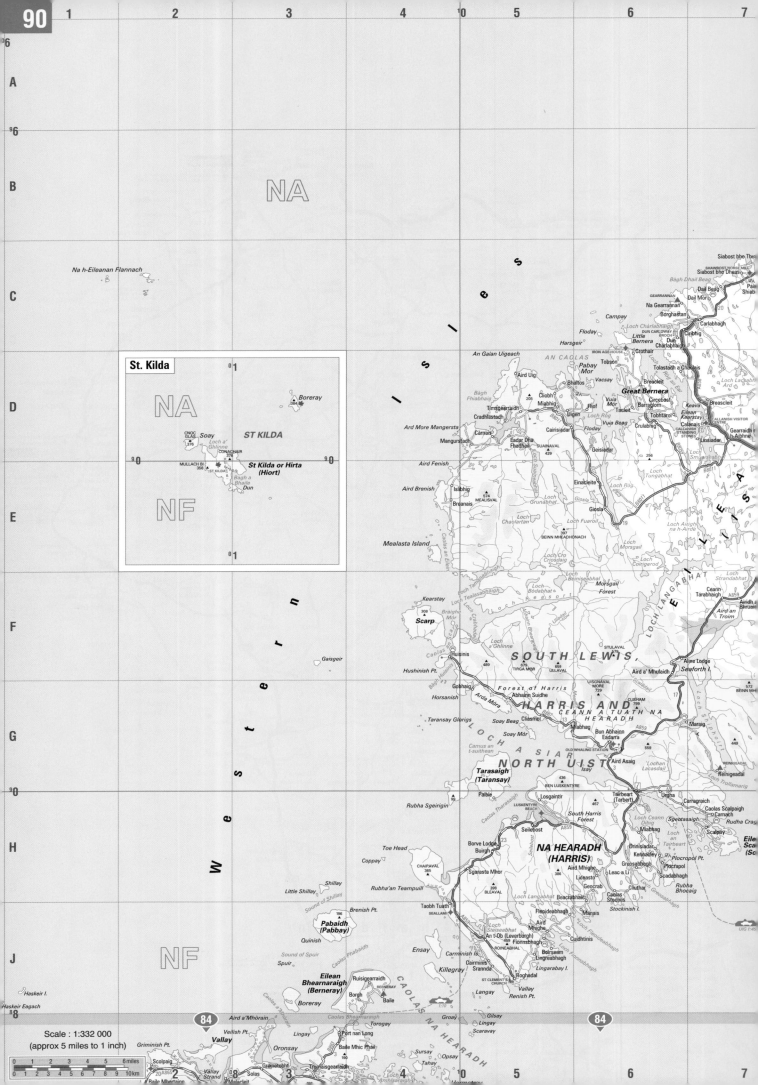

St. Kilda

NA

NF

NA

ST KILDA

Boreray

CNOC GLAS
376

Soay

Loch a' Ghlinne

CONACHAIR
376

MULLACH BI
358

ST KILDA

St Kilda or Hirta
(Hiort)

Bagh a Bhaile

Dun

NA

W e s t e r n   I s l e s

Na h-Eileanan Flannach

Gaisgeir

Scarp

Kearstay

Braighe Mor

308

Huisinis

Hushinish Pt.

Gobhaig

Horsanish

Arda Mora

Taransay Glorigs

Soay Beag

Soay Mor

Camus an t-suidhean

Tarasaigh
(Taransay)

Paible

Rubha Sgeirigin

Caolas Tharasaigh

NF

Haskeir I.

Haskeir Eagach

Siabost bho Thuas
SHAWBOST NORSE MILL
Siabost bho Dheas
Bagh Dhail Beag
Dail Beag
Dail Mor

GEARRANNAN
Na Gearrannan
Borghastan

Campay
Loch Charlabhaigh
DUN CARLOWAY BROCH
Little Bernera
Dun Charlabhaigh

Carlabhagh

Ciribhig

Floday

Harsgeir

IRON AGE HOUSE

An Galan Uigeach

Aird Uig

Pabay Mor

Vacsay

Bhaltos

Great Bernera

Breacleit

Tobson

Barraglom
Circebost

Keava

Breascleit

Bagh Fhlabhaig

Timsgearraidh

Cliobh
Miabhig

Uigen

Riof

Vuia Mor

Tobhtarol

Eilean Kearstay

Tacleit

Loch Rog

CALLANISH VISITOR CENTRE

Ard More Mangersta

Carnais

Eadar Dha Fhadhail

Cairisiadar

Floday

Crulabhig

CALLANISH STANDING STONES

Gearraidh na h-Aibhne

Mangurstadh

205

SUAINAVAL
429

Geisiadar

Vuia Beag

Linsiadar

256

Aird Fenish

Loch Suainabhal

Loch Rog

Loch Tungabhat

Aird Brenish

Islibhig

Breanais

574
MEALISVAL

Einacleite

Gisola

19

Loch Fuaroil

Loch Airigh na h-Airde

Loch Grunabhat

397

BEINN MHEADHONACH

Loch Chaolartan

Loch Morsgail

Loch Strandabhat

Mealasta Island

Loch Cro Criosdaig

Loch Bodabhat

Morsgail Forest

Ceann Tarabhaigh

A859

Airidh a Bhruaich

Aird an Troim

Loch Tealasabhaigh

Reasort

A859

Loch Langabhat

Loch Beinisabhal

Loch Coirigerod

EILEAN LIS

Aline Lodge

Seaforth I.

SOUTH LEWIS,

489

679
TIRGA MOR

659
ULLAVAL

Aird a' Mhulaidh

UISGNAVAL MORE
729

572
BEINN MH

Forest of Harris

Abhainn Suidhe

HARRIS AND

799
CUSHAM

17

Cliasmol

13

Miabhag

Bun Abhainn Eadarra

Aird Asaig

Isay

CEANN A TUATH NA HEARADH

A859

Maraig

OLD WHALING STATION

559

449

REINIGEADAL

NORTH UIST

Reinigeadal

BEN LUSKENTYRE
436

Loch Trollamarig

99

Losgaintir

LUSKENTYRE BEACH

South Harris Forest

A859

Tairbeart
(Tarbert)

467

Urgha

Carragraich

Caolas Scalpaigh

Camach

Rudha Crag

Loch Ceann Dibig

Sgeotasaigh

Scalpay

Eile Sca

Seilebost

Miabhag

Loch an Tairbeart

Toe Head

Coppay

Borve Lodge
Buirgh

23

Drinisiadar

Kennacley

NA HEARADH
(HARRIS)

386

Plocropol Pt.

Greosabhagh

Plocrapol

Aird Mhighe

Liceasto

Leac a Li

Scadabhagh

CHAIPAVAL
365

Sgarasta Mhor

398
BLEAVAL

Geocrab

Caolas Stochinis

Cluthat

Rubha Bhocaig

Shillay

Little Shillay

Rubha 'an Teampuill

Manais

Stockinish I.

Sound of Shillay

196

Brenish Pt.

Taobh Tuath

SEALLAM

459

Beacrabhaic

Aird Mhighe

UIG 1:45

Pabaidh
(Pabbay)

Quinish

Sound of Spuir

An t-Ob (Leverburgh)

Fionnsbhagh

Loch Steiseabhat

Aird Mhighe

Boirseam
Lingreabhagh

Loch Fleoideabhagh

Spuir

Ensay

Carminish Is.

ROINEABHAL

Cuidhtinis

Lingarabay I.

Caolas Phabaidh

Killegray

Cairminis
Srannda

Roghadal

Eilean Bhearnaraigh
(Berneray)

Ruisigearraidh

BERNERAY

ST CLEMENT'S CHURCH

Langay

Vallay

Borgh

Baile

Renish Pt.

Boreray

1:10

CAOLAS NA HEARADH

Aird a'Mhorain

Groay

Gilsay

Veilish Pt.

Torogay

Lingay

Scaravay

Scale : 1:332 000
(approx 5 miles to 1 inch)

Valley

Griminish Pt.

Lingay

Port nan Long

Sursay

Opsay

0 1 2 3 4 5 6 miles
0 1 2 3 4 5 6 7 8 9 10km

Scolpaig

20 A865

Oronsay

Baile Mhic Phail

Tahay

190

Valley Strand

Valley

Solas

Greinetobht

Malaclet

Griminis

Baile Mhartainn

Scolpaig

8

Map labels

RUBHA ROBHANAIS
(BUTT OF LEWIS)
CHURCH OF ST MOLVAG
Cunndal
Coig Peighinnean
Eòropaich
HARBOUR VIEW GALLERY
Lional
Port Nis
Cross Sands
Suainebost
Tabost
Aird Dhail
Cros
Sgiogarstaigh
Dail bho Dheas
Dail bho Thuath
Glen Cross
Gabhsann bho Thuath
Cuiashader
Gabhsann bho Dheas
Mealabost Bhuirgh
Bail Àrd Bhuirgh
Cellar Head
Coig Peighinnean Bhuirgh
Siadar
Loch Langabhat
Rubha Leathann
Siadar Tàrach
Aird Barvas
Siadar Uarach
TRUSHAL STONE
Baile an Truiseil
Loch Mòr, Shanndabhat

L E W I S

BLACK HOUSE MUSEUM
Barabhas Iarach
Barabhas Uarach
Labost
Arnol
Brù
Bragar
Barabhas
248 MUIRNEAG
Bail' Ur Tholastaidh
Tolastadh bho Thuath
Loch Urghag
Loch Breibhat
Tolsta Head
Loch Sgeireach Mòr
Gleann Tholàstaidh
Port Bun a'Ghlinne
Griais
Creag Fhraoch
Loch Scarabhat Mhòr
Bac
Loch Mòr an Stàrr
Col
Vatisker Pt.
292 BEINN MHOLACH
Col Uarach
Breibhig
Coll Sands
Aird Thunga
BROAD BAY OR LOCH A TUATH
Port Nan Giùran
Rubha an t-Siumpain
A857
Grianan
Tunga
Cnoc Amhlaigh
Newmarket
Sròn Ruadh
Aird
Port Mholair
An Gleann Ur
Sulaisiadar
NB
Lacasdal
STORNOWAY
Garrabost
Seisiadar
Stornoway
Mealabost
EYE PENINSULA
MUSEUM NAN EILEAN
Aiginis
Sanndabhaig
St COLUMBA'S
Pabail Uarach
AN LANNTAIR GALLERY
An Cnoc
Pabail Iarach
223
Tolm
Suardail
Bàgh Phabail
Loch a' Ghainmhich
Holm I.
A'Chearc
Acha Mòr
Arnish Moor
Loch Tobhta Brideis
Loch Orasaigh
ULLAPOOL 2:40
Loch m Falcag
Griomsidar
Ben Casgro
Lurbost
Raerinish Pt.
Ranais
Soval Lodge
Crosbost
Loch Trealabhal
Barkin Is.
Tabhaidh Mhor
Lacasaidh
Ceos
Eilean Chaluim Chille
Sildinis
Gearraidh Bhaird
Cromor
Cearsadar
Cabharstadh
Eilean Orasaidh
Tabost
CEARSIADAIR
Eilean Thoraidh
Ceann Shiphoirt
Marbhig
Loch Sgibacleit
Calbost
Taobh a' Ghlinne
Grabhair
Loch nan Eilean
Loch Shanndabhat
Kebock Head
PARK OR PAIRC
Orasaigh
Leumrabhagh
Eisgean
470 CRIONAIG
Loch Shell or Loch Sealg
Srianach
Eilean Iubhard
Mol Truisg
Gob Rubh'Uisenis
92
Rubha Bhrollum
Priest I.
Rubha a'Bhaird
Garbh Eilean
Eilean Mhuire
CAOLAS NAN EILEAN
Na h-Eileanan Mòra
(Shiant Islands)
Eilean an Tighe

NG

Greenstone Point
Rubha Beag
Opinan
Rubha Mòr
Mellon Udrigle
Sròn a' Gheodha Dhuibh
Eilean Furadh Mór
Gruinard I.
Rubha Reidh
Camas Mòr
Achgarve
155
Mellon Charles
Loch an Draing
Ormiscaig
Laide
296 AN CUAIDH
Cove
Isle of Ewe
Tighnafiline
Sand
Second Coast
First Co
86
Aultbea
Drumchork
Litt Gruir
Melvaig
Inverasdale
LOCH EWE
Aultgrishan
Midtown
Loch Sguod
Brae
Rubha 'Ard na Bà
Naast
Tournaig
INVEREWE GARDEN
Loch Bad a'Chreamh
FIONN LOCH
Fladda-chùain
Peterburn
Loch Fada
Air Dub
North Erradale
Londubh
Port Erradale
Loch Tollaidh
Poolewe
Rubha Bàn
Big Sand
85
Longa Island
Smithstown
GAIRLOCH HERITAGE MUSEUM
Caolas Beag
Gairloch
Eilean Troddav
CARN DEARG
Rubha Hunish
Rubha na h-Aiseig
Strath
MEALL AN DOIREAN 420
LOCH GAIRLOCH
BEINN AIRIGH CH.
DUNTULM CASTLE
Macqueen
Port Henderson
Aird
Duntulm
Kilmaluag
Badachro
Charlestown
Kerrysdale

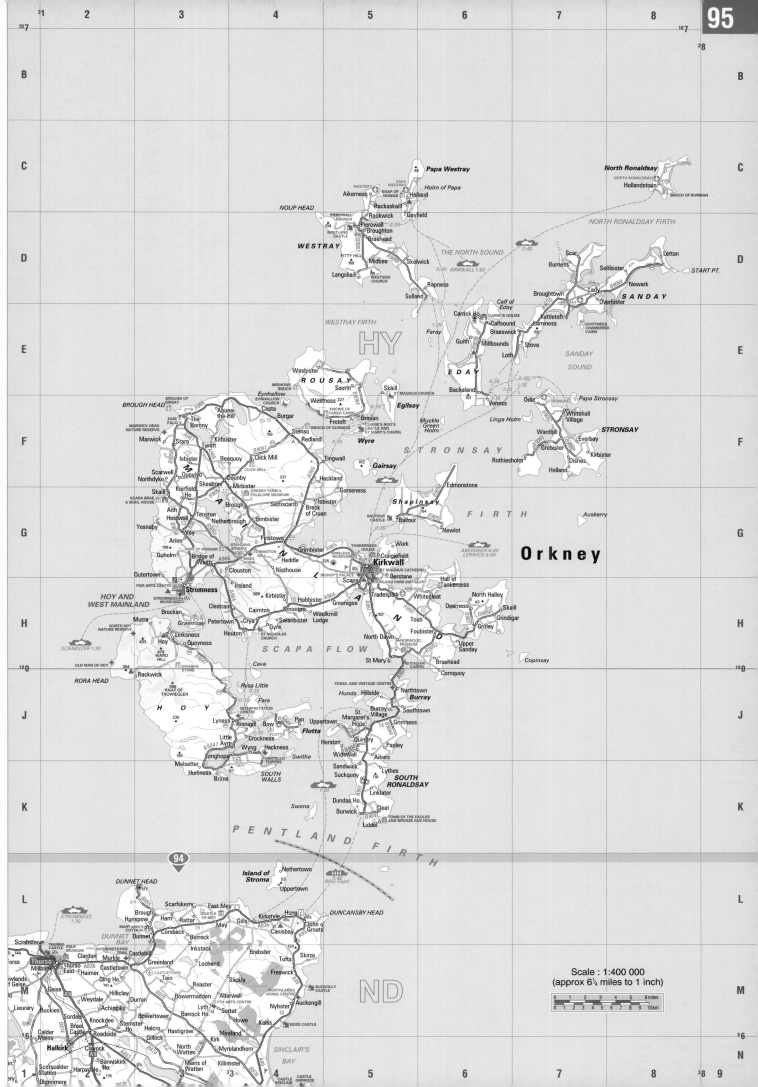

Key to Town Plan Symbols

	Motorway		Shopping Streets
	Primary Route Dual/Single		Railway
	Main Road Dual/Single		Tramway with Station
	Secondary Road Dual/Single		Railway/ Bus Station
	Minor Through Road/ One Way Street		Shopping Precinct/ Retail Park
	Pedestrian Roads		Park

✝	Abbey/Cathedral	⇄	Railway Station
	Ancient Monument		Roman Antiquity
	Aquarium		Safari Park
Ⓖ	Art Gallery	♿	Shopmobility
	Bird Garden		Theatre
	Building of Public Interest	ⓘ	Tourist Information Centre (open all year)
	Castle	ⓘ	Tourist Information Centre (open summer only)
	Church of interest		Zoo
	Cinema	◆	Other Place of Interest
	Garden		Underground/ Metro Station
	Historic Ship	Ⓗ	Hospital
	House	Ⓟ	Parking
	House & Garden		Police
	Museum	PO	Post Office
	Preserved Railway	▲	Youth Hostel

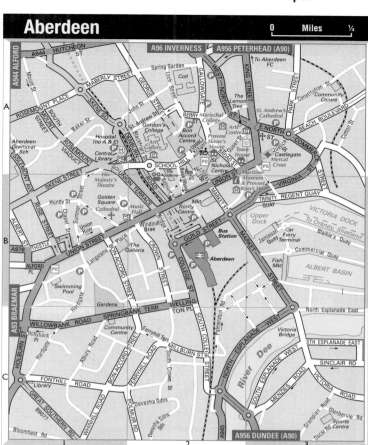

Aberdeen

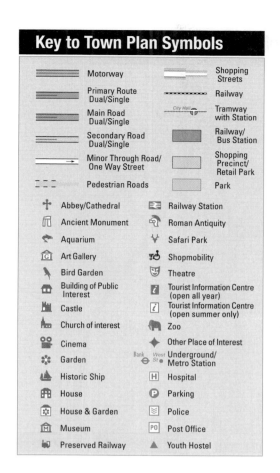

Bath

Blackpool

Birmingham

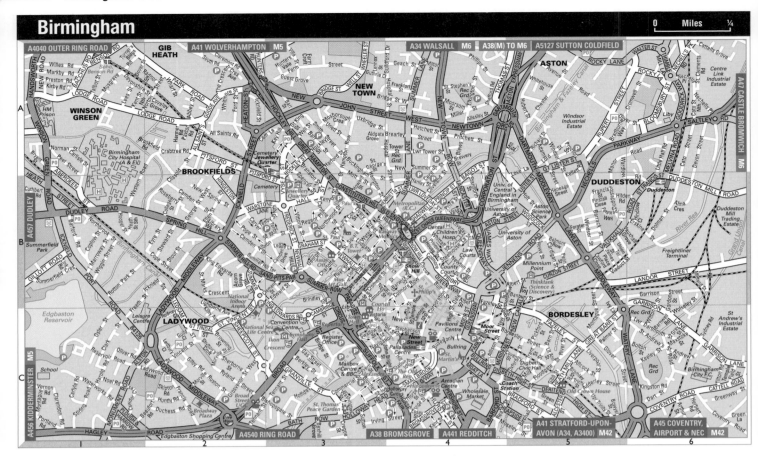

Bournemouth

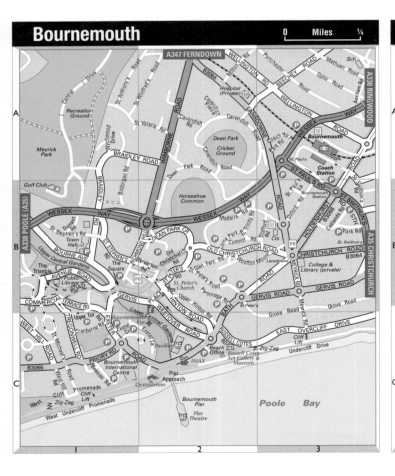

Bradford

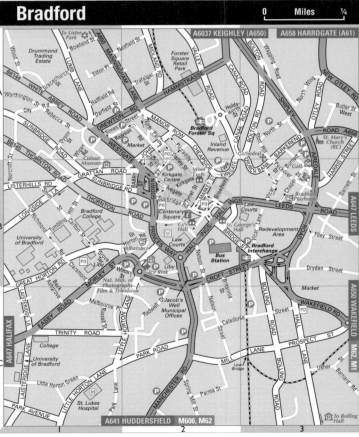

Bristol

0 Miles ¼

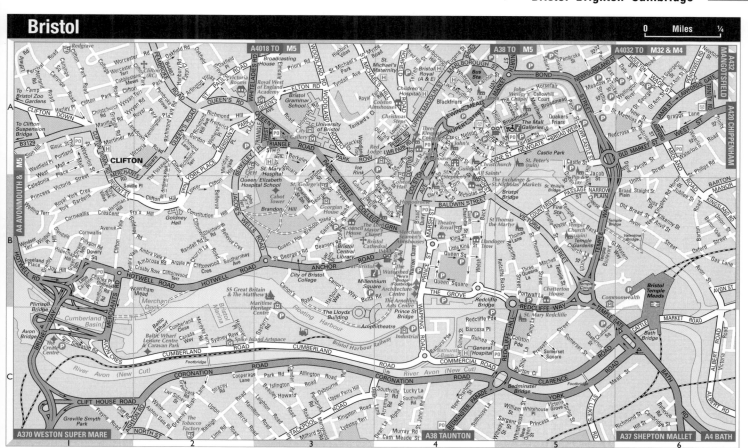

Brighton

0 Miles ¼

Cambridge

0 Miles ¼

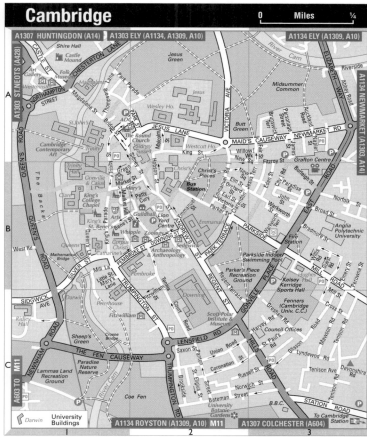

Cardiff / Caerdydd

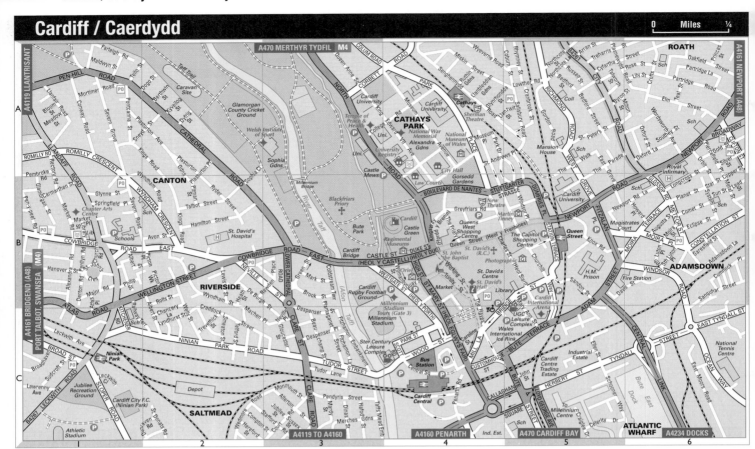

Canterbury

Cheltenham

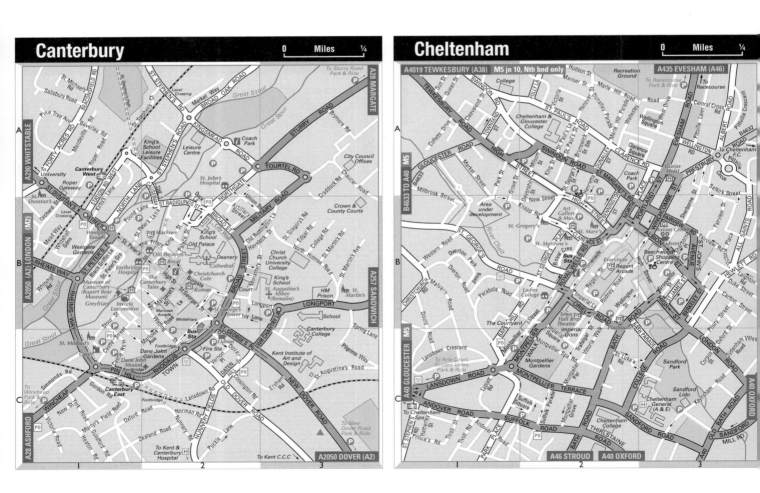

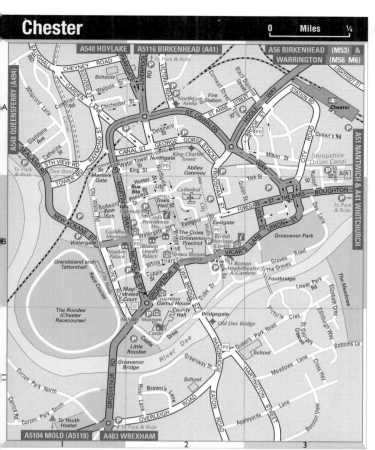

Chester

0 Miles ¼

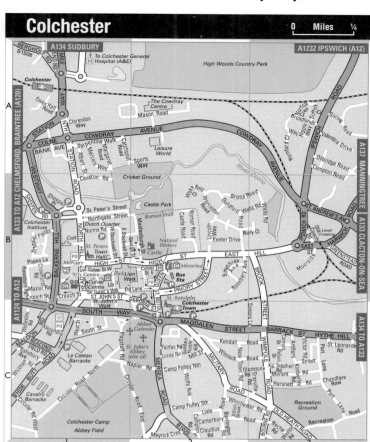

Colchester

0 Miles ¼

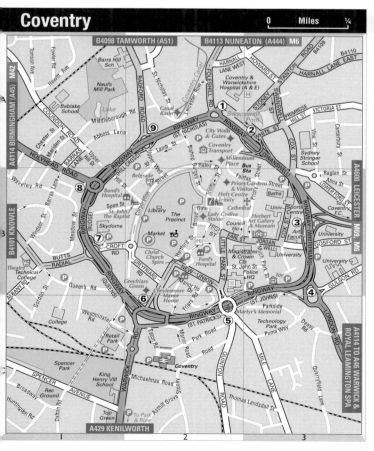

Coventry

0 Miles ¼

Croydon

0 Miles ¼

Derby

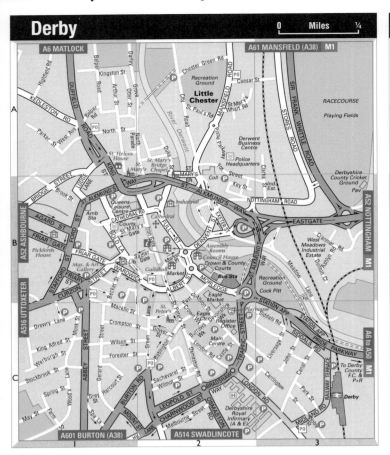

Durham

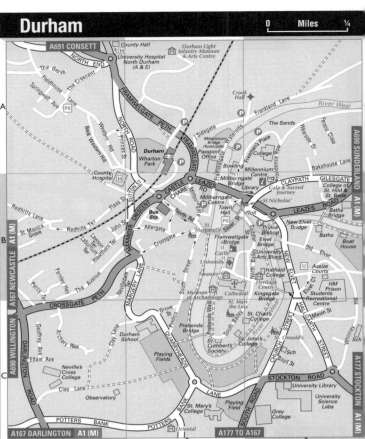

Edinburgh

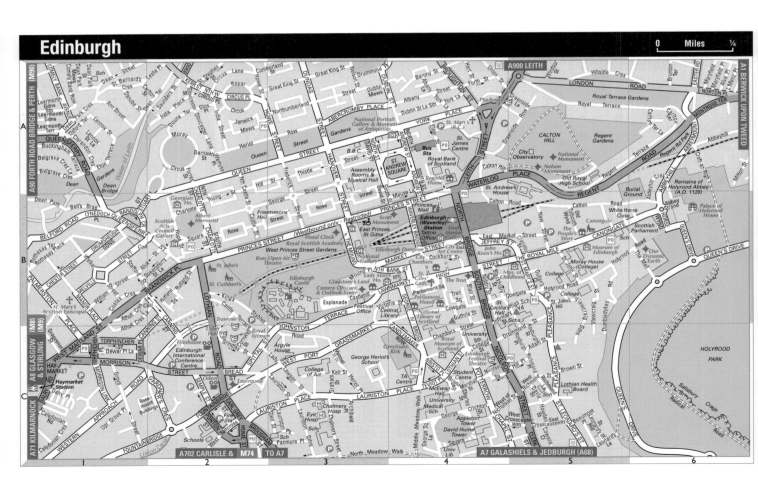

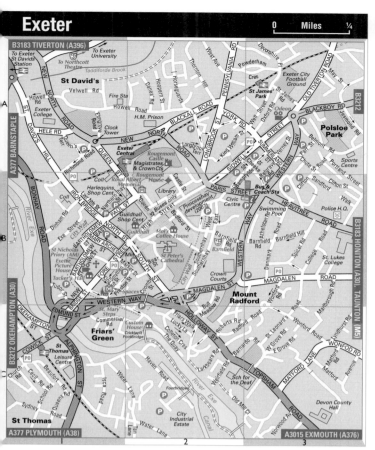

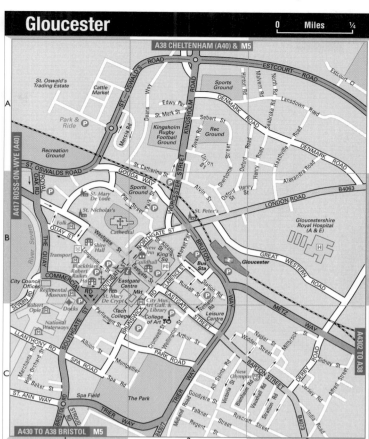

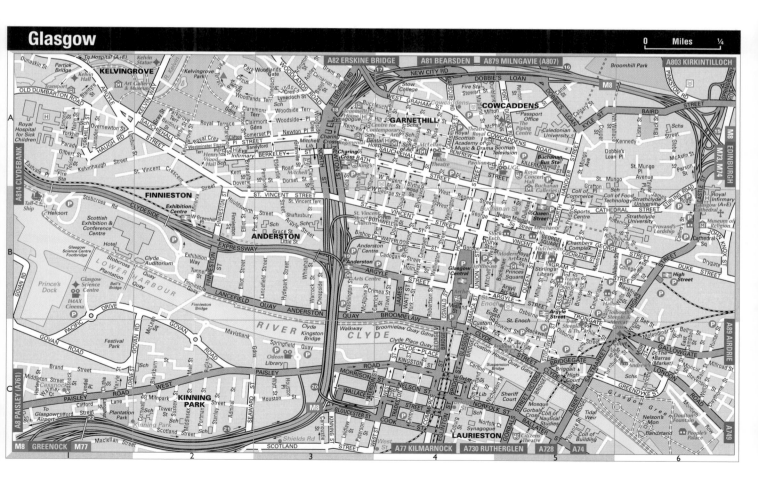

Hull

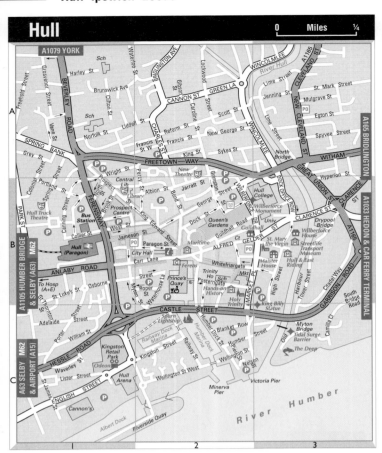

Ipswich

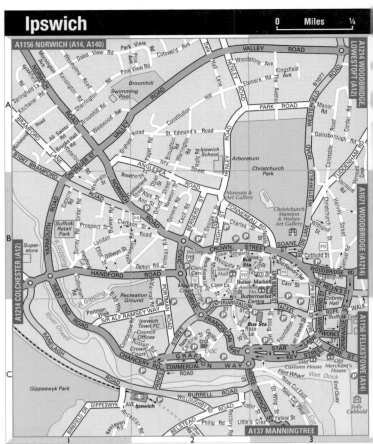

Leeds

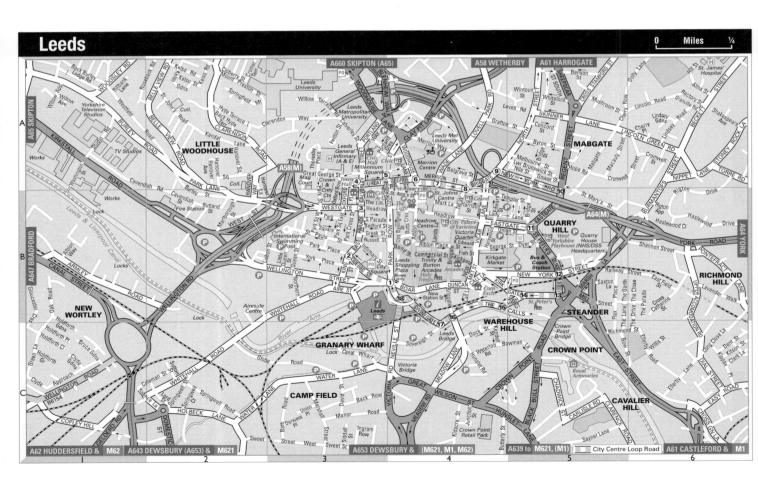

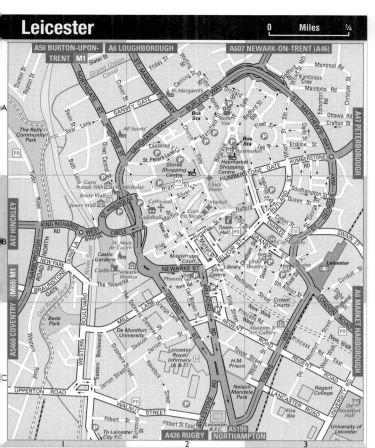

Leicester

0 Miles ¼

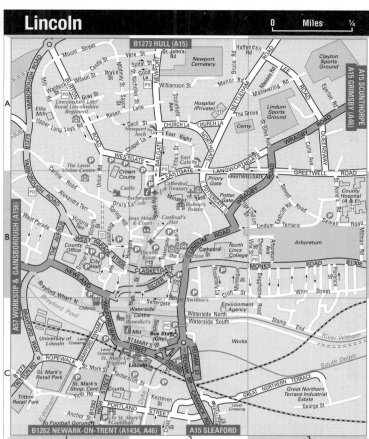

Lincoln

0 Miles ¼

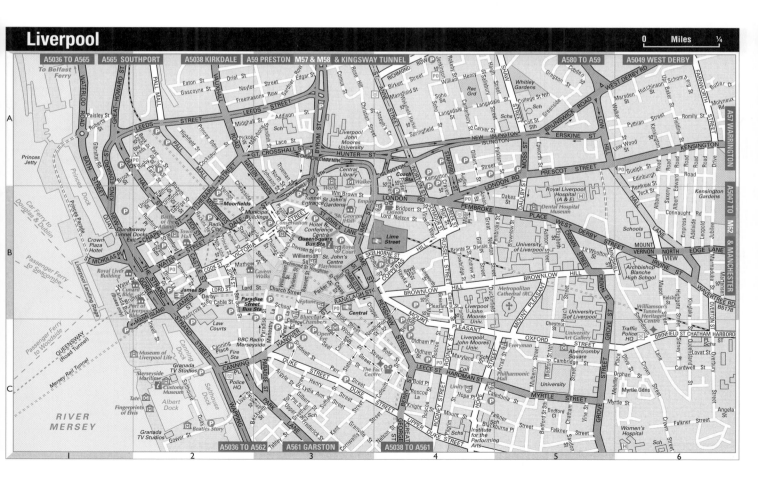

Liverpool

0 Miles ¼

Manchester

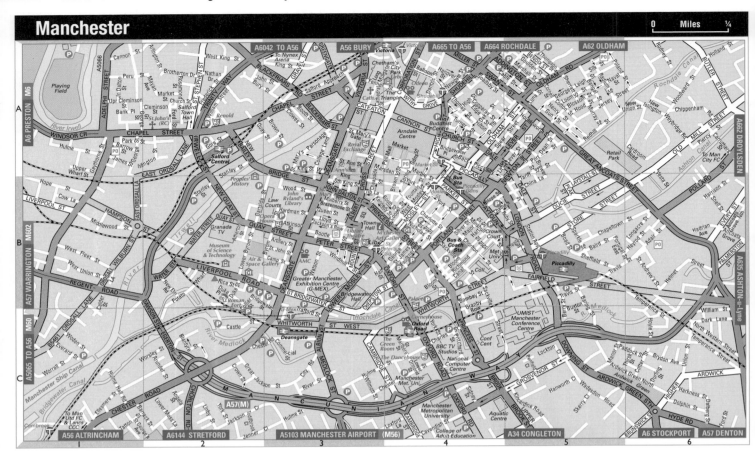

Middlesbrough

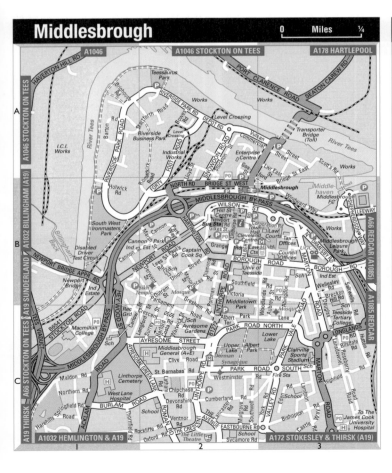

Milton Keynes

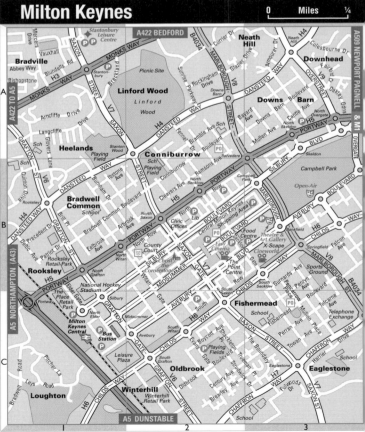

Newcastle upon Tyne

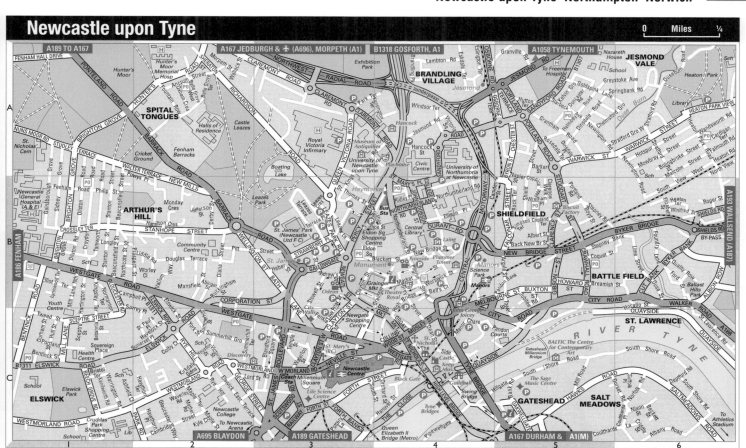

Northampton

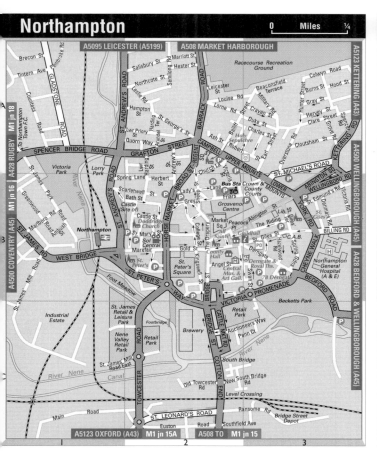

Norwich

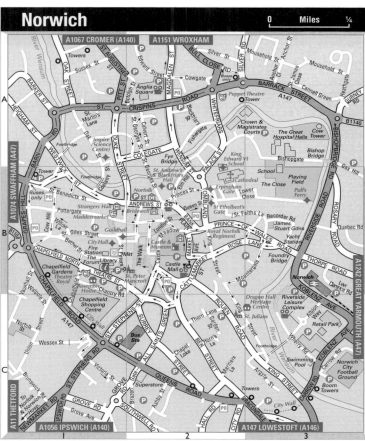

Nottingham

0   Miles   ¼

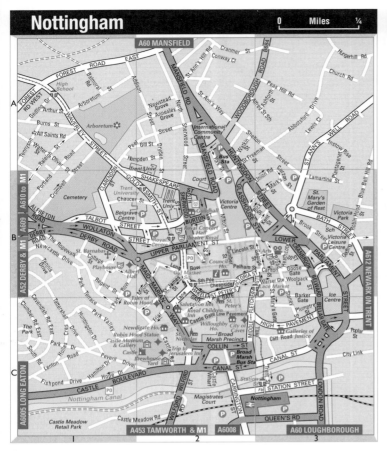

Oxford

0   Miles   ¼

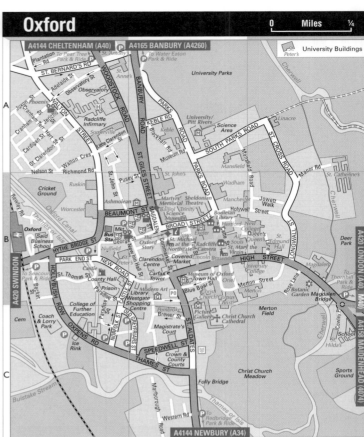

Plymouth

0   Miles   ¼

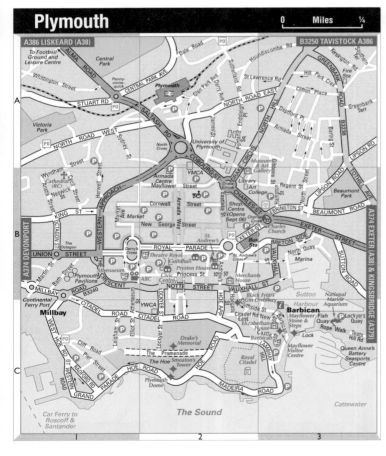

Portsmouth

0   Miles   ¼

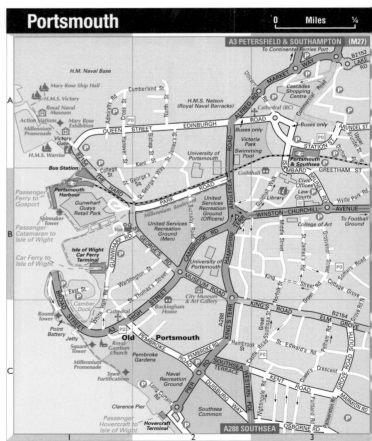

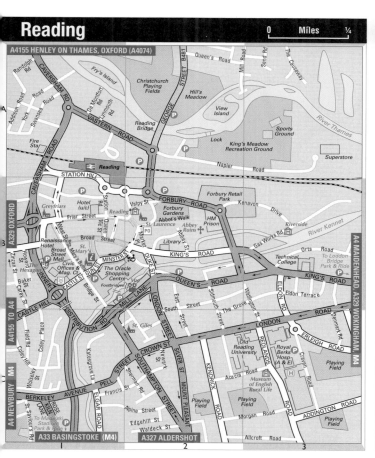

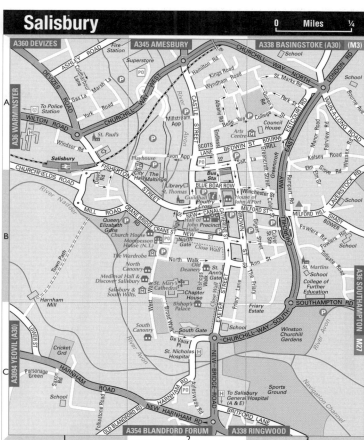

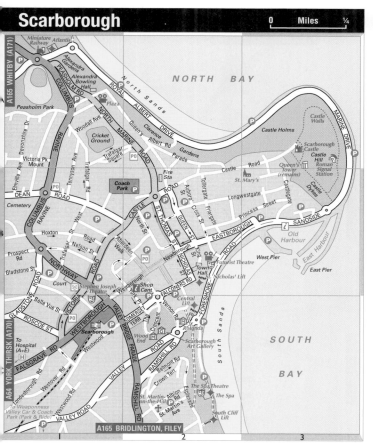

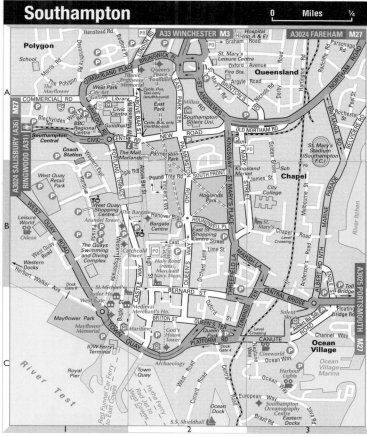

Sheffield

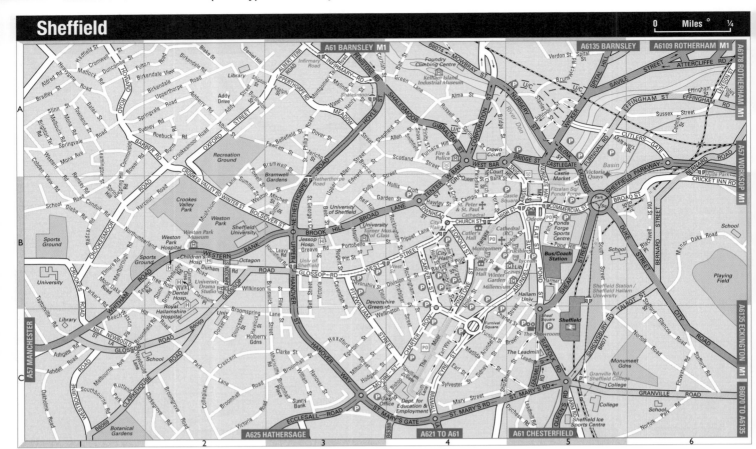

Stoke-on-Trent (Hanley)

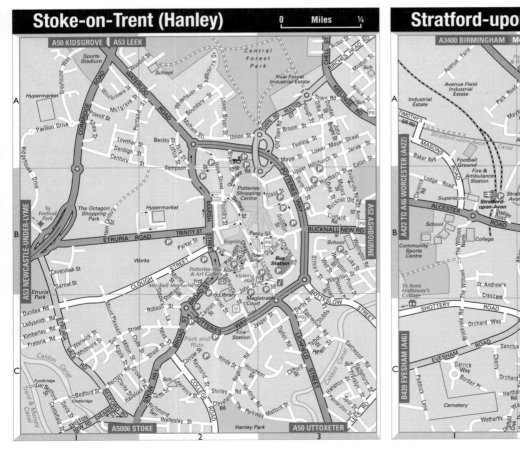

Stratford-upon-Avon

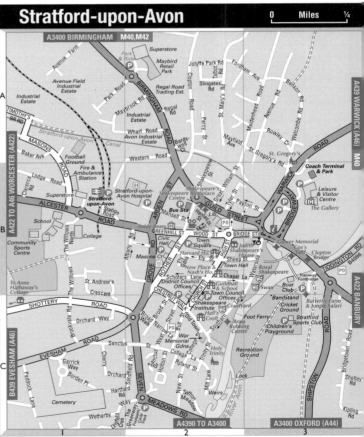

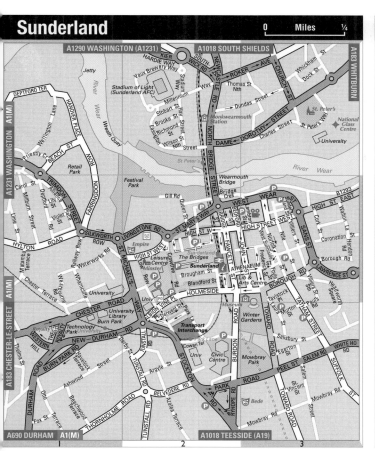

Sunderland

Miles 0 — ¼

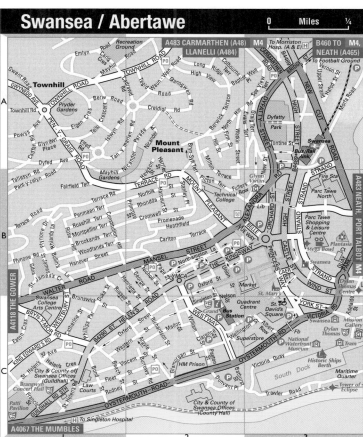

Swansea / Abertawe

Miles 0 — ¼

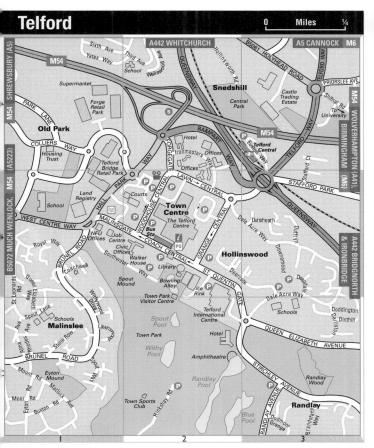

Telford

Miles 0 — ¼

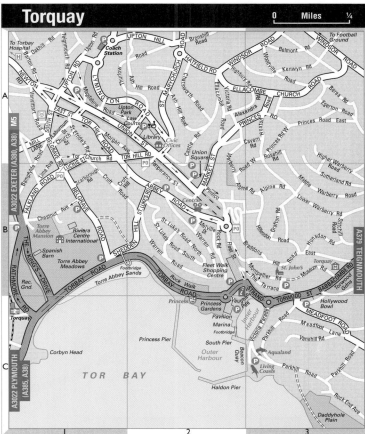

Torquay

Miles 0 — ¼

Winchester

0 Miles ¼

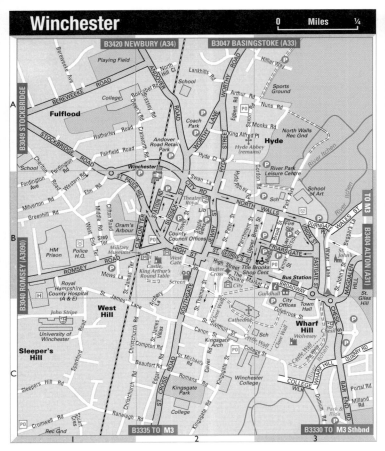

Windsor

0 Miles ¼

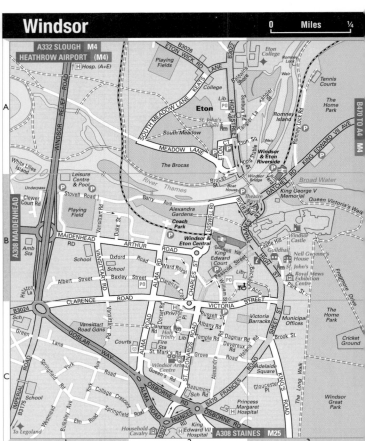

Worcester

0 Miles ¼

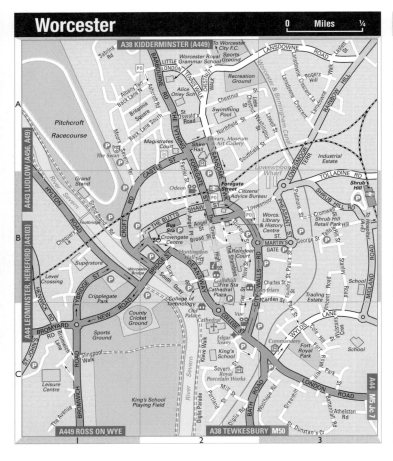

York

0 Miles ¼

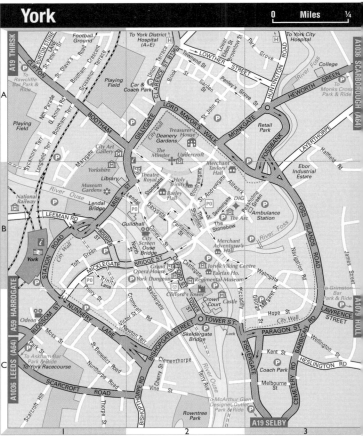

How to use the index

Example: Westcott *Devon* **7** F9

- F9 – grid square
- 7 – page number
- Devon – county or unitary authority

Abbreviations

Abbreviation	Name
Aberd C	**Aberdeen City**
Aberds	**Aberdeenshire**
Angl	**Isle of Anglesey**
Arg/Bute	**Argyll & Bute**
Bath/NE Som'set	**Bath & North East Somerset**
Beds	**Bedfordshire**
Bl Gwent	**Blaenau Gwent**
Blackb'n	**Blackburn with Darwen**
Blackp'l	**Blackpool**
Bournem'th	**Bournemouth**
Brackn'l	**Bracknell Forest**
Bridg	**Bridgend**
Brighton/Hove	**City of Brighton and Hove**
Bristol	**City and County of Bristol**
Bucks	**Buckinghamshire**
C/Edinb	**City of Edinburgh**
C/Glasg	**Glasgow City**
C/York	**City of York**
Caerph	**Caerphilly**
Cambs	**Cambridgeshire**
Card	**Cardiff**
Carms	**Carmarthenshire**
Ceredig'n	**Ceredigion**
Ches	**Cheshire**
Clack	**Clackmannanshire**
Cornw'l	**Cornwall**
Cumb	**Cumbria**
D'lington	**Darlington**
Denbs	**Denbighshire**
Derby	**Derbyshire**
Derby C	**Derby City**
Dumf/Gal	**Dumfries & Galloway**
Dundee C	**Dundee City**
E Ayrs	**East Ayrshire**
E Dunb	**East Dunbartonshire**
E Loth	**East Lothian**
E Renf	**East Renfrewshire**
ER Yorks	**East Riding of Yorkshire**
E Sussex	**East Sussex**
Falk	**Falkirk**
Flints	**Flintshire**
Glos	**Gloucestershire**
Gtr Man	**Greater Manchester**
Gwyn	**Gwynedd**
H'land	**Highland**
Hants	**Hampshire**
Hartlep'l	**Hartlepool**
Heref'd	**Herefordshire**
Herts	**Hertfordshire**
I/Man	**Isle of Man**
I/Scilly	**Isles of Scilly**
I/Wight	**Isle of Wight**
Invercl	**Inverclyde**
Kingston/Hull	**Kingston upon Hull**
Lancs	**Lancashire**
Leics	**Leicestershire**
Leics C	**Leicester City**
Lincs	**Lincolnshire**
London	**Greater London**
M/Keynes	**Milton Keynes**
Mersey	**Merseyside**
Merth Tyd	**Merthyr Tydfil**
Middlesbro	**Middlesbrough**
Midloth	**Midlothian**
Monmouths	**Monmouthshire**
N Ayrs	**North Ayrshire**
N Lanarks	**North Lanarkshire**
N Lincs	**North Lincolnshire**
N Som'set	**North Somerset**
N Yorks	**North Yorkshire**
NE Lincs	**North East Lincolnshire**
Neath P Talb	**Neath Port Talbot**
Newp	**City and County of Newport**
Northants	**Northamptonshire**
Northum	**Northumberland**
Nott'ham	**City of Nottingham**
Notts	**Nottinghamshire**
Oxon	**Oxfordshire**
Pembs	**Pembrokeshire**
Perth/Kinr	**Perth and Kinross**
Peterbro	**Peterborough**
Plym'th	**Plymouth**
Portsm'th	**Portsmouth**
Redcar/Clevel'd	**Redcar and Cleveland**
Renf	**Renfrewshire**
Rh Cyn Taff	**Rhondda Cynon Taff**
Rutl'd	**Rutland**
S'thampton	**Southampton**
S Ayrs	**South Ayrshire**
S Gloucs	**South Gloucestershire**
S Lanarks	**South Lanarkshire**
S Yorks	**South Yorkshire**
Scot Borders	**Scottish Borders**
Shetl'd	**Shetland**
Shrops	**Shropshire**
Som'set	**Somerset**
Southend	**Southend-on-Sea**
Staffs	**Staffordshire**
Stirl	**Stirling**
Stockton	**Stockton on Tees**
Stoke	**Stoke-on-Trent**
Swan	**Swansea**
Telford	**Telford and Wrekin**
Thurr'k	**Thurrock**
Torf	**Torfaen**
Tyne/Wear	**Tyne and Wear**
V/Glam	**Vale of Glamorgan**
W Berks	**West Berkshire**
W Dunb	**West Dunbartonshire**
W Isles	**Western Isles**
W Loth	**West Lothian**
W Midlands	**West Midlands**
W Sussex	**West Sussex**
W Yorks	**West Yorkshire**
Warwick	**Warwickshire**
Wilts	**Wiltshire**
Windsor	**Windsor and Maidenhead**
Worcs	**Worcestershire**
Wrex	**Wrexham**

A

Ab Kettleby *Leics* **36** C3
Ab Lench *Worcs* **27** C7
Abbas Combe *Som'set* **8** B6
Abberley *Worcs* **26** B4
Abberton *Essex* **31** G7
Abberton *Worcs* **26** C6
Abberwick *Northum* **63** B7
Abbess Roding *Essex* **30** G2
Abbey *Devon* **7** E10
Abbey-cwm-hir *Powys* **25** A7
Abbey Dore *Heref'd* **25** E10
Abbey Field *Essex* **30** F6
Abbey Hulton *Stoke* **44** H3
Abbey St Bathans *Scot Borders* **70** D6
Abbey Village *Lancs* **50** G2
Abbey Wood *London* **19** D11
Abbeydale *S Yorks* **45** D7
Abbeystead *Lancs* **50** D1
Abbeytown *Cumb* **56** A3
Abbots Bickington *Devon* **6** E2
Abbots Bromley *Staffs* **35** C6
Abbots Langley *Herts* **19** A7
Abbots Leigh *N Som'set* **15** D11
Abbots Morton *Worcs* **27** C7
Abbots Ripton *Cambs* **37** H8
Abbots Salford *Warwick* **27** C7
Abbotsbury *Dorset* **8** F4
Abbotsham *Devon* **6** D3
Abbotskerswell *Devon* **5** E9
Abbotsley *Cambs* **29** C9
Abbotswood *Hants* **10** B2
Abbotts Ann *Hants* **17** G10
Abcott *Shrops* **33** H9
Abdon *Shrops* **34** G1
Aber *Ceredig'n* **23** B9
Aber-Arad *Carms* **23** C8
Aber-banc *Ceredig'n* **23** B8
Aber Cowarch *Gwyn* **32** D4
Aber-Giâr *Carms* **23** B10
Aber-gwynfi *Neath P Talb* **14** B4
Aber-Hirnant *Gwyn* **32** B5
Aber-nant *Rh Cyn Taff* **14** A6
Aber-Rhiwlech *Gwyn* **32** C5
Aber-Village *Powys* **25** F8
Aberaeron *Ceredig'n* **24** B1
Aberaman *Rh Cyn Taff* **14** A6
Aberangell *Gwyn* **32** D4
Aberarder *H'land* **81** E6
Aberarder House *H'land* **81** A8
Aberarder Lodge *H'land* **81** E7
Aberargie *Perth/Kinr* **76** F4
Aberarth *Ceredig'n* **24** B1
Aberavon *Neath P Talb* **14** B3
Aberbeeg *Bl Gwent* **15** A8
Abercanaid *Merth Tyd* **14** A6
Abercarn *Caerph* **15** B8
Abercastle *Pembs* **22** C3
Abercegir *Powys* **32** E4
Aberchirder *Aberds* **88** C6
Abercraf *Powys* **24** G5
Abercrombie *Fife* **77** G8
Abercych *Pembs* **23** B7
Abercynafon *Powys* **25** G7
Abercynon *Rh Cyn Taff* **14** B6
Aberdalgie *Perth/Kinr* **76** E3
Aberdâr = Aberdare *Rh Cyn Taff* **14** A5
Aberdare = Aberdâr *Rh Cyn Taff* **14** A5
Aberdaron *Gwyn* **40** H3
Aberdaugleddau = Milford Haven *Pembs* **22** F4
Aberdeen *Aberd C* **83** C11
Aberdesach *Gwyn* **40** E6
Aberdour *Fife* **69** B10
Aberdovey *Gwyn* **32** F2
Aberdulais *Neath P Talb* **14** A3
Aberedw *Powys* **25** D7
Abereiddy *Pembs* **22** C2
Abererch *Gwyn* **40** G5
Aberfan *Merth Tyd* **14** A6
Aberfeldy *Perth/Kinr* **75** C11
Aberffraw *Angl* **40** D5
Aberffrwd *Ceredig'n* **32** H2
Aberford *W Yorks* **51** F10
Aberfoyle *Stirl* **75** G8
Abergavenny = Y Fenni *Monmouths* **25** G9
Abergele *Conwy* **42** E2
Abergorlech *Carms* **23** C10
Abergwaun = Fishguard *Pembs* **22** C4
Abergwesyn *Powys* **24** C5
Abergwili *Carms* **23** D9
Abergwynant *Gwyn* **32** D2
Abergwyngregyn *Gwyn* **41** C8
Abergynolwyn *Gwyn* **32** E2
Aberhonddu = Brecon *Powys* **25** F7
Aberhosan *Powys* **32** F4
Aberkenfig *Bridg* **14** C4
Aberlady *E Loth* **70** B3
Aberlemno *Angus* **77** B8
Aberllefenni *Gwyn* **32** E3
Abermagwr *Ceredig'n* **24** A3
Abermaw = Barmouth *Gwyn* **32** D2
Abermeurig *Ceredig'n* **23** A10
Abermule *Powys* **33** F7
Abernaint *Powys* **33** C7
Abernant *Carms* **23** D8
Abernethy *Perth/Kinr* **76** F4
Abernyte *Perth/Kinr* **76** D5
Aberpennar = Mountain Ash *Rh Cyn Taff* **14** B6
Aberporth *Ceredig'n* **23** A7
Abersoch *Gwyn* **40** H5
Abersychan *Torf* **15** A8
Abertawe = Swansea *Swan* **14** B2
Aberteifi = Cardigan *Ceredig'n* **22** B6
Aberthin *V/Glam* **14** D6
Abertillery = Abertyleri *Bl Gwent* **15** A8
Abertridwr *Caerph* **15** C7
Abertridwr *Powys* **32** D6
Abertyleri = Abertillery *Bl Gwent* **15** A8
Abertysswg *Caerph* **25** H8
Aberuthven *Perth/Kinr* **76** F2
Aberyscir *Powys* **24** F6
Aberystwyth *Ceredig'n* **32** G1
Abhainn Suidhe *W Isles* **90** G5
Abingdon *Oxon* **17** B11
Abinger Common *Surrey* **19** G8
Abinger Hammer *Surrey* **19** G7
Abington *S Lanarks* **60** A5
Abington Piggotts *Cambs* **29** D10
Ablington *Glos* **27** H8
Ablington *Wilts* **17** G8
Abney *Derby* **44** E5
Aboyne *Aberds* **83** D7
Abram *Gtr Man* **43** B9
Abriachan *H'land* **87** H8
Abridge *Essex* **19** B11
Abronhill *N Lanarks* **68** C6
Abson *S Gloucs* **16** D4
Abthorpe *Northants* **28** D3
Abune-the-Hill *Orkney* **95** F3
Aby *Lincs* **47** E8
Acaster Malbis *C/York* **52** E1
Acaster Selby *N Yorks* **52** E1
Accrington *Lancs* **50** G3
Acha *Arg/Bute* **78** F4
Acha Mor *W Isles* **91** E8
Achabraid *Arg/Bute* **73** E7
Achachork *H'land* **85** D9
Achafolla *Arg/Bute* **72** B6
Achagary *H'land* **93** D10
Achahoish *Arg/Bute* **72** F6
Achalader *Perth/Kinr* **76** C4
Achallader *Arg/Bute* **74** C6
Ach'an Todhair *H'land* **80** F2
Achanalt *H'land* **86** E5
Achanamara *Arg/Bute* **72** E6
Achandunie *H'land* **87** D9
Achany *H'land* **93** J8
Achaphubuil *H'land* **80** F2
Acharacle *H'land* **79** E9
Acharn *H'land* **79** F10
Acharn *Perth/Kinr* **75** C10
Acharole *H'land* **94** E4
Achath *Aberds* **83** B9
Achavanich *H'land* **94** F3
Achavraat *H'land* **87** G12
Achddu *Carms* **23** F9
Achduart *H'land* **92** J3
Achentoul *H'land* **93** F11
Achfary *H'land* **92** F5
Achgarve *H'land* **91** H13
Achiemore *H'land* **92** C6
Achiemore *H'land* **93** D11
A'Chill *H'land* **84** H7
Achiltibuie *H'land* **92** J3
Achina *H'land* **93** C10
Achinduich *H'land* **93** J8
Achinduin *Arg/Bute* **79** H11
Achingills *H'land* **94** D3
Achintee *H'land* **80** F3
Achintee *H'land* **86** G2
Achintraid *H'land* **85** E13
Achlean *H'land* **81** D10
Achleck *Arg/Bute* **78** G7
Achluachrach *H'land* **80** E4
Achlyness *H'land* **92** D5
Achmelvich *H'land* **92** G3
Achmore *H'land* **85** E13
Achmore *Stirl* **75** D8
Achnaba *Arg/Bute* **74** D2
Achnaba *Arg/Bute* **73** E8
Achnabat *H'land* **87** H8
Achnacarnin *H'land* **92** F3
Achnacarry *H'land* **80** E3
Achnacloich *Arg/Bute* **74** D2
Achnacloich *H'land* **85** H10
Achnaconeran *H'land* **80** B6
Achnacraig *Arg/Bute* **78** G7
Achnacroish *Arg/Bute* **79** G11
Achnadrish *Arg/Bute* **78** F7
Achnafalnich *Arg/Bute* **74** E5
Achnagarron *H'land* **87** E9
Achnaha *H'land* **78** E7
Achnahanat *H'land* **87** B8
Achnahannet *H'land* **82** A1
Achnairn *H'land* **93** H8
Achnaluachrach *H'land* **93** J9
Achnasaul *H'land* **80** E3
Achnasheen *H'land* **86** F4
Achosnich *H'land* **78** E7
Achranich *H'land* **79** G10
Achreamie *H'land* **93** C13
Achriabhach *H'land* **80** G3
Achriesgill *H'land* **92** D5
Achrimsdale *H'land* **93** J12
Achtoty *H'land* **93** C9
Achurch *Northants* **36** G6
Achuvoldrach *H'land* **93** D8
Achvaich *H'land* **87** B10
Achvarasdal *H'land* **93** C12
Ackergill *H'land* **94** E5
Acklam *Middlesbro'* **58** E5
Acklam *N Yorks* **52** C3
Ackleton *Shrops* **34** F3
Acklington *Northum* **63** C8
Ackton *W Yorks* **51** G10
Ackworth Moor Top *W Yorks* **51** H10
Acle *Norfolk* **39** D10
Acock's Green *W Midlands* **35** G7
Acol *Kent* **21** E10
Acomb *Northum* **62** G5
Acomb *C/York* **52** D1
Aconbury *Heref'd* **26** E2
Acre *Lancs* **50** G3
Acre Street *W Sussex* **11** E6
Acrefair *Wrex* **33** A8
Acton *Ches* **43** G9
Acton *Dorset* **9** G8
Acton *London* **19** C9
Acton *Shrops* **33** G9
Acton *Suffolk* **30** D5
Acton *Wrex* **42** G6
Acton Beauchamp *Heref'd* **26** C3
Acton Bridge *Ches* **43** E8
Acton Burnell *Shrops* **33** E11
Acton Green *Heref'd* **26** C3
Acton Pigott *Shrops* **33** E11
Acton Round *Shrops* **34** F2
Acton Scott *Shrops* **33** G10
Acton Trussell *Staffs* **34** D5
Acton Turville *S Gloucs* **16** C5
Adbaston *Staffs* **34** C3
Adber *Dorset* **8** B4
Adderley *Shrops* **34** A2
Adderstone *Northum* **71** G10
Addiewell *W Loth* **69** D8
Addingham *W Yorks* **51** E6
Addington *Bucks* **28** F4
Addington *London* **19** E10
Addington *Kent* **20** F3
Addinston *Scot Borders* **70** E4
Addiscombe *London* **19** E10
Addlestone *Surrey* **19** E7
Addlethorpe *Lincs* **47** F9
Adel *W Yorks* **51** F8
Adeney *Telford* **34** D3
Adfa *Powys* **33** E6
Adforton *Heref'd* **25** A11
Adisham *Kent* **21** F9
Adlestrop *Glos* **27** F9
Adlingfleet *ER Yorks* **52** G4
Adlington *Lancs* **43** A9
Admaston *Staffs* **34** C6
Admaston *Telford* **34** D2
Admington *Warwick* **27** D9
Adstock *Bucks* **28** E4
Adstone *Northants* **28** C2
Adversane *W Sussex* **11** B9
Advie *H'land* **88** E1
Adwalton *W Yorks* **51** G8
Adwell *Oxon* **18** B3
Adwick le Street *S Yorks* **45** B9
Adwick upon Dearne *S Yorks* **45** B8
Adziel *Aberds* **89** C9
Ae Village *Dumf/Gal* **60** E5
Affleck *Aberds* **89** F8
Affpuddle *Dorset* **9** E7
Affric Lodge *H'land* **80** A3
Afon-wen *Flints* **42** E4
Afton *I/Wight* **10** F2
Agglethorpe *N Yorks* **58** H1
Agneash *I/Man* **48** D4
Aigburth *Mersey* **43** D6
Aiginis *W Isles* **91** D9
Aike *ER Yorks* **52** E6
Aikerness *Orkney* **95** C5
Aikers *Orkney* **95** J5
Aiketgate *Cumb* **57** B6
Aikton *Cumb* **56** A4
Ailey *Heref'd* **25** D10
Ailstone *Warwick* **27** C9
Ailsworth *Peterbro* **37** F7
Ainderby Quernhow *N Yorks* **51** A9
Ainderby Steeple *N Yorks* **58** G4
Aingers Green *Essex* **31** F8
Ainsdale *Mersey* **42** A6
Ainsdale-on-Sea *Mersey* **42** A6
Ainstable *Cumb* **57** B7
Ainsworth *Gtr Man* **43** A10
Ainthorpe *N Yorks* **59** F8
Aintree *Mersey* **43** C6
Aird *Arg/Bute* **72** C6
Aird *Dumf/Gal* **54** C3
Aird *H'land* **85** A12
Aird *W Isles* **91** D10
Aird a Mhachair *W Isles* **84** D2
Aird a'Mhulaidh *W Isles* **90** F6
Aird Asaig *W Isles* **90** G6
Aird Dhail *W Isles* **91** A9
Aird Mhidhinis *W Isles* **84** H2
Aird Mhighe *W Isles* **90** H6
Aird Mhighe *W Isles* **90** J5
Aird Mhor *W Isles* **84** H2
Aird of Sleat *H'land* **85** H10
Aird Thunga *W Isles* **91** D9
Aird Uig *W Isles* **90** D5
Airdens *H'land* **87** B9
Airdrie *N Lanarks* **68** D6
Airdtorrisdale *H'land* **93** C9
Airidh a Bhruaich *W Isles* **90** F7
Airieland *Dumf/Gal* **55** D10
Airmyn *ER Yorks* **52** G3
Airntully *Perth/Kinr* **76** D3
Airor *H'land* **85** H12
Airth *Falk* **69** B7
Airton *N Yorks* **50** D5
Airyhassen *Dumf/Gal* **54** E6
Aisby *Lincs* **46** C2
Aisby *Lincs* **36** B6
Aisgernis *W Isles* **84** F2
Aiskew *N Yorks* **58** H3
Aislaby *N Yorks* **59** H8
Aislaby *N Yorks* **59** F9
Aislaby *Stockton* **58** E5
Aisthorpe *Lincs* **46** D3
Aith *Orkney* **95** G3
Aith *Shetl'd* **96** H5
Aith *Shetl'd* **96** D8
Aithsetter *Shetl'd* **96** K6
Aitkenhead *S Ayrs* **66** F6
Aitnoch *H'land* **87** H12
Akeld *Northum* **71** H8
Akeley *Bucks* **28** E4
Akenham *Suffolk* **31** D8
Albaston *Cornw'l* **4** D5
Alberbury *Shrops* **33** D9
Albourne *W Sussex* **12** E1
Albrighton *Shrops* **33** D10
Albrighton *Shrops* **34** E4
Alburgh *Norfolk* **39** G8
Albury *Herts* **29** F11
Albury *Surrey* **19** G7
Albury End *Herts* **29** F11
Alby Hill *Norfolk* **39** B7
Alcaig *H'land* **87** F8
Alcaston *Shrops* **33** G10
Alcester *Warwick* **27** C7
Alciston *E Sussex* **12** F4
Alcombe *Som'set* **7** B8
Alcombe *Wilts* **16** E5
Alconbury *Cambs* **37** H7
Alconbury Weston *Cambs* **37** H7
Aldbar Castle *Angus* **77** B8
Aldborough *Norfolk* **39** B7
Aldborough *N Yorks* **51** C10
Aldbourne *Wilts* **17** D9
Aldbrough *ER Yorks* **53** F8
Aldbrough St John *N Yorks* **58** E3
Aldbury *Herts* **28** G6
Aldcliffe *Lancs* **49** C4
Aldclune *Perth/Kinr* **76** A2
Aldeburgh *Suffolk* **31** C11
Aldeby *Norfolk* **39** F10
Aldenham *Herts* **19** B8
Alderbury *Wilts* **9** B10
Aldercar *Derby* **45** H8
Alderford *Norfolk* **39** D7
Alderholt *Dorset* **9** C10
Alderley *Glos* **16** B4
Alderley Edge *Ches* **44** E2
Aldermaston *W Berks* **18** E2
Aldermaston Wharf *W Berks* **18** E3
Alderminster *Warwick* **27** D9
Alder's End *Heref'd* **26** D3
Aldersey Green *Ches* **43** G7
Aldershot *Hants* **18** F5
Alderton *Glos* **27** E7
Alderton *Northants* **28** D4
Alderton *Shrops* **33** C10
Alderton *Suffolk* **31** D10
Alderton *Wilts* **16** C5
Alderwasley *Derby* **45** G7
Aldfield *N Yorks* **51** C8
Aldford *Ches* **43** G7
Aldham *Essex* **30** F6
Aldham *Suffolk* **31** D7
Aldie *H'land* **87** C10
Aldingbourne *W Sussex* **11** D8
Aldingham *Cumb* **49** B2
Aldington *Kent* **13** C9
Aldington *Worcs* **27** D7
Aldington Frith *Kent* **13** C9
Aldochlay *Arg/Bute* **68** A2
Aldreth *Cambs* **29** A11
Aldridge *W Midlands* **35** E6
Aldringham *Suffolk* **31** B11
Aldsworth *Glos* **27** G8
Aldunie *Moray* **82** A5
Aldwark *Derby* **44** G6
Aldwark *N Yorks* **51** C10
Aldwick *W Sussex* **11** E8
Aldwincle *Northants* **36** G6
Aldworth *W Berks* **18** D2
Alexandria *W Dunb* **68** C2
Alfardisworthy *Devon* **6** E1
Alfington *Devon* **7** G10
Alfold *Surrey* **11** A9
Alfold Bars *W Sussex* **11** A9
Alfold Crossways *Surrey* **19** H7
Alford *Aberds* **83** B7
Alford *Lincs* **47** E8
Alford *Som'set* **8** A5
Alfreton *Derby* **45** G8
Alfrick *Worcs* **26** C4
Alfrick Pound *Worcs* **26** C4
Alfriston *E Sussex* **12** F4
Algaltraig *Arg/Bute* **73** F9
Algarkirk *Lincs* **37** B8
Alhampton *Som'set* **8** A5
Aline Lodge *W Isles* **90** F6
Alisary *H'land* **79** D10
Alkborough *N Lincs* **52** G4
Alkerton *Oxon* **27** D10
Alkham *Kent* **21** G9
Alkington *Shrops* **33** B11
Alkmonton *Derby* **35** B7
All Cannings *Wilts* **17** E7
All Saints South Elmham *Suffolk* **39** G9
All Stretton *Shrops* **33** F10
Alladale Lodge *H'land* **86** C7
Allaleigh *Devon* **5** F9
Allanaquoich *Aberds* **82** D3
Allangrange Mains *H'land* **87** F9
Allanton *Scot Borders* **71** E7
Allanton *N Lanarks* **69** E7
Allathasdal *W Isles* **84** H1
Allendale Town *Northum* **62** H4
Allenheads *Northum* **57** B10
Allens Green *Herts* **29** G11
Allensford *Durham* **58** A1
Allensmore *Heref'd* **25** E11
Allenton *Derby C* **35** B9
Aller *Som'set* **8** B3
Allerby *Cumb* **56** C2
Allerford *Som'set* **7** B8
Allerston *N Yorks* **52** A4
Allerthorpe *ER Yorks* **52** E3
Allerton *Mersey* **43** D7
Allerton *W Yorks* **51** F7
Allerton Bywater *W Yorks* **51** G10
Allerton Mauleverer *N Yorks* **51** D10
Allesley *W Midlands* **35** G9
Allestree *Derby C* **35** B9
Allet *Cornw'l* **3** E6
Allexton *Leics* **36** E4
Allgreave *Ches* **44** F3
Allhallows *Medway* **20** D5
Allhallows-on-Sea *Medway* **20** D5
Alligin Shuas *H'land* **85** C13
Allimore Green *Staffs* **34** D4
Allington *Lincs* **36** A4
Allington *Wilts* **17** H9
Allington *Wilts* **17** E7
Allithwaite *Cumb* **49** B3
Alloa *Clack* **69** A7
Allonby *Cumb* **56** B2
Alloway *S Ayrs* **66** E6
Allt *Carms* **23** F10
Allt na h-Airbhe *H'land* **86** B4
Allt-nan-sùgh *H'land* **85** F14
Alltchaorunn *H'land* **74** B4
Alltforgan *Powys* **32** C5
Alltmawr *Powys* **25** D7
Alltnacaillich *H'land* **92** E7
Alltsigh *H'land* **81** B6
Alltwalis *Carms* **23** C9
Alltwen *Neath P Talb* **14** A3
Alltyblaca *Ceredig'n* **23** B10
Allwood Green *Suffolk* **31** A7
Almeley *Heref'd* **25** C10
Almer *Dorset* **9** E8
Almholme *S Yorks* **45** B9
Almington *Staffs* **34** B3
Alminstone Cross *Devon* **6** D2
Almondbank *Perth/Kinr* **76** E3
Almondbury *W Yorks* **51** H7
Almondsbury *S Gloucs* **16** C3
Alne *N Yorks* **51** C10
Alness *H'land* **87** E9
Alnham *Northum* **62** B5
Alnmouth *Northum* **63** B8
Alnwick *Northum* **63** B7
Alperton *London* **19** C8
Alphamstone *Essex* **30** E5
Alpheton *Suffolk* **30** C5
Alphington *Devon* **7** G8
Alport *Derby* **44** F6
Alpraham *Ches* **43** G8
Alresford *Essex* **31** F7
Alrewas *Staffs* **35** D7
Alsager *Ches* **43** G10
Alsagers Bank *Staffs* **44** H2
Alsop en le Dale *Derby* **44** G5
Alston *Cumb* **57** B9
Alston *Devon* **8** D2
Alstone *Glos* **26** E6
Alstonefield *Staffs* **44** G5
Alswear *Devon* **7** D6
Altandhu *H'land* **92** H2
Altanduin *H'land* **93** G11
Altarnun *Cornw'l* **4** C3
Altass *H'land* **92** J7
Alterwall *H'land* **94** D4
Altham *Lancs* **50** F3
Althorne *Essex* **20** B6
Althorpe *N Lincs* **46** B2
Alticry *Dumf/Gal* **54** D5
Altnabreac Station *H'land* **93** E13
Altnacealgach Hotel *H'land* **92** H5
Altnacraig *Arg/Bute* **79** J11
Altnafeadh *H'land* **74** B5
Altnaharra *H'land* **93** F8
Altofts *W Yorks* **51** G9
Alton *Derby* **45** F7
Alton *Hants* **18** H4
Alton *Staffs* **35** A6
Alton Pancras *Dorset* **8** D6
Alton Priors *Wilts* **17** E8
Altrincham *Gtr Man* **43** D10
Altrua *H'land* **80** E4
Altskeith *Stirl* **75** G7
Altyre Ho. *Moray* **87** F13
Alva *Clack* **75** H11
Alvanley *Ches* **43** E7
Alvaston *Derby C* **35** B9
Alvechurch *Worcs* **27** A7
Alvecote *Warwick* **35** E8
Alvediston *Wilts* **9** B8
Alveley *Shrops* **34** G3
Alverdiscott *Devon* **6** D4
Alverstoke *Hants* **10** E5
Alverstone *I/Wight* **10** F4
Alverton *Notts* **36** A3
Alves *Moray* **88** B1
Alvescot *Oxon* **17** A9
Alveston *S Gloucs* **16** C3
Alveston *Warwick* **27** C9
Alvie *H'land* **81** C10
Alvingham *Lincs* **47** C7
Alvington *Glos* **16** A3
Alwalton *Cambs* **37** F7
Alweston *Dorset* **8** C5
Alwinton *Northum* **62** C5
Alwoodley *W Yorks* **51** E8
Alyth *Perth/Kinr* **76** C5
Am Baile *W Isles* **84** G2
Am Buth *Arg/Bute* **79** J11
Amatnatua *H'land* **86** B7
Amber Hill *Lincs* **46** H6
Ambergate *Derby* **45** G7
Amberley *Glos* **16** A5
Amberley *W Sussex* **11** C9
Amble *Northum* **63** C8
Amblecote *W Midlands* **34** G4
Ambler Thorn *W Yorks* **51** G6
Ambleside *Cumb* **56** F5
Ambleston *Pembs* **22** D5
Ambrosden *Oxon* **28** G3
Amcotts *N Lincs* **46** A2
Amersham *Bucks* **18** B6
Amesbury *Wilts* **17** G8
Amington *Staffs* **35** E8
Amisfield *Dumf/Gal* **60** E5
Amlwch *Angl* **40** A6
Amlwch Port *Angl* **40** A6
Ammanford = Rhydaman *Carms* **24** G3
Amod *Arg/Bute* **65** E8
Amotherby *N Yorks* **52** B3
Ampfield *Hants* **10** B3
Ampleforth *N Yorks* **52** B1
Ampney Crucis *Glos* **17** A7
Ampney St Mary *Glos* **17** A7
Ampney St Peter *Glos* **17** A7
Amport *Hants* **17** G9
Ampthill *Beds* **29** E7
Ampton *Suffolk* **30** A5
Amroth *Pembs* **22** F6
Amulree *Perth/Kinr* **75** D11
An Caol *H'land* **85** C11
An Cnoc *W Isles* **91** D9
An Gleann Ur *W Isles* **91** D9
An t-Ob = Leverburgh *W Isles* **90** J5
Anagach *H'land* **82** A2
Anaheilt *H'land* **79** E11
Anancaun *H'land* **86** E3
Ancaster *Lincs* **36** A5
Anchor *Shrops* **33** G7
Anchorsholme *Blackp'l* **49** E3
Ancroft *Northum* **71** F8
Ancrum *Scot Borders* **62** A2
Anderby *Lincs* **47** E9
Anderson *Dorset* **9** E7
Anderton *Ches* **43** E9
Andover *Hants* **17** G10
Andover Down *Hants* **17** G10
Andoversford *Glos* **27** G7
Andreas *I/Man* **48** C4
Anfield *Mersey* **43** C6
Angersleigh *Som'set* **7** E10
Angle *Pembs* **22** F3
Angmering *W Sussex* **11** D9
Angram *N Yorks* **51** E11
Angram *N Yorks* **57** G10
Anie *Stirl* **75** F8
Ankerville *H'land* **87** D11
Anlaby *ER Yorks* **52** G6
Anmer *Norfolk* **38** C3
Anna Valley *Hants* **17** G10
Annan *Dumf/Gal* **61** G7
Annat *Arg/Bute* **74** E3
Annat *H'land* **85** C13
Annbank *S Ayrs* **67** D7
Annesley *Notts* **45** G9
Annesley Woodhouse *Notts* **45** G8
Annfield Plain *Durham* **58** A2
Annifirth *Shetl'd* **96** J3
Annitsford *Tyne/Wear* **63** F8
Annscroft *Shrops* **33** E10
Ansdell *Lancs* **49** G3
Ansford *Som'set* **8** A5
Ansley *Warwick* **35** F8
Anslow *Staffs* **35** C8
Anslow Gate *Staffs* **35** C7
Anstey *Herts* **29** E11
Anstey *Leics* **35** E11
Anstruther Easter *Fife* **77** G8
Anstruther Wester *Fife* **77** G8
Ansty *Hants* **18** G4
Ansty *Warwick* **35** G9
Ansty *Wilts* **9** B8
Ansty *W Sussex* **12** D1
Anthill Common *Hants* **10** C5
Anthorn *Cumb* **61** H7
Antingham *Norfolk* **39** B8
Anton's Gowt *Lincs* **46** H6
Antonshill *Falk* **69** B7
Antony *Cornw'l* **4** F4
Anwick *Lincs* **46** G5
Anwoth *Dumf/Gal* **55** D8
Aoradh *Arg/Bute* **64** B3
Apes Hall *Cambs* **38** F1
Apethorpe *Northants* **36** F6
Apeton *Staffs* **34** D4
Apley *Lincs* **46** E5
Apperknowle *Derby* **45** E7
Apperley *Glos* **26** F5
Apperley Bridge *W Yorks* **51** F7
Appersett *N Yorks* **57** G10
Appin *Arg/Bute* **74** C2
Appin House *Arg/Bute* **74** C2
Appleby *N Lincs* **46** A3
Appleby-in-Westmorland *Cumb* **57** D8
Appleby Magna *Leics* **35** E9
Appleby Parva *Leics* **35** E9
Applecross *H'land* **85** D12
Applecross Ho. *H'land* **85** D12
Appledore *Devon* **6** C3
Appledore *Devon* **7** E9
Appledore *Kent* **13** D8
Appledore Heath *Kent* **13** C8
Appleford *Oxon* **18** B2
Applegarthtown *Dumf/Gal* **61** E7
Appleshaw *Hants* **17** G10
Applethwaite *Cumb* **56** D4
Appleton *Halton* **43** D8
Appleton *Oxon* **17** A11
Appleton-le-Moors *N Yorks* **59** H8
Appleton-le-Street *N Yorks* **52** B3
Appleton Roebuck *N Yorks* **52** E1
Appleton Thorn *Warrington* **43** D9
Appleton Wiske *N Yorks* **58** F4
Appletreehall *Scot Borders* **61** B11
Appletreewick *N Yorks* **51** C6
Appley *Som'set* **7** D9
Appley Bridge *Lancs* **43** B8
Apse Heath *I/Wight* **10** F4
Apsley End *Beds* **29** E8
Apuldram *W Sussex* **11** D7
Aquhythie *Aberds* **83** B9
Arabella *H'land* **87** D11
Arbeadie *Aberds* **83** D8
Arberth = Narberth *Pembs* **22** E6
Arbirlot *Angus* **77** C9
Arboll *H'land* **87** C11
Arborfield *Wokingham* **18** E4
Arborfield Cross *Wokingham* **18** E4
Arborfield Garrison *Wokingham* **18** E4
Arbour-thorne *S Yorks* **45** D7
Arbroath *Angus* **77** C9
Arbuthnott *Aberds* **83** F9
Archiestown *Moray* **88** D2
Arclid *Ches* **43** F10
Ard-dhubh *H'land* **85** D12
Ardachu *H'land* **93** J9
Ardalanish *Arg/Bute* **78** K6
Ardanaiseig *Arg/Bute* **74** E3
Ardaneaskan *H'land* **85** E13
Ardanstur *Arg/Bute* **73** B7
Ardargie House Hotel *Perth/Kinr* **76** F3
Ardarroch *H'land* **85** E13
Ardbeg *Arg/Bute* **64** D5
Ardbeg *Arg/Bute* **73** E10
Ardcharnich *H'land* **86** C4
Ardchiavaig *Arg/Bute* **78** K6
Ardchullarie More *Stirl* **75** F8
Ardchyle *Stirl* **75** E8
Arddleen *Powys* **33** D8
Ardechvie *H'land* **80** D3
Ardeley *Herts* **29** F10
Ardelve *H'land* **85** F13
Arden *Arg/Bute* **68** B2
Ardens Grafton *Warwick* **27** C8
Ardentinny *Arg/Bute* **73** E10
Ardentraive *Arg/Bute* **73** F9
Ardeonaig *Stirl* **75** D9
Ardersier *H'land* **87** F10
Ardessie *H'land* **86** C3
Ardfern *Arg/Bute* **73** C7
Ardgartan *Arg/Bute* **74** G5
Ardgay *H'land* **87** B8
Ardgour *H'land* **74** A3
Ardheslaig *H'land* **85** C12
Ardiecow *Moray* **88** B5
Ardindrean *H'land* **86** C4
Ardingly *W Sussex* **12** D2
Ardington *Oxon* **17** C11
Ardlair *Aberds* **83** A7
Ardlamont Ho. *Arg/Bute* **73** G8
Ardleigh *Essex* **31** F7
Ardler *Perth/Kinr* **76** C5
Ardley *Oxon* **28** F2
Ardlui *Arg/Bute* **74** F6
Ardlussa *Arg/Bute* **72** E5
Ardmair *H'land* **86** B4
Ardmay *Arg/Bute* **74** G5
Ardminish *Arg/Bute* **65** D7
Ardmolich *H'land* **79** D10
Ardmore *Arg/Bute* **79** J10
Ardmore *H'land* **92** D5
Ardmore *H'land* **87** C10
Ardnacross *Arg/Bute* **79** G8
Ardnadam *Arg/Bute* **73** F10
Ardnagrask *H'land* **87** G8
Ardnarff *H'land* **85** E13
Ardnastang *H'land* **79** E11
Ardnave *Arg/Bute* **64** A3
Ardno *Arg/Bute* **73** C10
Ardo *Aberds* **89** E8
Ardo Ho. *Aberds* **89** F9
Ardoch *Perth/Kinr* **76** D3
Ardochy House *H'land* **80** C4
Ardoyne *Aberds* **83** A8
Ardpatrick *Arg/Bute* **72** G6
Ardpatrick Ho. *Arg/Bute* **72** H6
Ardpeaton *Arg/Bute* **73** E11
Ardrishaig *Arg/Bute* **73** E7
Ardross *Fife* **77** G8
Ardross *H'land* **87** D9
Ardross Castle *H'land* **87** D9
Ardrossan *N Ayrs* **66** B5
Ardshealach *H'land* **79** E9
Ardsley *S Yorks* **45** B7
Ardslignish *H'land* **79** E8
Ardtalla *Arg/Bute* **64** C5
Ardtalnaig *Perth/Kinr* **75** D10
Ardtoe *H'land* **79** D9
Ardtrostan *Perth/Kinr* **75** E9
Arduaine *Arg/Bute* **72** B6
Ardullie *H'land* **87** E8
Ardvasar *H'land* **85** H11
Ardvorlich *Perth/Kinr* **75** E9
Ardwell *Dumf/Gal* **54** E4
Ardwell Mains *Dumf/Gal* **54** E4
Ardwick *Gtr Man* **44** C2
Areley Kings *Worcs* **26** A5
Arford *Hants* **18** H5
Argoed *Caerph* **15** B7
Argoed Mill *Powys* **24** B6
Arichamish *Arg/Bute* **73** C8
Arichastlich *Arg/Bute* **74** D5
Aridhglas *Arg/Bute* **78** J6
Arileod *Arg/Bute* **78** F4
Arinacrinachd *H'land* **85** C12
Arinagour *Arg/Bute* **78** F5
Arion *Orkney* **95** G3
Arisaig *H'land* **79** C9
Ariundle *H'land* **79** E11
Arkendale *N Yorks* **51** C9
Arkesden *Essex* **29** E11
Arkholme *Lancs* **50** B1
Arkle Town *N Yorks* **58** F1
Arkley *London* **19** B9
Arksey *S Yorks* **45** B9
Arkwright Town *Derby* **45** E8
Arle *Glos* **26** F6
Arlecdon *Cumb* **56** E2
Arlesey *Beds* **29** E8
Arleston *Telford* **34** D2
Arley *Ches* **43** D9
Arlingham *Glos* **26** G4
Arlington *Devon* **6** B5
Arlington *E Sussex* **12** F4
Arlington *Glos* **27** H8
Armadale *H'land* **93** C10
Armadale *W Loth* **69** D8
Armadale Castle *H'land* **85** H11
Armathwaite *Cumb* **57** B7
Arminghall *Norfolk* **39** E8
Armitage *Staffs* **35** D6
Armley *W Yorks* **51** F8
Armscote *Warwick* **27** D9
Armthorpe *S Yorks* **45** B10
Arnabost *Arg/Bute* **78** F5
Arncliffe *N Yorks* **50** B5
Arncroach *Fife* **77** G8
Arne *Dorset* **9** F8
Arnesby *Leics* **36** F2
Arngask *Perth/Kinr* **76** F4
Arnisdale *H'land* **85** G13
Arnish *H'land* **85** D10
Arniston Engine *Midloth* **70** D2
Arnol *W Isles* **91** C8
Arnold *ER Yorks* **53** E7
Arnold *Notts* **45** H9
Arnprior *Stirl* **68** A5
Arnside *Cumb* **49** B4
Aros Mains *Arg/Bute* **79** G8
Arowry *Wrex* **33** B10
Arpafeelie *H'land* **87** F9
Arrad Foot *Cumb* **49** A3
Arram *ER Yorks* **52** E6
Arrathorne *N Yorks* **58** G3
Arreton *I/Wight* **10** F4
Arrington *Cambs* **29** C10
Arrivain *Arg/Bute* **74** D5
Arrochar *Arg/Bute* **74** G5
Arrow *Warwick* **27** C7
Arthington *W Yorks* **51** E8
Arthingworth *Northants* **36** G3
Arthog *Gwyn* **32** D2
Arthrath *Aberds* **89** E9
Arthurstone *Perth/Kinr* **76** C5
Artrochie *Aberds* **89** E10
Arundel *W Sussex* **11** D9
Aryhoulan *H'land* **80** G2
Asby *Cumb* **56** D2
Ascog *Arg/Bute* **73** G10
Ascot *Windsor* **18** E6
Ascott *Warwick* **27** E10
Ascott-under-Wychwood *Oxon* **27** G10
Asenby *N Yorks* **51** B9
Asfordby *Leics* **36** D3
Asfordby Hill *Leics* **36** D3
Asgarby *Lincs* **46** H5

Asgarby *Lincs* 47 F7
Ash *Kent* 20 E2
Ash *Kent* 21 F9
Ash *Som'set* 8 B3
Ash *Surrey* 18 F5
Ash Bullayne *Devon* 7 F6
Ash Green *Warwick* 35 G9
Ash Magna *Shrops* 34 B1
Ash Mill *Devon* 7 D6
Ash Priors *Som'set* 7 D10
Ash Street *Suffolk* 31 D7
Ash Thomas *Devon* 7 E9
Ash Vale *Surrey* 18 F5
Ashampstead *W Berks* 18 D2
Ashbocking *Suffolk* 31 C8
Ashbourne *Derby* 44 H5
Ashbrittle *Som'set* 7 D9
Ashburton *Devon* 5 E8
Ashbury *Devon* 6 G4
Ashbury *Oxon* 17 C9
Ashby *N Lincs* 46 B3
Ashby by Partney *Lincs* 47 F8
Ashby cum Fenby *NE Lincs* 46 B6
Ashby de la Launde *Lincs* 46 G4
Ashby-de-la-Zouch *Leics* 35 D9
Ashby Folville *Leics* 36 D3
Ashby Magna *Leics* 36 F1
Ashby Parva *Leics* 35 G11
Ashby Puerorum *Lincs* 47 E7
Ashby St Ledgers *Northants* 28 B2
Ashby St Mary *Norfolk* 39 E9
Ashchurch *Glos* 26 E6
Ashcombe *Devon* 5 D10
Ashcott *Som'set* 15 H10
Ashdon *Essex* 30 D2
Ashe *Hants* 18 G2
Asheldham *Essex* 20 A6
Ashen *Essex* 30 D4
Ashendon *Bucks* 28 G4
Ashfield *Carms* 24 F3
Ashfield *Stirl* 75 G10
Ashfield *Suffolk* 31 B9
Ashfield Green *Suffolk* 31 A9
Ashfold Crossways *W Sussex* 11 B11
Ashford *Devon* 6 C4
Ashford *Hants* 9 C10
Ashford *Kent* 13 B9
Ashford *Surrey* 19 D7
Ashford Bowdler *Shrops* 26 A2
Ashford Carbonell *Shrops* 26 A2
Ashford Hill *Hants* 18 E2
Ashford in the Water *Derby* 44 F5
Ashgill *S Lanarks* 68 F6
Ashill *Devon* 7 E9
Ashill *Norfolk* 38 E4
Ashill *Som'set* 8 C2
Ashingdon *Essex* 20 B5
Ashington *Northum* 63 E8
Ashington *Som'set* 8 B4
Ashington *W Sussex* 11 C10
Ashintully Castle *Perth/Kinr* 76 A4
Ashkirk *Scot Borders* 61 A10
Ashlett *Hants* 10 D3
Ashleworth *Glos* 26 F5
Ashley *Cambs* 30 B3
Ashley *Ches* 43 D10
Ashley *Devon* 6 E5
Ashley *Dorset* 9 D10
Ashley *Glos* 16 B6
Ashley *Hants* 10 E1
Ashley *Hants* 10 A2
Ashley *Northants* 36 F3
Ashley *Staffs* 34 B3
Ashley Green *Bucks* 28 H6
Ashley Heath *Dorset* 9 D10
Ashley Heath *Staffs* 34 B3
Ashmanhaugh *Norfolk* 39 C9
Ashmansworth *Hants* 17 F11
Ashmansworthy *Devon* 6 E2
Ashmore *Dorset* 9 C8
Ashorne *Warwick* 27 C10
Ashover *Derby* 45 F7
Ashow *Warwick* 27 A10
Ashprington *Devon* 5 F9
Ashreigney *Devon* 6 E5
Ashtead *Surrey* 19 F8
Ashton *Ches* 43 F8
Ashton *Cornw'l* 2 G5
Ashton *Hants* 10 C4
Ashton *Heref'd* 26 B2
Ashton *Invercl* 73 F11
Ashton *Northants* 28 D4
Ashton *Northants* 37 G6
Ashton Common *Wilts* 16 F5
Ashton-In-Makerfield *Gtr Man* 43 C8
Ashton Keynes *Wilts* 17 B7
Ashton under Hill *Worcs* 26 E6
Ashton-under-Lyne *Gtr Man* 44 C3
Ashton upon Mersey *Gtr Man* 43 C10
Ashurst *Hants* 10 C2
Ashurst *Kent* 12 C4
Ashurst *W Sussex* 11 C10
Ashurstwood *W Sussex* 12 C3
Ashwater *Devon* 6 G2
Ashwell *Herts* 29 E9
Ashwell *Rutl'd* 36 D4
Ashwell *Som'set* 8 C2
Ashwellthorpe *Norfolk* 39 F7
Ashwick *Som'set* 16 G3
Ashwicken *Norfolk* 38 D3
Ashybank *Scot Borders* 61 B11
Askam in Furness *Cumb* 49 B2
Askern *S Yorks* 45 A9
Askerswell *Dorset* 8 E4
Askett *Bucks* 28 H5
Askham *Cumb* 57 D7
Askham *Notts* 45 E11
Askham Bryan *C/York* 52 E1
Askham Richard *C/York* 51 E11
Asknish *Arg/Bute* 73 D8
Askrigg *N Yorks* 57 G11
Askwith *N Yorks* 51 E7
Aslackby *Lincs* 37 B6
Aslacton *Norfolk* 39 F7
Aslockton *Notts* 36 B3
Asloun *Aberds* 83 B7
Aspatria *Cumb* 56 B3
Aspenden *Herts* 29 F10
Asperton *Lincs* 37 B8
Aspley Guise *Beds* 28 E6
Aspley Heath *Beds* 28 E6
Aspull *Gtr Man* 43 B9
Asselby *ER Yorks* 52 G3
Asserby *Lincs* 47 E8
Assington *Suffolk* 30 E6
Assynt Ho. *H'land* 87 E8
Astbury *Ches* 44 F2
Astcote *Northants* 28 C3
Asterley *Shrops* 33 E9
Asterton *Shrops* 33 F9
Asthall *Oxon* 27 G9
Asthall Leigh *Oxon* 27 G10
Astley *Shrops* 33 D11
Astley *Warwick* 35 G9
Astley *Worcs* 26 B4
Astley Abbotts *Shrops* 34 F3
Astley Bridge *Gtr Man* 43 A10
Astley Cross *Worcs* 26 B5
Astley Green *Gtr Man* 43 C10
Aston *Ches* 43 H9
Aston *Ches* 43 E8
Aston *Derby* 44 D5
Aston *Heref'd* 25 A11
Aston *Herts* 29 F9
Aston *Oxon* 17 A10
Aston *Shrops* 33 C11
Aston *Staffs* 34 A3
Aston *S Yorks* 45 D8
Aston *Telford* 34 E2
Aston *W Midlands* 35 G6
Aston *Wokingham* 18 C4
Aston Abbotts *Bucks* 28 F5
Aston Botterell *Shrops* 34 G2
Aston-by-Stone *Staffs* 34 B5
Aston Cantlow *Warwick* 27 C8
Aston Clinton *Bucks* 28 G5
Aston Crews *Heref'd* 26 F3
Aston Cross *Glos* 26 E6
Aston End *Herts* 29 F9
Aston Eyre *Shrops* 34 F2
Aston Fields *Worcs* 26 B6
Aston Flamville *Leics* 35 F10
Aston Ingham *Heref'd* 26 F3
Aston juxta Mondrum *Ches* 43 G9
Aston le Walls *Northants* 27 C11
Aston Magna *Glos* 27 E8
Aston Munslow *Shrops* 33 G11
Aston on Clun *Shrops* 33 G9
Aston-on-Trent *Derby* 35 C10
Aston Rogers *Shrops* 33 E9
Aston Rowant *Oxon* 18 B4
Aston Sandford *Bucks* 28 H4
Aston Somerville *Worcs* 27 E7
Aston Subedge *Glos* 27 D8
Aston Tirrold *Oxon* 18 C2
Aston Upthorpe *Oxon* 18 C2
Astrop *Northants* 28 E2
Astwick *Beds* 29 E9
Astwood *M/Keynes* 28 D6
Astwood *Worcs* 26 C5
Astwood Bank *Worcs* 27 B7
Aswarby *Lincs* 37 B6
Aswardby *Lincs* 47 E7
Atch Lench *Worcs* 27 C7
Atcham *Shrops* 33 E11
Athelhampton *Dorset* 9 E6
Athelington *Suffolk* 31 A9
Athelney *Som'set* 8 B2
Athelstaneford *E Loth* 70 C4
Atherington *Devon* 6 D4
Atherstone *Warwick* 35 F9
Atherstone on Stour *Warwick* 27 C9
Atherton *Gtr Man* 43 B9
Atley Hill *N Yorks* 58 F3
Atlow *Derby* 44 H6
Attadale *H'land* 86 H2
Attadale Ho. *H'land* 86 H2
Attenborough *Notts* 35 B11
Atterby *Lincs* 46 C3
Attercliffe *S Yorks* 45 D7
Attleborough *Norfolk* 38 F6
Attleborough *Warwick* 35 F9
Attlebridge *Norfolk* 39 D7
Atwick *ER Yorks* 53 D7
Atworth *Wilts* 16 E5
Aubourn *Lincs* 46 F3
Auchagallon *N Ayrs* 66 C1
Auchallater *Aberds* 82 E3
Aucharnie *Aberds* 89 D6
Auchattie *Aberds* 83 D8
Auchavan *Angus* 82 G3
Auchbreck *Moray* 82 A4
Auchenback *E Renf* 68 E4
Auchenbainzie *Dumf/Gal* 60 D4
Auchenblae *Aberds* 83 F9
Auchenbrack *Dumf/Gal* 60 D3
Auchenbreck *Arg/Bute* 73 E9
Auchencairn *Dumf/Gal* 55 D10
Auchencairn *Dumf/Gal* 60 E5
Auchencairn *N Ayrs* 66 D3
Auchencrosh *S Ayrs* 54 B4
Auchencrow *Scot Borders* 71 D7
Auchendinny *Midloth* 69 D11
Auchengray *S Lanarks* 69 E8
Auchenhalrig *Moray* 88 B3
Auchenheath *S Lanarks* 69 F7
Auchenlochan *Arg/Bute* 73 F8
Auchenmalg *Dumf/Gal* 54 D5
Auchensoul *S Ayrs* 66 G5
Auchentiber *N Ayrs* 67 B6
Auchertyre *H'land* 85 F13
Auchgourish *H'land* 81 B11
Auchincarroch *W Dunb* 68 B3
Auchindrain *Arg/Bute* 73 C9
Auchindrean *H'land* 86 C4
Auchininna *Aberds* 89 D6
Auchinleck *E Ayrs* 67 D8
Auchinloch *N Lanarks* 68 C5
Auchinroath *Moray* 88 C2
Auchintoul *Aberds* 83 B7
Auchiries *Aberds* 89 E10
Auchlee *Aberds* 83 D10
Auchleven *Aberds* 83 A8
Auchlochan *S Lanarks* 69 G7
Auchlossan *Aberds* 83 C7
Auchlunies *Aberds* 83 D10
Auchlyne *Stirl* 75 E8
Auchmacoy *Aberds* 89 E9
Auchmair *Moray* 82 A5
Auchmantle *Dumf/Gal* 54 C4
Auchmillan *E Ayrs* 67 D8
Auchmithie *Angus* 77 C9
Auchmuirbridge *Fife* 76 G5
Auchmull *Angus* 83 F7
Auchnacree *Angus* 77 A7
Auchnagallin *H'land* 87 H13
Auchnagatt *Aberds* 89 D9
Auchnaha *Arg/Bute* 73 E8
Auchnashelloch *Perth/Kinr* 75 F10
Aucholzie *Aberds* 82 D5
Auchrannie *Angus* 76 B5
Auchroisk *H'land* 82 A2
Auchronie *Angus* 82 E6
Auchterarder *Perth/Kinr* 76 F2
Auchteraw *H'land* 80 C5
Auchterderran *Fife* 76 H5
Auchterhouse *Angus* 76 D6
Auchtermuchty *Fife* 76 F5
Auchterneed *H'land* 86 F7
Auchtertool *Fife* 69 A11
Auchtertyre *Moray* 88 C1
Auchtubh *Stirl* 75 E8
Auckengill *H'land* 94 D5
Auckley *S Yorks* 45 B10
Audenshaw *Gtr Man* 44 C3
Audlem *Ches* 34 A2
Audley *Staffs* 43 G10
Audley End *Essex* 30 E5
Auds *Aberds* 89 B6
Aughton *ER Yorks* 52 F3
Aughton *Lancs* 43 B6
Aughton *Lancs* 50 C1
Aughton *S Yorks* 45 D8
Aughton *Wilts* 17 F9
Aughton Park *Lancs* 43 B7
Auldearn *H'land* 87 F12
Aulden *Heref'd* 25 C11
Auldgirth *Dumf/Gal* 60 E5
Auldhame *E Loth* 70 B4
Auldhouse *S Lanarks* 68 E5
Ault a'chruinn *H'land* 80 A1
Aultanrynie *H'land* 92 F6
Aultbea *H'land* 91 J13
Aultdearg *H'land* 86 E5
Aultgrishan *H'land* 91 J12
Aultguish Inn *H'land* 86 D6
Aultibea *H'land* 93 G13
Aultiphurst *H'land* 93 C11
Aultmore *Moray* 88 C4
Aultnagoire *H'land* 81 A7
Aultnamain Inn *H'land* 87 C9
Aultnaslat *H'land* 80 C3
Aulton *Aberds* 83 A8
Aundorach *H'land* 82 B1
Aunsby *Lincs* 36 B6
Auquhorthies *Aberds* 89 F8
Aust *S Gloucs* 16 C2
Austendike *Lincs* 37 C8
Austerfield *S Yorks* 45 C10
Austrey *Warwick* 35 E8
Austwick *N Yorks* 50 C3
Authorpe *Lincs* 47 D8
Authorpe Row *Lincs* 47 E9
Avebury *Wilts* 17 E8
Aveley *Thurr'k* 20 C2
Avening *Glos* 16 B5
Averham *Notts* 45 G11
Aveton Gifford *Devon* 5 G7
Avielochan *H'land* 81 B11
Aviemore *H'land* 81 B10
Avington *Hants* 10 A4
Avington *W Berks* 17 E10
Avoch *H'land* 87 F10
Avon *Hants* 9 E10
Avon Dassett *Warwick* 27 D11
Avonbridge *Falk* 69 C8
Avonmouth *Bristol* 15 D11
Avonwick *Devon* 5 F8
Awbridge *Hants* 10 B2
Awhirk *Dumf/Gal* 54 D3
Awkley *S Gloucs* 16 C2
Awliscombe *Devon* 7 F10
Awre *Glos* 26 H4
Awsworth *Notts* 35 A10
Axbridge *Som'set* 15 F10
Axford *Hants* 18 G3
Axford *Wilts* 17 D9
Axminster *Devon* 8 E1
Axmouth *Devon* 8 E1
Axton *Flints* 42 D4
Aycliff *Kent* 21 G10
Aycliffe *Durham* 58 D3
Aydon *Northum* 62 G6
Aylburton *Glos* 16 A3
Ayle *Northum* 57 B9
Aylesbeare *Devon* 7 G9
Aylesbury *Bucks* 28 G5
Aylesby *NE Lincs* 46 B6
Aylesford *Kent* 20 F4
Aylesham *Kent* 21 F9
Aylestone *Leics C* 36 E1
Aylmerton *Norfolk* 39 B7
Aylsham *Norfolk* 39 C7
Aylton *Heref'd* 26 E3
Aymestrey *Heref'd* 25 B11
Aynho *Northants* 28 E2
Ayot St Lawrence *Herts* 29 G8
Ayot St Peter *Herts* 29 G9
Ayr *S Ayrs* 66 D6
Aysgarth *N Yorks* 58 H1
Ayside *Cumb* 49 A3
Ayston *Rutl'd* 36 E4
Aythorpe Roding *Essex* 30 G2
Ayton *Scot Borders* 71 D8
Aywick *Shetl'd* 96 E7
Azerley *N Yorks* 51 B8

B

Babbacombe *Torbay* 5 E10
Babbinswood *Shrops* 33 B9
Babcary *Som'set* 8 B4
Babel *Carms* 24 E5
Babell *Flints* 42 E4
Babraham *Cambs* 30 C2
Babworth *Notts* 45 D10
Bac *W Isles* 91 C9
Bachau *Angl* 40 B6
Back of Keppoch *H'land* 79 C9
Back Rogerton *E Ayrs* 67 D8
Backaland *Orkney* 95 E6
Backaskaill *Orkney* 95 C5
Backbarrow *Cumb* 49 A3
Backe *Carms* 23 E7
Backfolds *Aberds* 89 C10
Backford *Ches* 43 E7
Backford Cross *Ches* 43 E6
Backhill *Aberds* 89 E7
Backhill *Aberds* 89 E10
Backhill of Clackriach *Aberds* 89 D9
Backhill of Fortree *Aberds* 89 D9
Backhill of Trustach *Aberds* 83 D8
Backies *H'land* 93 J11
Backlass *H'land* 94 E4
Backwell *N Som'set* 15 E10
Backworth *Tyne/Wear* 63 F9
Bacon End *Essex* 30 G3
Baconsthorpe *Norfolk* 39 B7
Bacton *Heref'd* 25 E10
Bacton *Norfolk* 39 B9
Bacton *Suffolk* 31 B7
Bacton Green *Suffolk* 31 B7
Bacup *Lancs* 50 G4
Badachro *H'land* 85 A12
Badanloch Lodge *H'land* 93 F10
Badavanich *H'land* 86 F4
Badbury *Swindon* 17 C8
Badby *Northants* 28 C2
Badcall *H'land* 92 D5
Badcaul *H'land* 86 B3
Baddeley Green *Stoke* 44 G3
Baddesley Clinton *Warwick* 27 A9
Baddesley Ensor *Warwick* 35 F8
Baddidarach *H'land* 92 G3
Baddoch *Aberds* 82 E3
Baddock *H'land* 87 F10
Badenscoth *Aberds* 89 E7
Badenyon *Aberds* 82 B5
Badger *Shrops* 34 F3
Badger's Mount *Kent* 19 E11
Badgeworth *Glos* 26 G6
Badgworth *Som'set* 15 F9
Badicaul *H'land* 85 F12
Badingham *Suffolk* 31 B10
Badlesmere *Kent* 21 F7
Badlipster *H'land* 94 F4
Badluarach *H'land* 86 B2
Badminton *S Gloucs* 16 C5
Badnaban *H'land* 92 G3
Badninish *H'land* 87 B10
Badrallach *H'land* 86 B3
Badsey *Worcs* 27 D7
Badshot Lea *Surrey* 18 G5
Badsworth *W Yorks* 45 A8
Badwell Ash *Suffolk* 30 B6
Bae Colwyn = Colwyn Bay *Conwy* 41 C10
Bag Enderby *Lincs* 47 E7
Bagby *N Yorks* 51 A10
Bagendon *Glos* 27 H7
Bagh a Chaisteil = Castlebay *W Isles* 84 J1
Bagh Mor *W Isles* 84 C3
Bagh Shiarabhagh *W Isles* 84 H2
Baghasdal *W Isles* 84 G2
Bagillt *Flints* 42 E5
Baginton *Warwick* 27 A10
Baglan *Neath P Talb* 14 B3
Bagley *Shrops* 33 C10
Bagnall *Staffs* 44 G3
Bagnor *W Berks* 17 E11
Bagshot *Surrey* 18 E6
Bagshot *Wilts* 17 E10
Bagthorpe *Norfolk* 38 B3
Bagthorpe *Notts* 45 G8
Bagworth *Leics* 35 E10
Bagwy Llydiart *Heref'd* 25 F11
Bail Àrd Bhuirgh *W Isles* 91 B9
Bail Uachdraich *W Isles* 84 B3
Baildon *W Yorks* 51 F7
Baile *W Isles* 90 J4
Baile a Mhanaich *W Isles* 84 C2
Baile Ailein *W Isles* 91 E7
Baile an Truiseil *W Isles* 91 B8
Baile Boidheach *Arg/Bute* 72 F6
Baile Glas *W Isles* 84 C3
Baile Mhartainn *W Isles* 84 A2
Baile Mhic Phail *W Isles* 84 A3
Baile Mor *Arg/Bute* 78 J5
Baile Mor *W Isles* 84 B2
Baile na Creige *W Isles* 84 H1
Baile nan Cailleach *W Isles* 84 C2
Baile Raghaill *W Isles* 84 A2
Bailebeag *H'land* 81 B7
Baileyhead *Cumb* 61 F11
Bailiesward *Aberds* 88 E4
Baillieston *C/Glasg* 68 D5
Bail'lochdrach *W Isles* 84 C3
Bail'Ur Tholastaidh *W Isles* 91 C10
Bainbridge *N Yorks* 57 G11
Bainsford *Falk* 69 B7
Bainshole *Aberds* 88 E6
Bainton *ER Yorks* 52 D5
Bainton *Peterbro* 37 E6
Bairnkine *Scot Borders* 62 B2
Baker Street *Thurr'k* 20 C3
Baker's End *Herts* 29 G10
Bakewell *Derby* 44 F6
Bala = Y Bala *Gwyn* 32 B5
Balachuirn *H'land* 85 D10
Balavil *H'land* 81 C9
Balbeg *H'land* 81 A6
Balbeg *H'land* 86 H7
Balbeggie *Perth/Kinr* 76 E4
Balbithan *Aberds* 83 B9
Balbithan Ho. *Aberds* 83 B10
Balblair *H'land* 87 E10
Balblair *H'land* 87 B8
Balby *S Yorks* 45 B9
Balchladich *H'land* 92 F3
Balchraggan *H'land* 87 H8
Balchraggan *H'land* 87 G8
Balchrick *H'land* 92 D4
Balchrystie *Fife* 77 G7
Balcladaich *H'land* 80 A4
Balcombe *W Sussex* 12 C2
Balcombe Lane *W Sussex* 12 C2
Balcomie *Fife* 77 F9
Balcurvie *Fife* 76 G6
Baldersby *N Yorks* 51 B9
Baldersby St James *N Yorks* 51 B9
Balderstone *Lancs* 50 F2
Balderton *Ches* 42 F6
Balderton *Notts* 46 G2
Baldhu *Cornw'l* 3 E6
Baldinnie *Fife* 77 F7
Baldock *Herts* 29 E9
Baldovie *Dundee C* 77 D7
Baldrine *I/Man* 48 D4
Baldslow *E Sussex* 13 E6
Baldwin *I/Man* 48 D3
Baldwinholme *Cumb* 56 A5
Baldwin's Gate *Staffs* 34 A3
Bale *Norfolk* 38 B6
Balearn *Aberds* 89 C10
Balemartine *Arg/Bute* 78 G2
Balephuil *Arg/Bute* 78 G2
Balerno *C/Edinb* 69 D10
Balevullin *Arg/Bute* 78 G2
Balfield *Angus* 83 G7
Balfour *Orkney* 95 G5
Balfron *Stirl* 68 B4
Balfron Station *Stirl* 68 B4
Balgaveny *Aberds* 89 D6
Balgavies *Angus* 77 B8
Balgonar *Fife* 69 A9
Balgove *Aberds* 89 E8
Balgowan *H'land* 81 D8
Balgown *H'land* 85 B8
Balgrochan *E Dunb* 68 C5
Balgy *H'land* 85 C13
Balhaldie *Stirl* 75 G11
Balhalgardy *Aberds* 83 A9
Balham *London* 19 D9
Balhary *Perth/Kinr* 76 C5
Baliasta *Shetl'd* 96 C8
Baligill *H'land* 93 C11
Balintore *Angus* 76 B5
Balintore *H'land* 87 D11
Balintraid *H'land* 87 D10
Balk *N Yorks* 51 A10
Balkeerie *Angus* 76 C6
Balkemback *Angus* 76 D6
Balkholme *ER Yorks* 52 G3
Balkissock *S Ayrs* 54 A4
Ball *Shrops* 33 C9
Ball Haye Green *Staffs* 44 G3
Ball Hill *Hants* 17 E11
Ballabeg *I/Man* 48 E2
Ballacannel *I/Man* 48 D4
Ballachulish *H'land* 74 B3
Ballajora *I/Man* 48 C4
Ballaleigh *I/Man* 48 D3
Ballamodha *I/Man* 48 E2
Ballantrae *S Ayrs* 54 A3
Ballaquine *I/Man* 48 D4
Ballards Gore *Essex* 20 B6
Ballasalla *I/Man* 48 C3
Ballasalla *I/Man* 48 E2
Ballater *Aberds* 82 D5
Ballaugh *I/Man* 48 C3
Ballaveare *I/Man* 48 E3
Ballcorach *Moray* 82 A3
Ballechin *Perth/Kinr* 76 B2
Balleigh *H'land* 87 C10
Ballencrieff *E Loth* 70 C3
Ballentoul *Perth/Kinr* 81 G10
Ballidon *Derby* 44 G6
Balliemore *Arg/Bute* 73 E9
Balliemore *Arg/Bute* 79 J11
Ballikinrain *Stirl* 68 B4
Ballimeanoch *Arg/Bute* 73 B9
Ballimore *Arg/Bute* 73 E8
Ballimore *Stirl* 75 F8
Ballinaby *Arg/Bute* 64 B3
Ballindean *Perth/Kinr* 76 E5
Ballingdon *Suffolk* 30 D5
Ballinger Common *Bucks* 18 A6
Ballingham *Heref'd* 26 E2
Ballingry *Fife* 76 H4
Ballinlick *Perth/Kinr* 76 C2
Ballinluig *Perth/Kinr* 76 B2
Ballintuim *Perth/Kinr* 76 B4
Balloch *Angus* 76 B6
Balloch *H'land* 87 G10
Balloch *N Lanarks* 68 C6
Balloch *W Dunb* 68 B2
Ballochan *Aberds* 83 D7
Ballochford *Moray* 88 E3
Ballochmorrie *S Ayrs* 54 A5
Balls Cross *W Sussex* 11 B8
Balls Green *Essex* 31 F7
Ballygown *Arg/Bute* 78 G7
Ballygrant *Arg/Bute* 64 B4
Ballyhaugh *Arg/Bute* 78 F4
Balmacara *H'land* 85 F13
Balmacara Square *H'land* 85 F13
Balmaclellan *Dumf/Gal* 55 B9
Balmacneil *Perth/Kinr* 76 B2
Balmacqueen *H'land* 85 A9
Balmae *Dumf/Gal* 55 E9
Balmaha *Stirl* 68 A3
Balmalcolm *Fife* 76 G6
Balmeanach *H'land* 85 D10
Balmedie *Aberds* 83 B11
Balmer Heath *Shrops* 33 B10
Balmerino *Fife* 76 E6
Balmerlawn *Hants* 10 D2
Balmichael *N Ayrs* 66 C2
Balmirmer *Angus* 77 D8
Balmore *H'land* 85 D7
Balmore *H'land* 86 H6
Balmore *H'land* 87 G11
Balmore *Perth/Kinr* 76 B2
Balmule *Fife* 69 B11
Balmullo *Fife* 77 E7
Balmungie *H'land* 87 F10
Balnaboth *Angus* 82 G5
Balnabruaich *H'land* 87 E10
Balnabruich *H'land* 94 H3
Balnacoil *H'land* 93 H11
Balnacra *H'land* 86 G2
Balnafoich *H'land* 87 H9
Balnagall *H'land* 87 C11
Balnaguard *Perth/Kinr* 76 B2
Balnahard *Arg/Bute* 72 D3
Balnahard *Arg/Bute* 78 H7
Balnain *H'land* 86 H7
Balnakeil *H'land* 92 C6
Balnaknock *H'land* 85 B9
Balnapaling *H'land* 87 E10
Balne *N Yorks* 52 H1
Balochroy *Arg/Bute* 65 C8
Balone *Fife* 77 F7
Balornock *C/Glasg* 68 D5
Balquharn *Perth/Kinr* 76 D3
Balquhidder *Stirl* 75 E8
Balsall *W Midlands* 35 H8
Balsall Common *W Midlands* 35 H8
Balsall Heath *W Midlands* 35 G6
Balscott *Oxon* 27 D10
Balsham *Cambs* 30 C2
Baltasound *Shetl'd* 96 C8
Balterley *Staffs* 43 G10
Baltersan *Dumf/Gal* 55 C7
Balthangie *Aberds* 89 C8
Baltonsborough *Som'set* 8 A4
Balvaird *H'land* 87 F8
Balvicar *Arg/Bute* 72 B6
Balvraid *H'land* 85 G13
Balvraid *H'land* 87 H11
Bamber Bridge *Lancs* 50 G1
Bambers Green *Essex* 30 F2
Bamburgh *Northum* 71 G10
Bamff *Perth/Kinr* 76 B5
Bamford *Derby* 44 D6
Bamford *Gtr Man* 44 A2
Bampton *Cumb* 57 E7
Bampton *Devon* 7 D8
Bampton *Oxon* 17 A10
Bampton Grange *Cumb* 57 E7
Banavie *H'land* 80 F3
Banbury *Oxon* 27 D11
Bancffosfelen *Carms* 23 E9
Banchory *Aberds* 83 D8
Banchory-Devenick *Aberds* 83 C11
Bancycapel *Carms* 23 E9
Bancyfelin *Carms* 23 E8
Bancyffordd *Carms* 23 C9
Bandirran *Perth/Kinr* 76 D5
Banff *Aberds* 89 B6
Bangor *Gwyn* 41 C7
Bangor-is-y-coed *Wrex* 43 H6
Banham *Norfolk* 39 G6
Bank *Hants* 10 D1
Bank Newton *N Yorks* 50 D5
Bank Street *Worcs* 26 B3
Bankend *Dumf/Gal* 60 G6
Bankfoot *Perth/Kinr* 76 D3
Bankglen *E Ayrs* 67 E9
Bankhead *Aberd C* 83 B10
Bankhead *Aberds* 83 C8
Banknock *Falk* 68 C6
Banks *Cumb* 61 G11
Banks *Lancs* 49 G3
Bankshill *Dumf/Gal* 61 E7
Banningham *Norfolk* 39 C8
Banniskirk Ho. *H'land* 94 E3
Bannister Green *Essex* 30 F3
Bannockburn *Stirl* 69 A7
Banstead *Surrey* 19 F9
Bantham *Devon* 5 G7
Banton *N Lanarks* 68 C6
Banwell *N Som'set* 15 F9
Banyard's Green *Suffolk* 31 A9
Bapchild *Kent* 20 E6
Bar Hill *Cambs* 29 B10
Barabhas *W Isles* 91 C8
Barabhas Iarach *W Isles* 91 C8
Barabhas Uarach *W Isles* 91 B8
Barachandroman *Arg/Bute* 79 J9
Barassie *S Ayrs* 66 C6
Baravullin *Arg/Bute* 79 H11
Barbaraville *H'land* 87 D10
Barber Booth *Derby* 44 D5
Barbieston *S Ayrs* 67 E7
Barbon *Cumb* 50 A2
Barbridge *Ches* 43 G9
Barbrook *Devon* 6 B6
Barby *Northants* 28 A2
Barcaldine *Arg/Bute* 74 C2
Barcheston *Warwick* 27 E9
Barcombe *E Sussex* 12 E3
Barcombe Cross *E Sussex* 12 E3
Barden *N Yorks* 58 G2
Barden Scale *N Yorks* 51 D6
Bardennoch *Dumf/Gal* 67 G8
Bardfield Saling *Essex* 30 F3
Bardister *Shetl'd* 96 F5
Bardney *Lincs* 46 F5
Bardon *Leics* 35 D10
Bardon Mill *Northum* 62 G3
Bardowie *E Dunb* 68 C4
Bardrainney *Invercl* 68 C2
Bardsea *Cumb* 49 B3
Bardsey *W Yorks* 51 E9
Bardwell *Suffolk* 30 A6
Bare *Lancs* 49 C4
Barfad *Arg/Bute* 73 G7
Barford *Norfolk* 39 E7
Barford *Warwick* 27 B9
Barford St John *Oxon* 27 E11
Barford St Martin *Wilts* 9 A9
Barford St Michael *Oxon* 27 E11
Barfreston *Kent* 21 F9
Bargod = Bargoed *Caerph* 15 B7
Bargoed = Bargod *Caerph* 15 B7
Bargrennan *Dumf/Gal* 54 B6
Barham *Cambs* 37 H7
Barham *Kent* 21 F9
Barham *Suffolk* 31 C8
Barharrow *Dumf/Gal* 55 D9
Barhill *Dumf/Gal* 55 C11
Barholm *Lincs* 37 D6
Barkby *Leics* 36 E2
Barkestone-le-Vale *Leics* 36 B3
Barkham *Wokingham* 18 E4
Barking *London* 19 C11
Barking *Suffolk* 31 C7
Barking Tye *Suffolk* 31 C7
Barkingside *London* 19 C11
Barkisland *W Yorks* 51 H6
Barkston *Lincs* 36 A5
Barkston *N Yorks* 51 F10
Barkway *Herts* 29 E10
Barlaston *Staffs* 34 B4
Barlavington *W Sussex* 11 C8
Barlborough *Derby* 45 E8
Barlby *N Yorks* 52 F2
Barlestone *Leics* 35 E10
Barley *Herts* 29 E10
Barley *Lancs* 50 E4
Barley Mow *Tyne/Wear* 58 A3
Barleythorpe *Rutl'd* 36 E4
Barling *Essex* 20 C6
Barlow *Derby* 45 E7
Barlow *N Yorks* 52 G2
Barlow *Tyne/Wear* 63 G7
Barmby Moor *ER Yorks* 52 E3
Barmby on the Marsh *ER Yorks* 52 G2
Barmer *Norfolk* 38 B4
Barmoor Castle *Northum* 71 G8
Barmoor Lane End *Northum* 71 G9
Barmouth = Abermaw *Gwyn* 32 D2
Barmpton *D'lington* 58 E4
Barmston *ER Yorks* 53 D7
Barnack *Peterbro* 37 E6
Barnacle *Warwick* 35 G9
Barnard Castle *Durham* 58 E1
Barnard Gate *Oxon* 27 G11
Barnardiston *Suffolk* 30 D4
Barnbarroch *Dumf/Gal* 55 D11
Barnburgh *S Yorks* 45 B8
Barnby *Suffolk* 39 G10
Barnby Dun *S Yorks* 45 B10
Barnby in the Willows *Notts* 46 G2
Barnby Moor *Notts* 45 D10
Barnes Street *Kent* 20 G3
Barnet *London* 19 B9
Barnetby le Wold *N Lincs* 46 B4
Barney *Norfolk* 38 B5
Barnham *Suffolk* 38 H4
Barnham *W Sussex* 11 D8
Barnham Broom *Norfolk* 39 E6
Barnhead *Angus* 77 B9
Barnhill *Ches* 43 G7
Barnhill *Dundee C* 77 D7
Barnhill *Moray* 88 C1
Barnhills *Dumf/Gal* 54 B2
Barningham *Durham* 58 E1
Barningham *Suffolk* 38 H5
Barnoldby le Beck *NE Lincs* 46 B6
Barnoldswick *Lancs* 50 E4
Barns Green *W Sussex* 11 B10
Barnsley *Glos* 27 H7
Barnsley *S Yorks* 45 B7
Barnstaple *Devon* 6 C4
Barnston *Essex* 30 G3
Barnston *Mersey* 42 D5
Barnstone *Notts* 36 B3
Barnt Green *Worcs* 27 A7
Barnton *Ches* 43 E9
Barnton *C/Edinb* 69 C10
Barnwell All Saints *Northants* 36 G6
Barnwell St Andrew *Northants* 36 G6
Barnwood *Glos* 26 G5
Barochreal *Arg/Bute* 79 J11
Barons Cross *Heref'd* 25 C11
Barr *S Ayrs* 66 G5
Barra Castle *Aberds* 83 A9
Barrachan *Dumf/Gal* 54 E6
Barrack *Aberds* 89 D8
Barraglom *W Isles* 90 D6
Barrahormid *Arg/Bute* 72 E6
Barran *Arg/Bute* 79 J11
Barrapol *Arg/Bute* 78 G2
Barras *Aberds* 83 E10
Barras *Cumb* 57 E10
Barrasford *Northum* 62 F5
Barravullin *Arg/Bute* 73 C7
Barregarrow *I/Man* 48 D3
Barrhead *E Renf* 68 E3
Barrhill *S Ayrs* 54 A5
Barrington *Cambs* 29 D10
Barrington *Som'set* 8 C2
Barripper *Cornw'l* 2 F5
Barrmill *N Ayrs* 67 A6
Barrock *H'land* 94 C4
Barrock Ho. *H'land* 94 D4
Barrow *Lancs* 50 F3
Barrow *Rutl'd* 36 D4
Barrow *Suffolk* 30 B4
Barrow Green *Kent* 20 E6
Barrow Gurney *N Som'set* 15 E11
Barrow Haven *N Lincs* 53 G6
Barrow-in-Furness *Cumb* 49 C2
Barrow Island *Cumb* 49 C1
Barrow Nook *Lancs* 43 B7
Barrow Street *Wilts* 9 A7
Barrow upon Humber *N Lincs* 53 G6
Barrow upon Soar *Leics* 36 D1
Barrow upon Trent *Derby* 35 C9
Barroway Drove *Norfolk* 38 E1
Barrowburn *Northum* 62 B4
Barrowby *Lincs* 36 B4
Barrowcliff *N Yorks* 59 H11
Barrowden *Rutl'd* 36 E5
Barrowford *Lancs* 50 F4
Barrows Green *Ches* 43 G9
Barrows Green *Cumb* 57 H7
Barrow's Green *Mersey* 43 D8
Barry *Angus* 77 D8
Barry = Y Barri *V/Glam* 15 E7
Barry Island *V/Glam* 15 E7
Barsby *Leics* 36 D2
Barsham *Suffolk* 39 G9
Barston *W Midlands* 35 H8
Bartestree *Heref'd* 26 D2
Barthol Chapel *Aberds* 89 E8
Barthomley *Ches* 43 G10
Bartley *Hants* 10 C2
Bartley Green *W Midlands* 34 G6
Bartlow *Cambs* 30 D2
Barton *Cambs* 29 C11
Barton *Ches* 43 G7
Barton *Glos* 27 F8
Barton *Lancs* 42 B6
Barton *Lancs* 49 F5
Barton *N Yorks* 58 F3
Barton *Oxon* 28 H2
Barton *Torbay* 5 E10
Barton *Warwick* 27 C8
Barton Bendish *Norfolk* 38 E3
Barton Hartshorn *Bucks* 28 E3
Barton in Fabis *Notts* 35 B11
Barton in the Beans *Leics* 35 E9
Barton-le-Clay *Beds* 29 E7
Barton-le-Street *N Yorks* 52 B3
Barton-le-Willows *N Yorks* 52 C3
Barton Mills *Suffolk* 30 A4
Barton on Sea *Hants* 9 E11
Barton on the Heath *Warwick* 27 E9
Barton St David *Som'set* 8 A4
Barton Seagrave *Northants* 36 H4
Barton Stacey *Hants* 17 G11
Barton Turf *Norfolk* 39 C9
Barton-under-Needwood *Staffs* 35 D7
Barton-upon-Humber *N Lincs* 52 G6
Barton Waterside *N Lincs* 52 G6
Barugh *S Yorks* 45 B7
Barway *Cambs* 37 H11
Barwell *Leics* 35 F10
Barwick *Herts* 29 G10
Barwick *Som'set* 8 C4
Barwick in Elmet *W Yorks* 51 F9
Baschurch *Shrops* 33 C10
Bascote *Warwick* 27 B11
Basford Green *Staffs* 44 G3
Bashall Eaves *Lancs* 50 E2
Bashley *Hants* 9 E11
Basildon *Essex* 20 C4
Basingstoke *Hants* 18 F3
Baslow *Derby* 44 E6
Bason Bridge *Som'set* 15 G9
Bassaleg *Newp* 15 C8
Bassenthwaite *Cumb* 56 C4
Bassett *S'thampton* 10 C3
Bassingbourn *Cambs* 29 D10
Bassingfield *Notts* 36 B2
Bassingham *Lincs* 46 F3
Bassingthorpe *Lincs* 36 C5
Basta *Shetl'd* 96 D7
Baston *Lincs* 37 D7
Bastwick *Norfolk* 39 D10
Baswick Steer *ER Yorks* 53 E6
Batchworth Heath *Herts* 19 B7
Batcombe *Dorset* 8 D5
Batcombe *Som'set* 16 H3
Bate Heath *Ches* 43 E9
Batford *Herts* 29 G8
Bath *Bath/NE Som'set* 16 E4
Bathampton *Bath/NE Som'set* 16 E4
Bathealton *Som'set* 7 D9
Batheaston *Bath/NE Som'set* 16 E4
Bathford *Bath/NE Som'set* 16 E4
Bathgate *W Loth* 69 D8
Bathley *Notts* 45 G11
Bathpool *Cornw'l* 4 D3
Bathpool *Som'set* 8 B1
Bathville *W Loth* 69 D8
Batley *W Yorks* 51 G8
Batsford *Glos* 27 E8
Battersby *N Yorks* 59 F6
Battersea *London* 19 D9
Battisborough Cross *Devon* 5 G6
Battisford *Suffolk* 31 C7
Battisford Tye *Suffolk* 31 C7
Battle *E Sussex* 12 E6
Battle *Powys* 25 E7
Battledown *Glos* 26 F6
Battlefield *Shrops* 33 D11
Battlesbridge *Essex* 20 B4
Battlesden *Beds* 28 F6
Battlesea Green *Suffolk* 39 H8
Battleton *Som'set* 7 D8
Battram *Leics* 35 E10
Battramsley *Hants* 10 E2
Baughton *Worcs* 26 D5
Baughurst *Hants* 18 F2
Baulking *Oxon* 17 B10
Baumber *Lincs* 46 E6
Baunton *Glos* 17 A7
Baverstock *Wilts* 9 A9
Bawburgh *Norfolk* 39 E7
Bawdeswell *Norfolk* 38 C6
Bawdrip *Som'set* 15 H9
Bawdsey *Suffolk* 31 D10
Bawtry *S Yorks* 45 C10
Baxenden *Lancs* 50 G3
Baxterley *Warwick* 35 F8
Baybridge *Hants* 10 B4
Baycliff *Cumb* 49 B2
Baydon *Wilts* 17 D9
Bayford *Herts* 29 H10
Bayford *Som'set* 8 B6
Bayles *Cumb* 57 B9
Baylham *Suffolk* 31 C8
Baynard's Green *Oxon* 28 F2
Bayston Hill *Shrops* 33 E10
Baythorn End *Essex* 30 D4
Bayton *Worcs* 26 A3
Beach *H'land* 79 F10
Beachampton *Bucks* 28 E4
Beachamwell *Norfolk* 38 E3
Beachans *Moray* 87 G13
Beacharr *Arg/Bute* 65 D7
Beachborough *Kent* 21 H8
Beachley *Glos* 16 B2
Beacon *Devon* 7 F10
Beacon End *Essex* 30 F6
Beacon Hill *Surrey* 18 H5
Beacon's Bottom *Bucks* 18 B4
Beaconsfield *Bucks* 18 C6
Beacrabhaic *W Isles* 90 H6
Beadlam *N Yorks* 52 A2
Beadlow *Beds* 29 E8
Beadnell *Northum* 71 H11
Beaford *Devon* 6 E4
Beal *Northum* 71 F9
Beal *N Yorks* 51 G11
Beamhurst *Staffs* 35 B6
Beaminster *Dorset* 8 D3
Beamish *Durham* 58 A3
Beamsley *N Yorks* 51 D6
Bean *Kent* 20 D2
Beanacre *Wilts* 16 E6
Beanley *Northum* 62 B6
Beaquoy *Orkney* 95 F4
Bear Cross *Bournem'th* 9 E9
Beardwood *Blackb'n* 50 G2
Beare Green *Surrey* 19 G8
Bearley *Warwick* 27 B8
Bearnus *Arg/Bute* 78 G6
Bearpark *Durham* 58 B3
Bearsbridge *Northum* 62 H3
Bearsden *E Dunb* 68 C4
Bearsted *Kent* 20 F4
Bearstone *Shrops* 34 B3
Bearwood *Heref'd* 25 C10
Bearwood *Poole* 9 E9
Bearwood *W Midlands* 34 G6
Beattock *Dumf/Gal* 60 C6
Beauchamp Roding *Essex* 30 G2
Beauchief *S Yorks* 45 D7
Beaufort *Bl Gwent* 25 G8
Beaufort Castle *H'land* 87 G8
Beaulieu *Hants* 10 D2
Beauly *H'land* 87 G8
Beaumaris *Angl* 41 C8
Beaumont *Cumb* 61 H9
Beaumont *Essex* 31 F8
Beaumont Hill *D'lington* 58 E3
Beausale *Warwick* 27 A9
Beauworth *Hants* 10 B4
Beaworthy *Devon* 6 G3
Beazley End *Essex* 30 F4
Bebington *Mersey* 42 D6
Bebside *Northum* 63 E8
Beccles *Suffolk* 39 F10
Becconsall *Lancs* 49 G4
Beck Foot *Cumb* 57 G8
Beck Hole *N Yorks* 59 F9
Beck Row *Suffolk* 38 H2
Beck Side *Cumb* 49 A2
Beckbury *Shrops* 34 E3
Beckenham *London* 19 E10
Beckermet *Cumb* 56 F2
Beckfoot *Cumb* 56 F3
Beckfoot *Cumb* 56 B2
Beckford *Worcs* 26 E6
Beckhampton *Wilts* 17 E7
Beckingham *Lincs* 46 G2
Beckingham *Notts* 45 D11
Beckington *Som'set* 16 F5
Beckley *E Sussex* 13 D7
Beckley *Hants* 9 E11
Beckley *Oxon* 28 G2
Beckton *London* 19 C11
Beckwithshaw *N Yorks* 51 D8
Becontree *London* 19 C11
Bed-y-coedwr *Gwyn* 32 C3
Bedale *N Yorks* 58 H3
Bedburn *Durham* 58 C2
Bedchester *Dorset* 9 C7
Beddau *Rh Cyn Taff* 14 C6
Beddgelert *Gwyn* 41 F7
Beddingham *E Sussex* 12 F3
Beddington *London* 19 E10
Bedfield *Suffolk* 31 B9
Bedford *Beds* 29 C7
Bedham *W Sussex* 11 B9
Bedhampton *Hants* 10 D6
Bedingfield *Suffolk* 31 B8
Bedlam *N Yorks* 51 C8
Bedlington *Northum* 63 E8
Bedlington Station *Northum* 63 E8
Bedlinog *Merth Tyd* 14 A6
Bedminster *Bristol* 16 D2
Bedmond *Herts* 19 A7
Bednall *Staffs* 34 D5
Bedrule *Scot Borders* 62 B2
Bedstone *Shrops* 33 H9
Bedwas *Caerph* 15 C7
Bedworth *Warwick* 35 G9
Bedworth Little Heath *Warwick* 35 G9
Beeby *Leics* 36 E2
Beech *Hants* 18 H3
Beech *Staffs* 34 B4
Beech Hill *Gtr Man* 43 B8
Beech Hill *W Berks* 18 E3
Beechingstoke *Wilts* 17 F7
Beedon *W Berks* 17 D11
Beeford *ER Yorks* 53 D7
Beeley *Derby* 44 F6
Beelsby *NE Lincs* 46 B6
Beenham *W Berks* 18 E2
Beeny *Cornw'l* 4 B2
Beer *Devon* 7 H11
Beer Hackett *Dorset* 8 C4
Beercrocombe *Som'set* 8 B2
Beesands *Devon* 5 G9
Beesby *Lincs* 47 D8
Beeson *Devon* 5 G9
Beeston *Beds* 29 D8
Beeston *Ches* 43 G8
Beeston *Norfolk* 38 D5
Beeston *Notts* 35 B11
Beeston *W Yorks* 51 F8
Beeston Regis *Norfolk* 39 A7
Beeswing *Dumf/Gal* 55 C11
Beetham *Cumb* 49 B4
Beetley *Norfolk* 38 D5
Begbroke *Oxon* 27 G11
Begelly *Pembs* 22 F6
Beggar's Bush *Powys* 25 B9
Beguildy *Powys* 33 H7
Beighton *Norfolk* 39 E9
Beighton *S Yorks* 45 D8
Beighton Hill *Derby* 44 G6
Beith *N Ayrs* 66 A6
Bekesbourne *Kent* 21 F8
Belaugh *Norfolk* 39 D8
Belbroughton *Worcs* 34 H5
Belchamp Otten *Essex* 30 D5
Belchamp St Paul *Essex* 30 D4
Belchamp Walter *Essex* 30 D5
Belchford *Lincs* 46 E6
Belford *Northum* 71 G10
Belhaven *E Loth* 70 C5
Belhelvie *Aberds* 83 B11
Belhinnie *Aberds* 82 A6
Bell Bar *Herts* 29 H9
Bell Busk *N Yorks* 50 D5
Bell End *Worcs* 34 H5
Bell o'th'Hill *Ches* 43 H8
Bellabeg *Aberds* 82 B5
Bellamore *S Ayrs* 66 H5
Bellanoch *Arg/Bute* 72 D6
Bellaty *Angus* 76 B5
Belleau *Lincs* 47 E8
Bellehiglash *Moray* 88 E1
Bellerby *N Yorks* 58 G2
Bellever *Devon* 5 D7
Belliehill *Angus* 77 A8
Bellingdon *Bucks* 28 H6
Bellingham *Northum* 62 E4
Belloch *Arg/Bute* 65 E7
Bellochantuy *Arg/Bute* 65 E7
Bells Yew Green *E Sussex* 12 C5
Bellsbank *E Ayrs* 67 F7
Bellshill *N Lanarks* 68 D6
Bellshill *Northum* 71 G10
Bellspool *Scot Borders* 69 G10
Bellsquarry *W Loth* 69 D9
Belmaduthy *H'land* 87 F9
Belmesthorpe *Rutl'd* 36 D6
Belmont *Blackb'n* 50 H2
Belmont *London* 19 E9
Belmont *S Ayrs* 66 D6
Belmont *Shetl'd* 96 C7
Belnacraig *Aberds* 82 B5
Belowda *Cornw'l* 3 C8
Belper *Derby* 45 H7
Belper Lane End *Derby* 45 H7
Belsay *Northum* 63 F7

Caldwell Derby 35 D8
Caldwell N Yorks 58 E2
Caldy Mersey 42 D5
Caledrhydiau Ceredig'n 23 A9
Calfsound Orkney 95 E6
Calgary Arg/Bute 78 F6
Califer Moray 87 F13
California Falk 69 C8
California Norfolk 39 D11
Calke Derby 35 C9
Callakille H'land 85 C11
Callaly Northum 62 C6
Callander Stirl 75 G9
Callaughton Shrops 34 F2
Callestick Cornw'l 3 D6
Calligarry H'land 85 H11
Callington Cornw'l 4 E4
Callow Heref'd 25 E11
Callow End Worcs 26 D5
Callow Hill Wilts 17 C7
Callow Hill Worcs 26 A4
Callows Grave Worcs 26 B2
Calmore Hants 10 C2
Calmsden Glos 27 H7
Calne Wilts 17 D7
Calow Derby 45 E8
Calshot Hants 10 D3
Calstock Cornw'l 4 E5
Calstone Wellington Wilts 17 E7
Calthorpe Norfolk 39 B7
Calthwaite Cumb 56 B6
Calton N Yorks 50 D5
Calton Staffs 44 G5
Calveley Ches 43 G8
Calver Derby 44 E6
Calver Hill Heref'd 25 D10
Calverhall Shrops 34 B2
Calverleigh Devon 7 E8
Calverley W Yorks 51 F8
Calvert Bucks 28 F3
Calverton M/Keynes 28 E4
Calverton Notts 45 H10
Calvine Perth/Kinr 81 G10
Calvo Cumb 56 A3
Cam Glos 16 B4
Camas-luinie H'land 80 A1
Camasnacroise H'land 79 F11
Camastianavaig H'land 85 E10
Camasunary H'land 85 G10
Camault Muir H'land 87 G8
Camb Shetl'd 96 D7
Camber E Sussex 13 E8
Camberley Surrey 18 E5
Camberwell London 19 D10
Camblesforth N Yorks 52 G2
Cambo Northum 62 E6
Cambois Northum 63 E9
Camborne Cornw'l 2 E5
Cambourne Cambs 29 C10
Cambridge Cambs 29 C11
Cambridge Glos 16 A4
Cambridge Town Southend 20 C6
Cambus Clack 69 A7
Cambusavie Farm H'land 87 B10
Cambusbarron Stirl 68 A6
Cambuskenneth Stirl 69 A7
Cambuslang S Lanarks 68 D5
Cambusmore Lodge H'land 87 B10
Camden London 19 C9
Camelford Cornw'l 4 C2
Camelsdale W Sussex 11 A7
Camerory H'land 87 H13
Camer's Green Worcs 26 E4
Camerton Bath/NE Som'set 16 F3
Camerton Cumb 56 C2
Camerton ER Yorks 53 G8
Camghouran Perth/Kinr 75 B8
Cammachmore Aberds 83 D11
Cammeringham Lincs 46 D3
Camore H'land 87 B10
Camp Hill Warwick 35 F9
Campbeltown Arg/Bute 65 F8
Camperdown Tyne/Wear 63 F8
Campmuir Perth/Kinr 76 D5
Campsall S Yorks 45 A9
Campsey Ash Suffolk 31 C10
Campton Beds 29 E8
Camptown Scot Borders 62 B3
Camrose Pembs 22 D4
Camserney Perth/Kinr 75 C11
Camster H'land 94 F4
Camuschoirk H'land 79 E10
Camuscross H'land 85 G11
Camusnagaul H'land 80 F2
Camusnagaul H'land 86 C3
Camusrory H'land 79 B11
Camusteel H'land 85 D12
Camusterrach H'land 85 D12
Camusvrachan Perth/Kinr 75 C9
Canada Hants 10 C1
Canadia E Sussex 12 E6
Canal Side S Yorks 45 A10
Candacraig Ho. Aberds 82 B5
Candlesby Lincs 47 F8
Candy Mill S Lanarks 69 F9
Cane End Oxon 18 D3
Canewdon Essex 20 B5
Canford Bottom Dorset 9 D9
Canford Cliffs Poole 9 F9
Canford Magna Poole 9 E9
Canham's Green Suffolk 31 B7
Canholes Derby 44 E4
Canisbay H'land 94 C5
Cann Dorset 9 B7
Cann Common Dorset 9 B7
Cannard's Grave Som'set 16 G3
Cannich H'land 86 H6
Cannington Som'set 15 H8
Cannock Staffs 34 E5
Cannock Wood Staffs 34 D6
Canon Bridge Heref'd 25 D11
Canon Frome Heref'd 26 D3
Canon Pyon Heref'd 25 D11
Canonbie Dumf/Gal 61 F9
Canons Ashby Northants 28 C2
Canonstown Cornw'l 2 F4
Canterbury Kent 21 F8
Cantley Norfolk 39 E9
Cantley S Yorks 45 B10
Cantlop Shrops 33 E11
Canton Card 15 D7
Cantraybruich H'land 87 G10
Cantraydoune H'land 87 G10
Cantraywood H'land 87 G10
Cantsfield Lancs 50 B2
Canvey Island Essex 20 C4
Canwick Lincs 46 F3
Canworthy Water Cornw'l 4 B3
Caol H'land 80 F3
Caol Ila Arg/Bute 64 A5
Caolas Arg/Bute 78 G3
Caolas Scalpaigh W Isles 90 H7
Caolas Stocinis W Isles 90 H6
Capel Surrey 19 G8
Capel Bangor Ceredig'n 32 G2
Capel Betws Lleucu Ceredig'n 24 C3
Capel Carmel Gwyn 40 H3
Capel Coch Angl 40 B6
Capel Curig Conwy 41 E9
Capel Cynon Ceredig'n 23 B8
Capel Dewi Ceredig'n 23 B9
Capel Dewi Ceredig'n 32 G2
Capel Dewi Carms 23 D9
Capel Garmon Conwy 41 E10
Capel-gwyn Angl 40 C5
Capel Gwyn Carms 23 D9
Capel Gwynfe Carms 24 F4
Capel Hendre Carms 23 E10
Capel Hermon Gwyn 32 C3
Capel Isaac Carms 23 D10
Capel Iwan Carms 23 C7
Capel le Ferne Kent 21 H9
Capel Llanilltern Card 14 C6
Capel Mawr Angl 40 C6
Capel St Andrew Suffolk 31 D10
Capel St Mary Suffolk 31 E7
Capel Seion Ceredig'n 32 H2
Capel Tygwydd Ceredig'n 23 B7
Capel Uchaf Gwyn 41 F7
Capel-y-graig Gwyn 41 D7
Capelulo Conwy 41 C9
Capenhurst Ches 42 E6
Capernwray Lancs 49 B5
Capheaton Northum 62 E6
Cappercleuch Scot Borders 61 A8
Capplegill Dumf/Gal 61 C7
Capton Devon 5 F9
Caputh Perth/Kinr 76 D3
Car Colston Notts 36 A3
Carbis Bay Cornw'l 2 F4
Carbost H'land 85 E8
Carbost H'land 85 D9
Carbrook S Yorks 45 D7
Carbrooke Norfolk 38 E5
Carburton Notts 45 E10
Carcant Scot Borders 70 E2
Carcary Angus 77 B9
Carclaze Cornw'l 3 D9
Carcroft S Yorks 45 A9
Cardenden Fife 69 A11
Cardeston Shrops 33 D9
Cardiff = Caerdydd Card 15 D7
Cardigan = Aberteifi Ceredig'n 22 B6
Cardington Beds 29 D7
Cardington Shrops 33 F11
Cardinham Cornw'l 4 E2
Cardonald C/Glasg 68 D4
Cardow Moray 88 D1
Cardrona Scot Borders 70 G2
Cardross Arg/Bute 68 C2
Cardurnock Cumb 61 H7
Careby Lincs 36 D6
Careston Angus 77 B8
Carew Pembs 22 F5
Carew Cheriton Pembs 22 F5
Carew Newton Pembs 22 F5
Carey Heref'd 26 E2
Carfrae E Loth 70 D4
Cargenbridge Dumf/Gal 60 F5
Cargill Perth/Kinr 76 D4
Cargo Cumb 61 H9
Cargreen Cornw'l 4 E5
Carham Northum 71 G7
Carhampton Som'set 7 B9
Carharrack Cornw'l 2 E6
Carie Perth/Kinr 75 D9
Carie Perth/Kinr 75 B9
Carines Cornw'l 3 D6
Carisbrooke I/Wight 10 F3
Cark Cumb 49 B3
Carlabhagh W Isles 90 C7
Carland Cross Cornw'l 3 D7
Carlby Lincs 37 D6
Carlecotes S Yorks 44 B5
Carlesmoor N Yorks 51 B7
Carleton Cumb 57 D7
Carleton Cumb 56 A6
Carleton Lancs 49 F3
Carleton N Yorks 50 E5
Carleton Forehoe Norfolk 39 E6
Carleton Rode Norfolk 39 F7
Carlin How Redcar/Clevel'd 59 E8
Carlingcott Bath/NE Som'set 16 F3
Carlisle Cumb 61 H10
Carlops Scot Borders 69 E10
Carlton Beds 28 C6
Carlton Cambs 30 C3
Carlton Leics 35 E9
Carlton Notts 36 A2
Carlton N Yorks 59 H7
Carlton N Yorks 52 G2
Carlton N Yorks 51 A6
Carlton N Yorks 58 E2
Carlton Stockton 58 D4
Carlton Suffolk 31 B10
Carlton S Yorks 45 A7
Carlton W Yorks 51 G9
Carlton Colville Suffolk 39 G11
Carlton Curlieu Leics 36 F2
Carlton Husthwaite N Yorks 51 B10
Carlton in Cleveland N Yorks 58 F6
Carlton in Lindrick Notts 45 D9
Carlton le Moorland Lincs 46 G3
Carlton Miniott N Yorks 51 A9
Carlton on Trent Notts 45 F11
Carlton Scroop Lincs 36 A5
Carluke S Lanarks 69 E7
Carmarthen = Caerfyrddin Carms 23 D9
Carmel Angl 40 B5
Carmel Carms 23 E10
Carmel Flints 42 E4
Carmel Guernsey 11
Carmel Gwyn 40 E6
Carmont Aberds 83 E10
Carmunnock C/Glasg 68 E5
Carmyle C/Glasg 68 D5
Carmyllie Angus 77 C8
Carn-gorm H'land 80 A1
Carnaby ER Yorks 53 C7
Carnach H'land 86 B3
Carnach H'land 80 A2
Carnach W Isles 90 H7
Carnachy H'land 93 D10
Carnais W Isles 90 D5
Carnbee Fife 77 G8
Carnbo Perth/Kinr 76 G3
Carnbrea Cornw'l 2 E5
Carnduff S Lanarks 68 F5
Carnduncan Arg/Bute 64 B3
Carne Cornw'l 3 F8
Carnforth Lancs 49 B4
Carnhedryn Pembs 22 D3
Carnhell Green Cornw'l 2 F5
Carnkie Cornw'l 2 F6
Carnkie Cornw'l 2 F5
Carno Powys 32 F5
Carnoch H'land 86 H6
Carnoch H'land 86 F5
Carnock Fife 69 B9
Carnon Downs Cornw'l 3 E6
Carnousie Aberds 89 C6
Carnoustie Angus 77 D8
Carnwath S Lanarks 69 F8
Carnyorth Cornw'l 2 F2
Carperby N Yorks 58 H1
Carpley Green N Yorks 57 H11
Carr S Yorks 45 C9
Carr Hill Tyne/Wear 63 G8
Carradale Arg/Bute 65 E9
Carragraich W Isles 90 H6
Carrbridge H'land 81 A11
Carrefour Selous Jersey 11
Carreg-wen Pembs 23 B7
Carreglefn Angl 40 B5
Carrick Arg/Bute 73 E8
Carrick Fife 77 E7
Carrick Castle Arg/Bute 73 D10
Carrick Ho. Orkney 95 E6
Carriden Falk 69 B9
Carrington Gtr Man 43 C10
Carrington Lincs 47 G7
Carrington Midloth 70 D2
Carrog Conwy 41 F9
Carrog Denbs 33 A7
Carron Falk 69 B7
Carron Moray 88 D2
Carron Bridge N Lanarks 68 B6
Carronbridge Dumf/Gal 60 D4
Carrshield Northum 57 B10
Carrutherstown Dumf/Gal 61 F7
Carrville Durham 58 B4
Carsaig Arg/Bute 79 J8
Carsaig Arg/Bute 72 E6
Carscreugh Dumf/Gal 54 D5
Carse Gray Angus 77 B7
Carse Ho. Arg/Bute 72 G6
Carsegowan Dumf/Gal 55 D7
Carseriggan Dumf/Gal 54 C6
Carsethorn Dumf/Gal 60 H5
Carshalton London 19 E9
Carsington Derby 44 G6
Carskiey Arg/Bute 65 H7
Carsluith Dumf/Gal 55 D7
Carsphairn Dumf/Gal 67 G8
Carstairs S Lanarks 69 F8
Carstairs Junction S Lanarks 69 F8
Carswell Marsh Oxon 17 B10
Carter's Clay Hants 10 B2
Carterton Oxon 27 H9
Carterway Heads Northum 58 A1
Carthew Cornw'l 3 D9
Carthorpe N Yorks 51 A9
Cartington Northum 62 C6
Cartland S Lanarks 69 F7
Cartmel Cumb 49 B3
Cartmel Fell Cumb 56 H6
Carway Carms 23 F9
Cary Fitzpaine Som'set 8 B4
Cas-gwent = Chepstow Monmouths 15 B11
Cascob Powys 25 B9
Cashlie Perth/Kinr 75 C7
Cashmoor Dorset 9 C8
Casnewydd = Newport Newp 15 C9
Cassey Compton Glos 27 G7
Cassington Oxon 27 G11
Cassop Durham 58 C4
Castell Denbs 42 F4
Castell-Howell Ceredig'n 23 B9
Castell-Nedd = Neath Neath P Talb 14 B3
Castell Newydd Emlyn = Newcastle Emlyn Carms 23 B8
Castell-y-bwch Torf 15 B8
Castellau Rh Cyn Taff 14 C6
Casterton Cumb 50 B2
Castle Acre Norfolk 38 D4
Castle Ashby Northants 28 C5
Castle Bolton N Yorks 58 G1
Castle Bromwich W Midlands 35 G7
Castle Bytham Lincs 36 D5
Castle Caereinion Powys 33 E7
Castle Camps Cambs 30 D3
Castle Carrock Cumb 61 H11
Castle Cary Som'set 8 A5
Castle Combe Wilts 16 D5
Castle Donington Leics 35 C10
Castle Douglas Dumf/Gal 55 C10
Castle Eaton Swindon 17 B8
Castle Eden Durham 58 C5
Castle Forbes Aberds 83 B8
Castle Frome Heref'd 26 D3
Castle Green Surrey 18 E6
Castle Gresley Derby 35 D8
Castle Heaton Northum 71 F8
Castle Hedingham Essex 30 E4
Castle Hill Kent 12 B5
Castle Huntly Perth/Kinr 76 E6
Castle Kennedy Dumf/Gal 54 D4
Castle O'er Dumf/Gal 61 D8
Castle Pulverbatch Shrops 33 E10
Castle Rising Norfolk 38 C2
Castle Stuart H'land 87 G10
Castlebay = Bagh a Chaisteil W Isles 84 J1
Castlebythe Pembs 22 D5
Castlecary N Lanarks 68 C6
Castlecraig H'land 87 E11
Castlefairn Dumf/Gal 60 E3
Castleford W Yorks 51 G10
Castlehill Scot Borders 69 G11
Castlehill H'land 94 D3
Castlehill W Dunb 68 C2
Castlemaddy Dumf/Gal 67 H8
Castlemartin Pembs 22 G4
Castlemilk Dumf/Gal 61 F7
Castlemilk C/Glasg 68 E5
Castlemorris Pembs 22 C4
Castlemorton Worcs 26 E4
Castleside Durham 58 B1
Castlethorpe M/Keynes 28 D5
Castleton Angus 76 C6
Castleton Arg/Bute 73 E7
Castleton Derby 44 D5
Castleton Gtr Man 44 A2
Castleton Newp 15 C8
Castleton N Yorks 59 F7
Castletown Ches 43 G7
Castletown H'land 94 D3
Castletown H'land 87 G10
Castletown I/Man 48 F2
Castletown Tyne/Wear 63 H9
Castleweary Scot Borders 61 C10
Castley N Yorks 51 E8
Caston Norfolk 38 F5
Castor Peterbro 37 F7
Catacol N Ayrs 66 B2
Catbrain S Glocs 16 C2
Catbrook Monmouths 15 A11
Catchall Cornw'l 2 G3
Catchems Corner W Midlands 35 H8
Catchgate Durham 58 A2
Catcleugh Northum 62 C3
Catcliffe S Yorks 45 D8
Catcott Som'set 15 H9
Caterham Surrey 19 F10
Catfield Norfolk 39 C9
Catfirth Shetl'd 96 H6
Catford London 19 D10
Catforth Lancs 49 F4
Cathays Card 15 D7
Cathcart C/Glasg 68 D4
Cathedine Powys 25 F8
Catherington Hants 10 C5
Catherton Shrops 34 H2
Catlodge H'land 81 D8
Catlowdy Cumb 61 F10
Catmore W Berks 17 C11
Caton Lancs 49 C5
Caton Green Lancs 49 C5
Catrine E Ayrs 67 D8
Cat's Ash Newp 15 B9
Catsfield E Sussex 12 E6
Catshill Worcs 26 A6
Cattal N Yorks 51 D10
Cattawade Suffolk 31 E8
Catterall Lancs 49 E4
Catterick N Yorks 58 G3
Catterick Bridge N Yorks 58 G3
Catterick Garrison N Yorks 58 G2
Catterlen Cumb 57 C6
Catterline Aberds 83 F10
Catterton N Yorks 51 E11
Catthorpe Leics 36 H1
Cattistock Dorset 8 E4
Catton Northum 62 H4
Catton N Yorks 51 B9
Catwick ER Yorks 53 E7
Catworth Cambs 29 A7
Caudlesprings Norfolk 38 E5
Caulcott Oxon 28 F2
Cauldcots Angus 77 C9
Cauldhame Stirl 68 A5
Cauldmill Scot Borders 61 B11
Cauldon Staffs 44 H4
Caulkerbush Dumf/Gal 60 H5
Caulside Dumf/Gal 61 E10
Caunsall Worcs 34 G4
Caunton Notts 45 F11
Causeway End Dumf/Gal 55 C7
Causeway Foot W Yorks 51 F6
Causeway-head Stirl 75 H10
Causewayend S Lanarks 69 G9
Causewayhead Cumb 56 A3
Causey Park Bridge Northum 63 D7
Causeyend Aberds 83 B11
Cautley Cumb 57 G8
Cavendish Suffolk 30 D5
Cavendish Bridge Leics 35 C10
Cavenham Suffolk 30 B4
Caversfield Oxon 28 F2
Caversham Reading 18 D4
Caverswall Staffs 34 A5
Cavil ER Yorks 52 F3
Cawdor H'land 87 F11
Cawkwell Lincs 46 E6
Cawood N Yorks 52 F1
Cawsand Cornw'l 4 F5
Cawston Norfolk 39 C7
Cawthorne S Yorks 44 B6
Cawthorpe Lincs 37 C6
Cawton N Yorks 52 B2
Caxton Cambs 29 C10
Caynham Shrops 26 A2
Caythorpe Lincs 46 H3
Caythorpe Notts 45 H10
Cayton N Yorks 59 H11
Ceann a Bhaigh W Isles 84 B2
Ceann a Deas Loch Baghasdail W Isles 84 G2
Ceann Shiphoirt W Isles 91 F7
Ceann Tarabhaigh W Isles 90 F7
Ceannacroc Lodge H'land 80 B4
Cearsiadair W Isles 91 E8
Cefn Berain Conwy 42 F2
Cefn-brith Conwy 42 G2
Cefn Canol Powys 33 B8
Cefn-coch Conwy 41 D10
Cefn Coch Powys 33 C7
Cefn-coed-y-cymmer Merth Tyd 25 H7
Cefn Cribbwr Bridg 14 C4
Cefn Cross Bridg 14 C4
Cefn-ddwysarn Gwyn 32 B5
Cefn Einion Shrops 33 G8
Cefn-gorwydd Powys 24 D6
Cefn-mawr Wrex 33 A8
Cefn-y-bedd Flints 42 G6
Cefn-y-pant Carms 22 D6
Cefneithin Carms 23 E10
Cei-bach Ceredig'n 23 A9
Ceinewydd = New Quay Ceredig'n 23 A8
Ceint Angl 40 C6
Cellan Ceredig'n 24 D3
Cellarhead Staffs 44 H3
Cemaes Angl 40 A5
Cemmaes Powys 32 E4
Cemmaes Road Powys 32 E4
Cenarth Carms 23 B7
Cenin Gwyn 40 F6
Central Invercl 73 F11
Ceos W Isles 91 E8
Ceres Fife 77 F7
Cerne Abbas Dorset 8 D5
Cerney Wick Glos 17 B7
Cerrigceinwen Angl 40 C6
Cerrigydrudion Conwy 42 H2
Cessford Scot Borders 62 A3
Ceunant Gwyn 41 D7
Chaceley Glos 26 E5
Chacewater Cornw'l 3 E6
Chackmore Bucks 28 E3
Chacombe Northants 27 D11
Chad Valley W Midlands 34 G6
Chadderton Gtr Man 44 B3
Chadderton Fold Gtr Man 44 B2
Chaddesden Derby C 35 B9
Chaddesley Corbett Worcs 26 A5
Chaddleworth W Berks 17 D11
Chadlington Oxon 27 F10
Chadshunt Warwick 27 C10
Chadwell Leics 36 C3
Chadwell St Mary Thurr'k 20 D3
Chadwick End W Midlands 27 A9
Chadwick Green Mersey 43 C8
Chaffcombe Som'set 8 C2
Chagford Devon 5 C8
Chailey E Sussex 12 E2
Chain Bridge Lincs 37 A9
Chainbridge Cambs 37 E10
Chainhurst Kent 20 G4
Chalbury Dorset 9 D9
Chalbury Common Dorset 9 D9
Chaldon Surrey 19 F10
Chaldon Herring or Dorset 9 F6
Chale I/Wight 10 G3
Chale Green I/Wight 10 G3
Chalfont Common Bucks 19 B7
Chalfont St Giles Bucks 18 B6
Chalfont St Peter Bucks 19 B7
Chalford Glos 16 A5
Chalgrove Oxon 18 B3
Chalk Kent 20 D3
Challacombe Devon 6 B5
Challoch Dumf/Gal 54 C6
Challock Kent 21 F7
Chalton Beds 29 F7
Chalton Hants 10 C6
Chalvington E Sussex 12 F4
Chancery Ceredig'n 32 H1
Chandler's Ford Hants 10 B3
Channel Tunnel Kent 21 H8
Channerwick Shetl'd 96 L6
Chantry Som'set 16 G4
Chantry Suffolk 31 D8
Chapel Fife 69 A11
Chapel Allerton Som'set 15 F10
Chapel Allerton W Yorks 51 F9
Chapel Amble Cornw'l 3 B8
Chapel Brampton Northants 28 B4
Chapel Choriton Staffs 34 B4
Chapel-en-le-Frith Derby 44 D4
Chapel End Warwick 35 F9
Chapel Green Warwick 35 G8
Chapel Green Warwick 27 B11
Chapel Haddlesey N Yorks 52 G1
Chapel Head Cambs 37 G9
Chapel Hill Aberds 89 E10
Chapel Hill Lincs 46 G6
Chapel Hill Monmouths 15 B11
Chapel Hill N Yorks 51 E9
Chapel Lawn Shrops 33 H9
Chapel-le-Dale N Yorks 50 B3
Chapel Milton Derby 44 D4
Chapel of Garioch Aberds 83 A9
Chapel Row W Berks 18 E2
Chapel St Leonards Lincs 47 E9
Chapel Stile Cumb 56 F5
Chapelgate Lincs 37 C10
Chapelhall N Lanarks 68 D6
Chapelhill Dumf/Gal 60 D6
Chapelhill H'land 87 D11
Chapelhill N Ayrs 66 B5
Chapelhill Perth/Kinr 76 E5
Chapelhill Perth/Kinr 76 D3
Chapelknowe Dumf/Gal 61 F9
Chapelton Angus 77 C9
Chapelton Devon 6 D4
Chapelton H'land 81 B11
Chapelton S Lanarks 68 F5
Chapeltown Blackb'n 50 H3
Chapeltown Moray 82 A4
Chapeltown S Yorks 45 C7
Chapmans Well Devon 6 G2
Chapmanslade Wilts 16 G5
Chapmore End Herts 29 G10
Chappel Essex 30 F5
Chard Som'set 8 D2
Chardstock Devon 8 D2
Charfield S Glocs 16 B4
Charford Worcs 26 B6
Charing Kent 20 G6
Charing Cross Dorset 9 C10
Charing Heath Kent 20 G6
Charingworth Glos 27 E9
Charlbury Oxon 27 G10
Charlcombe Bath/NE Som'set 16 E4
Charlecote Warwick 27 C9
Charles Devon 6 C5
Charles Tye Suffolk 31 C7
Charlesfield Dumf/Gal 61 G7
Charleston Angus 76 C6
Charleston Renf 68 D3
Charlestown Aberd C 83 C11
Charlestown Cornw'l 3 D9
Charlestown Derby 44 C4
Charlestown Dorset 8 G5
Charlestown Fife 69 B9
Charlestown Gtr Man 44 B2
Charlestown H'land 87 G9
Charlestown H'land 85 A13
Charlestown W Yorks 50 G5
Charlestown of Aberlour Moray 88 D2
Charlesworth Derby 44 C4
Charleton Devon 5 G8
Charlton London 19 D11
Charlton Hants 17 G10
Charlton Herts 29 F8
Charlton Northants 28 E2
Charlton Northum 62 E4
Charlton Som'set 16 F3
Charlton Telford 34 D1
Charlton Wilts 9 B8
Charlton Wilts 17 F8
Charlton Wilts 16 C6
Charlton Worcs 27 D7
Charlton W Sussex 11 C7
Charlton Abbots Glos 27 F7
Charlton Adam Som'set 8 B4
Charlton-All-Saints Wilts 9 B10
Charlton Horethorne Som'set 8 B5
Charlton Kings Glos 26 F6
Charlton Mackerell Som'set 8 B4
Charlton Marshall Dorset 9 D7
Charlton Musgrove Som'set 8 B6
Charlton on Otmoor Oxon 28 G2
Charltons Redcar/Clevel'd 59 E7
Charlwood Surrey 19 G9
Charlynch Som'set 7 C11
Charminster Dorset 8 E5
Charmouth Dorset 8 E2
Charndon Bucks 28 F3
Charney Bassett Oxon 17 B10
Charnock Richard Lancs 50 H1
Charsfield Suffolk 31 C9
Chart Corner Kent 20 F4
Chart Sutton Kent 20 G5
Charter Alley Hants 18 F2
Charterhouse Som'set 15 F10
Charterville Allotments Oxon 27 G10
Chartham Kent 21 F8
Chartham Hatch Kent 21 F8
Chartridge Bucks 18 A6
Charvil Wokingham 18 D4
Charwelton Northants 28 C2
Chasetown Staffs 34 E6
Chastleton Oxon 27 F9
Chasty Devon 6 F2
Chatburn Lancs 50 E3
Chatcull Staffs 34 B3
Chatham Medway 20 E4
Chathill Northum 71 H10
Chattenden Medway 20 D4
Chatteris Cambs 37 G9
Chattisham Suffolk 31 D7
Chatto Scot Borders 62 B3
Chatton Northum 71 H9
Chawleigh Devon 6 E6
Chawley Oxon 17 A11
Chawston Beds 29 C8
Chawton Hants 18 H4
Cheadle Gtr Man 44 D2
Cheadle Staffs 34 A6
Cheadle Heath Gtr Man 44 D2
Cheadle Hulme Gtr Man 44 D2
Cheam London 19 E9
Cheapside Surrey 19 F7
Chearsley Bucks 28 G4
Chebsey Staffs 34 C4
Checkendon Oxon 18 C3
Checkley Ches 43 H10
Checkley Heref'd 26 E2
Checkley Staffs 34 B6
Chedburgh Suffolk 30 C4
Cheddar Som'set 15 F10
Cheddington Bucks 28 G6
Cheddleton Staffs 44 G3
Cheddon Fitzpaine Som'set 8 B1
Chedglow Wilts 16 B6
Chedgrave Norfolk 39 F9
Chedington Dorset 8 D3
Chediston Suffolk 39 H9
Chedworth Glos 27 G7
Chedzoy Som'set 15 H9
Cheeklaw Scot Borders 70 E6
Cheeseman's Green Kent 13 C9
Cheglinch Devon 6 B4
Cheldon Devon 7 E6
Chelford Ches 44 E2
Chell Heath Stoke 44 G2
Chellaston Derby C 35 B9
Chellington Beds 28 C6
Chelmarsh Shrops 34 G3
Chelmer Village Essex 30 H4
Chelmondiston Suffolk 31 E9
Chelmorton Derby 44 F5
Chelmsford Essex 30 H4
Chelsea London 19 D9
Chelsfield London 19 E11
Chelsworth Suffolk 30 D6
Cheltenham Glos 26 F6
Chelveston Northants 28 B6
Chelvey N Som'set 15 E10
Chelwood Bath/NE Som'set 16 E3
Chelwood Common E Sussex 12 D3
Chelwood Gate E Sussex 12 D3
Chelworth Wilts 16 B6
Chelworth Green Wilts 17 B7
Chemistry Shrops 33 A11
Chenies Bucks 19 B7
Cheny Longville Shrops 33 G10
Chepstow = Cas-gwent Monmouths 15 B11
Chequerfield W Yorks 51 G10
Cherhill Wilts 17 D7
Cherington Glos 16 B6
Cherington Warwick 27 E9
Cheriton Devon 7 B6
Cheriton Hants 10 B4
Cheriton Kent 21 H8
Cheriton Swan 23 G9
Cheriton Bishop Devon 7 G6
Cheriton Fitzpaine Devon 7 F7
Cheriton or Stackpole Elidor Pembs 22 G4
Cherrington Telford 34 C2
Cherry Burton ER Yorks 52 E5
Cherry Hinton Cambs 29 C11
Cherry Orchard Worcs 26 C5
Cherry Willingham Lincs 46 E4
Cherrybank Perth/Kinr 76 E4
Chertsey Surrey 19 E7
Cheselbourne Dorset 9 E6
Chesham Bucks 18 A6
Chesham Bois Bucks 18 B6
Cheshunt Herts 19 A10
Cheslyn Hay Staffs 34 E5
Chessington London 19 E8
Chester Ches 43 F7
Chester-Le-Street Durham 58 A3
Chester Moor Durham 58 B3
Chesterblade Som'set 16 G3
Chesterfield Derby 45 E7
Chesters Scot Borders 62 B2
Chesters Scot Borders 62 A2
Chesterton Cambs 37 F7
Chesterton Cambs 29 B11
Chesterton Glos 17 A7
Chesterton Oxon 28 F2
Chesterton Shrops 34 F3
Chesterton Staffs 44 H2
Chesterton Warwick 27 C10
Chesterwood Northum 62 G4
Chestfield Kent 21 E8
Cheston Devon 5 F7
Cheswardine Shrops 34 C3
Cheswick Northum 71 F9
Chetnole Dorset 8 D5
Chettiscombe Devon 7 E8
Chettisham Cambs 37 G11
Chettle Dorset 9 C8
Chetton Shrops 34 F2
Chetwode Bucks 28 F3
Chetwynd Aston Telford 34 D3
Cheveley Cambs 30 B3
Chevening Kent 19 F11
Chevington Suffolk 30 C4
Chevithorne Devon 7 E8
Chew Magna Bath/NE Som'set 16 E2
Chew Stoke Bath/NE Som'set 16 E2
Chewton Keynsham Bath/NE Som'set 16 E3
Chewton Mendip Som'set 16 F2
Chicheley M/Keynes 28 D6
Chichester W Sussex 11 D7
Chickerell Dorset 8 F5
Chicklade Wilts 9 A8
Chicksgrove Wilts 9 A8
Chidden Hants 10 C5
Chiddingfold Surrey 18 H6
Chiddingly E Sussex 12 E4
Chiddingstone Kent 19 G11
Chiddingstone Causeway Kent 20 G2
Chiddingstone Hoath Kent 12 B3
Chideock Dorset 8 E3
Chidham W Sussex 11 D6
Chidswell W Yorks 51 G8
Chieveley W Berks 17 D11
Chignall St James Essex 30 H3
Chignall Smealy Essex 30 G3
Chigwell Essex 19 B11
Chigwell Row Essex 19 B11
Chilbolton Hants 17 H10
Chilcomb Hants 10 B4
Chilcombe Dorset 8 E4
Chilcompton Som'set 16 F3
Chilcote Leics 35 D8
Child Okeford Dorset 9 C7
Childer Thornton Ches 42 E6
Childrey Oxon 17 C10
Child's Ercall Shrops 34 C2
Childswickham Worcs 27 E7
Childwall Mersey 43 D7
Childwick Green Herts 29 G8
Chilfrome Dorset 8 E4
Chilgrove W Sussex 11 C7
Chilham Kent 21 F7
Chilhampton Wilts 9 A9
Chilla Devon 6 F3
Chillaton Devon 4 C5
Chillenden Kent 21 F9
Chillerton I/Wight 10 F3
Chillesford Suffolk 31 C10
Chillingham Northum 71 H9
Chillington Devon 5 G8
Chillington Som'set 8 C2
Chilmark Wilts 9 A8
Chilson Oxon 27 G10
Chilsworthy Cornw'l 4 D5
Chilsworthy Devon 6 F2
Chilthorne Domer Som'set 8 C4
Chiltington E Sussex 12 E2
Chilton Bucks 28 G3
Chilton Durham 58 D3
Chilton Oxon 17 C11
Chilton Cantelo Som'set 8 B4
Chilton Foliat Wilts 17 D10
Chilton Lane Durham 58 C4
Chilton Polden Som'set 15 H9
Chilton Street Suffolk 30 D4
Chilton Trinity Som'set 15 H8
Chilvers Coton Warwick 35 F9
Chilwell Notts 35 B11
Chilworth Hants 10 C3
Chilworth Surrey 19 G7
Chimney Oxon 17 A10
Chineham Hants 18 F3
Chingford London 19 B10
Chinley Derby 44 D4
Chinley Head Derby 44 D4
Chinnor Oxon 18 A4
Chipnall Shrops 34 B3
Chippenhall Green Suffolk 39 H8
Chippenham Cambs 30 B3
Chippenham Wilts 16 D6
Chipperfield Herts 19 A7
Chipping Herts 29 E10
Chipping Lancs 50 E2
Chipping Campden Glos 27 E8
Chipping Hill Essex 30 G5
Chipping Norton Oxon 27 F10
Chipping Ongar Essex 20 A2
Chipping Sodbury S Glocs 16 C4
Chipping Warden Northants 27 D11
Chipstable Som'set 7 D9
Chipstead Kent 19 F11
Chipstead Surrey 19 F9
Chirbury Shrops 33 F8
Chirk = Y Waun Wrex 33 B8
Chirk Bank Shrops 33 B8
Chirmorrie S Ayrs 54 B5
Chirnside Scot Borders 71 E7
Chirnsidebridge Scot Borders 71 E7
Chirton Wilts 17 F7
Chisbury Wilts 17 E9
Chiselborough Som'set 8 C3
Chiseldon Swindon 17 D8
Chiserley W Yorks 50 G6
Chislehampton Oxon 18 B2
Chislehurst London 19 D11
Chislet Kent 21 E9
Chiswell Green Herts 19 A8
Chiswick London 19 D9
Chiswick End Cambs 29 D10
Chisworth Derby 44 C3
Chithurst W Sussex 11 B7
Chittering Cambs 29 A11
Chitterne Wilts 16 G6
Chittlehamholt Devon 6 D5
Chittlehampton Devon 6 D5
Chittoe Wilts 16 E6
Chivenor Devon 6 C4
Chobham Surrey 18 E6
Choicelee Scot Borders 70 E6
Cholderton Wilts 17 G9
Cholesbury Bucks 28 H6
Chollerford Northum 62 F5
Chollerton Northum 62 F5
Cholmondeston Ches 43 F9
Cholsey Oxon 18 C2
Cholstrey Heref'd 25 C11
Chop Gate N Yorks 59 G6
Choppington Northum 63 E8
Chopwell Tyne/Wear 63 H7
Chorley Ches 43 G8
Chorley Lancs 50 H1
Chorley Shrops 34 G2
Chorley Staffs 35 D6
Chorleywood Herts 19 B7
Chorlton cum Hardy Gtr Man 44 C2
Chorlton Lane Ches 43 H7
Choulton Shrops 33 G9
Chowdene Tyne/Wear 63 H8
Chowley Ches 43 G7
Chrishall Essex 29 E11
Christchurch Cambs 37 F10
Christchurch Dorset 9 E10
Christchurch Glos 26 G2
Christchurch Newp 15 C9
Christian Malford Wilts 16 D6
Christleton Ches 43 F7
Christmas Common Oxon 18 B4
Christon N Som'set 15 F9
Christon Bank Northum 63 A8
Christow Devon 5 C9
Chryston N Lanarks 68 C5
Chudleigh Devon 5 D9
Chudleigh Knighton Devon 5 D9
Chulmleigh Devon 6 E5
Chunal Derby 44 C4
Church Lancs 50 G3
Church Aston Telford 34 D3
Church Brampton Northants 28 B4
Church Broughton Derby 35 B8
Church Crookham Hants 18 F5
Church Eaton Staffs 34 D4
Church End Beds 28 F6
Church End Beds 29 E8
Church End Beds 28 E6
Church End Cambs 37 G8
Church End Cambs 37 E9
Church End ER Yorks 53 D6
Church End Essex 30 D2
Church End Essex 30 F4
Church End Hants 18 F3
Church End Lincs 37 B8
Church End Warwick 35 F8
Church End Warwick 35 F8
Church End Wilts 17 D7
Church Enstone Oxon 27 F10
Church Fenton N Yorks 51 F11
Church Green Devon 7 G10
Church Green Norfolk 39 F6
Church Gresley Derby 35 D8
Church Hanborough Oxon 27 G11
Church Hill Ches 43 F9
Church Houses N Yorks 59 G7
Church Knowle Dorset 9 F8
Church Laneham Notts 46 E2
Church Langton Leics 36 F3
Church Lawford Warwick 35 H10
Church Lawton Ches 44 G2
Church Leigh Staffs 34 B6
Church Lench Worcs 27 C7
Church Mayfield Staffs 35 A7
Church Minshull Ches 43 F9
Church Norton W Sussex 11 E7
Church Preen Shrops 33 F11
Church Pulverbatch Shrops 33 E10
Church Stoke Powys 33 F8
Church Stowe Northants 28 C3
Church Street Kent 20 D4
Church Stretton Shrops 33 F10
Church Town N Lincs 45 B11
Church Town Surrey 19 F10
Church Village Rh Cyn Taff 14 C6
Church Warsop Notts 45 F9
Churcham Glos 26 G4
Churchbridge Staffs 34 E5
Churchdown Glos 26 G5
Churchend Essex 30 F3
Churchend Essex 21 B7
Churchend S Glocs 16 B4
Churchfield W Midlands 34 F6
Churchgate Street Essex 29 G11
Churchill Devon 6 B4
Churchill Devon 8 D2
Churchill N Som'set 15 F10
Churchill Oxon 27 F9
Churchill Worcs 34 H4
Churchill Worcs 26 C6
Churchinford Som'set 7 E11
Churchover Warwick 35 G11
Churchstanton Som'set 7 E10
Churchstow Devon 5 G8
Churchtown Derby 44 F6
Churchtown I/Man 48 C4
Churchtown Lancs 49 E4
Churchtown Mersey 49 H3
Churnsike Lodge Northum 62 F2
Churston Ferrers Torbay 5 F10
Churt Surrey 18 H5
Churton Ches 43 G7
Churwell W Yorks 51 G8
Chute Standen Wilts 17 F10
Chwilog Gwyn 40 G6
Chyandour Cornw'l 2 F3
Cilan Uchaf Gwyn 40 H4
Cilcain Flints 42 F4
Cilcennin Ceredig'n 24 B2
Cilfor Gwyn 41 G8
Cilfrew Neath P Talb 14 A3
Cilfynydd Rh Cyn Taff 14 B6
Cilgerran Pembs 22 B6
Cilgwyn Carms 24 F4
Cilgwyn Gwyn 40 E6
Cilgwyn Pembs 22 C5
Ciliau Aeron Ceredig'n 23 A9
Cill Donnain W Isles 84 F2
Cille Bhrighde W Isles 84 G2
Cille Pheadair W Isles 84 G2
Cilmery Powys 25 C7
Cilsan Carms 23 D10
Ciltalgarth Gwyn 41 F10
Cilwendeg Pembs 23 C7
Cilybebyll Neath P Talb 14 A3
Cilycwm Carms 24 E4
Cimla Neath P Talb 14 B3
Cinderford Glos 26 G3
Cippyn Pembs 22 B6
Circebost W Isles 90 D6
Cirencester Glos 17 A7
Ciribhig W Isles 90 C6
City London 19 C10
City Powys 33 G8
City Dulas Angl 40 B6
Clachaig Arg/Bute 73 E10
Clachan Arg/Bute 72 H6
Clachan Arg/Bute 72 B6
Clachan Arg/Bute 79 G11
Clachan Arg/Bute 74 F4
Clachan H'land 85 E10
Clachan W Isles 84 D2
Clachan na Luib W Isles 84 B3
Clachan of Campsie E Dunb 68 C5
Clachan of Glendaruel Arg/Bute 73 E8
Clachan-Seil Arg/Bute 72 B6
Clachan Strachur Arg/Bute 73 C9
Clachaneasy Dumf/Gal 54 B6
Clachanmore Dumf/Gal 54 E3
Clachbreck Arg/Bute 72 F6
Clachnabrain Angus 82 G5
Clachtoll H'land 92 G3
Clackmannan Clack 69 A8
Clacton-on-Sea Essex 31 G8
Cladach Chireboist W Isles 84 B2
Claddach-knockline W Isles 84 B2
Cladich Arg/Bute 74 E3
Claggan H'land 79 G9
Claggan H'land 80 F3
Claigan H'land 84 C7
Claines Worcs 26 C5
Clandown Bath/NE Som'set 16 F3
Clanfield Hants 10 C5
Clanfield Oxon 17 A9
Clanville Hants 17 G10
Claonaig Arg/Bute 73 H7
Claonel H'land 93 J8
Clap Hill Kent 13 C9
Clapgate Dorset 9 D9
Clapgate Herts 29 F11
Clapham Beds 29 C7
Clapham London 19 D9
Clapham N Yorks 50 C3
Clapham W Sussex 11 D9
Clappers Scot Borders 71 E8
Clappersgate Cumb 56 F5
Clapton Som'set 8 D3
Clapton-in-Gordano N Som'set 15 D10
Clapton-on-the-Hill Glos 27 G8
Clapworthy Devon 6 D5
Clara Vale Tyne/Wear 63 G7
Clarach Ceredig'n 32 G2
Clarbeston Pembs 22 D5
Clarbeston Road Pembs 22 D5
Clarborough Notts 45 D11
Clardon H'land 94 D3
Clare Suffolk 30 D4
Clarebrand Dumf/Gal 55 C10
Clarencefield Dumf/Gal 60 G6
Clarilaw Scot Borders 61 B11
Clark's Green Surrey 19 H8
Clarkston E Renf 68 E4
Clashandorran H'land 87 G8
Clashcoig H'land 87 B9
Clashindarroch Aberds 88 E4
Clashmore H'land 92 F3
Clashmore H'land 87 C10
Clashnessie H'land 92 F3
Clashnoir Moray 82 A4
Clate Shetl'd 96 G7
Clathy Perth/Kinr 76 F2
Clatt Aberds 83 A7
Clatter Powys 32 F5
Clatterford I/Wight 10 F3
Clatterin Bridge Aberds 83 F8
Clatworthy Som'set 7 C9
Claughton Lancs 49 E5
Claughton Lancs 50 C1
Claughton Mersey 42 D6
Claverdon Warwick 27 B8
Claverham N Som'set 15 E10
Clavering Essex 29 E11
Claverley Shrops 34 F3
Claverton Bath/NE Som'set 16 E4
Clawdd-newydd Denbs 42 G3
Clawthorpe Cumb 49 B5
Clawton Devon 6 G2
Claxby Lincs 46 C5
Claxby Lincs 47 E8
Claxton Norfolk 39 E9
Claxton N Yorks 52 C2
Clay Common Suffolk 39 G10
Clay Coton Northants 36 H1
Clay Cross Derby 45 F7
Clay Hill W Berks 18 D2
Clay Lake Lincs 37 C8

Crosshill *E Ayrs* 67 D7
Crosshill *Fife* 76 H4
Crosshill *S Ayrs* 66 F6
Crosshouse *E Ayrs* 67 C6
Crossings *Cumb* 61 F11
Crosskeys *Caerph* 15 B8
Crosskirk *H'land* 93 B13
Crosslanes *Shrops* 33 D9
Crosslee *Scot Borders* 61 B9
Crosslee *Renf* 68 D3
Crossmichael *Dumf/Gal* 55 C10
Crossmoor *Lancs* 49 F4
Crossroads *Aberds* 83 D9
Crossroads *E Ayrs* 67 C7
Crossway *Heref'd* 26 E3
Crossway *Monmouths* 25 G11
Crossway *Powys* 25 C7
Crossway Green *Worcs* 26 B5
Crossways *Dorset* 9 F6
Crosswell *Pembs* 22 C6
Crosswood *Ceredig'n* 24 A3
Crosthwaite *Cumb* 56 G6
Croston *Lancs* 49 H4
Crostwick *Norfolk* 39 D8
Crostwight *Norfolk* 39 C9
Crothair *W Isles* 90 D6
Crouch *Kent* 20 F3
Crouch Hill *Dorset* 8 C6
Crouch House Green *Kent* 19 G11
Croucheston *Wilts* 9 B9
Croughton *Northants* 28 E2
Crovie *Aberds* 89 B8
Crow Edge *S Yorks* 44 B5
Crow Hill *Heref'd* 26 F3
Crowan *Cornw'l* 2 F5
Crowborough *E Sussex* 12 C4
Crowcombe *Som'set* 7 C10
Crowdecote *Derby* 44 F5
Crowden *Derby* 44 C4
Crowell *Oxon* 18 B4
Crowfield *Northants* 28 D3
Crowfield *Suffolk* 31 C8
Crowhurst *E Sussex* 13 E6
Crowhurst *Surrey* 19 G10
Crowhurst Lane End *Surrey* 19 G10
Crowland *Lincs* 37 D8
Crowlas *Cornw'l* 2 F4
Crowle *N Lincs* 45 A11
Crowle *Worcs* 26 C6
Crowmarsh Gifford *Oxon* 18 C3
Crown Corner *Suffolk* 31 A9
Crownhill *Plym'th* 4 F5
Crownland *Suffolk* 31 B7
Crownthorpe *Norfolk* 39 E6
Crowntown *Cornw'l* 2 F5
Crows-an-wra *Cornw'l* 2 G2
Crowshill *Norfolk* 38 E5
Crowsnest *Shrops* 33 E9
Crowthorne *Brackn'l* 18 E5
Crowton *Ches* 43 E8
Croxall *Staffs* 35 D7
Croxby *Lincs* 46 C5
Croxdale *Durham* 58 C3
Croxden *Staffs* 35 B6
Croxley Green *Herts* 19 B7
Croxton *Cambs* 29 B9
Croxton *N Lincs* 46 A4
Croxton *Norfolk* 38 G4
Croxton *Staffs* 34 B3
Croxton Kerrial *Leics* 36 C4
Croxtonbank *Staffs* 34 B3
Croy *H'land* 87 G10
Croy *N Lanarks* 68 C6
Croyde *Devon* 6 C3
Croydon *Cambs* 29 D10
Croydon *London* 19 E10
Crubenmore Lodge *H'land* 81 D8
Cruckmeole *Shrops* 33 E10
Cruckton *Shrops* 33 D10
Cruden Bay *Aberds* 89 E10
Crudgington *Telford* 34 D2
Crudwell *Wilts* 16 B6
Crug *Powys* 25 A8
Crugmeer *Cornw'l* 3 B8
Crugybar *Carms* 24 E3
Crulabhig *W Isles* 90 D6
Crumlin = Crymlyn *Caerph* 15 B8
Crumpsall *Gtr Man* 44 B2
Crundale *Kent* 21 G7
Crundale *Pembs* 22 E4
Cruwys Morchard *Devon* 7 E7
Crux Easton *Hants* 17 F11
Crwbin *Carms* 23 E9
Crya *Orkney* 95 H4
Cryers Hill *Bucks* 18 B5
Crymlyn *Gwyn* 41 C8
Crymlyn = Crumlin *Caerph* 15 B8
Crymych *Pembs* 22 C6
Crynant *Neath P Talb* 14 A3
Crynfryn *Ceredig'n* 24 B2
Cuaig *H'land* 85 C12
Cuan *Arg/Bute* 72 B6
Cubbington *Warwick* 27 B10
Cubeck *N Yorks* 57 H11
Cubert *Cornw'l* 3 D6
Cubley *S Yorks* 44 B6
Cubley Common *Derby* 35 B7
Cublington *Bucks* 28 F5
Cublington *Heref'd* 25 E11
Cuckfield *W Sussex* 12 D2
Cucklington *Som'set* 9 B6
Cuckney *Notts* 45 E9
Cuckoo Hill *Notts* 45 C11
Cuddesdon *Oxon* 18 A3
Cuddington *Bucks* 28 G4
Cuddington *Ches* 43 E9
Cuddington Heath *Ches* 43 H7
Cuddy Hill *Lancs* 49 F4
Cudham *London* 19 F11
Cudliptown *Devon* 4 D6
Cudworth *Som'set* 8 C2
Cudworth *S Yorks* 45 B7
Cuffley *Herts* 19 A10
Cuiashader *W Isles* 91 B10
Cuidhir *W Isles* 84 H1
Cuidhtinis *W Isles* 90 J5
Culbo *H'land* 87 E9
Culbokie *H'land* 87 F9
Culburnie *H'land* 86 G7
Culcabock *H'land* 87 G9
Culcairn *H'land* 87 E9
Culcharry *H'land* 87 F11
Culcheth *Warrington* 43 C9
Culdrain *Aberds* 88 E5
Culduie *H'land* 85 D12
Culford *Suffolk* 30 A5
Culgaith *Cumb* 57 D8
Culham *Oxon* 18 B2
Culkein *H'land* 92 F3
Culkein Drumbeg *H'land* 92 F4
Culkerton *Glos* 16 B6
Cullachie *H'land* 81 A11
Cullen *Moray* 88 B5
Cullercoats *Tyne/Wear* 63 F9
Cullicudden *H'land* 87 E9
Cullingworth *W Yorks* 51 F6
Cullipool *Arg/Bute* 72 B6
Cullivoe *Shetl'd* 96 C7
Culloch *Perth/Kinr* 75 F10
Culloden *H'land* 87 G10
Cullompton *Devon* 7 F9
Culmaily *H'land* 87 B11
Culmazie *Dumf/Gal* 54 D6
Culmington *Shrops* 33 G10
Culmstock *Devon* 7 E10
Culnacraig *H'land* 92 J3
Culnaknock *H'land* 85 B10
Culpho *Suffolk* 31 D9
Culrain *H'land* 87 B8
Culross *Fife* 69 B8
Culroy *S Ayrs* 66 E6
Culsh *Aberds* 89 D8
Culsh *Aberds* 82 D5
Culshabbin *Dumf/Gal* 54 D6
Culswick *Shetl'd* 96 J4
Cultercullen *Aberds* 89 F9
Cults *Aberd C* 83 C10
Cults *Aberds* 88 E5
Cults *Dumf/Gal* 55 E7
Culverstone Green *Kent* 20 E3
Culverthorpe *Lincs* 36 A6
Culworth *Northants* 28 D2
Culzie Lodge *H'land* 87 D8
Cumbernauld *N Lanarks* 68 C6
Cumbernauld Village *N Lanarks* 68 C6
Cumberworth *Lincs* 47 E9
Cuminestown *Aberds* 89 C8
Cumlewick *Shetl'd* 96 L6
Cummersdale *Cumb* 56 A5
Cummertrees *Dumf/Gal* 61 G7
Cummingston *Moray* 88 B1
Cumnock *E Ayrs* 67 D8
Cumnor *Oxon* 17 A11
Cumrew *Cumb* 57 A7
Cumwhinton *Cumb* 56 A6
Cumwhitton *Cumb* 57 A7
Cundall *N Yorks* 51 B10
Cunninghamhead *N Ayrs* 67 B6
Cunnister *Shetl'd* 96 D7
Cupar *Fife* 76 F6
Cupar Muir *Fife* 76 F6
Cupernham *Hants* 10 B2
Curbar *Derby* 44 E6
Curbridge *Hants* 10 C4
Curbridge *Oxon* 27 H10
Curdridge *Hants* 10 C4
Curdworth *Warwick* 35 F7
Curland *Som'set* 8 C1
Curlew Green *Suffolk* 31 B10
Currarie *S Ayrs* 66 G4
Curridge *W Berks* 17 D11
Currie *C/Edinb* 69 D10
Curry Mallet *Som'set* 8 B2
Curry Rivel *Som'set* 8 B2
Curtisden Green *Kent* 12 B6
Curtisknowle *Devon* 5 F8
Cury *Cornw'l* 2 G5
Cushnie *Aberds* 89 B7
Cushuish *Som'set* 7 C10
Cusop *Heref'd* 25 D9
Cutcloy *Dumf/Gal* 55 F7
Cutcombe *Som'set* 7 C8
Cutgate *Gtr Man* 44 A2
Cutiau *Gwyn* 32 D2
Cutlers Green *Essex* 30 E2
Cutnall Green *Worcs* 26 B5
Cutsdean *Glos* 27 E7
Cutthorpe *Derby* 45 E7
Cutts *Shetl'd* 96 K6
Cuxham *Oxon* 18 B3
Cuxton *Medway* 20 E4
Cuxwold *Lincs* 46 B5
Cwm *Bl Gwent* 25 H8
Cwm *Denbs* 42 E3
Cwm *Swan* 14 B2
Cwm-byr *Carms* 24 E3
Cwm-Cewydd *Gwyn* 32 D4
Cwm-cou *Ceredig'n* 23 B7
Cwm-Dulais *Swan* 14 A2
Cwm-felin-fach *Caerph* 15 B7
Cwm Ffrwd-oer *Torf* 15 A8
Cwm-hesgen *Gwyn* 32 C3
Cwm-hwnt *Rh Cyn Taff* 24 H6
Cwm Irfon *Powys* 24 D5
Cwm-Llinau *Powys* 32 E4
Cwm-mawr *Carms* 23 E10
Cwm-parc *Rh Cyn Taff* 14 B5
Cwm Penmachno *Conwy* 41 F9
Cwm-y-glo *Carms* 23 E10
Cwm-y-glo *Gwyn* 41 D7
Cwmafan *Neath P Talb* 14 B3
Cwmaman *Rh Cyn Taff* 14 B6
Cwmann *Carms* 23 B10
Cwmavon *Torf* 25 H9
Cwmbach *Carms* 23 D7
Cwmbach *Carms* 23 F9
Cwmbach *Powys* 25 C7
Cwmbach *Powys* 25 E8
Cwmbâch *Rh Cyn Taff* 14 A6
Cwmbelan *Powys* 32 G5
Cwmbran = Cwmbrân *Torf* 15 B8
Cwmbrân = Cwmbran *Torf* 15 B8
Cwmbrwyno *Ceredig'n* 32 G3
Cwmcarn *Caerph* 15 B8
Cwmcarvan *Monmouths* 25 H11
Cwmcych *Pembs* 23 C7
Cwmdare *Rh Cyn Taff* 14 A5
Cwmderwen *Powys* 32 E5
Cwmdu *Carms* 24 E3
Cwmdu *Powys* 25 F8
Cwmdu *Swan* 14 B2
Cwmduad *Carms* 23 C8
Cwmdwr *Carms* 24 E4
Cwmfelin *Bridg* 14 C4
Cwmfelin *Merth Tyd* 14 A6
Cwmfelin Boeth *Carms* 22 E6
Cwmfelin Mynach *Carms* 23 D7
Cwmffrwd *Carms* 23 E9
Cwmgiedd *Powys* 24 G4
Cwmgors *Neath P Talb* 24 G4
Cwmgwili *Carms* 23 E10
Cwmgwrach *Neath P Talb* 14 A4
Cwmhiraeth *Carms* 23 C8
Cwmifor *Carms* 24 F3
Cwmisfael *Carms* 23 E9
Cwmllynfell *Neath P Talb* 24 G4
Cwmorgan *Carms* 23 C7
Cwmpengraig *Carms* 23 C8
Cwmrhos *Powys* 25 F8
Cwmsychpant *Ceredig'n* 23 B9
Cwmtillery *Bl Gwent* 25 H9
Cwmwysg *Powys* 24 F5
Cwmyoy *Monmouths* 25 F9
Cwmystwyth *Ceredig'n* 24 A4
Cwrt *Gwyn* 32 E2
Cwrt-newydd *Ceredig'n* 23 B9
Cwrt-y-cadno *Carms* 24 D3
Cwrt-y-gollen *Powys* 25 G9
Cydweli = Kidwelly *Carms* 23 F9
Cyffordd Llandudno = Llandudno Junction *Conwy* 41 C9
Cyffylliog *Denbs* 42 G3
Cyfronydd *Powys* 33 E7
Cymer *Neath P Talb* 14 B4
Cyncoed *Card* 15 C7
Cynghordy *Carms* 24 D5
Cynheidre *Carms* 23 F9
Cynwyd *Denbs* 33 A6
Cynwyl Elfed *Carms* 23 D8
Cywarch *Gwyn* 32 D4

D

Dacre *Cumb* 56 D6
Dacre *N Yorks* 51 C7
Dacre Banks *N Yorks* 51 C7
Daddry Shield *Durham* 57 C10
Dadford *Bucks* 28 E3
Dadlington *Leics* 35 F10
Dafarn Faig *Gwyn* 40 F6
Dafen *Carms* 23 F10
Daffy Green *Norfolk* 38 E5
Dagenham *London* 19 C11
Daglingworth *Glos* 26 H6
Dagnall *Bucks* 28 G6
Dail Beag *W Isles* 90 C7
Dail bho Dheas *W Isles* 91 A9
Dail bho Thuath *W Isles* 91 A9
Dail Mor *W Isles* 90 C7
Daill *Arg/Bute* 64 B4
Dailly *S Ayrs* 66 F5
Dairsie or Osnaburgh *Fife* 77 F7
Daisy Hill *Gtr Man* 43 B9
Dalabrog *W Isles* 84 F2
Dalavich *Arg/Bute* 73 B8
Dalbeattie *Dumf/Gal* 55 C11
Dalblair *E Ayrs* 67 E9
Dalbog *Angus* 83 F7
Dalbury *Derby* 35 B8
Dalby *I/Man* 48 E2
Dalby *N Yorks* 52 B2
Dalchalloch *Perth/Kinr* 75 A10
Dalchalm *H'land* 93 J12
Dalchenna *Arg/Bute* 73 C9
Dalchirach *Moray* 88 E1
Dalchork *H'land* 93 H8
Dalchreichart *H'land* 80 B4
Dalchruin *Perth/Kinr* 75 F10
Dalderby *Lincs* 46 F6
Dale *Pembs* 22 F3
Dale Abbey *Derby* 35 B10
Dale Head *Cumb* 56 E6
Dale of Walls *Shetl'd* 96 H3
Dalelia *H'land* 79 E10
Daless *H'land* 87 H11
Dalfaber *H'land* 81 B11
Dalgarven *N Ayrs* 66 B5
Dalgety Bay *Fife* 69 B10
Dalginross *Perth/Kinr* 75 E10
Dalguise *Perth/Kinr* 76 C2
Dalhalvaig *H'land* 93 D11
Dalham *Suffolk* 30 B4
Dalinlongart *Arg/Bute* 73 E10
Dalkeith *Midloth* 70 D2
Dallam *Warrington* 43 C8
Dallas *Moray* 87 F14
Dalleagles *E Ayrs* 67 E8
Dallinghoo *Suffolk* 31 C9
Dallington *E Sussex* 12 E5
Dallington *Northants* 28 B4
Dallow *N Yorks* 51 B7
Dalmadilly *Aberds* 83 B9
Dalmally *Arg/Bute* 74 E4
Dalmarnock *C/Glasg* 68 D5
Dalmary *Stirl* 75 H8
Dalmellington *E Ayrs* 67 F7
Dalmeny *C/Edinb* 69 C10
Dalmigavie *H'land* 81 B9
Dalmigavie Lodge *H'land* 81 A9
Dalmore *H'land* 87 E9
Dalmuir *W Dunb* 68 C3
Dalnabreck *H'land* 79 E9
Dalnacardoch Lodge *Perth/Kinr* 81 F9
Dalnacroich *H'land* 86 F6
Dalnaglar Castle *Perth/Kinr* 76 A4
Dalnahaitnach *H'land* 81 A10
Dalnaspidal Lodge *Perth/Kinr* 81 F8
Dalnavaid *Perth/Kinr* 76 A3
Dalnavie *H'land* 87 D9
Dalnawillan Lodge *H'land* 93 E13
Dalness *H'land* 74 B4
Dalnessie *H'land* 93 H9
Dalqueich *Perth/Kinr* 76 G3
Dalreavoch *H'land* 93 J10
Dalry *N Ayrs* 66 B5
Dalrymple *E Ayrs* 67 E6
Dalserf *S Lanarks* 69 E7
Dalston *Cumb* 56 A5
Dalswinton *Dumf/Gal* 60 E5
Dalton *Dumf/Gal* 61 F7
Dalton *Lancs* 43 B7
Dalton *Northum* 62 H5
Dalton *Northum* 63 F7
Dalton *N Yorks* 51 B10
Dalton *N Yorks* 58 F2
Dalton *S Yorks* 45 C8
Dalton-in-Furness *Cumb* 49 B2
Dalton-le-Dale *Durham* 58 B5
Dalton-on-Tees *N Yorks* 58 F3
Dalton Piercy *Hartlep'l* 58 C5
Dalveich *Stirl* 75 E9
Dalvina Lodge *H'land* 93 E9
Dalwhinnie *H'land* 81 E8
Dalwood *Devon* 8 D1
Dalwyne *S Ayrs* 66 G6
Dam Green *Norfolk* 39 G6
Dam Side *Lancs* 49 E4
Damerham *Hants* 9 C10
Damgate *Norfolk* 39 E10
Damnaglaur *Dumf/Gal* 54 F4
Damside *Scot Borders* 69 F10
Danbury *Essex* 30 H4
Danby *N Yorks* 59 F8
Danby Wiske *N Yorks* 58 G4
Dandaleith *Moray* 88 D2
Danderhall *Midloth* 70 D2
Dane End *Herts* 29 F10
Danebridge *Ches* 44 F3
Danehill *E Sussex* 12 D3
Danemoor Green *Norfolk* 39 E6
Danesford *Shrops* 34 F3
Daneshill *Hants* 18 F3
Dangerous Corner *Lancs* 43 A8
Danskine *E Loth* 70 D4
Darcy Lever *Gtr Man* 43 B10
Darenth *Kent* 20 D2
Daresbury *Halton* 43 D8
Darfield *S Yorks* 45 B8
Darfoulds *Notts* 45 E9
Dargate *Kent* 21 E7
Darite *Cornw'l* 4 E3
Darlaston *W Midlands* 34 F5
Darley *N Yorks* 51 D8
Darley Bridge *Derby* 44 F6
Darley Head *N Yorks* 51 D7
Darlingscott *Warwick* 27 D9
Darlington *D'lington* 58 E3
Darliston *Shrops* 34 B1
Darlton *Notts* 45 E11
Darnall *S Yorks* 45 D7
Darnick *Scot Borders* 70 G4
Darowen *Powys* 32 E4
Darra *Aberds* 89 D7
Darracott *Devon* 6 C3
Darras Hall *Northum* 63 F7
Darrington *W Yorks* 51 G10
Darsham *Suffolk* 31 B11
Dartford *Kent* 20 D2
Dartford Crossing *Kent* 20 D2
Dartington *Devon* 5 E8
Dartmeet *Devon* 5 D7
Dartmouth *Devon* 5 F9
Darton *S Yorks* 45 B7
Darvel *E Ayrs* 68 G4
Darwell Hole *E Sussex* 12 E5
Darwen *Blackb'n* 50 G2
Datchet *Windsor* 18 D6
Datchworth *Herts* 29 G9
Datchworth Green *Herts* 29 G9
Daubhill *Gtr Man* 43 B10
Daugh of Kinermony *Moray* 88 D2
Dauntsey *Wilts* 16 C6
Dava *Moray* 87 H13
Davenham *Ches* 43 E9
Davenport Green *Ches* 44 E2
Daventry *Northants* 28 B2
David's Well *Powys* 33 H6
Davidson's Mains *C/Edinb* 69 C11
Davidstow *Cornw'l* 4 C2
Davington *Dumf/Gal* 61 C8
Daviot *Aberds* 83 A9
Daviot *H'land* 87 H10
Davoch of Grange *Moray* 88 C4
Davyhulme *Gtr Man* 43 C10
Dawley *Telford* 34 E2
Dawlish *Devon* 5 D10
Dawlish Warren *Devon* 5 D10
Dawn *Conwy* 41 C10
Daws Heath *Essex* 20 C5
Daw's House *Cornw'l* 4 C4
Dawsmere *Lincs* 37 B10
Dayhills *Staffs* 34 B5
Daylesford *Glos* 27 F9
Ddôl-Cownwy *Powys* 32 D6
Ddrydwy *Angl* 40 C5
Deadwater *Northum* 62 D2
Deaf Hill *Durham* 58 C4
Deal *Kent* 21 F10
Deal Hall *Essex* 21 B7
Dean *Cumb* 56 D2
Dean *Devon* 5 E8
Dean *Devon* 6 B4
Dean *Dorset* 9 C8
Dean *Hants* 10 C4
Dean *Som'set* 16 G3
Dean Prior *Devon* 5 E8
Dean Row *Ches* 44 D2
Deanburnhaugh *Scot Borders* 61 B9
Deane *Gtr Man* 43 B9
Deane *Hants* 18 F2
Deanich Lodge *H'land* 86 C6
Deanland *Dorset* 9 C8
Deans *W Loth* 69 D9
Deanscales *Cumb* 56 D2
Deanshanger *Northants* 28 E4
Deanston *Stirl* 75 G10
Dearham *Cumb* 56 C2
Debach *Suffolk* 31 C9
Debden *Essex* 30 E2
Debden *Essex* 19 B11
Debden Cross *Essex* 30 E2
Debenham *Suffolk* 31 B8
Dechmont *W Loth* 69 C9
Deddington *Oxon* 27 E11
Dedham *Essex* 31 E7
Dedham Heath *Essex* 31 E7
Deebank *Aberds* 83 D8
Deene *Northants* 36 F5
Deenethorpe *Northants* 36 F5
Deepcar *S Yorks* 44 C6
Deepcut *Surrey* 18 F6
Deepdale *Cumb* 50 A3
Deeping Gate *Lincs* 37 E7
Deeping St James *Lincs* 37 E7
Deeping St Nicholas *Lincs* 37 D8
Deerhill *Moray* 88 C4
Deerhurst *Glos* 26 F5
Deerness *Orkney* 95 H6
Defford *Worcs* 26 D6
Defynnog *Powys* 24 F6
Deganwy *Conwy* 41 C9
Deighton *N Yorks* 58 F4
Deighton *W Yorks* 51 H7
Deighton *C/York* 52 E2
Deiniolen *Gwyn* 41 D7
Delabole *Cornw'l* 4 C1
Delamere *Ches* 43 F8
Delfrigs *Aberds* 89 F9
Dell Lodge *H'land* 82 B2
Delliefure *H'land* 87 H13
Delnabo *Moray* 82 B3
Delnadamph *Aberds* 82 C4
Delph *Gtr Man* 44 B3
Delves *Durham* 58 B2
Delvine *Perth/Kinr* 76 C4
Dembleby *Lincs* 36 B6
Denaby Main *S Yorks* 45 C8
Denbigh = Dinbych *Denbs* 42 F3
Denbury *Devon* 5 E9
Denby *Derby* 45 H7
Denby Dale *W Yorks* 44 B6
Denchworth *Oxon* 17 B10
Dendron *Cumb* 49 B2
Denel End *Beds* 29 E7
Denend *Aberds* 88 E6
Denford *Northants* 36 H5
Dengie *Essex* 20 A6
Denham *Bucks* 19 C7
Denham *Suffolk* 30 B4
Denham *Suffolk* 31 A8
Denham Green *Bucks* 19 C7
Denham Street *Suffolk* 31 A8
Denhead *Aberds* 89 C9
Denhead *Fife* 77 F7
Denhead of Arbilot *Angus* 77 C8
Denhead of Gray *Dundee C* 76 D6
Denholm *Scot Borders* 61 B11
Denholme *W Yorks* 51 F6
Denholme Clough *W Yorks* 51 F6
Denio *Gwyn* 40 G5
Denmead *Hants* 10 C5
Denmore *Aberd C* 83 B11
Denmoss *Aberds* 89 D6
Dennington *Suffolk* 31 B9
Denny *Falk* 69 B7
Denny Lodge *Hants* 10 D2
Dennyloanhead *Falk* 69 B7
Denshaw *Gtr Man* 44 A3
Denside *Aberds* 83 D10
Densole *Kent* 21 G9
Denston *Suffolk* 30 C4
Denstone *Staffs* 35 A7
Dent *Cumb* 57 H9
Denton *Cambs* 37 G7
Denton *D'lington* 58 E3
Denton *E Sussex* 12 F3
Denton *Gtr Man* 44 C3
Denton *Kent* 21 G9
Denton *Lincs* 36 B4
Denton *Norfolk* 39 G8
Denton *Northants* 28 C5
Denton *N Yorks* 51 E7
Denton *Oxon* 18 A2
Denton's Green *Mersey* 43 C7
Denver *Norfolk* 38 E2
Denwick *Northum* 63 B8
Deopham *Norfolk* 39 E6
Deopham Green *Norfolk* 38 F6
Depden *Suffolk* 30 C4
Depden Green *Suffolk* 30 C4
Deptford *London* 19 D10
Deptford *Wilts* 17 H7
Derby *Derby C* 35 B9
Derbyhaven *I/Man* 48 F2
Dereham *Norfolk* 38 D5
Deri *Caerph* 15 A7
Derril *Devon* 6 F2
Derringstone *Kent* 21 G9
Derrington *Staffs* 34 C4
Derriton *Devon* 6 F2
Derry Hill *Wilts* 16 D6
Derryguaig *Arg/Bute* 78 H7
Derrythorpe *N Lincs* 46 B2
Dersingham *Norfolk* 38 B2
Dervaig *Arg/Bute* 78 F7
Derwen *Denbs* 42 G3
Derwenlas *Powys* 32 F3
Desborough *Northants* 36 G4
Desford *Leics* 35 E10
Detchant *Northum* 71 G9
Detling *Kent* 20 F4
Deuddwr *Powys* 33 D8
Devauden *Monmouths* 15 B10
Devil's Bridge *Ceredig'n* 32 H3
Devizes *Wilts* 17 E7
Devol *Invercl* 68 C2
Devonport *Plym'th* 4 F5
Devonside *Clack* 76 H2
Devoran *Cornw'l* 3 F6
Dewar *Scot Borders* 70 F2
Dewlish *Dorset* 9 E6
Dewsbury *W Yorks* 51 G8
Dewsbury Moor *W Yorks* 51 G8
Dewshall Court *Heref'd* 25 E11
Dhoon *I/Man* 48 D4
Dhoor *I/Man* 48 C4
Dhowin *I/Man* 48 B4
Dial Post *W Sussex* 11 C10
Dibden *Hants* 10 D3
Dibden Purlieu *Hants* 10 D3
Dickleburgh *Norfolk* 39 G7
Didbrook *Glos* 27 E7
Didcot *Oxon* 18 C2
Diddington *Cambs* 29 B8
Diddlebury *Shrops* 33 G11
Didley *Heref'd* 25 E11
Didling *W Sussex* 11 C7
Didmarton *Glos* 16 C5
Didsbury *Gtr Man* 44 C2
Didworthy *Devon* 5 E7
Digby *Lincs* 46 G4
Digg *H'land* 85 B9
Diggle *Gtr Man* 44 B4
Digmoor *Lancs* 43 B7
Digswell Park *Herts* 29 G9
Dihewid *Ceredig'n* 23 A9
Dilham *Norfolk* 39 C9
Dilhorne *Staffs* 34 A5
Dillarburn *S Lanarks* 69 F7
Dillington *Cambs* 29 B8
Dilston *Northum* 62 G5
Dilton Marsh *Wilts* 16 G5
Dilwyn *Heref'd* 25 C11
Dinas *Carms* 23 C7
Dinas *Gwyn* 40 G4
Dinas Cross *Pembs* 22 C5
Dinas Dinlle *Gwyn* 40 E6
Dinas-Mawddwy *Gwyn* 32 D4
Dinas Powys *V/Glam* 15 D7
Dinbych = Denbigh *Denbs* 42 F3
Dinbych-y-Pysgod = Tenby *Pembs* 22 F6
Dinder *Som'set* 16 G2
Dinedor *Heref'd* 26 E2
Dingestow *Monmouths* 25 G11
Dingle *Mersey* 42 D6
Dingleden *Kent* 13 C7
Dingley *Northants* 36 G3
Dingwall *H'land* 87 F8
Dinlabyre *Scot Borders* 61 D11
Dinmael *Conwy* 32 A6
Dinnet *Aberds* 82 D6
Dinnington *Som'set* 8 C3
Dinnington *S Yorks* 45 D9
Dinnington *Tyne/Wear* 63 F8
Dinorwic *Gwyn* 41 D7
Dinton *Bucks* 28 G4
Dinton *Wilts* 9 A9
Dinwoodie Mains *Dumf/Gal* 61 D7
Dinworthy *Devon* 6 E2
Dippen *N Ayrs* 66 D3
Dippenhall *Surrey* 18 G5
Dipple *Moray* 88 C3
Dipple *S Ayrs* 66 F5
Diptford *Devon* 5 F8
Dipton *Durham* 58 A2
Dirdhu *H'land* 82 A2
Dirleton *E Loth* 70 B4
Dirt Pot *Northum* 57 B10
Discoed *Powys* 25 B9
Diseworth *Leics* 35 C10
Dishes *Orkney* 95 F7
Dishforth *N Yorks* 51 B9
Disley *Ches* 44 D3
Diss *Norfolk* 39 H7
Disserth *Powys* 25 C7
Distington *Cumb* 56 D2
Ditchampton *Wilts* 9 A9
Ditcheat *Som'set* 16 H3
Ditchingham *Norfolk* 39 F9
Ditchling *E Sussex* 12 E2
Ditherington *Shrops* 33 D11
Dittisham *Devon* 5 F9
Ditton *Halton* 43 D7
Ditton *Kent* 20 F4
Ditton Green *Cambs* 30 C3
Ditton Priors *Shrops* 34 G2
Divach *H'land* 81 A6
Divlyn *Carms* 24 E4
Dixton *Glos* 26 E6
Dixton *Monmouths* 26 G2
Dobcross *Gtr Man* 44 B3
Dobwalls *Cornw'l* 4 E3
Doc Penfro = Pembroke Dock *Pembs* 22 F4
Doccombe *Devon* 5 C8
Dochfour Ho. *H'land* 87 H9
Dochgarroch *H'land* 87 G9
Docking *Norfolk* 38 B3
Docklow *Heref'd* 26 C2
Dockray *Cumb* 56 D5
Dockroyd *W Yorks* 50 F6
Dodburn *Scot Borders* 61 C10
Doddinghurst *Essex* 20 B2
Doddington *Cambs* 37 F9
Doddington *Kent* 20 F6
Doddington *Lincs* 46 E3
Doddington *Northum* 71 G8
Doddington *Shrops* 34 H2
Doddiscombsleigh *Devon* 5 C9
Dodford *Northants* 28 B3
Dodford *Worcs* 26 A6
Dodington *S Gloucs* 16 C4
Dodleston *Ches* 42 F6
Dods Leigh *Staffs* 34 B6
Dodworth *S Yorks* 45 B7
Doe Green *Warrington* 43 D8
Doe Lea *Derby* 45 F8
Dog Village *Devon* 7 G8
Dogdyke *Lincs* 46 G6
Dogmersfield *Hants* 18 F4
Dogridge *Wilts* 17 C7
Dogsthorpe *Peterbro* 37 E7
Dol-fôr *Powys* 32 E4
Dôl-y-Bont *Ceredig'n* 32 G2
Dol-y-cannau *Powys* 25 D9
Dolanog *Powys* 33 D6
Dolau *Powys* 25 B8
Dolau *Rh Cyn Taff* 14 C5
Dolbenmaen *Gwyn* 41 F7
Dolfach *Powys* 32 E5
Dolfor *Powys* 33 G7
Dolgarrog *Conwy* 41 D9
Dolgellau *Gwyn* 32 D3
Dolgran *Carms* 23 C9
Dolhendre *Gwyn* 41 G10
Doll *H'land* 93 J11
Dollar *Clack* 76 H2
Dolley Green *Powys* 25 B9
Dollwen *Ceredig'n* 32 G2
Dolphin *Flints* 42 E4
Dolphinholme *Lancs* 49 D5
Dolphinton *S Lanarks* 69 F10
Dolton *Devon* 6 E4
Dolwen *Conwy* 41 C10
Dolwen *Powys* 32 E5
Dolwyd *Conwy* 41 C10
Dolwyddelan *Conwy* 41 E9
Dolyhir *Powys* 25 C9
Doncaster *S Yorks* 45 B9
Dones Green *Ches* 43 E9
Donhead St Andrew *Wilts* 9 B8
Donhead St Mary *Wilts* 9 B8
Donibristle *Fife* 69 B10
Donington *Lincs* 37 B8
Donington on Bain *Lincs* 46 D6
Donington South Ing *Lincs* 37 B8
Donisthorpe *Leics* 35 D9
Donkey Town *Surrey* 18 E6
Donnington *Glos* 27 F8
Donnington *Heref'd* 26 E4
Donnington *Shrops* 34 E1
Donnington *Telford* 34 D3
Donnington *W Berks* 17 E11
Donnington *W Sussex* 11 D7
Donnington Wood *Telford* 34 D3
Donyatt *Som'set* 8 C2
Doonfoot *S Ayrs* 66 E6
Dorback Lodge *H'land* 82 B2
Dorchester *Dorset* 8 E5
Dorchester *Oxon* 18 B2
Dordon *Warwick* 35 E8
Dore *S Yorks* 45 D7
Dores *H'land* 87 H8
Dorking *Surrey* 19 G8
Dormansland *Surrey* 12 B3
Dormanstown *Redcar/Clevel'd* 59 D6
Dormington *Heref'd* 26 D2
Dormston *Worcs* 26 C6
Dornal *S Ayrs* 54 B5
Dorney *Bucks* 18 D6
Dornie *H'land* 85 F13
Dornoch *H'land* 87 C10
Dornock *Dumf/Gal* 61 G8
Dorrery *H'land* 94 E2
Dorridge *W Midlands* 35 H7
Dorrington *Lincs* 46 G4
Dorrington *Shrops* 33 E10
Dorsington *Warwick* 27 D8
Dorstone *Heref'd* 25 D10
Dorton *Bucks* 28 G3
Dorusduain *H'land* 80 A1
Dosthill *Staffs* 35 F8
Dottery *Dorset* 8 E3
Doublebois *Cornw'l* 4 E2
Dougarie *N Ayrs* 66 C1
Doughton *Glos* 16 B5
Douglas *I/Man* 48 E3
Douglas *S Lanarks* 69 G7
Douglas & Angus *Dundee C* 77 D7
Douglas Water *S Lanarks* 69 G7
Douglas West *S Lanarks* 69 G7
Douglastown *Angus* 77 C7
Doulting *Som'set* 16 G3
Dounby *Orkney* 95 F3
Doune *H'land* 92 J7
Doune *Stirl* 75 G10
Doune Park *Aberds* 89 B7
Douneside *Aberds* 82 C6
Dounie *H'land* 87 B8
Dounreay *H'land* 93 C12
Dousland *Devon* 4 E6
Dovaston *Shrops* 33 C9
Dove Holes *Derby* 44 E4
Dovenby *Cumb* 56 C2
Dover *Kent* 21 G10
Dovercourt *Essex* 31 E9
Doverdale *Worcs* 26 B5
Doveridge *Derby* 35 B7
Doversgreen *Surrey* 19 G9
Dowally *Perth/Kinr* 76 C3
Dowbridge *Lancs* 49 F4
Dowdeswell *Glos* 26 G6
Dowlais *Merth Tyd* 25 H7
Dowland *Devon* 6 E4
Dowlish Wake *Som'set* 8 C2
Down Ampney *Glos* 17 B8
Down Hatherley *Glos* 26 F5
Down St Mary *Devon* 7 F6
Down Thomas *Devon* 4 F6
Downcraig Ferry *N Ayrs* 73 H10
Downderry *Cornw'l* 4 F4
Downe *London* 19 E11
Downend *I/Wight* 10 F4
Downend *S Gloucs* 16 D3
Downend *W Berks* 17 D11
Downfield *Dundee C* 76 D6
Downgate *Cornw'l* 4 D4
Downham *Essex* 20 B4
Downham *Lancs* 50 E3
Downham *Northum* 71 G7
Downham Market *Norfolk* 38 E2
Downhead *Som'set* 16 G3
Downhill *Perth/Kinr* 76 D3
Downhill *Tyne/Wear* 63 H9
Downholland Cross *Lancs* 42 B6
Downholme *N Yorks* 58 G2
Downies *Aberds* 83 D11
Downley *Bucks* 18 B5
Downside *Som'set* 16 G3
Downside *Surrey* 19 F8
Downton *Hants* 10 E1
Downton *Wilts* 9 B10
Downton on the Rock *Heref'd* 25 A11
Dowsby *Lincs* 37 C7
Dowsdale *Lincs* 37 D8
Dowthwaitehead *Cumb* 56 D5
Doxey *Staffs* 34 C5
Doxford *Northum* 63 A7
Doxford Park *Tyne/Wear* 58 A4
Doynton *S Gloucs* 16 D4
Draffan *S Lanarks* 68 F6
Dragonby *N Lincs* 46 A3
Drakeland Corner *Devon* 5 F6
Drakemyre *N Ayrs* 66 A5
Drake's Broughton *Worcs* 26 D6
Drakes Cross *Worcs* 35 H6
Drakewalls *Cornw'l* 4 D5
Draughton *Northants* 36 H3
Draughton *N Yorks* 50 D6
Drax *N Yorks* 52 G2
Draycote *Warwick* 27 A11
Draycott *Derby* 35 B10
Draycott *Glos* 27 E8
Draycott *Som'set* 15 F10
Draycott in the Clay *Staffs* 35 C7
Draycott in the Moors *Staffs* 34 A5
Drayford *Devon* 7 E6
Drayton *Leics* 36 F4
Drayton *Lincs* 37 B8
Drayton *Norfolk* 39 D7
Drayton *Oxon* 27 D11
Drayton *Oxon* 17 B11
Drayton *Portsm'th* 10 D5
Drayton *Som'set* 8 B3
Drayton *Worcs* 34 H5
Drayton Bassett *Staffs* 35 E7
Drayton Beauchamp *Bucks* 28 G6
Drayton Parslow *Bucks* 28 F5
Drayton St Leonard *Oxon* 18 B2
Dre-fach *Ceredig'n* 23 B10
Dre-fach *Carms* 24 G3
Drebley *N Yorks* 51 D6
Dreemskerry *I/Man* 48 C4
Dreenhill *Pembs* 22 E4
Drefach *Carms* 23 C8
Drefach *Carms* 23 E10
Drefelin *Carms* 23 C8
Dreghorn *N Ayrs* 67 C6
Drellingore *Kent* 21 G9
Drem *E Loth* 70 C4
Dresden *Stoke* 34 A5
Dreumasdal *W Isles* 84 E2
Drewsteignton *Devon* 7 G6
Driby *Lincs* 47 E7
Driffield *ER Yorks* 52 D6
Driffield *Glos* 17 B7
Drigg *Cumb* 56 G2
Drighlington *W Yorks* 51 G8
Drimnin *H'land* 79 F8
Drimpton *Dorset* 8 D3
Drimsynie *Arg/Bute* 74 G4
Drinisiadar *W Isles* 90 H6
Drinkstone *Suffolk* 30 B6
Drinkstone Green *Suffolk* 30 B6
Drishaig *Arg/Bute* 74 F4
Drissaig *Arg/Bute* 73 B8
Drochil *Scot Borders* 69 F10
Drointon *Staffs* 34 C6
Droitwich Spa *Worcs* 26 B5
Droman *H'land* 92 D4
Dron *Perth/Kinr* 76 F4
Dronfield *Derby* 45 E7
Dronfield Woodhouse *Derby* 45 E7
Drongan *E Ayrs* 67 E7
Dronley *Angus* 76 D6
Droxford *Hants* 10 C5
Droylsden *Gtr Man* 44 C3
Druid *Denbs* 32 A6
Druidston *Pembs* 22 E3
Druimarbin *H'land* 80 F2
Druimavuic *Arg/Bute* 74 C3
Druimdrishaig *Arg/Bute* 72 F6
Druimindarroch *H'land* 79 C9
Druimyeon More *Arg/Bute* 65 C7
Drum *Arg/Bute* 73 F8
Drum *Perth/Kinr* 76 G3
Drumbeg *H'land* 92 F4
Drumblade *Aberds* 88 D5
Drumblair *Aberds* 89 D6
Drumbuie *Dumf/Gal* 55 A8
Drumbuie *H'land* 85 E12
Drumburgh *Cumb* 61 H8
Drumburn *Dumf/Gal* 60 G5
Drumchapel *C/Glasg* 68 C4
Drumchardine *H'land* 87 G8
Drumchork *H'land* 91 J13
Drumclog *S Lanarks* 68 G5
Drumderfit *H'land* 87 F9
Drumeldrie *Fife* 77 G7
Drumelzier *Scot Borders* 69 G10
Drumfearn *H'land* 85 G11
Drumgask *H'land* 81 D8
Drumgley *Angus* 77 B7
Drumguish *H'land* 81 D9
Drumin *Moray* 88 E1
Drumlasie *Aberds* 83 C8
Drumlemble *Arg/Bute* 65 G7
Drumligair *Aberds* 83 B11
Drumlithie *Aberds* 83 E9
Drummoddie *Dumf/Gal* 54 E6
Drummond *H'land* 87 E9
Drummore *Dumf/Gal* 54 F4
Drummuir *Moray* 88 D3
Drummuir Castle *Moray* 88 D3
Drumnadrochit *H'land* 81 A7
Drumnagorrach *Moray* 88 C5
Drumoak *Aberds* 83 D9
Drumpark *Dumf/Gal* 60 E4
Drumphail *Dumf/Gal* 54 C5
Drumrash *Dumf/Gal* 55 B9
Drumrunie *H'land* 92 J4
Drums *Aberds* 89 F9
Drumsallie *H'land* 80 F1
Drumstinchall *Dumf/Gal* 55 D11
Drumsturdy *Angus* 77 D7
Drumtochty Castle *Aberds* 83 F8
Drumtroddan *Dumf/Gal* 54 E6
Drumuie *H'land* 85 D9
Drumuillie *H'land* 81 A11
Drumvaich *Stirl* 75 G9
Drumwhindle *Aberds* 89 E9
Drunkendub *Angus* 77 C9
Drury *Flints* 42 F5
Drury Square *Norfolk* 38 D5
Dry Doddington *Lincs* 46 H2
Dry Drayton *Cambs* 29 B10
Drybeck *Cumb* 57 E8
Drybridge *Moray* 88 B4
Drybridge *N Ayrs* 67 C6
Drybrook *Glos* 26 G3
Dryburgh *Scot Borders* 70 G4
Dryhope *Scot Borders* 61 A8
Drylaw *C/Edinb* 69 C11
Drym *Cornw'l* 2 F5
Drymen *Stirl* 68 B3
Drymuir *Aberds* 89 D9
Drynoch *H'land* 85 E9
Dryslwyn *Carms* 23 D10
Dryton *Shrops* 34 E1
Dubford *Aberds* 89 B8
Dubton *Angus* 77 B8
Duchally *H'land* 92 H6
Duchlage *Arg/Bute* 68 B2
Duck Corner *Suffolk* 31 D10
Duckington *Ches* 43 G7
Ducklington *Oxon* 27 H10
Duckmanton *Derby* 45 E8
Duck's Cross *Beds* 29 C8
Duddenhoe End *Essex* 29 E11
Duddingston *C/Edinb* 69 C11
Duddington *Northants* 36 E5
Duddleswell *E Sussex* 12 D3
Duddo *Northum* 71 F8
Duddon *Ches* 43 F8
Duddon Bridge *Cumb* 56 H4
Dudleston *Shrops* 33 B9
Dudleston Heath *Shrops* 33 B9
Dudley *Tyne/Wear* 63 F8
Dudley *W Midlands* 34 F5
Dudley Port *W Midlands* 34 F5
Duffield *Derby* 35 A9
Duffryn *Newp* 15 C8
Duffryn *Neath P Talb* 14 B4
Dufftown *Moray* 88 E3
Duffus *Moray* 88 B1
Dufton *Cumb* 57 D8
Duggleby *N Yorks* 52 C4
Duirinish *H'land* 85 E12
Duisdalemore *H'land* 85 G12
Duisky *H'land* 80 F2
Dukestown *Bl Gwent* 25 G8
Dukinfield *Gtr Man* 44 C3
Dulas *Angl* 40 B6
Dulcote *Som'set* 16 G2
Dulford *Devon* 7 F9
Dull *Perth/Kinr* 75 C11
Dullatur *N Lanarks* 68 C6
Dullingham *Cambs* 30 C3
Dulnain Bridge *H'land* 82 A1
Duloe *Beds* 29 B8
Duloe *Cornw'l* 4 F3
Dulsie *H'land* 87 G12
Dulverton *Som'set* 7 D8
Dulwich *London* 19 D10
Dumbarton *W Dunb* 68 C2
Dumbleton *Glos* 27 E7
Dumcrieff *Dumf/Gal* 61 C7
Dumfries *Dumf/Gal* 60 F5
Dumgoyne *Stirl* 68 B4
Dummer *Hants* 18 G2
Dumpford *W Sussex* 11 B7
Dumpton *Kent* 21 E10
Dun *Angus* 77 B9
Dun Charlabhaigh *W Isles* 90 C6
Dunain Ho. *H'land* 87 G9
Dunalastair *Perth/Kinr* 75 B10
Dunan *H'land* 85 F10
Dunans *Arg/Bute* 73 D9
Dunball *Som'set* 15 G9
Dunbar *E Loth* 70 C5
Dunbeath *H'land* 94 H3
Dunbeg *Arg/Bute* 79 H11
Dunblane *Stirl* 75 G10
Dunbog *Fife* 76 F5
Duncanston *Aberds* 83 A7
Duncanston *H'land* 87 F8
Dunchurch *Warwick* 27 A11
Duncote *Northants* 28 C3
Duncow *Dumf/Gal* 60 E5
Duncraggan *Stirl* 75 G8
Duncrievie *Perth/Kinr* 76 G4
Duncton *W Sussex* 11 C8
Dundas Ho. *Orkney* 95 K5
Dundee *Dundee C* 77 D7
Dundeugh *Dumf/Gal* 67 H8
Dundon *Som'set* 8 A3
Dundonald *S Ayrs* 67 C6
Dundonnell *H'land* 86 C3
Dundonnell Hotel *H'land* 86 C3
Dundonnell House *H'land* 86 C4
Dundraw *Cumb* 56 B4
Dundreggan *H'land* 80 B5
Dundreggan Lodge *H'land* 80 B5
Dundrennan *Dumf/Gal* 55 E10
Dundry *N Som'set* 16 E2
Dunecht *Aberds* 83 C9
Dunfermline *Fife* 69 B9
Dunfield *Glos* 17 B8
Dunford Bridge *S Yorks* 44 B5
Dungworth *S Yorks* 44 D6
Dunham *Notts* 46 E2
Dunham-on-the-Hill *Ches* 43 E7
Dunham Town *Gtr Man* 43 D10
Dunhampton *Worcs* 26 B5
Dunholme *Lincs* 46 E4
Dunino *Fife* 77 F8
Dunipace *Falk* 69 B7
Dunira *Perth/Kinr* 75 E10
Dunkeld *Perth/Kinr* 76 C3
Dunkerton *Bath/NE Som'set* 16 F4
Dunkeswell *Devon* 7 F10
Dunkeswick *N Yorks* 51 E9
Dunkirk *Kent* 21 F7
Dunkirk *Norfolk* 39 C8
Dunk's Green *Kent* 20 F3
Dunlappie *Angus* 83 G7
Dunley *Hants* 17 F11
Dunley *Worcs* 26 B4
Dunlichity Lodge *H'land* 87 H9
Dunlop *E Ayrs* 67 B7
Dunmaglass Lodge *H'land* 81 A7
Dunmore *Arg/Bute* 72 G6
Dunmore *Falk* 69 B7
Dunnet *H'land* 94 C4
Dunnichen *Angus* 77 C8
Dunninald *Angus* 77 B10
Dunning *Perth/Kinr* 76 F3
Dunnington *ER Yorks* 53 D7
Dunnington *Warwick* 27 C7
Dunnington *C/York* 52 D2
Dunnockshaw *Lancs* 50 G4
Dunollie *Arg/Bute* 79 H11
Dunoon *Arg/Bute* 73 F10
Dunragit *Dumf/Gal* 54 D4
Dunrostan *Arg/Bute* 72 E6
Duns *Scot Borders* 70 E6
Duns Tew *Oxon* 27 F11
Dunsby *Lincs* 37 C7
Dunscore *Dumf/Gal* 60 E4
Dunscroft *S Yorks* 45 B10
Dunsdale *Redcar/Clevel'd* 59 E7
Dunsden Green *Oxon* 18 D4
Dunsfold *Surrey* 19 H7
Dunsford *Devon* 5 C9
Dunshalt *Fife* 76 F5
Dunshillock *Aberds* 89 D9
Dunskey Ho. *Dumf/Gal* 54 D3
Dunsley *N Yorks* 59 E9
Dunsmore *Bucks* 28 H5
Dunsop Bridge *Lancs* 50 D2
Dunstable *Beds* 29 F7
Dunstall *Staffs* 35 C7
Dunstall Common *Worcs* 26 D5
Dunstall Green *Suffolk* 30 B4
Dunstan *Northum* 63 B8
Dunstan Steads *Northum* 63 A8
Dunster *Som'set* 7 B8
Dunston *Lincs* 46 F4
Dunston *Norfolk* 39 E8
Dunston *Staffs* 34 D5
Dunston *Tyne/Wear* 63 G8
Dunsville *S Yorks* 45 B10
Dunswell *ER Yorks* 53 F6
Dunsyre *S Lanarks* 69 F9
Dunterton *Devon* 4 D4
Duntisbourne Abbots *Glos* 26 H6
Duntisbourne Leer *Glos* 26 H6
Duntisbourne Rouse *Glos* 26 H6
Duntish *Dorset* 8 D5
Duntocher *W Dunb* 68 C3
Dunton *Beds* 29 D9
Dunton *Bucks* 28 F5
Dunton *Norfolk* 38 B4
Dunton Bassett *Leics* 35 F11
Dunton Green *Kent* 20 F2

Dunton Wayletts *Essex* 20 B3
Duntulm *H'land* 85 A9
Dunure *S Ayrs* 66 E5
Dunvant *Swan* 23 G10
Dunvegan *H'land* 84 D7
Dunwich *Suffolk* 31 A11
Dunwood *Staffs* 44 G3
Dupplin Castle *Perth/Kinr* 76 F3
Durdar *Cumb* 56 A6
Durgates *E Sussex* 12 C5
Durham *Durham* 58 B3
Durisdeer *Dumf/Gal* 60 C4
Durisdeermill *Dumf/Gal* 60 C4
Durkar *W Yorks* 51 H9
Durleigh *Som'set* 15 H8
Durley *Hants* 10 C4
Durley *Wilts* 17 E9
Durnamuck *H'land* 86 B3
Durness *H'land* 92 C7
Durno *Aberds* 83 A9
Duror *H'land* 74 B2
Durran *Arg/Bute* 73 C8
Durran *H'land* 94 D3
Durrington *Wilts* 17 G8
Durrington *W Sussex* 11 D10
Dursley *Glos* 16 B4
Durston *Som'set* 8 B1
Durweston *Dorset* 9 D7
Dury *Shetl'd* 96 G6
Duston *Northants* 28 B4
Duthil *H'land* 81 A11
Dutlas *Powys* 33 H8
Duton Hill *Essex* 30 F3
Dutson *Cornw'l* 4 C4
Dutton *Ches* 43 E8
Duxford *Cambs* 29 D11
Duxford *Oxon* 17 B10
Dwygyfylchi *Conwy* 41 C9
Dwyran *Angl* 40 D6
Dyce *Aberd C* 83 B10
Dye House *Northum* 62 H5
Dyffryn *Bridg* 14 B4
Dyffryn *Carms* 23 D8
Dyffryn *Pembs* 22 C4
Dyffryn Ardudwy *Gwyn* 32 C1
Dyffryn Castell *Ceredig'n* 32 G3
Dyffryn Ceidrych *Carms* 24 F4
Dyffryn Cellwen *Neath P Talb* 24 H5
Dyke *Lincs* 37 C7
Dyke *Moray* 87 F12
Dykehead *Angus* 76 A6
Dykehead *N Lanarks* 69 E7
Dykehead *Stirl* 75 H8
Dykelands *Aberds* 83 G9
Dykends *Angus* 76 B5
Dykeside *Aberds* 89 D7
Dykesmains *N Ayrs* 66 B5
Dylife *Powys* 32 F4
Dymchurch *Kent* 13 D9
Dymock *Glos* 26 E4
Dyrham *S Gloucs* 16 D4
Dysart *Fife* 70 A2
Dyserth *Denbs* 42 E3

E

Eachwick *Northum* 63 F7
Eadar Dha Fhadhail *W Isles* 90 D5
Eagland Hill *Lancs* 49 E4
Eagle *Lincs* 46 F2
Eagle Barnsdale *Lincs* 46 F2
Eagle Moor *Lincs* 46 F2
Eaglescliffe *Stockton* 58 E5
Eaglesfield *Cumb* 56 D2
Eaglesfield *Dumf/Gal* 61 F8
Eaglesham *E Renf* 68 E4
Eaglethorpe *Northants* 37 F6
Eairy *I/Man* 48 E2
Eakley Lanes *M/Keynes* 28 C5
Eakring *Notts* 45 F10
Ealand *N Lincs* 45 A11
Ealing *London* 19 C8
Eals *Northum* 62 H2
Eamont Bridge *Cumb* 57 D7
Earby *Lancs* 50 E5
Earcroft *Blackb'n* 50 G2
Eardington *Shrops* 34 F3
Eardisland *Heref'd* 25 C11
Eardisley *Heref'd* 25 D10
Eardiston *Shrops* 33 C9
Eardiston *Worcs* 26 B3
Earith *Cambs* 29 A10
Earl Shilton *Leics* 35 F10
Earl Soham *Suffolk* 31 B9
Earl Sterndale *Derby* 44 F4
Earl Stonham *Suffolk* 31 C8
Earle *Northum* 71 H8
Earley *Wokingham* 18 D4
Earlham *Norfolk* 39 E8
Earlish *H'land* 85 B8
Earls Barton *Northants* 28 B5
Earls Colne *Essex* 30 F5
Earl's Croome *Worcs* 26 D5
Earl's Green *Suffolk* 31 B7
Earlsdon *W Midlands* 35 H9
Earlsferry *Fife* 77 H7
Earlsfield *Lincs* 36 B5
Earlsford *Aberds* 89 E8
Earlsheaton *W Yorks* 51 G8
Earlsmill *Moray* 87 F12
Earlston *Scot Borders* 70 G4
Earlston *E Ayrs* 67 C7
Earlswood *Monmouths* 15 B10
Earlswood *Surrey* 19 G9
Earlswood *Warwick* 27 A8
Earnley *W Sussex* 11 E7
Earsairidh *W Isles* 84 J2
Earsdon *Tyne/Wear* 63 F9
Earsham *Norfolk* 39 G9
Earswick *C/York* 52 D2
Eartham *W Sussex* 11 D8
Easby *N Yorks* 59 F6
Easby *N Yorks* 58 F2
Easdale *Arg/Bute* 72 B6
Easebourne *W Sussex* 11 B7
Easenhall *Warwick* 35 H10
Eashing *Surrey* 18 G6
Easington *Bucks* 28 G3
Easington *Durham* 58 B5
Easington *ER Yorks* 53 H9
Easington *Northum* 71 G10
Easington *Oxon* 27 E11
Easington *Oxon* 18 B3
Easington *Redcar/Clevel'd* 59 E8
Easington Colliery *Durham* 58 B5
Easington Lane *Tyne/Wear* 58 B4
Easingwold *N Yorks* 51 C11
Easole Street *Kent* 21 F9
Eassie *Angus* 76 C6
East Aberthaw *V/Glam* 14 E6
East Adderbury *Oxon* 27 E11
East Allington *Devon* 5 G8
East Anstey *Devon* 7 D7
East Appleton *N Yorks* 58 G3
East Ardsley *W Yorks* 51 G9
East Ashling *W Sussex* 11 D7
East Auchronie *Aberds* 83 C10
East Ayton *N Yorks* 59 H10
East Bank *Bl Gwent* 25 H9
East Barkwith *Lincs* 46 D5
East Barming *Kent* 20 F4
East Barnby *N Yorks* 59 E9
East Barnet *London* 19 B9
East Barns *E Loth* 70 C6
East Barsham *Norfolk* 38 B5
East Beckham *Norfolk* 39 B7
East Bedfont *London* 19 D7
East Bergholt *Suffolk* 31 E7
East Bilney *Norfolk* 38 D5
East Blatchington *E Sussex* 12 F3
East Boldre *Hants* 10 D2
East Brent *Som'set* 15 F9
East Bridgford *Notts* 36 A2
East Buckland *Devon* 6 C5
East Budleigh *Devon* 7 H9
East Burrafirth *Shetl'd* 96 H5
East Burton *Dorset* 9 F7
East Butsfield *Durham* 58 B2
East Butterwick *N Lincs* 46 B2
East Cairnbeg *Aberds* 83 F9
East Calder *W Loth* 69 D9
East Carleton *Norfolk* 39 E7
East Carlton *Northants* 36 G4
East Carlton *W Yorks* 51 E8
East Chaldon *Dorset* 9 F6
East Challow *Oxon* 17 C10
East Chiltington *E Sussex* 12 E2
East Chinnock *Som'set* 8 C3
East Chisenbury *Wilts* 17 F8
East Clandon *Surrey* 19 F7
East Claydon *Bucks* 28 F4
East Clyne *H'land* 93 J12
East Coker *Som'set* 8 C4
East Combe *Som'set* 7 C10
East Common *N Yorks* 52 F2
East Compton *Som'set* 16 G3
East Cottingwith *ER Yorks* 52 E3
East Cowes *I/Wight* 10 E4
East Cowick *ER Yorks* 52 G2
East Cowton *N Yorks* 58 F4
East Cramlington *Northum* 63 F8
East Cranmore *Som'set* 16 G3
East Creech *Dorset* 9 F8
East Croachy *H'land* 81 A8
East Croftmore *H'land* 81 B11
East Curthwaite *Cumb* 56 B5
East Dean *E Sussex* 12 G4
East Dean *Hants* 10 B1
East Dean *W Sussex* 11 C8
East Down *Devon* 6 B5
East Drayton *Notts* 45 E11
East Ella *Kingston/Hull* 53 G6
East End *Dorset* 9 E8
East End *ER Yorks* 53 G8
East End *Hants* 10 E2
East End *Hants* 10 B5
East End *Hants* 17 E11
East End *Herts* 29 F11
East End *Kent* 13 C7
East End *N Som'set* 15 D10
East End *Oxon* 27 G10
East Farleigh *Kent* 20 F4
East Farndon *Northants* 36 G3
East Ferry *Lincs* 46 C2
East Fortune *E Loth* 70 C4
East Garston *W Berks* 17 D10
East Ginge *Oxon* 17 C11
East Goscote *Leics* 36 D2
East Grafton *Wilts* 17 E9
East Grimstead *Wilts* 9 B11
East Grinstead *W Sussex* 12 C2
East Guldeford *E Sussex* 13 D8
East Haddon *Northants* 28 B3
East Hagbourne *Oxon* 18 C2
East Halton *N Lincs* 53 H7
East Ham *London* 19 C11
East Hanney *Oxon* 17 B11
East Hanningfield *Essex* 20 A4
East Hardwick *W Yorks* 51 H10
East Harling *Norfolk* 38 G5
East Harlsey *N Yorks* 58 G5
East Harnham *Wilts* 9 B10
East Harptree *Bath/NE Som'set* 16 F2
East Hartford *Northum* 63 F8
East Harting *W Sussex* 11 C6
East Hatley *Cambs* 29 C9
East Hauxwell *N Yorks* 58 G2
East Haven *Angus* 77 D8
East Heckington *Lincs* 37 A7
East Hedleyhope *Durham* 58 B2
East Hendred *Oxon* 17 C11
East Herrington *Tyne/Wear* 58 A4
East Heslerton *N Yorks* 52 B5
East Hoathly *E Sussex* 12 E4
East Horrington *Som'set* 16 G2
East Horsley *Surrey* 19 F7
East Horton *Northum* 71 G9
East Huntspill *Som'set* 15 G9
East Hyde *Beds* 29 G8
East Ilkerton *Devon* 6 B6
East Ilsley *W Berks* 17 C11
East Keal *Lincs* 47 F7
East Kennett *Wilts* 17 E8
East Keswick *W Yorks* 51 E9
East Kilbride *S Lanarks* 68 E5
East Kirkby *Lincs* 47 F7
East Knapton *N Yorks* 52 B4
East Knighton *Dorset* 9 F7
East Knoyle *Wilts* 9 A7
East Kyloe *Northum* 71 G9
East Lambrook *Som'set* 8 C3
East Lamington *H'land* 87 D10
East Langdon *Kent* 21 G10
East Langton *Leics* 36 F3
East Langwell *H'land* 93 J10
East Lavant *W Sussex* 11 D7
East Lavington *W Sussex* 11 C8
East Layton *N Yorks* 58 F2
East Leake *Notts* 36 C1
East Learmouth *Northum* 71 G7
East Leigh *Devon* 6 F5
East Lexham *Norfolk* 38 D4
East Lilburn *Northum* 62 A6
East Linton *E Loth* 70 C4
East Liss *Hants* 11 B6
East Looe *Cornw'l* 4 F3
East Lound *N Lincs* 45 C11
East Lulworth *Dorset* 9 F7
East Lutton *N Yorks* 52 C5
East Lydford *Som'set* 8 A4
East Mains *Aberds* 83 D8
East Malling *Kent* 20 F4
East March *Angus* 77 D7
East Marden *W Sussex* 11 C7
East Markham *Notts* 45 E11
East Marton *N Yorks* 50 D5
East Meon *Hants* 10 B5
East Mere *Devon* 7 E8
East Mersea *Essex* 31 G7
East Mey *H'land* 94 C5
East Molesey *Surrey* 19 E8
East Morden *Dorset* 9 E8
East Morton *W Yorks* 51 E6
East Ness *N Yorks* 52 B2
East Newton *ER Yorks* 53 F8
East Norton *Leics* 36 E3
East Nynehead *Som'set* 7 D10
East Oakley *Hants* 18 F2
East Ogwell *Devon* 5 D9
East Orchard *Dorset* 9 C7
East Ord *Northum* 71 E8
East Panson *Devon* 6 G2
East Peckham *Kent* 20 G3
East Pennard *Som'set* 16 H2
East Perry *Cambs* 29 B8
East Portlemouth *Devon* 5 H8
East Prawle *Devon* 5 H8
East Preston *W Sussex* 11 D9
East Putford *Devon* 6 E2
East Quantoxhead *Som'set* 7 B10
East Rainton *Tyne/Wear* 58 B4
East Ravendale *NE Lincs* 46 C6
East Raynham *Norfolk* 38 C4
East Rhidorroch Lodge *H'land* 86 B5
East Rigton *W Yorks* 51 E9
East Rounton *N Yorks* 58 F5
East Row *N Yorks* 59 E9
East Rudham *Norfolk* 38 C4
East Runton *Norfolk* 39 A7
East Ruston *Norfolk* 39 C9
East Saltoun *E Loth* 70 D3
East Sleekburn *Northum* 63 E8
East Somerton *Norfolk* 39 D10
East Stockwith *Lincs* 45 C11
East Stoke *Dorset* 9 F7
East Stoke *Notts* 45 H11
East Stour *Dorset* 9 B7
East Stourmouth *Kent* 21 E9
East Stowford *Devon* 6 D5
East Stratton *Hants* 18 H2
East Studdal *Kent* 21 G10
East Suisnish *H'land* 85 E10
East Taphouse *Cornw'l* 4 E2
East-the-Water *Devon* 6 D3
East Thirston *Northum* 63 D7
East Tilbury *Thurr'k* 20 D3
East Tisted *Hants* 10 A6
East Torrington *Lincs* 46 D5
East Tuddenham *Norfolk* 39 D6
East Tytherley *Hants* 10 B1
East Tytherton *Wilts* 16 D6
East Village *Devon* 7 F7
East Wall *Shrops* 33 F11
East Walton *Norfolk* 38 D3
East Wellow *Hants* 10 B2
East Wemyss *Fife* 76 H6
East Whitburn *W Loth* 69 D8
East Williamston *Pembs* 22 F5
East Winch *Norfolk* 38 D2
East Winterslow *Wilts* 9 A11
East Wittering *W Sussex* 11 E6
East Witton *N Yorks* 58 H2
East Woodburn *Northum* 62 E5
East Woodhay *Hants* 17 E11
East Worldham *Hants* 18 H4
East Worlington *Devon* 7 E6
East Worthing *W Sussex* 11 D10
Eastbourne *E Sussex* 12 G5
Eastbridge *Suffolk* 31 B11
Eastburn *W Yorks* 50 E6
Eastbury *Herts* 19 B7
Eastbury *W Berks* 17 D10
Eastby *N Yorks* 50 D6
Eastchurch *Kent* 20 D6
Eastcombe *Glos* 16 A5
Eastcote *London* 19 C8
Eastcote *Northants* 28 C3
Eastcote *W Midlands* 35 H7
Eastcott *Cornw'l* 6 E1
Eastcott *Wilts* 17 F7
Eastcourt *Wilts* 16 B6
Eastcourt *Wilts* 17 E9
Easter Ardross *H'land* 87 D9
Easter Balmoral *Aberds* 82 D4
Easter Boleskine *H'land* 81 A7
Easter Compton *S Gloucs* 16 C2
Easter Cringate *Stirl* 68 B6
Easter Davoch *Aberds* 82 C6
Easter Earshaig *Dumf/Gal* 60 C6
Easter Fearn *H'land* 87 C9
Easter Galcantray *H'land* 87 G11
Easter Howgate *Midloth* 69 D11
Easter Howlaws *Scot Borders* 70 F6
Easter Kinkell *H'land* 87 F8
Easter Lednathie *Angus* 76 A6
Easter Milton *H'land* 87 F12
Easter Moniack *H'land* 87 G8
Easter Ord *Aberds* 83 C10
Easter Quarff *Shetl'd* 96 K6
Easter Rhynd *Perth/Kinr* 76 F4
Easter Row *Stirl* 75 H10
Easter Silverford *Aberds* 89 B7
Easter Skeld *Shetl'd* 96 J5
Easter Whyntie *Aberds* 88 B6
Eastergate *W Sussex* 11 D8
Easterhouse *C/Glasg* 68 D5
Eastern Green *W Midlands* 35 G8
Easterton *Wilts* 17 F7
Eastertown *Som'set* 15 F9
Eastertown of Auchleuchries *Aberds* 89 E10
Eastfield *N Lanarks* 69 D7
Eastfield *N Yorks* 52 A6
Eastfield Hall *Northum* 63 C8
Eastgate *Durham* 57 C11
Eastgate *Norfolk* 39 C7
Eastham *Mersey* 42 D6
Eastham Ferry *Mersey* 42 D6
Easthampstead *Brackn'l* 18 E5
Eastheath *Wokingham* 18 E5
Easthope *Shrops* 34 F1
Easthorpe *Essex* 30 F6
Easthorpe *Leics* 36 B4
Easthorpe *Notts* 45 G11
Easthouses *Midloth* 70 D2
Eastington *Devon* 7 F6
Eastington *Glos* 26 H4
Eastington *Glos* 27 G8
Eastleach Martin *Glos* 27 H9
Eastleach Turville *Glos* 27 H8
Eastleigh *Devon* 6 D3
Eastleigh *Hants* 10 C3
Eastling *Kent* 20 F6
Eastmoor *Derby* 45 E7
Eastmoor *Norfolk* 38 E3
Eastney *Portsm'th* 10 E5
Eastnor *Heref'd* 26 E4
Eastoft *N Lincs* 52 H4
Eastoke *Hants* 10 E6
Easton *Cambs* 29 A8
Easton *Cumb* 61 H8
Easton *Cumb* 61 F10
Easton *Devon* 5 C8
Easton *Dorset* 8 G5
Easton *Hants* 10 A4
Easton *Lincs* 36 C5
Easton *Norfolk* 39 D7
Easton *Som'set* 15 G11
Easton *Suffolk* 31 C9
Easton *Wilts* 16 D5
Easton Grey *Wilts* 16 C5
Easton-in-Gordano *N Som'set* 15 D11
Easton Maudit *Northants* 28 C5
Easton on the Hill *Northants* 36 E6
Easton Royal *Wilts* 17 E9
Eastpark *Dumf/Gal* 60 G6
Eastrea *Cambs* 37 F8
Eastriggs *Dumf/Gal* 61 G8
Eastrington *ER Yorks* 52 G3
Eastry *Kent* 21 F10
Eastville *Bristol* 16 D3
Eastville *Lincs* 47 G8
Eastwell *Leics* 36 C3
Eastwick *Herts* 29 G11
Eastwick *Shetl'd* 96 F5
Eastwood *Notts* 45 H8
Eastwood *Southend* 20 C5
Eastwood *W Yorks* 50 G5
Eathorpe *Warwick* 27 B10
Eaton *Ches* 43 F8
Eaton *Ches* 44 F2
Eaton *Leics* 36 C3
Eaton *Norfolk* 39 E8
Eaton *Notts* 45 E11
Eaton *Oxon* 17 A11
Eaton *Shrops* 33 G9
Eaton *Shrops* 33 G11
Eaton Bishop *Heref'd* 25 E11
Eaton Bray *Beds* 28 F6
Eaton Constantine *Shrops* 34 E1
Eaton Green *Beds* 28 F6
Eaton Hastings *Oxon* 17 B9
Eaton on Tern *Shrops* 34 C2
Eaton Socon *Cambs* 29 C8
Eavestone *N Yorks* 51 C8
Ebberston *N Yorks* 52 A4
Ebbesbourne Wake *Wilts* 9 B8
Ebbw Vale = Glyn Ebwy *Bl Gwent* 25 H8
Ebchester *Durham* 63 H7
Ebford *Devon* 5 C10
Ebley *Glos* 26 H5
Ebnal *Ches* 43 H7
Ebrington *Glos* 27 D8
Ecchinswell *Hants* 17 F11
Ecclaw *Scot Borders* 70 D6
Ecclefechan *Dumf/Gal* 61 F7
Eccles *Scot Borders* 70 F6
Eccles *Gtr Man* 43 C10
Eccles *Kent* 20 E4
Eccles on Sea *Norfolk* 39 C10
Eccles Road *Norfolk* 38 F6
Ecclesall *S Yorks* 45 D7
Ecclesfield *S Yorks* 45 C7
Ecclesgreig *Aberds* 83 G9
Eccleshall *Staffs* 34 C4
Eccleshill *W Yorks* 51 F7
Ecclesmachan *W Loth* 69 C9
Eccleston *Ches* 43 F7
Eccleston *Lancs* 49 H5
Eccleston *Mersey* 43 C7
Eccleston Park *Mersey* 43 C7
Eccup *W Yorks* 51 E8
Echt *Aberds* 83 C9
Eckford *Scot Borders* 70 H6
Eckington *Derby* 45 E8
Eckington *Worcs* 26 D6
Ecton *Northants* 28 B5
Edale *Derby* 44 D5
Edburton *W Sussex* 11 C11
Edderside *Cumb* 56 B2
Edderton *H'land* 87 C10
Eddistone *Devon* 6 D1
Eddleston *Scot Borders* 69 F11
Eden Park *London* 19 E10
Edenbridge *Kent* 19 G11
Edenfield *Lancs* 50 H3
Edenhall *Cumb* 57 C7
Edenham *Lincs* 37 C6
Edensor *Derby* 44 F6
Edentaggart *Arg/Bute* 68 A2
Edenthorpe *S Yorks* 45 B10
Edentown *Cumb* 61 H9
Ederline *Arg/Bute* 73 C7
Edern *Gwyn* 40 G4
Edgarley *Som'set* 15 H11
Edgbaston *W Midlands* 35 G6
Edgcott *Bucks* 28 F3
Edgcott *Som'set* 7 C7
Edge *Shrops* 33 E9
Edge End *Glos* 26 G2
Edge Green *Ches* 43 G7
Edge Hill *Mersey* 42 D6
Edgebolton *Shrops* 34 C1
Edgefield *Norfolk* 39 B6
Edgefield Street *Norfolk* 39 B6
Edgeside *Lancs* 50 G4
Edgeworth *Glos* 26 H6
Edgmond *Telford* 34 D3
Edgmond Marsh *Telford* 34 C3
Edgton *Shrops* 33 G9
Edgware *London* 19 B8
Edgworth *Blackb'n* 50 H3
Edinample *Stirl* 75 E8
Edinbane *H'land* 85 C8
Edinburgh *C/Edinb* 69 C11
Edingale *Staffs* 35 D8
Edingight Ho. *Moray* 88 C5
Edingley *Notts* 45 G10
Edingthorpe *Norfolk* 39 B9
Edingthorpe Green *Norfolk* 39 B9
Edington *Som'set* 15 H9
Edington *Wilts* 16 F6
Edintore *Moray* 88 D4
Edith Weston *Rutl'd* 36 E5
Edithmead *Som'set* 15 G9
Edlesborough *Bucks* 28 G6
Edlingham *Northum* 63 C7
Edlington *Lincs* 46 E6
Edmondsham *Dorset* 9 C9
Edmondsley *Durham* 58 B3
Edmondthorpe *Leics* 36 D4
Edmonstone *Orkney* 95 F6
Edmonton *London* 19 B10
Edmundbyers *Durham* 58 A1
Ednam *Scot Borders* 70 G6
Ednaston *Derby* 35 A8
Edradynate *Perth/Kinr* 75 B11
Edrom *Scot Borders* 71 E7
Edstaston *Shrops* 33 B11
Edstone *Warwick* 27 B8
Edvin Loach *Heref'd* 26 C3
Edwalton *Notts* 36 B1
Edwardstone *Suffolk* 30 D6
Edwinsford *Carms* 24 E3
Edwinstowe *Notts* 45 F10
Edworth *Beds* 29 D9
Edwyn Ralph *Heref'd* 26 C3
Edzell *Angus* 83 G7
Efail Isaf *Rh Cyn Taff* 14 C6
Efailnewydd *Gwyn* 40 G5
Efailwen *Carms* 22 D6
Efenechtyd *Denbs* 42 G4
Effingham *Surrey* 19 F8
Effirth *Shetl'd* 96 H5
Efford *Devon* 7 F7
Egdon *Worcs* 26 C6
Egerton *Gtr Man* 43 A10
Egerton *Kent* 20 G6
Egerton Forstal *Kent* 20 G5
Eggborough *N Yorks* 52 G1
Eggbuckland *Plym'th* 4 F6
Eggington *Beds* 28 F6
Egginton *Derby* 35 C8
Egglescliffe *Stockton* 58 E5
Eggleston *Durham* 57 D11
Egham *Surrey* 19 D7
Egleton *Rutl'd* 36 E4
Eglingham *Northum* 63 B7
Egloshayle *Cornw'l* 3 B8
Egloskerry *Cornw'l* 4 C3
Eglwys-Brewis *V/Glam* 14 E6
Eglwys Cross *Wrex* 33 A10
Eglwys Fach *Ceredig'n* 32 F2
Eglwysbach *Conwy* 41 C10
Eglwyswen *Pembs* 22 C6
Eglwyswrw *Pembs* 22 C6
Egmanton *Notts* 45 F11
Egremont *Cumb* 56 E2
Egremont *Mersey* 42 C6
Egton *N Yorks* 59 F9
Egton Bridge *N Yorks* 59 F9
Eight Ash Green *Essex* 30 F6
Eignaig *H'land* 79 G10
Eil *H'land* 81 B10
Eilanreach *H'land* 85 G13
Eilean Darach *H'land* 86 C4
Eileanach Lodge *H'land* 87 E8
Einacleite *W Isles* 90 E6
Eisgean *W Isles* 91 F8
Eisingrug *Gwyn* 41 G8
Elan Village *Powys* 24 B6
Elberton *S Gloucs* 16 C3
Elburton *Plym'th* 4 F6
Elcho *Perth/Kinr* 76 E4
Elcombe *Swindon* 17 C8
Eldernell *Cambs* 37 F9
Eldersfield *Worcs* 26 E5
Elderslie *Renf* 68 D3
Eldon *Durham* 58 D3
Eldrick *S Ayrs* 54 A5
Eldroth *N Yorks* 50 C3
Eldwick *W Yorks* 51 E7
Elfhowe *Cumb* 56 G6
Elford *Northum* 71 G10
Elford *Staffs* 35 D7
Elgin *Moray* 88 B2
Elgol *H'land* 85 G10
Elham *Kent* 21 G8
Elie *Fife* 77 G7
Elim *Angl* 40 B5
Eling *Hants* 10 C2
Elishader *H'land* 85 B10
Elishaw *Northum* 62 D4
Elkesley *Notts* 45 E10
Elkstone *Glos* 26 G6
Ellan *H'land* 81 A10
Elland *W Yorks* 51 G7
Ellary *Arg/Bute* 72 F6
Ellastone *Staffs* 35 A7
Ellemford *Scot Borders* 70 D6
Ellenbrook *I/Man* 48 E3
Ellenhall *Staffs* 34 C4
Ellen's Green *Surrey* 19 H7
Ellerbeck *N Yorks* 58 G5
Ellerburn *N Yorks* 52 A4
Ellerby *N Yorks* 59 E8
Ellerdine Heath *Telford* 34 C2
Ellerhayes *Devon* 7 F8
Elleric *Arg/Bute* 74 C3
Ellerker *ER Yorks* 52 G5
Ellerton *ER Yorks* 52 F3
Ellerton *Shrops* 34 C3
Ellesborough *Bucks* 28 H5
Ellesmere *Shrops* 33 B10
Ellesmere Port *Ches* 43 E7
Ellingham *Norfolk* 39 F9
Ellingham *Northum* 71 H10
Ellingstring *N Yorks* 51 A7
Ellington *Cambs* 29 A8
Ellington *Northum* 63 D8
Elliot *Angus* 77 D9
Ellisfield *Hants* 18 G3
Ellistown *Leics* 35 D10
Ellon *Aberds* 89 E9
Ellonby *Cumb* 56 C6
Ellough *Suffolk* 39 G10
Elloughton *ER Yorks* 52 G5
Ellwood *Glos* 26 H2
Elm *Cambs* 37 E10
Elm Hill *Dorset* 9 B7
Elm Park *London* 20 C2
Elmbridge *Worcs* 26 B6
Elmdon *Essex* 29 E11
Elmdon *W Midlands* 35 G7
Elmdon Heath *W Midlands* 35 G7
Elmers End *London* 19 E10
Elmesthorpe *Leics* 35 F10
Elmfield *I/Wight* 10 E5
Elmhurst *Staffs* 35 D7
Elmley Castle *Worcs* 26 D6
Elmley Lovett *Worcs* 26 B5
Elmore *Glos* 26 G4
Elmore Back *Glos* 26 G4
Elmscott *Devon* 6 D1
Elmsett *Suffolk* 31 D7
Elmstead Market *Essex* 31 F7
Elmsted *Kent* 13 B10
Elmstone *Kent* 21 E9
Elmstone Hardwicke *Glos* 26 F6
Elmswell *ER Yorks* 52 D5
Elmswell *Suffolk* 30 B6
Elmton *Derby* 45 E9
Elphin *H'land* 92 H5
Elphinstone *E Loth* 70 C2
Elrick *Aberds* 83 C10
Elrig *Dumf/Gal* 54 E6
Elsdon *Northum* 62 D5
Elsecar *S Yorks* 45 C7
Elsenham *Essex* 30 F2
Elsfield *Oxon* 28 G2
Elsham *N Lincs* 46 A4
Elsing *Norfolk* 39 D6
Elslack *N Yorks* 50 E5
Elson *Shrops* 33 B9
Elsrickle *S Lanarks* 69 F9
Elstead *Surrey* 18 G6
Elsted *W Sussex* 11 C7
Elsthorpe *Lincs* 37 C6
Elstob *Durham* 58 D4
Elston *Notts* 45 H11
Elston *Wilts* 17 G7
Elstone *Devon* 6 E5
Elstow *Beds* 29 D7
Elstree *Herts* 19 B8
Elstronwick *ER Yorks* 53 F8
Elswick *Lancs* 49 F4
Elsworth *Cambs* 29 B10
Elterwater *Cumb* 56 F5
Eltham *London* 19 D11
Eltisley *Cambs* 29 C9
Elton *Cambs* 37 F6
Elton *Ches* 43 E7
Elton *Derby* 44 F6
Elton *Glos* 26 G4
Elton *Heref'd* 25 A11
Elton *Notts* 36 B3
Elton *Stockton* 58 E5
Elton Green *Ches* 43 E7
Elvanfoot *S Lanarks* 60 B5
Elvaston *Derby* 35 B10
Elveden *Suffolk* 38 H4
Elvingston *E Loth* 70 C3
Elvington *Kent* 21 F9
Elvington *C/York* 52 E2
Elwick *Hartlep'l* 58 C5
Elwick *Northum* 71 G10
Elworth *Ches* 43 F10
Elworthy *Som'set* 7 C9
Ely *Cambs* 37 G11
Ely *Card* 15 D7
Emberton *M/Keynes* 28 D5
Embleton *Cumb* 56 C3
Embleton *Northum* 63 A8
Embo *H'land* 87 B11
Embo Street *H'land* 87 B11
Emborough *Som'set* 16 F3
Embsay *N Yorks* 50 D6
Emery Down *Hants* 10 D1
Emley *W Yorks* 44 A6
Emmbrook *Wokingham* 18 E4
Emmer Green *Reading* 18 D4
Emmington *Oxon* 18 A4
Emneth *Norfolk* 37 E10
Emneth Hungate *Norfolk* 37 E11
Empingham *Rutl'd* 36 E5
Empshott *Hants* 11 A6
Emstrey *Shrops* 33 D11
Emsworth *Hants* 10 D6
Enborne *W Berks* 17 E11
Enchmarsh *Shrops* 33 F11
Enderby *Leics* 35 F11
Endmoor *Cumb* 49 A5
Endon *Staffs* 44 G3
Endon Bank *Staffs* 44 G3
Enfield *London* 19 B10
Enfield Wash *London* 19 B10
Enford *Wilts* 17 F8
Engamoor *Shetl'd* 96 H4
Engine Common *S Gloucs* 16 C3
Englefield *W Berks* 18 D3
Englefield Green *Surrey* 18 D6
Englesea-brook *Ches* 43 G10
English Bicknor *Glos* 26 G2
English Frankton *Shrops* 33 C10
Englishcombe *Bath/NE Som'set* 16 E4
Enham-Alamein *Hants* 17 G10
Enmore *Som'set* 8 A1
Ennerdale Bridge *Cumb* 56 E2
Enoch *Dumf/Gal* 60 C4
Enochdhu *Perth/Kinr* 76 A3
Ensay *Arg/Bute* 78 G6
Ensbury *Bournem'th* 9 E9
Ensdon *Shrops* 33 D10
Ensis *Devon* 6 D4
Enstone *Oxon* 27 F10
Enterkinfoot *Dumf/Gal* 60 C4
Enterpen *N Yorks* 58 F5
Enville *Staffs* 34 G4
Eolaigearraidh *W Isles* 84 H2
Eorabus *Arg/Bute* 78 J6
Eòropaidh *W Isles* 91 A10
Epperstone *Notts* 45 H10
Epping *Essex* 19 A11
Epping Green *Essex* 29 H11
Epping Green *Herts* 29 H9
Epping Upland *Essex* 19 A11
Eppleby *N Yorks* 58 E2
Eppleworth *ER Yorks* 52 F6
Epsom *Surrey* 19 E9
Epwell *Oxon* 27 D10
Epworth *N Lincs* 45 B11
Epworth Turbary *N Lincs* 45 B11
Erbistock *Wrex* 33 A9
Erbusaig *H'land* 85 F12
Erchless Castle *H'land* 86 G7
Erdington *W Midlands* 35 F7
Eredine *Arg/Bute* 73 C8
Eriboll *H'land* 92 D7
Ericstane *Dumf/Gal* 60 B6
Eridge Green *E Sussex* 12 C4
Erines *Arg/Bute* 73 F7
Eriswell *Suffolk* 38 H3
Erith *London* 20 D2
Erlestoke *Wilts* 16 F6
Ermine *Lincs* 46 E3
Ermington *Devon* 5 F7
Erpingham *Norfolk* 39 B7
Errogie *H'land* 81 A7
Errol *Perth/Kinr* 76 E5
Erskine *Renf* 68 C3
Erskine Bridge *Renf* 68 C3
Ervie *Dumf/Gal* 54 C3
Erwarton *Suffolk* 31 E9
Erwood *Powys* 25 D7
Eryholme *N Yorks* 58 F4
Eryrys *Denbs* 42 G5
Escomb *Durham* 58 D2
Escrick *N Yorks* 52 E2
Esgairdawe *Carms* 24 D3
Esgairgeiliog *Powys* 32 E3
Esh *Durham* 58 B2
Esh Winning *Durham* 58 B2
Esher *Surrey* 19 E8
Esholt *W Yorks* 51 E7
Eshott *Northum* 63 D8
Eshton *N Yorks* 50 D5
Esk Valley *N Yorks* 59 F9
Eskadale *H'land* 86 H7
Eskbank *Midloth* 70 D2
Eskdale Green *Cumb* 56 F3
Eskdalemuir *Dumf/Gal* 61 D8
Eske *ER Yorks* 53 E6
Eskham *Lincs* 47 C7
Esprick *Lancs* 49 F4
Essendine *Rutl'd* 36 D6
Essendon *Herts* 29 H9
Essich *H'land* 87 H9
Essington *Staffs* 34 E5
Esslemont *Aberds* 89 F9
Eston *Redcar/Clevel'd* 59 E6
Eswick *Shetl'd* 96 H6
Etal *Northum* 71 G8
Etchilhampton *Wilts* 17 E7
Etchingham *E Sussex* 12 D6
Etchinghill *Kent* 21 H8
Etchinghill *Staffs* 34 D6
Ethie Castle *Angus* 77 C9
Ethie Mains *Angus* 77 C9
Etling Green *Norfolk* 38 D6
Eton *Windsor* 18 D6
Eton Wick *Windsor* 18 D6
Etteridge *H'land* 81 D8
Ettersgill *Durham* 57 D10
Ettingshall *W Midlands* 34 F5
Ettington *Warwick* 27 D9
Etton *ER Yorks* 52 E5
Etton *Peterbro* 37 E7
Ettrick *Scot Borders* 61 B8
Ettrickbridge *Scot Borders* 61 A9
Ettrickhill *Scot Borders* 61 B8
Etwall *Derby* 35 B8
Euston *Suffolk* 38 H4
Euximoor Drove *Cambs* 37 F10
Euxton *Lancs* 50 H1
Evanstown *Bridg* 14 C5
Evanton *H'land* 87 E9
Evedon *Lincs* 46 H4
Evelix *H'land* 87 B10
Evenjobb *Powys* 25 B9
Evenley *Northants* 28 E2
Evenlode *Glos* 27 F9
Evenwood *Durham* 58 D2
Evenwood Gate *Durham* 58 D2
Everbay *Orkney* 95 F7
Evercreech *Som'set* 16 H3
Everdon *Northants* 28 C2
Everingham *ER Yorks* 52 E4
Everleigh *Wilts* 17 F9
Everley *N Yorks* 59 H10
Eversholt *Beds* 28 E6
Evershot *Dorset* 8 D4
Eversley *Hants* 18 E4
Eversley Cross *Hants* 18 E4
Everthorpe *ER Yorks* 52 F5
Everton *Beds* 29 C9
Everton *Hants* 10 E1
Everton *Mersey* 42 C6
Everton *Notts* 45 C10
Evertown *Dumf/Gal* 61 F9
Evesbatch *Heref'd* 26 D3
Evesham *Worcs* 27 D7
Evington *Leics C* 36 E2
Ewden Village *S Yorks* 44 C6
Ewell *Surrey* 19 E9
Ewell Minnis *Kent* 21 G9
Ewelme *Oxon* 18 B3
Ewen *Glos* 17 B7
Ewenny *V/Glam* 14 D5
Ewerby *Lincs* 46 H5
Ewerby Thorpe *Lincs* 46 H5
Ewes *Dumf/Gal* 61 D9
Ewesley *Northum* 62 D6
Ewhurst *Surrey* 19 G7
Ewhurst Green *E Sussex* 13 D6
Ewhurst Green *Surrey* 19 H7
Ewloe *Flints* 42 F6
Ewloe Green *Flints* 42 F5
Ewood *Blackb'n* 50 G2
Eworthy *Devon* 6 G3
Ewshot *Hants* 18 G5
Ewyas Harold *Heref'd* 25 F10
Exbourne *Devon* 6 F5
Exbury *Hants* 10 E3
Exebridge *Som'set* 7 D8
Exelby *N Yorks* 58 H3
Exeter *Devon* 7 G8
Exford *Som'set* 7 C7
Exhall *Warwick* 27 C8
Exley Head *W Yorks* 50 F6
Exminster *Devon* 5 C10
Exmouth *Devon* 5 C11
Exnaboe *Shetl'd* 96 M5
Exning *Suffolk* 30 B3
Exton *Devon* 5 C10
Exton *Hants* 10 B5
Exton *Rutl'd* 36 D5
Exton *Som'set* 7 C8
Exwick *Devon* 7 G8
Eyam *Derby* 44 E6
Eydon *Northants* 28 C2
Eye *Heref'd* 25 B11
Eye *Peterbro* 37 E8
Eye *Suffolk* 31 A8
Eye Green *Peterbro* 37 E8
Eyemouth *Scot Borders* 71 D8
Eyeworth *Beds* 29 D9
Eyhorne Street *Kent* 20 F5
Eyke *Suffolk* 31 C10
Eynesbury *Cambs* 29 C8
Eynort *H'land* 85 F8
Eynsford *Kent* 20 E2
Eynsham *Oxon* 27 H11
Eype *Dorset* 8 E3
Eyre *H'land* 85 C9
Eyre *H'land* 85 E10
Eythorne *Kent* 21 G9
Eyton *Heref'd* 25 B11
Eyton *Shrops* 33 G9
Eyton *Wrex* 33 A9
Eyton upon the Weald Moors *Telford* 34 D2

F

Faccombe *Hants* 17 F10
Faceby *N Yorks* 58 F5
Facit *Lancs* 50 H4
Faddiley *Ches* 43 G8
Fadmoor *N Yorks* 59 H7
Faerdre *Swan* 14 A2
Failford *S Ayrs* 67 D7
Failsworth *Gtr Man* 44 B2
Fain *H'land* 86 D4
Fair Green *Norfolk* 38 D2
Fair Hill *Cumb* 57 C7
Fair Oak *Hants* 10 C3
Fair Oak Green *Hants* 18 E3
Fairbourne *Gwyn* 32 D2
Fairburn *N Yorks* 51 G10
Fairfield *Derby* 44 E4
Fairfield *Stockton* 58 E5
Fairfield *Worcs* 27 D7
Fairfield *Worcs* 34 H5
Fairford *Glos* 17 A8
Fairhaven *Lancs* 49 G3
Fairlie *N Ayrs* 73 H11
Fairlight *E Sussex* 13 E7
Fairlight Cove *E Sussex* 13 E7
Fairmile *Devon* 7 G9
Fairmilehead *C/Edinb* 69 D11
Fairoak *Staffs* 34 B3
Fairseat *Kent* 20 E3
Fairstead *Essex* 30 G4
Fairstead *Norfolk* 38 D2
Fairwarp *E Sussex* 12 D3
Fairy Cottage *I/Man* 48 D4
Fairy Cross *Devon* 6 D3
Fakenham *Norfolk* 38 C5
Fala *Midloth* 70 D3
Fala Dam *Midloth* 70 D3
Falahill *Scot Borders* 70 E2
Falcon *Heref'd* 26 E3
Faldingworth *Lincs* 46 D4
Falfield *S Gloucs* 16 B3
Falkenham *Suffolk* 31 E9
Falkirk *Falk* 69 C7
Falkland *Fife* 76 G5
Falla *Scot Borders* 62 B3
Fallgate *Derby* 45 F7
Fallin *Stirl* 69 A7
Fallowfield *Gtr Man* 44 C2
Fallsidehill *Scot Borders* 70 F5
Falmer *E Sussex* 12 F2
Falmouth *Cornw'l* 3 F7
Falsgrave *N Yorks* 59 H11
Falstone *Northum* 62 E3
Fanagmore *H'land* 92 E4
Fangdale Beck *N Yorks* 59 G6
Fangfoss *ER Yorks* 52 D3
Fankerton *Falk* 68 B6
Fanmore *Arg/Bute* 78 G7
Fannich Lodge *H'land* 86 E5
Fans *Scot Borders* 70 F5
Far Bank *S Yorks* 45 A10
Far Bletchley *M/Keynes* 28 E5
Far Cotton *Northants* 28 C4
Far Forest *Worcs* 26 A4
Far Laund *Derby* 45 H7
Far Sawrey *Cumb* 56 G5
Farcet *Cambs* 37 F8
Farden *Shrops* 34 H1
Fareham *Hants* 10 D4
Farewell *Staffs* 35 D6
Farforth *Lincs* 47 E7
Faringdon *Oxon* 17 B9
Farington *Lancs* 49 G5
Farlam *Cumb* 61 H11
Farlary *H'land* 93 J10
Farleigh *N Som'set* 15 E10
Farleigh *Surrey* 19 E10
Farleigh Hungerford *Som'set* 16 F5
Farleigh Wallop *Hants* 18 G3
Farlesthorpe *Lincs* 47 E8
Farleton *Cumb* 49 A5
Farleton *Lancs* 50 C1
Farley *Shrops* 33 E9
Farley *Staffs* 35 A6
Farley *Wilts* 9 B11
Farley Green *Surrey* 19 G7
Farley Hill *Luton* 29 F7
Farley Hill *Wokingham* 18 E4
Farleys End *Glos* 26 G4
Farlington *N Yorks* 52 C2
Farlow *Shrops* 34 G2
Farmborough *Bath/NE Som'set* 16 E3
Farmcote *Glos* 27 F7
Farmcote *Shrops* 34 F3
Farmington *Glos* 27 G8
Farmoor *Oxon* 27 H11
Farmtown *Moray* 88 C5
Farnborough *London* 19 E11
Farnborough *Hants* 18 F5
Farnborough *Warwick* 27 D11
Farnborough *W Berks* 17 C11
Farnborough Green *Hants* 18 F5
Farncombe *Surrey* 18 G6
Farndish *Beds* 28 B6
Farndon *Ches* 43 G7
Farndon *Notts* 45 G11
Farnell *Angus* 77 B9
Farnham *Dorset* 9 C8
Farnham *Essex* 29 F11
Farnham *N Yorks* 51 C9
Farnham *Suffolk* 31 B10
Farnham *Surrey* 18 G5
Farnham Common *Bucks* 18 C6
Farnham Green *Essex* 29 F11
Farnham Royal *Bucks* 18 C6
Farnhill *N Yorks* 50 E6
Farningham *Kent* 20 E2
Farnley *N Yorks* 51 E8
Farnley *W Yorks* 51 F8
Farnley Tyas *W Yorks* 44 A5
Farnsfield *Notts* 45 G10
Farnworth *Gtr Man* 43 B10
Farnworth *Halton* 43 D8
Farr *H'land* 87 H9
Farr *H'land* 81 C10
Farr *H'land* 93 C10
Farr House *H'land* 87 H9
Farringdon *Devon* 7 G9
Farrington Gurney *Bath/NE Som'set* 16 F3
Farsley *W Yorks* 51 F8
Farthinghoe *Northants* 28 E2
Farthingloe *Kent* 21 G9
Farthingstone *Northants* 28 C3
Fartown *W Yorks* 51 H7
Farway *Devon* 7 G10
Fasag *H'land* 85 C13
Fascadale *H'land* 79 D8
Faslane Port *Arg/Bute* 73 E11
Fasnacloich *Arg/Bute* 74 C3
Fasnakyle Ho. *H'land* 80 A5
Fassfern *H'land* 80 F2
Fatfield *Tyne/Wear* 58 A4
Fattahead *Aberds* 89 C6
Faugh *Cumb* 57 A7
Fauldhouse *W Loth* 69 D8
Faulkbourne *Essex* 30 G4
Faulkland *Som'set* 16 F4
Fauls *Shrops* 34 B1
Faversham *Kent* 21 E7
Favillar *Moray* 88 E2
Fawdington *N Yorks* 51 B10
Fawfieldhead *Staffs* 44 F4
Fawkham Green *Kent* 20 E2
Fawler *Oxon* 27 G10
Fawley *Bucks* 18 C4
Fawley *Hants* 10 D3
Fawley *W Berks* 17 C10
Fawley Chapel *Heref'd* 26 F2
Faxfleet *ER Yorks* 52 G4
Faygate *W Sussex* 11 A11
Fazakerley *Mersey* 43 C6
Fazeley *Staffs* 35 E8
Fearby *N Yorks* 51 A7
Fearn *H'land* 87 D11
Fearn Lodge *H'land* 87 C9
Fearn Station *H'land* 87 D11
Fearnan *Perth/Kinr* 75 C10
Fearnbeg *H'land* 85 C12
Fearnhead *Warrington* 43 C9
Fearnmore *H'land* 85 B12
Featherstone *Staffs* 34 E5
Featherstone *W Yorks* 51 G10
Featherwood *Northum* 62 C4
Feckenham *Worcs* 27 B7
Feering *Essex* 30 F5
Feetham *N Yorks* 57 G11
Feizor *N Yorks* 50 C3
Felbridge *Surrey* 12 C2
Felbrigg *Norfolk* 39 B8
Felcourt *Surrey* 12 B2
Felden *Herts* 19 A7
Felin-Crai *Powys* 24 F5
Felindre *Ceredig'n* 23 A10
Felindre *Carms* 23 D10
Felindre *Carms* 24 E3
Felindre *Carms* 24 F4
Felindre *Carms* 23 C8
Felindre *Powys* 33 G7
Felindre *Swan* 14 A2
Felindre Farchog *Pembs* 22 C6
Felinfach *Ceredig'n* 23 A10
Felinfach *Powys* 25 E7
Felinfoel *Carms* 23 F10
Felingwm isaf *Carms* 23 D10
Felingwm uchaf *Carms* 23 D10
Felinwynt *Ceredig'n* 23 A7
Felixkirk *N Yorks* 51 A10
Felixstowe *Suffolk* 31 E9
Felixstowe Ferry *Suffolk* 31 E10
Felkington *Northum* 71 F8
Felkirk *W Yorks* 45 A7
Fell Side *Cumb* 56 C5
Felling *Tyne/Wear* 63 G8
Felmersham *Beds* 28 C6
Felmingham *Norfolk* 39 C8
Felpham *W Sussex* 11 E8
Felsham *Suffolk* 30 C6
Felsted *Essex* 30 F3
Feltham *London* 19 D8
Felthorpe *Norfolk* 39 D7
Felton *Heref'd* 26 D2
Felton *Northum* 63 C7
Felton *N Som'set* 15 E11
Felton Butler *Shrops* 33 D9
Feltwell *Norfolk* 38 F3
Fen Ditton *Cambs* 29 B11
Fen Drayton *Cambs* 29 B10
Fen End *W Midlands* 35 H8
Fen Side *Lincs* 47 G7

H

How Green *Kent* 19 G11
Howbrook *S Yorks* 45 C7
Howden *Scot Borders* 62 A2
Howden *ER Yorks* 52 G3
Howden-le-Wear *Durham* 58 C2
Howe *H'land* 94 D5
Howe *Norfolk* 39 E8
Howe *N Yorks* 51 A9
Howe Bridge *Gtr Man* 43 B9
Howe Green *Essex* 20 A4
Howe of Teuchar *Aberds* 89 D7
Howe Street *Essex* 30 G3
Howe Street *Essex* 30 E3
Howell *Lincs* 46 H5
Howey *Powys* 25 C7
Howgate *Midloth* 69 E11
Howick *Northum* 63 B8
Howle *Durham* 58 D1
Howle *Telford* 34 C2
Howlett End *Essex* 30 E2
Howley *Som'set* 8 D1
Hownam *Scot Borders* 62 B3
Hownam Mains *Scot Borders* 62 A3
Howpasley *Scot Borders* 61 C9
Howsham *N Lincs* 46 B4
Howsham *N Yorks* 52 C3
Howslack *Dumf/Gal* 60 C6
Howtel *Northum* 71 G7
Howton *Heref'd* 25 F11
Howtown *Cumb* 56 E6
Howwood *Renf* 68 D2
Hoxne *Suffolk* 39 H7
Hoy *Orkney* 95 H3
Hoylake *Mersey* 42 D5
Hoyland *S Yorks* 45 B7
Hoylandswaine *S Yorks* 44 B6
Hubberholme *N Yorks* 50 B5
Hubbert's Bridge *Lincs* 37 A8
Huby *N Yorks* 51 E8
Huby *N Yorks* 52 C1
Hucclecote *Glos* 26 G5
Hucking *Kent* 20 F5
Hucknall *Notts* 45 H9
Huddersfield *W Yorks* 51 H7
Huddington *Worcs* 26 C6
Hudswell *N Yorks* 58 F2
Huggate *ER Yorks* 52 D4
Hugglescote *Leics* 35 D10
Hugh Town *I/Scilly* 2 C3
Hughenden Valley *Bucks* 18 B5
Hughley *Shrops* 34 F1
Huish *Devon* 6 E4
Huish *Wilts* 17 E8
Huish Champflower *Som'set* 7 D9
Huish Episcopi *Som'set* 8 B3
Huisinis *W Isles* 90 F4
Hulcott *Bucks* 28 G5
Hulland *Derby* 44 H6
Hulland Ward *Derby* 44 H6
Hullavington *Wilts* 16 C5
Hullbridge *Essex* 20 B5
Hulme *Gtr Man* 44 C2
Hulme End *Staffs* 44 G5
Hulme Walfield *Ches* 44 F2
Hulver Street *Suffolk* 39 G10
Hulverstone *I/Wight* 10 F2
Humber *Heref'd* 26 C2
Humber Bridge *ER Yorks* 52 G6
Humberston *NE Lincs* 47 B7
Humbie *E Loth* 70 D3
Humbleton *ER Yorks* 53 F8
Humbleton *Northum* 71 H8
Humby *Lincs* 36 B6
Hume *Scot Borders* 70 F6
Humshaugh *Northum* 62 F5
Huna *H'land* 94 C5
Huncoat *Lancs* 50 F3
Huncote *Leics* 35 F11
Hundalee *Scot Borders* 62 B2
Hunderthwaite *Durham* 57 D11
Hundle Houses *Lincs* 46 G6
Hundleby *Lincs* 47 F7
Hundleton *Pembs* 22 F4
Hundon *Suffolk* 30 D4
Hundred Acres *Hants* 10 C4
Hundred End *Lancs* 49 G4
Hundred House *Powys* 25 C8
Hungarton *Leics* 36 E2
Hungerford *Hants* 9 C10
Hungerford *W Berks* 17 E10
Hungerford Newtown *W Berks* 17 D10
Hungerton *Lincs* 36 C4
Hungladder *H'land* 85 A8
Hunmanby *N Yorks* 53 B6
Hunmanby Moor *N Yorks* 53 B7
Hunningham *Warwick* 27 B10
Hunny Hill *I/Wight* 10 F3
Hunsdon *Herts* 29 G11
Hunsingore *N Yorks* 51 D10
Hunslet *W Yorks* 51 F9
Hunsonby *Cumb* 57 C7
Hunspow *H'land* 94 C4
Hunstanton *Norfolk* 38 A2
Hunstanworth *Durham* 57 B11
Hunsterson *Ches* 43 H9
Hunston *Suffolk* 30 B6
Hunston *W Sussex* 11 D7
Hunstrete *Bath/NE Som'set* 16 E3
Hunt End *Worcs* 27 B7
Hunter's Quay *Arg/Bute* 73 F10
Hunthill Lodge *Angus* 82 F6
Hunting-tower *Perth/Kinr* 76 E3
Huntingdon *Cambs* 29 A9
Huntingfield *Suffolk* 31 A10
Huntingford *Dorset* 9 A7
Huntington *E Loth* 70 C3
Huntington *Heref'd* 25 C9
Huntington *Staffs* 34 D5
Huntington *C/York* 52 D2
Huntley *Glos* 26 G4
Huntly *Aberds* 88 E5
Huntlywood *Scot Borders* 70 F5
Hunton *Kent* 20 G4
Hunton *N Yorks* 58 G2
Hunt's Corner *Norfolk* 39 G6
Hunt's Cross *Mersey* 43 D7
Huntsham *Devon* 7 D9
Huntspill *Som'set* 15 G9
Huntworth *Som'set* 8 A2
Hunwick *Durham* 58 C2
Hunworth *Norfolk* 39 B6
Hurdsfield *Ches* 44 E3
Hurley *Warwick* 35 F8
Hurley *Windsor* 18 C5
Hurlford *E Ayrs* 67 C7
Hurliness *Orkney* 95 K3
Hurn *Dorset* 9 E10
Hurn's End *Lincs* 47 H8
Hursley *Hants* 10 B3
Hurst *N Yorks* 58 F1
Hurst *Som'set* 8 C3
Hurst *Wokingham* 18 D4
Hurst Green *E Sussex* 12 D6
Hurst Green *Lancs* 50 F2
Hurst Wickham *W Sussex* 12 E1
Hurstbourne Priors *Hants* 17 G11
Hurstbourne Tarrant *Hants* 17 F10
Hurstpierpoint *W Sussex* 12 E1
Hurstway Common *Heref'd* 25 D9
Hurstwood *Lancs* 50 F4
Hurtmore *Surrey* 18 G6
Hurworth Place *D'lington* 58 F3
Hury *Durham* 57 E11
Husabost *H'land* 84 C7
Husbands Bosworth *Leics* 36 G2
Husborne Crawley *Beds* 28 E6
Husthwaite *N Yorks* 51 B11
Hutchwns *Bridg* 14 D4
Huthwaite *Notts* 45 G8
Huttoft *Lincs* 47 E9
Hutton *Scot Borders* 71 E8
Hutton *Cumb* 56 D6
Hutton *ER Yorks* 52 D6
Hutton *Essex* 20 B3
Hutton *Lancs* 49 G4
Hutton *N Som'set* 15 F9
Hutton Buscel *N Yorks* 52 A5
Hutton Conyers *N Yorks* 51 B9
Hutton Cranswick *ER Yorks* 52 D6
Hutton End *Cumb* 56 C6
Hutton Gate *Redcar/Clevel'd* 59 E6
Hutton Henry *Durham* 58 C5
Hutton-le-Hole *N Yorks* 59 G8
Hutton Magna *Durham* 58 E2
Hutton Roof *Cumb* 56 C5
Hutton Roof *Cumb* 50 B1
Hutton Rudby *N Yorks* 58 F5
Hutton Sessay *N Yorks* 51 B10
Hutton Village *Redcar/Clevel'd* 59 E6
Hutton Wandesley *N Yorks* 51 D11
Huxley *Ches* 43 F8
Huxter *Shetl'd* 96 H5
Huxter *Shetl'd* 96 G7
Huxton *Scot Borders* 71 D7
Huyton *Mersey* 43 C7
Hwlffordd = Haverfordwest *Pembs* 22 E4
Hycemoor *Cumb* 56 H2
Hyde *Glos* 16 A5
Hyde *Gtr Man* 44 C3
Hyde *Hants* 9 C10
Hyde Heath *Bucks* 18 A6
Hyde Park *S Yorks* 45 B9
Hydestile *Surrey* 18 G6
Hylton Castle *Tyne/Wear* 63 H9
Hyndford Bridge *S Lanarks* 69 F8
Hynish *Arg/Bute* 78 H2
Hyssington *Powys* 33 F9
Hythe *Hants* 10 D3
Hythe *Kent* 21 H8
Hythe End *Windsor* 19 D7
Hythie *Aberds* 89 C10

I

Ibberton *Dorset* 9 D6
Ible *Derby* 44 G6
Ibsley *Hants* 9 D10
Ibstock *Leics* 35 D10
Ibstone *Bucks* 18 B4
Ibthorpe *Hants* 17 F10
Ibworth *Hants* 18 F2
Ichrachan *Arg/Bute* 74 D3
Ickburgh *Norfolk* 38 F4
Ickenham *London* 19 C7
Ickford *Bucks* 28 H3
Ickham *Kent* 21 F9
Ickleford *Herts* 29 E8
Icklesham *E Sussex* 13 E7
Ickleton *Cambs* 29 D11
Icklingham *Suffolk* 30 A4
Ickwell Green *Beds* 29 D8
Icomb *Glos* 27 F9
Idbury *Oxon* 27 G9
Iddesleigh *Devon* 6 F4
Ide *Devon* 7 G7
Ide Hill *Kent* 19 F11
Ideford *Devon* 5 D9
Iden *E Sussex* 13 D8
Iden Green *Kent* 13 C7
Iden Green *Kent* 12 C6
Idle *W Yorks* 51 F7
Idlicote *Warwick* 27 D9
Idmiston *Wilts* 17 H8
Idole *Carms* 23 E9
Idridgehay *Derby* 44 H6
Idrigill *H'land* 85 B8
Idstone *Oxon* 17 C9
Idvies *Angus* 77 C8
Iffley *Oxon* 18 A2
Ifield *W Sussex* 19 H9
Ifold *W Sussex* 11 A9
Iford *E Sussex* 12 F3
Ifton Heath *Shrops* 33 B9
Ightfield *Shrops* 34 B1
Ightham *Kent* 20 F2
Iken *Suffolk* 31 C11
Ilam *Staffs* 44 G5
Ilchester *Som'set* 8 B4
Ilderton *Northum* 62 A6
Ilford *London* 19 C11
Ilfracombe *Devon* 6 B4
Ilkeston *Derby* 35 A10
Ilketshall St Andrew *Suffolk* 39 G9
Ilketshall St Lawrence *Suffolk* 39 G9
Ilketshall St Margaret *Suffolk* 39 G9
Ilkley *W Yorks* 51 E7
Illey *W Midlands* 34 G5
Illingworth *W Yorks* 51 G6
Illogan *Cornw'l* 2 E5
Illston on the Hill *Leics* 36 F3
Ilmer *Bucks* 28 H4
Ilmington *Warwick* 27 D9
Ilminster *Som'set* 8 C2
Ilsington *Devon* 5 D8
Ilston *Swan* 23 G10
Ilton *N Yorks* 51 B7
Ilton *Som'set* 8 C2
Imachar *N Ayrs* 66 B1
Imeraval *Arg/Bute* 64 D4
Immingham *NE Lincs* 46 A5
Impington *Cambs* 29 B11
Ince *Ches* 43 E7
Ince Blundell *Mersey* 42 B6
Ince in Makerfield *Gtr Man* 43 B8
Inch of Arnhall *Aberds* 83 F8
Inchbare *Angus* 83 G8
Inchberry *Moray* 88 C3
Inchbraoch *Angus* 77 B10
Incheril *H'land* 86 E3
Inchgrundle *Angus* 82 F6
Inchina *H'land* 86 B2
Inchinnan *Renf* 68 D3
Inchkinloch *H'land* 93 E8
Inchlaggan *H'land* 80 C3
Inchlumpie *H'land* 87 D8
Inchmore *H'land* 86 G6
Inchnacardoch Hotel *H'land* 80 B5
Inchnadamph *H'land* 92 G5
Inchree *H'land* 74 A3
Inchture *Perth/Kinr* 76 E5
Inchyra *Perth/Kinr* 76 E4
Indian Queens *Cornw'l* 3 D8
Inerval *Arg/Bute* 64 D4
Ingatestone *Essex* 20 B3
Ingbirchworth *S Yorks* 44 B6
Ingestre *Staffs* 34 C5
Ingham *Lincs* 46 D3
Ingham *Norfolk* 39 C9
Ingham *Suffolk* 30 A5
Ingham Corner *Norfolk* 39 C9
Ingleborough *Norfolk* 37 D10
Ingleby *Derby* 35 C9
Ingleby *Lincs* 46 E2
Ingleby Arncliffe *N Yorks* 58 F5
Ingleby Barwick *Stockton* 58 E5
Ingleby Greenhow *N Yorks* 59 F6
Inglemire *Kingston/Hull* 53 F6
Inglesbatch *Bath/NE Som'set* 16 E4
Inglesham *Swindon* 17 B9
Ingleton *Durham* 58 D2
Ingleton *N Yorks* 50 B2
Inglewhite *Lancs* 49 E5
Ingliston *C/Edinb* 69 C10
Ingoe *Northum* 62 F6
Ingol *Lancs* 49 F5
Ingoldisthorpe *Norfolk* 38 B2
Ingoldmells *Lincs* 47 F9
Ingoldsby *Lincs* 36 B6
Ingon *Warwick* 27 C9
Ingram *Northum* 62 B6
Ingrave *Essex* 20 B3
Ingrow *W Yorks* 51 F6
Ings *Cumb* 56 G6
Ingst *S Gloucs* 16 C2
Ingworth *Norfolk* 39 C7
Inham's End *Cambs* 37 F8
Inkberrow *Worcs* 27 C7
Inkpen *W Berks* 17 E10
Inkstack *H'land* 94 C4
Inn *Cumb* 56 F6
Innellan *Arg/Bute* 73 F10
Innerleithen *Scot Borders* 70 G2
Innerleven *Fife* 76 G6
Innermessan *Dumf/Gal* 54 C3
Innerwick *E Loth* 70 C6
Innerwick *Perth/Kinr* 75 C8
Innis Chonain *Arg/Bute* 74 E4
Insch *Aberds* 83 A8
Insh *H'land* 81 C10
Inshore *H'land* 92 C6
Inskip *Lancs* 49 F4
Instoneville *S Yorks* 45 A9
Instow *Devon* 6 C3
Intake *S Yorks* 45 B9
Inver *Aberds* 82 D4
Inver *H'land* 87 C11
Inver *Perth/Kinr* 76 C3
Inver Mallie *H'land* 80 E3
Inverailort *H'land* 79 C10
Inveraldie *Angus* 77 D7
Inveralligin *H'land* 85 C13
Inverallochy *Aberds* 89 B10
Inveran *H'land* 87 B8
Inveraray *Arg/Bute* 73 C9
Inverarish *H'land* 85 E10
Inverarity *Angus* 77 C7
Inverarnan *Stirl* 74 F6
Inverasdale *H'land* 91 J13
Inverbeg *Arg/Bute* 74 H6
Inverbervie *Aberds* 83 F10
Inverboyndie *Aberds* 89 B6
Inverbroom *H'land* 86 C4
Invercassley *H'land* 92 J7
Invercauld House *Aberds* 82 D3
Inverchaolain *Arg/Bute* 73 F9
Invercharnan *H'land* 74 C4
Inverchoran *H'land* 86 F5
Invercreran *Arg/Bute* 74 C3
Inverdruie *H'land* 81 B11
Inverebrie *Aberds* 89 E9
Invereck *Arg/Bute* 73 E10
Inverernan Ho. *Aberds* 82 B5
Invereshie House *H'land* 81 C10
Inveresk *E Loth* 70 C2
Inverey *Aberds* 82 E2
Inverfarigaig *H'land* 81 A7
Invergarry *H'land* 80 C5
Invergelder *Aberds* 82 D4
Invergeldie *Perth/Kinr* 75 E10
Invergordon *H'land* 87 E10
Invergowrie *Perth/Kinr* 76 D6
Inverguseran *H'land* 85 H12
Inverhadden *Perth/Kinr* 75 B9
Inverharroch *Moray* 88 E3
Inverherive *Stirl* 74 E6
Inverie *H'land* 79 B10
Inverinan *Arg/Bute* 73 B8
Inverinate *H'land* 85 F14
Inverkeilor *Angus* 77 C9
Inverkeithing *Fife* 69 B10
Inverkeithny *Aberds* 89 D6
Inverkip *Invercl* 73 F11
Inverkirkaig *H'land* 92 H3
Inverlael *H'land* 86 C4
Inverlochlarig *Stirl* 75 F7
Inverlochy *Arg/Bute* 74 E4
Inverlochy *H'land* 80 F3
Inverlussa *Arg/Bute* 72 E5
Invermark Lodge *Angus* 82 E6
Invermoidart *H'land* 79 D9
Invermoriston *H'land* 80 B6
Invernaver *H'land* 93 C10
Inverneill *Arg/Bute* 73 E7
Inverness *H'land* 87 G9
Invernettie *Aberds* 89 D11
Invernoaden *Arg/Bute* 73 D10
Inveroran Hotel *Arg/Bute* 74 C5
Inverpolly Lodge *H'land* 92 H3
Inverquharity *Angus* 77 B7
Inverquhomery *Aberds* 89 D10
Inverroy *H'land* 80 E4
Inversanda *H'land* 74 B2
Invershiel *H'land* 80 B1
Invershin *H'land* 87 B8
Inversnaid Hotel *Stirl* 74 G6
Inverugie *Aberds* 89 D11
Inveruglas *Arg/Bute* 74 G6
Inveruglass *H'land* 81 C10
Inverurie *Aberds* 83 A9
Invervar *Perth/Kinr* 75 C9
Inverythan *Aberds* 89 D7
Inwardleigh *Devon* 6 G4
Inworth *Essex* 30 G5
Iochdar *W Isles* 84 D2
Iping *W Sussex* 11 B7
Ipplepen *Devon* 5 E9
Ipsden *Oxon* 18 C3
Ipsley *Worcs* 27 B7
Ipstones *Staffs* 44 G4
Ipswich *Suffolk* 31 D8
Irby *Mersey* 42 D5
Irby in the Marsh *Lincs* 47 F8
Irby upon Humber *NE Lincs* 46 B5
Irchester *Northants* 28 B6
Ireby *Cumb* 56 C4
Ireby *Lancs* 50 B2
Ireland *Orkney* 95 H4
Ireland *Shetl'd* 96 L5
Ireland's Cross *Shrops* 34 A3
Ireleth *Cumb* 49 B2
Ireshopeburn *Durham* 57 C10
Irlam *Gtr Man* 43 C10
Irnham *Lincs* 36 C6
Iron Acton *S Gloucs* 16 C3
Iron Cross *Warwick* 27 C7
Ironbridge *Telford* 34 E2
Ironmacannie *Dumf/Gal* 55 B9
Ironside *Aberds* 89 C8
Ironville *Derby* 45 G8
Irstead *Norfolk* 39 C9
Irthington *Cumb* 61 G10
Irthlingborough *Northants* 28 A6
Irton *N Yorks* 52 A6
Irvine *N Ayrs* 66 C6
Isauld *H'land* 93 C12
Isbister *Orkney* 95 F3
Isbister *Orkney* 95 G4
Isbister *Shetl'd* 96 D5
Isbister *Shetl'd* 96 G7
Isfield *E Sussex* 12 E3
Isham *Northants* 28 A5
Isle Abbotts *Som'set* 8 B2
Isle Brewers *Som'set* 8 B2
Isle of Whithorn *Dumf/Gal* 55 F7
Isleham *Cambs* 30 A3
Isleornsay *H'land* 85 G12
Islesburgh *Shetl'd* 96 G5
Islesteps *Dumf/Gal* 60 F5
Isleworth *London* 19 D8
Isley Walton *Leics* 35 C10
Islibhig *W Isles* 90 E4
Islington *London* 19 C10
Islip *Northants* 36 H5
Islip *Oxon* 28 G2
Istead Rise *Kent* 20 E3
Isycoed *Wrex* 43 G7
Itchen *S'thampton* 10 C3
Itchen Abbas *Hants* 10 A4
Itchen Stoke *Hants* 10 A4
Itchingfield *W Sussex* 11 B10
Itchington *S Gloucs* 16 C3
Itteringham *Norfolk* 39 B7
Itton *Devon* 6 G5
Itton Common *Monmouths* 15 B10
Ivegill *Cumb* 56 B6
Iver *Bucks* 19 C7
Iver Heath *Bucks* 19 C7
Iveston *Durham* 58 A2
Ivinghoe *Bucks* 28 G6
Ivinghoe Aston *Bucks* 28 G6
Ivington *Heref'd* 25 C11
Ivington Green *Heref'd* 25 C11
Ivy Chimneys *Essex* 19 A11
Ivy Cross *Dorset* 9 B7
Ivy Hatch *Kent* 20 F2
Ivybridge *Devon* 5 F7
Ivychurch *Kent* 13 D9
Iwade *Kent* 20 E6
Iwerne Courtney or Shroton *Dorset* 9 C7
Iwerne Minster *Dorset* 9 C7
Ixworth *Suffolk* 30 A6
Ixworth Thorpe *Suffolk* 30 A6

J

Jack Hill *N Yorks* 51 D8
Jack in the Green *Devon* 7 G9
Jacksdale *Notts* 45 G8
Jackstown *Aberds* 89 E7
Jacobstow *Cornw'l* 4 B2
Jacobstowe *Devon* 6 F4
Jameston *Pembs* 22 G5
Jamestown *Dumf/Gal* 61 D9
Jamestown *H'land* 86 F7
Jamestown *W Dunb* 68 B2
Jarrow *Tyne/Wear* 63 G9
Jarvis Brook *E Sussex* 12 D4
Jasper's Green *Essex* 30 F4
Java *Arg/Bute* 79 H10
Jawcraig *Falk* 69 C7
Jaywick *Essex* 31 G8
Jealott's Hill *Brackn'l* 18 D5
Jedburgh *Scot Borders* 62 A2
Jeffreyston *Pembs* 22 F5
Jellyhill *E Dunb* 68 C5
Jemimaville *H'land* 87 E10
Jersey Farm *Herts* 29 H8
Jesmond *Tyne/Wear* 63 G8
Jevington *E Sussex* 12 F4
Jockey End *Herts* 29 G7
John o'Groats *H'land* 94 C5
Johnby *Cumb* 56 C6
John's Cross *E Sussex* 12 D6
Johnshaven *Aberds* 83 G9
Johnston *Pembs* 22 E4
Johnstone *Renf* 68 D3
Johnstonebridge *Dumf/Gal* 60 D6
Johnstown *Carms* 23 E9
Johnstown *Wrex* 42 H6
Joppa *C/Edinb* 70 C2
Joppa *S Ayrs* 67 E7
Jordans *Bucks* 18 B6
Jordanthorpe *S Yorks* 45 D7
Jump *S Yorks* 45 B7
Jumpers Green *Dorset* 9 E10
Juniper Green *C/Edinb* 69 D10
Jurby East *I/Man* 48 C3
Jurby West *I/Man* 48 C3

K

Kaber *Cumb* 57 E9
Kaimend *S Lanarks* 69 F8
Kaimes *C/Edinb* 69 D11
Kalemouth *Scot Borders* 70 H6
Kames *Arg/Bute* 73 F8
Kames *Arg/Bute* 73 B7
Kames *E Ayrs* 68 H5
Kea *Cornw'l* 3 E7
Keadby *N Lincs* 46 A2
Keal Cotes *Lincs* 47 F7
Kearsley *Gtr Man* 43 B10
Kearstwick *Cumb* 50 A2
Kearton *N Yorks* 57 G11
Kearvaig *H'land* 92 B5
Keasden *N Yorks* 50 C3
Keckwick *Halton* 43 D8
Keddington *Lincs* 47 D7
Kedington *Suffolk* 30 D4
Kedleston *Derby* 35 A9
Keelby *Lincs* 46 A5
Keele *Staffs* 44 H2
Keeley Green *Beds* 29 D7
Keeston *Pembs* 22 E4
Keevil *Wilts* 16 F6
Kegworth *Leics* 35 C10
Kehelland *Cornw'l* 2 E5
Keig *Aberds* 83 B8
Keighley *W Yorks* 51 E6
Keil *H'land* 74 B2
Keilarsbrae *Clack* 69 A7
Keilhill *Aberds* 89 C7
Keillmore *Arg/Bute* 72 E5
Keillor *Perth/Kinr* 76 C5
Keillour *Perth/Kinr* 76 E2
Keills *Arg/Bute* 64 B5
Keils *Arg/Bute* 72 G4
Keinton Mandeville *Som'set* 8 A4
Keir Mill *Dumf/Gal* 60 D4
Keisby *Lincs* 36 C6
Keiss *H'land* 94 D5
Keith *Moray* 88 C4
Keith Inch *Aberds* 89 D11
Keithock *Angus* 77 A9
Kelbrook *Lancs* 50 E5
Kelby *Lincs* 36 A6
Keld *Cumb* 57 E7
Keld *N Yorks* 57 F10
Keldholme *N Yorks* 59 H8
Kelfield *N Lincs* 46 B2
Kelfield *N Yorks* 52 F1
Kelham *Notts* 45 G11
Kellan *Arg/Bute* 79 G8
Kellas *Angus* 77 D7
Kellas *Moray* 88 C1
Kellaton *Devon* 5 H9
Kelleth *Cumb* 57 F8
Kelleythorpe *ER Yorks* 52 D5
Kelling *Norfolk* 39 A6
Kellingley *N Yorks* 51 G11
Kellington *N Yorks* 52 G1
Kelloe *Durham* 58 C4
Kelloholm *Dumf/Gal* 60 B3
Kelly *Devon* 4 C4
Kelly Bray *Cornw'l* 4 D4
Kelmarsh *Northants* 36 H3
Kelmscot *Oxon* 17 B9
Kelsale *Suffolk* 31 B10
Kelsall *Ches* 43 F8
Kelsall Hill *Ches* 43 F8
Kelshall *Herts* 29 E10
Kelsick *Cumb* 56 A3
Kelso *Scot Borders* 70 G6
Kelstedge *Derby* 45 F7
Kelstern *Lincs* 46 C6
Kelston *Bath/NE Som'set* 16 E4
Keltneyburn *Perth/Kinr* 75 C10
Kelton *Dumf/Gal* 60 F5
Kelty *Fife* 69 A10
Kelvedon *Essex* 30 G5
Kelvedon Hatch *Essex* 20 B2
Kelvin *S Lanarks* 68 E5
Kelvinside *C/Glasg* 68 D4
Kelynack *Cornw'l* 2 F2
Kemback *Fife* 77 F7
Kemberton *Shrops* 34 E3
Kemble *Glos* 16 B6
Kemerton *Worcs* 26 E6
Kemeys Commander *Monmouths* 15 A9
Kemnay *Aberds* 83 B9
Kemp Town *Brighton/Hove* 12 F2
Kempley *Glos* 26 F3
Kemps Green *Warwick* 27 A8
Kempsey *Worcs* 26 D5
Kempsford *Glos* 17 B8
Kempshott *Hants* 18 F3
Kempston *Beds* 29 D7
Kempston Hardwick *Beds* 29 D7
Kempton *Shrops* 33 G9
Kemsing *Kent* 20 F2
Kemsley *Kent* 20 E6
Kenardington *Kent* 13 C8
Kenchester *Heref'd* 25 D11
Kencot *Oxon* 17 A9
Kendal *Cumb* 57 G7
Kendoon *Dumf/Gal* 67 H9
Kendray *S Yorks* 45 B7
Kenfig *Bridg* 14 C4
Kenfig Hill *Bridg* 14 C4
Kenilworth *Warwick* 27 A9
Kenknock *Stirl* 75 D7
Kenley *London* 19 F10
Kenley *Shrops* 34 E1
Kenmore *H'land* 85 C12
Kenmore *Perth/Kinr* 75 C10
Kenn *Devon* 5 C10
Kenn *N Som'set* 15 E10
Kennacley *W Isles* 90 H6
Kennacraig *Arg/Bute* 73 G7
Kennerleigh *Devon* 7 F7
Kennet *Clack* 69 A8
Kennethmont *Aberds* 83 A7
Kennett *Cambs* 30 B3
Kennford *Devon* 5 C10
Kenninghall *Norfolk* 38 G6
Kenninghall Heath *Norfolk* 38 G6
Kennington *Kent* 13 B9
Kennington *Oxon* 18 A2
Kennoway *Fife* 76 G6
Kenny Hill *Suffolk* 38 H2
Kennythorpe *N Yorks* 52 C3
Kenovay *Arg/Bute* 78 G2
Kensaleyre *H'land* 85 C9
Kensington *London* 19 D9
Kensworth *Beds* 29 G7
Kensworth Common *Beds* 29 G7
Kent Street *E Sussex* 13 E6
Kent Street *Kent* 20 F3
Kent Street *W Sussex* 11 B11
Kentallen *H'land* 74 B3
Kentchurch *Heref'd* 25 F11
Kentford *Suffolk* 30 B4
Kentisbeare *Devon* 7 F9
Kentisbury *Devon* 6 B5
Kentisbury Ford *Devon* 6 B5
Kentmere *Cumb* 56 F6
Kenton *Devon* 5 C10
Kenton *Suffolk* 31 B8
Kenton *Tyne/Wear* 63 G8
Kenton Bankfoot *Tyne/Wear* 63 G8
Kentra *H'land* 79 E9
Kents Bank *Cumb* 49 B3
Kent's Green *Glos* 26 F4
Kent's Oak *Hants* 10 B2
Kenwick *Shrops* 33 B10
Kenwyn *Cornw'l* 3 E7
Keoldale *H'land* 92 C6
Keppanach *H'land* 74 A3
Keppoch *H'land* 85 F14
Keprigan *Arg/Bute* 65 G7
Kepwick *N Yorks* 58 G5
Kerchesters *Scot Borders* 70 G6
Keresley *W Midlands* 35 G9
Kernborough *Devon* 5 G8
Kerne Bridge *Heref'd* 26 G2
Kerris *Cornw'l* 2 G3
Kerry *Powys* 33 G7
Kerrycroy *Arg/Bute* 73 G10
Kerry's Gate *Heref'd* 25 E10
Kerrysdale *H'land* 85 A13
Kersall *Notts* 45 F11
Kersey *Suffolk* 31 D7
Kershopefoot *Cumb* 61 E10
Kersoe *Worcs* 26 E6
Kerswell *Devon* 7 F9
Kerswell Green *Worcs* 26 D5
Kesgrave *Suffolk* 31 D9
Kessingland *Suffolk* 39 G11
Kessingland Beach *Suffolk* 39 G11
Kessington *E Dunb* 68 C4
Kestle *Cornw'l* 3 E8
Kestle Mill *Cornw'l* 3 D7
Keston *London* 19 E11
Keswick *Cumb* 56 D4
Keswick *Norfolk* 39 E8
Keswick *Norfolk* 39 B9
Ketley *Telford* 34 D2
Ketley Bank *Telford* 34 D2
Ketsby *Lincs* 47 E7
Kettering *Northants* 36 H4
Ketteringham *Norfolk* 39 E7
Kettins *Perth/Kinr* 76 D5
Kettlebaston *Suffolk* 30 C6
Kettlebridge *Fife* 76 G6
Kettleburgh *Suffolk* 31 B9
Kettlehill *Fife* 76 G6
Kettleholm *Dumf/Gal* 61 F7
Kettleness *N Yorks* 59 E9
Kettleshume *Ches* 44 E3
Kettlesing Bottom *N Yorks* 51 D8
Kettlesing Head *N Yorks* 51 D8
Kettlestone *Norfolk* 38 B5
Kettlethorpe *Lincs* 46 E2
Kettletoft *Orkney* 95 E7
Kettlewell *N Yorks* 50 B5
Ketton *Rutl'd* 36 E5
Kew *London* 19 D8
Kew Bridge *London* 19 D8
Kewstoke *N Som'set* 15 E9
Kexbrough *S Yorks* 45 B7
Kexby *Lincs* 46 D2
Kexby *C/York* 52 D3
Key Green *Ches* 44 F2
Keyham *Leics* 36 E2
Keyhaven *Hants* 10 E2
Keyingham *ER Yorks* 53 G8
Keymer *W Sussex* 12 E2
Keynsham *Bath/NE Som'set* 16 E3
Keysoe *Beds* 29 B7
Keysoe Row *Beds* 29 B7
Keyston *Cambs* 36 H6
Keyworth *Notts* 36 B2
Kibblesworth *Tyne/Wear* 63 H8
Kibworth Beauchamp *Leics* 36 F2
Kibworth Harcourt *Leics* 36 F2
Kidbrooke *London* 19 D11
Kiddemore Green *Staffs* 34 E4
Kidderminster *Worcs* 34 H4
Kiddington *Oxon* 27 F11
Kidlington *Oxon* 27 G11
Kidmore End *Oxon* 18 D3
Kidsgrove *Staffs* 44 G2
Kidstones *N Yorks* 50 A5
Kidwelly = Cydweli *Carms* 23 F9
Kiel Crofts *Arg/Bute* 74 D2
Kielder *Northum* 62 D2
Kierfiold Ho. *Orkney* 95 G3
Kilbagie *Clack* 69 B8
Kilbarchan *Renf* 68 D3
Kilbeg *H'land* 85 H11
Kilberry *Arg/Bute* 72 G6
Kilbirnie *N Ayrs* 66 A6
Kilbride *Arg/Bute* 79 J11
Kilbride *Arg/Bute* 74 E2
Kilbride *H'land* 85 F10
Kilburn *Angus* 82 G5
Kilburn *Derby* 45 H7
Kilburn *London* 19 C9
Kilburn *N Yorks* 51 B11
Kilby *Leics* 36 F2
Kilchamaig *Arg/Bute* 73 G7
Kilchattan *Arg/Bute* 72 D2
Kilchattan Bay *Arg/Bute* 66 A4
Kilchenzie *Arg/Bute* 65 F7
Kilcheran *Arg/Bute* 79 H11
Kilchiaran *Arg/Bute* 64 B3
Kilchoan *Arg/Bute* 72 B6
Kilchoan *H'land* 78 E7
Kilchoman *Arg/Bute* 64 B3
Kilchrenan *Arg/Bute* 74 E3
Kilconquhar *Fife* 77 G7
Kilcot *Glos* 26 F3
Kilcoy *H'land* 87 F8
Kilcreggan *Arg/Bute* 73 E11
Kildale *N Yorks* 59 F7
Kildalloig *Arg/Bute* 65 G8
Kildary *H'land* 87 D10
Kildermorie Lodge *H'land* 87 D8
Kildonan *N Ayrs* 66 D3
Kildonan Lodge *H'land* 93 G12
Kildonnan *H'land* 78 C7
Kildrummy *Aberds* 82 B6
Kildwick *N Yorks* 50 E6
Kilfinan *Arg/Bute* 73 F8
Kilfinnan *H'land* 80 D4
Kilgetty *Pembs* 22 F6
Kilgwrrwg Common *Monmouths* 15 B10
Kilham *ER Yorks* 53 C6
Kilham *Northum* 71 G7
Kilkenneth *Arg/Bute* 78 G2
Kilkerran *Arg/Bute* 65 G8
Kilkhampton *Cornw'l* 6 E1
Killamarsh *Derby* 45 D8
Killay *Swan* 14 B2
Killbeg *Arg/Bute* 79 G9
Killean *Arg/Bute* 65 D7
Killearn *Stirl* 68 B4
Killen *H'land* 87 F9
Killerby *D'lington* 58 E2
Killichonan *Perth/Kinr* 75 B8
Killiechonate *H'land* 80 E4
Killiechronan *Arg/Bute* 79 G8
Killiecrankie *Perth/Kinr* 76 A2
Killiemor *Arg/Bute* 78 H7
Killiemore House *Arg/Bute* 78 J7
Killilan *H'land* 86 H2
Killimster *H'land* 94 E5
Killin *Stirl* 75 D8
Killin Lodge *H'land* 81 C7
Killinallan *Arg/Bute* 64 A4
Killinghall *N Yorks* 51 D8
Killington *Cumb* 57 H8
Killingworth *Tyne/Wear* 63 F8
Killmahumaig *Arg/Bute* 72 D6
Killochyett *Scot Borders* 70 F3
Killocraw *Arg/Bute* 65 E7
Killundine *H'land* 79 G8
Kilmacolm *Invercl* 68 D2
Kilmaha *Arg/Bute* 73 C8
Kilmahog *Stirl* 75 G9
Kilmalieu *H'land* 79 F11
Kilmaluag *H'land* 85 A9
Kilmany *Fife* 76 E6
Kilmarie *H'land* 85 G10
Kilmarnock *E Ayrs* 67 C7
Kilmaron Castle *Fife* 76 F6
Kilmartin *Arg/Bute* 73 D7
Kilmaurs *E Ayrs* 67 B7
Kilmelford *Arg/Bute* 73 B7
Kilmeny *Arg/Bute* 64 B4
Kilmersdon *Som'set* 16 F3
Kilmeston *Hants* 10 B4
Kilmichael *Arg/Bute* 65 F7
Kilmichael Glassary *Arg/Bute* 73 D7
Kilmichael of Inverlussa *Arg/Bute* 72 E6
Kilmington *Devon* 8 E1
Kilmington *Wilts* 16 H4
Kilmonivaig *H'land* 80 E3
Kilmorack *H'land* 86 G7
Kilmore *Arg/Bute* 79 J11
Kilmore *H'land* 85 H11
Kilmory *Arg/Bute* 72 F6
Kilmory *H'land* 79 D8
Kilmory *H'land* 85 H8
Kilmory *N Ayrs* 66 D2
Kilmuir *H'land* 84 D7
Kilmuir *H'land* 87 G9
Kilmuir *H'land* 87 D10
Kilmuir *H'land* 85 A8
Kilmun *Arg/Bute* 73 E10
Kilmun *Arg/Bute* 73 B8
Kiln Pit Hill *Northum* 58 A1
Kilncadzow *S Lanarks* 69 F7
Kilndown *Kent* 12 C6
Kilnhurst *S Yorks* 45 C8
Kilninian *Arg/Bute* 78 G6
Kilninver *Arg/Bute* 79 J11
Kilnsea *ER Yorks* 53 H10
Kilnsey *N Yorks* 50 C5
Kilnwick *ER Yorks* 52 E5
Kilnwick Percy *ER Yorks* 52 D4
Kiloran *Arg/Bute* 72 D2
Kilpatrick *N Ayrs* 66 D2
Kilpeck *Heref'd* 25 E11
Kilphedir *H'land* 93 H12
Kilpin *ER Yorks* 52 G3
Kilpin Pike *ER Yorks* 52 G3
Kilrenny *Fife* 77 G8
Kilsby *Northants* 28 A2
Kilspindie *Perth/Kinr* 76 E5
Kilsyth *N Lanarks* 68 C6
Kiltarlity *H'land* 87 G8
Kilton *Notts* 45 E9
Kilton *Som'set* 7 B10
Kilton Thorpe *Redcar/Clevel'd* 59 E7
Kilvaxter *H'land* 85 B8
Kilve *Som'set* 7 B10
Kilvington *Notts* 36 A3
Kilwinning *N Ayrs* 66 B6
Kimber worth *S Yorks* 45 C8
Kimberley *Norfolk* 39 E6
Kimberley *Notts* 35 A11
Kimble Wick *Bucks* 28 H5
Kimblesworth *Durham* 58 B3
Kimbolton *Cambs* 29 B7
Kimbolton *Heref'd* 26 B2
Kimcote *Leics* 36 G1
Kimmeridge *Dorset* 9 G8
Kimmerston *Northum* 71 G8
Kimpton *Hants* 17 G9
Kimpton *Herts* 29 G8
Kinbrace *H'land* 93 F11
Kinbuck *Stirl* 75 G10
Kincaple *Fife* 77 F7
Kincardine *Fife* 69 B8
Kincardine *H'land* 87 C9
Kincardine Bridge *Fife* 69 B8
Kincardine O'Neil *Aberds* 83 D7
Kinclaven *Perth/Kinr* 76 D4
Kincorth *Aberd C* 83 C11
Kincorth Ho. *Moray* 87 E13
Kincraig *H'land* 81 C10
Kincraigie *Perth/Kinr* 76 C2
Kindallachan *Perth/Kinr* 76 C2
Kineton *Glos* 27 F7
Kineton *Warwick* 27 C10
Kinfauns *Perth/Kinr* 76 E4
King Edward *Aberds* 89 C7
King Sterndale *Derby* 44 E4
Kingairloch *H'land* 79 F11
Kingarth *Arg/Bute* 73 H9
Kingcoed *Monmouths* 25 H11
Kingerby *Lincs* 46 C4
Kingham *Oxon* 27 F9
Kingholm Quay *Dumf/Gal* 60 F5
Kinghorn *Fife* 69 B11
Kingie *H'land* 80 C3
Kinglassie *Fife* 76 H5
Kingoodie *Perth/Kinr* 76 E6
King's Acre *Heref'd* 25 D11
King's Bromley *Staffs* 35 D7
King's Caple *Heref'd* 26 F2
King's Cliffe *Northants* 36 F6
King's Coughton *Warwick* 27 C7
King's Heath *W Midlands* 35 G6
Kings Hedges *Cambs* 29 B11
Kings Langley *Herts* 19 A7
King's Lynn *Norfolk* 38 C2
King's Meaburn *Cumb* 57 D8
King's Mills *Wrex* 42 H6
Kings Muir *Scot Borders* 69 G11
King's Newnham *Warwick* 35 H10
King's Newton *Derby* 35 C9
King's Norton *Leics* 36 E2
King's Norton *W Midlands* 35 H6
King's Nympton *Devon* 6 E5
King's Pyon *Heref'd* 25 C11
King's Ripton *Cambs* 37 H8
King's Somborne *Hants* 10 A2
King's Stag *Dorset* 8 C6
King's Stanley *Glos* 16 A5
King's Sutton *Northants* 27 E11
King's Thorn *Heref'd* 26 E2
King's Walden *Herts* 29 F8
Kings Worthy *Hants* 10 A3
Kingsand *Cornw'l* 4 F5
Kingsbarns *Fife* 77 F8
Kingsbridge *Devon* 5 G8
Kingsbridge *Som'set* 7 C8
Kingsburgh *H'land* 85 C8
Kingsbury *London* 19 C9
Kingsbury *Warwick* 35 F8
Kingsbury Episcopi *Som'set* 8 B3
Kingsclere *Hants* 18 F2
Kingscote *Glos* 16 B5
Kingscott *Devon* 6 E4
Kingscross *N Ayrs* 66 D3
Kingsdon *Som'set* 8 B4
Kingsdown *Kent* 21 G10
Kingseat *Fife* 69 A10
Kingsey *Bucks* 28 H4
Kingsfold *W Sussex* 19 H8
Kingsford *E Ayrs* 67 B7
Kingsford *Worcs* 34 G4
Kingsforth *N Lincs* 52 H6
Kingsgate *Kent* 21 D10
Kingsheanton *Devon* 6 C4
Kingshouse Hotel *H'land* 74 B5
Kingside Hill *Cumb* 56 A3
Kingskerswell *Devon* 5 E9
Kingskettle *Fife* 76 G6
Kingsland *Angl* 40 B4
Kingsland *Heref'd* 25 B11
Kingsley *Ches* 43 E8
Kingsley *Hants* 18 H4
Kingsley *Staffs* 44 H4
Kingsley Green *W Sussex* 11 A7
Kingsley Holt *Staffs* 44 H4
Kingsley Park *Northants* 28 B4
Kingsmuir *Angus* 77 C7
Kingsmuir *Fife* 77 G8
Kingsnorth *Kent* 13 C9
Kingstanding *W Midlands* 35 F6
Kingsteignton *Devon* 5 D9
Kingsthorpe *Northants* 28 B4
Kingston *Cambs* 29 C10
Kingston *Devon* 5 G7
Kingston *Dorset* 9 D6
Kingston *Dorset* 9 G8
Kingston *E Loth* 70 B4
Kingston *Hants* 9 D10
Kingston *I/Wight* 10 F3
Kingston *Kent* 21 F8
Kingston *Moray* 88 B3
Kingston Bagpuize *Oxon* 17 B11
Kingston Blount *Oxon* 18 B4
Kingston by Sea *W Sussex* 11 D11
Kingston Deverill *Wilts* 16 H5
Kingston Gorse *W Sussex* 11 D9
Kingston Lisle *Oxon* 17 C10
Kingston Maurward *Dorset* 8 E6
Kingston near Lewes *E Sussex* 12 F2
Kingston on Soar *Notts* 35 C11
Kingston Russell *Dorset* 8 E4
Kingston St Mary *Som'set* 7 D11
Kingston Seymour *N Som'set* 15 E10
Kingston Upon Hull *Kingston/Hull* 53 G6
Kingston upon Thames *London* 19 E8
Kingston Vale *London* 19 D9
Kingstone *Heref'd* 25 E11
Kingstone *Som'set* 8 C2
Kingstone *Staffs* 35 C6
Kingstown *Cumb* 61 H9
Kingswear *Devon* 5 F9
Kingswells *Aberd C* 83 C10
Kingswinford *W Midlands* 34 G4
Kingswood *Bucks* 28 G3
Kingswood *Glos* 16 B4
Kingswood *Heref'd* 25 C9
Kingswood *Kent* 20 F5
Kingswood *Powys* 33 E8
Kingswood *S Gloucs* 16 D3
Kingswood *Surrey* 19 F9
Kingswood *Warwick* 27 A8
Kingthorpe *Lincs* 46 E5
Kington *Heref'd* 25 C9
Kington *Worcs* 26 C6
Kington Langley *Wilts* 16 D6
Kington Magna *Dorset* 9 B6
Kington St Michael *Wilts* 16 D6
Kingussie *H'land* 81 C9
Kingweston *Som'set* 8 A4
Kininvie Ho. *Moray* 88 D3
Kinkell Bridge *Perth/Kinr* 76 F2
Kinknockie *Aberds* 89 D10
Kinlet *Shrops* 34 G3
Kinloch *Fife* 76 F5
Kinloch *H'land* 78 B6
Kinloch *H'land* 92 F6
Kinloch *H'land* 85 G11
Kinloch *Perth/Kinr* 76 C4
Kinloch *Perth/Kinr* 76 C5
Kinloch Hourn *H'land* 80 C1
Kinloch Laggan *H'land* 81 E7
Kinloch Lodge *H'land* 93 D8
Kinloch Rannoch *Perth/Kinr* 75 B9
Kinlochan *H'land* 79 E11
Kinlochard *Stirl* 75 G7
Kinlochbeoraid *H'land* 79 C11
Kinlochbervie *H'land* 92 D5
Kinlocheil *H'land* 80 F1
Kinlochewe *H'land* 86 E3
Kinlochleven *H'land* 74 A4
Kinlochmoidart *H'land* 79 D10
Kinlochmorar *H'land* 79 B11
Kinlochmore *H'land* 74 A4
Kinlochspelve *Arg/Bute* 79 J9
Kinloid *H'land* 79 C9
Kinloss *Moray* 87 E13
Kinmel Bay *Conwy* 42 D2
Kinmuck *Aberds* 83 B10
Kinmundy *Aberds* 83 B10
Kinnadie *Aberds* 89 D9
Kinnaird *Perth/Kinr* 76 E5
Kinnaird Castle *Angus* 77 B9
Kinneff *Aberds* 83 F10
Kinnelhead *Dumf/Gal* 60 C6
Kinnell *Angus* 77 B9
Kinnerley *Shrops* 33 C9
Kinnersley *Heref'd* 25 D10
Kinnersley *Worcs* 26 D5
Kinnerton *Powys* 25 B9
Kinnesswood *Perth/Kinr* 76 G4
Kinninvie *Durham* 58 D1
Kinnordy *Angus* 76 B6
Kinoulton *Notts* 36 B2
Kinross *Perth/Kinr* 76 G4
Kinrossie *Perth/Kinr* 76 D4
Kinsbourne Green *Herts* 29 G8
Kinsey Heath *Ches* 34 A2
Kinsham *Heref'd* 25 B10
Kinsham *Worcs* 26 E6
Kinsley *W Yorks* 45 A8
Kinson *Bournem'th* 9 E9
Kintbury *W Berks* 17 E10
Kintessack *Moray* 87 E12
Kintillo *Perth/Kinr* 76 F4
Kintocher *Aberds* 83 C7
Kinton *Heref'd* 25 A11
Kinton *Shrops* 33 D9
Kintore *Aberds* 83 B9
Kintour *Arg/Bute* 64 C5
Kintra *Arg/Bute* 78 J6
Kintra *Arg/Bute* 64 D4
Kintraw *Arg/Bute* 73 C7
Kinuachdrachd *Arg/Bute* 72 D6
Kinveachy *H'land* 81 B11
Kinver *Staffs* 34 G4
Kippax *W Yorks* 51 F10
Kippen *Stirl* 68 A5
Kippford or Scaur *Dumf/Gal* 55 D11
Kirbister *Orkney* 95 H4
Kirbister *Orkney* 95 F7
Kirbuster *Orkney* 95 F3
Kirby Bedon *Norfolk* 39 E8
Kirby Bellars *Leics* 36 D3
Kirby Cane *Norfolk* 39 F9
Kirby Cross *Essex* 31 F9
Kirby Grindalythe *N Yorks* 52 C5
Kirby Hill *N Yorks* 51 C9
Kirby Hill *N Yorks* 58 F2
Kirby Knowle *N Yorks* 58 H5
Kirby-le-Soken *Essex* 31 F9
Kirby Misperton *N Yorks* 52 B3
Kirby Muxloe *Leics* 35 E11
Kirby Overblow *N Yorks* 51 E9
Kirby Row *Norfolk* 39 F9
Kirby Sigston *N Yorks* 58 G5
Kirby Underdale *ER Yorks* 52 D4
Kirby Wiske *N Yorks* 51 A9
Kirdford *W Sussex* 11 B9
Kirk *H'land* 94 E4
Kirk Bramwith *S Yorks* 45 A10
Kirk Deighton *N Yorks* 51 D9
Kirk Ella *ER Yorks* 52 G6
Kirk Hallam *Derby* 35 A10
Kirk Hammerton *N Yorks* 51 D10
Kirk Ireton *Derby* 44 G6
Kirk Langley *Derby* 35 B8
Kirk Merrington *Durham* 58 C3
Kirk Michael *I/Man* 48 C3
Kirk of Shotts *N Lanarks* 69 D7
Kirk Sandall *S Yorks* 45 B10
Kirk Smeaton *N Yorks* 51 H11
Kirk Yetholm *Scot Borders* 71 H7
Kirkabister *Shetl'd* 96 K6

Kirkandrews Dumf/Gal 55 E9
Kirkandrews upon Eden Cumb 61 H9
Kirkbampton Cumb 61 H9
Kirkbean Dumf/Gal 60 H5
Kirkbride Cumb 61 H8
Kirkbuddo Angus 77 C8
Kirkburn Scot Borders 69 G11
Kirkburn ER Yorks 52 D5
Kirkburton W Yorks 44 A5
Kirkby Lincs 46 C4
Kirkby Mersey 43 C7
Kirkby N Yorks 59 F6
Kirkby Fleetham N Yorks 58 G3
Kirkby Green Lincs 46 G4
Kirkby In Ashfield Notts 45 G9
Kirkby-in-Furness Cumb 49 A2
Kirkby la Thorpe Lincs 46 H5
Kirkby Lonsdale Cumb 50 B2
Kirkby Malham N Yorks 50 C4
Kirkby Mallory Leics 35 E10
Kirkby Malzeard N Yorks 51 B8
Kirkby Mills N Yorks 59 H8
Kirkby on Bain Lincs 46 F6
Kirkby Stephen Cumb 57 F9
Kirkby Thore Cumb 57 D8
Kirkby Underwood Lincs 37 C6
Kirkby Wharfe N Yorks 51 E11
Kirkbymoorside N Yorks 59 H7
Kirkcaldy Fife 69 A11
Kirkcambeck Cumb 61 G11
Kirkcarswell Dumf/Gal 55 E10
Kirkcolm Dumf/Gal 54 C3
Kirkconnel Dumf/Gal 60 B3
Kirkconnell Dumf/Gal 60 G5
Kirkcowan Dumf/Gal 54 C6
Kirkcudbright Dumf/Gal 55 D9
Kirkdale Mersey 42 C6
Kirkfieldbank S Lanarks 69 F7
Kirkgunzeon Dumf/Gal 55 C11
Kirkham Lancs 49 F4
Kirkham N Yorks 52 C3
Kirkhamgate W Yorks 51 G8
Kirkharle Northum 62 E6
Kirkheaton Northum 62 F6
Kirkheaton W Yorks 51 H7
Kirkhill Angus 77 A9
Kirkhill H'land 87 G8
Kirkhill Midloth 69 D11
Kirkhill Moray 88 E2
Kirkhope Scot Borders 61 A9
Kirkhouse Scot Borders 70 G2
Kirkiboll H'land 93 D8
Kirkibost H'land 85 G10
Kirkinch Angus 76 C6
Kirkinner Dumf/Gal 55 D7
Kirkintilloch E Dunb 68 C5
Kirkland Cumb 56 E2
Kirkland Cumb 57 C8
Kirkland Dumf/Gal 60 D4
Kirkland Dumf/Gal 60 B3
Kirkleatham Redcar/Clevel'd 59 D6
Kirklevington Stockton 58 F5
Kirkley Suffolk 39 F11
Kirklington Notts 45 G10
Kirklington N Yorks 51 A9
Kirklinton Cumb 61 G10
Kirkliston C/Edinb 69 C10
Kirkmaiden Dumf/Gal 54 F4
Kirkmichael Perth/Kinr 76 B3
Kirkmichael S Ayrs 66 F6
Kirkmuirhill S Lanarks 68 F6
Kirknewton Northum 71 G8
Kirknewton W Loth 69 D10
Kirkney Aberds 88 E5
Kirkoswald Cumb 57 B7
Kirkoswald S Ayrs 66 F5
Kirkpatrick Durham Dumf/Gal 60 F3
Kirkpatrick-Fleming Dumf/Gal 61 F8
Kirksanton Cumb 49 A1
Kirkstall W Yorks 51 F8
Kirkstead Lincs 46 F5
Kirkstile Aberds 88 E5
Kirkstyle H'land 94 C5
Kirkton Aberds 83 A8
Kirkton Aberds 89 D6
Kirkton Angus 77 C7
Kirkton Angus 77 D7
Kirkton Scot Borders 61 B11
Kirkton Dumf/Gal 60 E5
Kirkton Fife 76 E6
Kirkton H'land 85 F13
Kirkton H'land 86 G2
Kirkton H'land 87 B10
Kirkton H'land 87 F10
Kirkton Perth/Kinr 76 F2
Kirkton S Lanarks 60 A5
Kirkton Stirl 75 G8
Kirkton Manor Scot Borders 69 G11
Kirkton of Airlie Angus 76 B6
Kirkton of Auchterhouse Angus 76 D6
Kirkton of Auchterless Aberds 89 D7
Kirkton of Barevan H'land 87 G11
Kirkton of Bourtie Aberds 89 F8
Kirkton of Collace Perth/Kinr 76 D4
Kirkton of Craig Angus 77 B10
Kirkton of Culsalmond Aberds 89 E6
Kirkton of Durris Aberds 83 D9
Kirkton of Glenbuchat Aberds 82 B5
Kirkton of Glenisla Angus 76 A5
Kirkton of Kingoldrum Angus 76 B6
Kirkton of Largo Fife 77 G7
Kirkton of Lethendy Perth/Kinr 76 C4
Kirkton of Logie Buchan Aberds 89 F9
Kirkton of Maryculter Aberds 83 D10
Kirkton of Menmuir Angus 77 A8
Kirkton of Monikie Angus 77 D8
Kirkton of Oyne Aberds 83 A8
Kirkton of Rayne Aberds 83 A8
Kirkton of Skene Aberds 83 C10
Kirkton of Tough Aberds 83 B8
Kirktonhill Scot Borders 70 E3
Kirktown Aberds 89 C10
Kirktown of Alvah Aberds 89 B6
Kirktown of Deskford Moray 88 B5
Kirktown of Fetteresso Aberds 83 E10
Kirktown of Mortlach Moray 88 E3
Kirktown of Slains Aberds 89 F10
Kirkurd Scot Borders 69 F10
Kirkwall Orkney 95 G5
Kirkwhelpington Northum 62 E5
Kirmington N Lincs 46 A5
Kirmond le Mire Lincs 46 C5
Kirn Arg/Bute 73 F10
Kirriemuir Angus 76 B6
Kirstead Green Norfolk 39 F8
Kirtlebridge Dumf/Gal 61 F8
Kirtleton Dumf/Gal 61 E8
Kirtling Cambs 30 C3
Kirtling Green Cambs 30 C3
Kirtlington Oxon 27 G11
Kirtomy H'land 93 C10
Kirton Lincs 37 B9
Kirton Notts 45 F10
Kirton Suffolk 31 E9
Kirton End Lincs 37 A8
Kirton Holme Lincs 37 A8
Kirton in Lindsey N Lincs 46 C3
Kislingbury Northants 28 C3
Kites Hardwick Warwick 27 B11
Kittisford Som'set 7 D9
Kittle Swan 23 H10
Kitt's Green W Midlands 35 G7
Kitt's Moss Gtr Man 44 D2
Kittybrewster Aberd C 83 C11
Kitwood Hants 10 A5
Kivernoll Heref'd 25 E11
Kiveton Park S Yorks 45 D8
Knaith Lincs 46 D2
Knaith Park Lincs 46 D2
Knap Corner Dorset 9 B7
Knaphill Surrey 18 F6
Knapp Perth/Kinr 76 D5
Knapp Som'set 8 B2
Knapthorpe Notts 45 G11
Knapton Norfolk 39 B9
Knapton C/York 52 D1
Knapton Green Heref'd 25 C11
Knapwell Cambs 29 B10
Knaresborough N Yorks 51 D9
Knarsdale Northum 57 A8
Knauchland Moray 88 C5
Knaven Aberds 89 D8
Knayton N Yorks 58 H5
Knebworth Herts 29 F9
Knedlington ER Yorks 52 G3
Kneesall Notts 45 F11
Kneesworth Cambs 29 D10
Kneeton Notts 45 H11
Knelston Swan 23 H9
Knenhall Staffs 34 B5
Knettishall Suffolk 38 G5
Knightacott Devon 6 C5
Knightcote Warwick 27 C10
Knightley Dale Staffs 34 C4
Knighton Devon 4 G6
Knighton Leics C 36 E1
Knighton Staffs 34 C3
Knighton Staffs 34 A3
Knighton = Tref-y-Clawdd Powys 25 A9
Knightswood C/Glasg 68 D4
Knightwick Worcs 26 C4
Knill Heref'd 25 B9
Knipton Leics 36 B4
Knitsley Durham 58 B2
Kniveton Derby 44 G6
Knock Arg/Bute 79 H8
Knock Cumb 57 D8
Knock Moray 88 C5
Knockally H'land 94 H3
Knockan H'land 92 H5
Knockandhu Moray 82 A4
Knockando Moray 88 D1
Knockando Ho. Moray 88 D2
Knockbain H'land 87 F9
Knockbreck H'land 84 B7
Knockbrex Dumf/Gal 55 E8
Knockdee H'land 94 D3
Knockdolian S Ayrs 66 H4
Knockenkelly N Ayrs 66 D3
Knockentiber E Ayrs 67 C6
Knockespock Ho. Aberds 83 A7
Knockfarrel H'land 87 F8
Knockglass Dumf/Gal 54 D3
Knockholt Kent 19 F11
Knockholt Pound Kent 19 F11
Knockie Lodge H'land 80 B6
Knockin Shrops 33 C9
Knockinlaw E Ayrs 67 C7
Knocklearn Dumf/Gal 60 F3
Knocknaha Arg/Bute 65 G7
Knocknain Dumf/Gal 54 C2
Knockrome Arg/Bute 72 F4
Knocksharry I/Man 48 D2
Knodishall Suffolk 31 B11
Knolls Green Ches 44 E2
Knolton Wrex 33 B9
Knolton Bryn Wrex 33 B9
Knook Wilts 16 G6
Knossington Leics 36 E4
Knott End-on-Sea Lancs 49 E3
Knotting Beds 29 B7
Knotting Green Beds 29 B7
Knottingley W Yorks 51 G11
Knotts Cumb 56 D6
Knotts Lancs 50 D3
Knotty Ash Mersey 43 C7
Knotty Green Bucks 18 B6
Knowbury Shrops 26 A2
Knowe Dumf/Gal 54 B6
Knowehead Dumf/Gal 67 G9
Knowes of Elrick Aberds 88 C6
Knowesgate Northum 62 E5
Knoweton N Lanarks 68 E6
Knowhead Aberds 89 C9
Knowl Hill Windsor 18 D5
Knowle Bristol 16 D3
Knowle Devon 7 F6
Knowle Devon 7 H9
Knowle Devon 6 C3
Knowle Shrops 26 A2
Knowle W Midlands 35 H7
Knowle Green Lancs 50 F2
Knowle Park W Yorks 51 E6
Knowlton Dorset 9 C9
Knowlton Kent 21 F9
Knowsley Mersey 43 C7
Knowstone Devon 7 D7
Knox Bridge Kent 13 B6
Knucklas Powys 25 A9
Knuston Northants 28 B6
Knutsford Ches 43 E10
Knutton Staffs 44 H2
Knypersley Staffs 44 G2
Kuggar Cornw'l 2 H6
Kyle of Lochalsh H'land 85 F12
Kyleakin H'land 85 F12
Kylerhea H'land 85 F12
Kylesknoydart H'land 79 B11
Kylesku H'land 92 F5
Kylesmorar H'land 79 B11
Kylestrome H'land 92 F5
Kyllachy House H'land 81 A9
Kynaston Shrops 33 C9
Kynnersley Telford 34 D2
Kyre Magna Worcs 26 B3

L

La Fontenelle Guernsey 11
La Planque Guernsey 11
Labost W Isles 91 C7
Lacasaidh W Isles 91 E8
Lacasdal W Isles 91 D9
Laceby NE Lincs 46 B6
Lacey Green Bucks 18 B5
Lach Dennis Ches 43 E10
Lackford Suffolk 30 A4
Lacock Wilts 16 E6
Ladbroke Warwick 27 C11
Laddingford Kent 20 G3
Lade Bank Lincs 47 G7
Ladock Cornw'l 3 D7
Lady Orkney 95 D7
Ladybank Fife 76 F6
Ladykirk Scot Borders 71 F7
Ladysford Aberds 89 B9
Laga H'land 79 E9
Lagalochan Arg/Bute 73 B7
Lagavulin Arg/Bute 64 D5
Lagg Arg/Bute 72 F4
Lagg N Ayrs 66 D2
Laggan Arg/Bute 64 C3
Laggan H'land 80 D4
Laggan H'land 81 D8
Laggan H'land 79 D10
Laggan S Ayrs 54 A5
Lagganulva Arg/Bute 78 G7
Laide H'land 91 H13
Laigh Fenwick E Ayrs 67 B7
Laigh Glengall S Ayrs 66 E6
Laighmuir E Ayrs 67 B7
Laindon Essex 20 C3
Lair H'land 86 G3
Lairg H'land 93 J8
Lairg Lodge H'land 93 J8
Lairg Muir H'land 93 J8
Lairgmore H'land 87 H8
Laisterdyke W Yorks 51 F7
Laithes Cumb 56 C6
Lake I/Wight 10 F4
Lake Wilts 17 H8
Lakenham Norfolk 39 E8
Lakenheath Suffolk 38 G3
Lakesend Norfolk 37 F11
Lakeside Cumb 56 H5
Laleham Surrey 19 E7
Laleston Bridg 14 D4
Lamarsh Essex 30 E5
Lamas Norfolk 39 C8
Lambden Scot Borders 70 F6
Lamberhurst Kent 12 C5
Lamberhurst Quarter Kent 12 C5
Lamberton Scot Borders 71 E8
Lambeth London 19 D10
Lambhill C/Glasg 68 D4
Lambley Notts 45 H10
Lambley Northum 62 H2
Lamborough Hill Oxon 17 A11
Lambourn W Berks 17 D10
Lambourne End Essex 19 B11
Lambs Green W Sussex 19 H9
Lambston Pembs 22 E4
Lambton Tyne/Wear 58 A3
Lamerton Devon 4 D5
Lamesley Tyne/Wear 63 H8
Laminess Orkney 95 E7
Lamington H'land 87 D10
Lamington S Lanarks 69 G8
Lamlash N Ayrs 66 C3
Lamloch Dumf/Gal 67 G8
Lamonby Cumb 56 C6
Lamorna Cornw'l 2 G3
Lamorran Cornw'l 3 E7
Lampardbrook Suffolk 31 B9
Lampeter = Llanbedr Pont Steffan Ceredig'n 23 B10
Lampeter Velfrey Pembs 22 E6
Lamphey Pembs 22 F5
Lamplugh Cumb 56 D2
Lamport Northants 28 A4
Lamyatt Som'set 16 H3
Lana Devon 6 G2
Lanark S Lanarks 69 F7
Lancaster Lancs 49 C4
Lanchester Durham 58 B2
Lancing W Sussex 11 D10
Landbeach Cambs 29 B11
Landcross Devon 6 D3
Landerberry Aberds 83 C9
Landford Wilts 10 C1
Landford Manor Wilts 10 B1
Landimore Swan 23 G9
Landkey Devon 6 C4
Landore Swan 14 B2
Landrake Cornw'l 4 E4
Landscove Devon 5 E8
Landshipping Pembs 22 E5
Landshipping Quay Pembs 22 E5
Landulph Cornw'l 4 E5
Landwade Suffolk 30 B3
Lane Cornw'l 3 C7
Lane End Bucks 18 B5
Lane End Cumb 56 G3
Lane End Dorset 9 E7
Lane End Hants 10 B4
Lane End I/Wight 10 F5
Lane End Lancs 50 E4
Lane Ends Lancs 50 F3
Lane Ends Lancs 50 D3
Lane Ends N Yorks 50 E5
Lane Head Derby 44 E5
Lane Head Durham 58 E2
Lane Head Gtr Man 43 C9
Lane Head W Yorks 44 B5
Lane Side Lancs 50 G3
Laneast Cornw'l 4 C3
Laneham Notts 46 E2
Lanehead Durham 57 B10
Lanehead Northum 62 E3
Lanercost Cumb 61 G11
Laneshaw Bridge Lancs 50 E5
Lanfach Caerph 15 B8
Langar Notts 36 B3
Langbank Renf 68 C2
Langbar N Yorks 51 D6
Langburnshiels Scot Borders 61 C11
Langcliffe N Yorks 50 C4
Langdale H'land 93 E9
Langdale End N Yorks 59 G10
Langdon Cornw'l 4 C4
Langdon Beck Durham 57 C10
Langdon Hills Essex 20 C3
Langdyke Fife 76 G6
Langenhoe Essex 31 G7
Langford Beds 29 D8
Langford Devon 7 F9
Langford Essex 30 H5
Langford Notts 46 G2
Langford Oxon 17 A9
Langford Budville Som'set 7 D10
Langham Essex 31 E7
Langham Norfolk 38 A6
Langham Rutl'd 36 D4
Langham Suffolk 30 B6
Langhaugh Scot Borders 69 G11
Langho Lancs 50 F3
Langholm Dumf/Gal 61 E9
Langleeford Northum 62 A5
Langley Ches 44 E3
Langley Hants 10 D3
Langley Herts 29 F9
Langley Kent 20 F5
Langley Northum 62 G4
Langley Slough 19 D7
Langley Warwick 27 B8
Langley W Sussex 11 B7
Langley Burrell Wilts 16 D6
Langley Common Derby 35 B8
Langley Heath Kent 20 F5
Langley Lower Green Essex 29 E11
Langley Marsh Som'set 7 D9
Langley Park Durham 58 B3
Langley Street Norfolk 39 E9
Langley Upper Green Essex 29 E11
Langney E Sussex 12 F5
Langold Notts 45 D9
Langore Cornw'l 4 C4
Langport Som'set 8 B3
Langrick Lincs 46 H6
Langridge Bath/NE Som'set 16 E4
Langridge Ford Devon 6 D4
Langrigg Cumb 56 B3
Langrish Hants 10 B6
Langsett S Yorks 44 B6
Langshaw Scot Borders 70 G4
Langside Perth/Kinr 75 F10
Langskaill Orkney 95 D5
Langstone Hants 10 D6
Langstone Newp 15 B9
Langthorne N Yorks 58 G3
Langthorpe N Yorks 51 C9
Langthwaite N Yorks 58 F1
Langtoft ER Yorks 52 C6
Langtoft Lincs 37 D7
Langton Durham 58 E2
Langton Lincs 46 F6
Langton Lincs 47 E7
Langton N Yorks 52 C3
Langton by Wragby Lincs 46 E5
Langton Green Kent 12 C4
Langton Green Suffolk 31 A8
Langton Herring Dorset 8 F5
Langton Matravers Dorset 9 G9
Langtree Devon 6 E3
Langwathby Cumb 57 C7
Langwell Ho. H'land 94 H3
Langwell Lodge H'land 92 J4
Langwith Derby 45 F9
Langwith Junction Derby 45 F9
Langworth Lincs 46 E4
Lanivet Cornw'l 3 C9
Lanlivery Cornw'l 4 F1
Lanner Cornw'l 2 F6
Lanreath Cornw'l 4 F2
Lansallos Cornw'l 4 F2
Lansdown Glos 26 F6
Lanteglos Highway Cornw'l 4 F2
Lanton Scot Borders 62 A2
Lanton Northum 71 G8
Lapford Devon 7 F6
Laphroaig Arg/Bute 64 D4
Lapley Staffs 34 D4
Lapworth Warwick 27 A8
Larachbeg H'land 79 G9
Larbert Falk 69 B7
Larden Green Ches 43 G8
Largie Aberds 88 E6
Largiemore Arg/Bute 73 E8
Largoward Fife 77 G7
Largs N Ayrs 73 H11
Largybeg N Ayrs 66 D3
Largymore N Ayrs 66 D3
Larkfield Inverc'l 73 F11
Larkhall S Lanarks 68 E6
Larkhill Wilts 17 G8
Larling Norfolk 38 G5
Larriston Scot Borders 61 D11
Lartington Durham 58 E1
Lary Aberds 82 C5
Lasham Hants 18 G3
Lashenden Kent 13 B7
Lassington Glos 26 F4
Lassodie Fife 69 A10
Lastingham N Yorks 59 G8
Latcham Som'set 15 G10
Latchford Herts 29 F10
Latchford Warrington 43 D9
Latchingdon Essex 20 A5
Latchley Cornw'l 4 D5
Lately Common Warrington 43 C9
Lathbury M/Keynes 28 D5
Latheron H'land 94 G3
Latheronwheel H'land 94 G3
Latheronwheel Ho. H'land 94 G3
Lathones Fife 77 G7
Latimer Bucks 19 B7
Latteridge S Gloucs 16 C3
Lattiford Som'set 8 B5
Latton Wilts 17 B7
Latton Bush Essex 29 H11
Lauchintilly Aberds 83 B9
Lauder Scot Borders 70 F4
Laugharne Carms 23 E8
Laughterton Lincs 46 E2
Laughton E Sussex 12 E4
Laughton Leics 36 G2
Laughton Lincs 37 B6
Laughton Lincs 46 C2
Laughton Common S Yorks 45 D9
Laughton en le Morthen S Yorks 45 D9
Launcells Cornw'l 6 F1
Launceston Cornw'l 4 C4
Launton Oxon 28 F3
Laurencekirk Aberds 83 F9
Laurieston Dumf/Gal 55 C9
Laurieston Falk 69 C8
Lavendon M/Keynes 28 C6
Lavenham Suffolk 30 D6
Laverhay Dumf/Gal 61 D7
Laversdale Cumb 61 G10
Laverstock Wilts 9 A10
Laverstoke Hants 17 G11
Laverton Glos 27 E7
Laverton N Yorks 51 B8
Laverton Som'set 16 F4
Lavister Wrex 42 G6
Law S Lanarks 69 E7
Lawers Perth/Kinr 75 D9
Lawers Perth/Kinr 75 E10
Lawford Essex 31 E7
Lawhitton Cornw'l 4 C4
Lawkland N Yorks 50 C3
Lawley Telford 34 E2
Lawnhead Staffs 34 C4
Lawrenny Pembs 22 F5
Lawshall Suffolk 30 C5
Lawton Heref'd 25 C11
Laxey I/Man 48 D4
Laxfield Suffolk 31 A9
Laxfirth Shetl'd 96 J6
Laxfirth Shetl'd 96 H6
Laxford Bridge H'land 92 E5
Laxo Shetl'd 96 G6
Laxobigging Shetl'd 96 F6
Laxton ER Yorks 52 G3
Laxton Northants 36 F5
Laxton Notts 45 F11
Laycock W Yorks 50 E6
Layer Breton Essex 30 G6
Layer de la Haye Essex 30 G6
Layer Marney Essex 30 G6
Layham Suffolk 31 D7
Laylands Green W Berks 17 E10
Laytham ER Yorks 52 F3
Layton Blackp'l 49 F3
Lazenby Redcar/Clevel'd 59 D6
Lazonby Cumb 57 C7
Le Planel Guernsey 11
Le Villocq Guernsey 11
Lea Derby 45 G7
Lea Heref'd 26 F3
Lea Lincs 46 D2
Lea Shrops 33 G9
Lea Shrops 33 E10
Lea Wilts 16 C6
Lea Marston Warwick 35 F8
Lea Town Lancs 49 F4
Leabrooks Derby 45 G8
Leac a Li W Isles 90 H6
Leachkin H'land 87 G9
Leadburn Midloth 69 E11
Leaden Roding Essex 30 G2
Leadenham Lincs 46 G3
Leadgate Cumb 57 B9
Leadgate Durham 58 A2
Leadgate Northum 63 H7
Leadhills S Lanarks 60 B4
Leafield Oxon 27 G10
Leagrave Luton 29 F7
Leake N Yorks 58 G5
Leake Commonside Lincs 47 G7
Lealholm N Yorks 59 F8
Lealt Arg/Bute 72 D5
Lealt H'land 85 B10
Leamington Hastings Warwick 27 B11
Leamonsley Staffs 35 E7
Leamside Durham 58 B4
Leanaig H'land 87 F8
Leargybreck Arg/Bute 72 F4
Leasgill Cumb 49 A4
Leasingham Lincs 46 H4
Leasingthorne Durham 58 D3
Leasowe Mersey 42 C5
Leatherhead Surrey 19 F8
Leatherhead Common Surrey 19 F8
Leathley N Yorks 51 E8
Leaton Shrops 33 D10
Leaveland Kent 21 F7
Leavening N Yorks 52 C3
Leaves Green London 19 E11
Leazes Durham 63 H7
Lebberston N Yorks 53 A6
Lechlade-on-Thames Glos 17 B9
Leck Lancs 50 B2
Leckford Hants 17 H10
Leckfurin H'land 93 D10
Leckgruinart Arg/Bute 64 B3
Leckhampstead Bucks 28 E4
Leckhampstead W Berks 17 D11
Leckhampstead Thicket W Berks 17 D11
Leckhampton Glos 26 G6
Leckie H'land 86 E3
Leckmelm H'land 86 B4
Leckwith V/Glam 15 D7
Leconfield ER Yorks 52 E6
Ledaig Arg/Bute 74 D2
Ledburn Bucks 28 F6
Ledbury Heref'd 26 E4
Ledcharrie Stirl 75 E8
Ledgemoor Heref'd 25 C11
Ledicot Heref'd 25 B11
Ledmore H'land 92 H5
Lednagullin H'land 93 C10
Ledsham Ches 42 E6
Ledsham W Yorks 51 G10
Ledston W Yorks 51 G10
Ledston Luck W Yorks 51 F10
Ledwell Oxon 27 F11
Lee Arg/Bute 78 J7
Lee Devon 6 B3
Lee Hants 10 C2
Lee Lancs 50 D1
Lee Shrops 33 B10
Lee Brockhurst Shrops 33 C11
Lee Clump Bucks 18 A6
Lee Mill Devon 5 F7
Lee Moor Devon 5 E6
Lee-on-the-Solent Hants 10 D4
Leeans Shetl'd 96 J5
Leebotten Shetl'd 96 L6
Leebotwood Shrops 33 F10
Leece Cumb 49 C2
Leechpool Pembs 22 E4
Leeds Kent 20 F5
Leeds W Yorks 51 F8
Leedstown Cornw'l 2 F5
Leek Staffs 44 G3
Leek Wootton Warwick 27 B9
Leekbrook Staffs 44 G3
Leeming N Yorks 58 H3
Leeming Bar N Yorks 58 G3
Lees Derby 35 B8
Lees Gtr Man 44 B3
Lees W Yorks 50 F6
Leeswood Flints 42 F5
Legbourne Lincs 47 D7
Legerwood Scot Borders 70 F4
Legsby Lincs 46 D5
Leicester Leics C 36 E1
Leicester Forest East Leics 35 E11
Leigh Dorset 8 D5
Leigh Glos 26 F5
Leigh Gtr Man 43 B9
Leigh Kent 20 G2
Leigh Shrops 33 E9
Leigh Surrey 19 G9
Leigh Wilts 17 B7
Leigh Worcs 26 C4
Leigh Beck Essex 20 C5
Leigh Common Som'set 8 B6
Leigh Delamere Wilts 16 D5
Leigh Green Kent 13 C8
Leigh on Sea Southend 20 C5
Leigh Park Hants 10 D6
Leigh Sinton Worcs 26 C4
Leigh upon Mendip Som'set 16 G3
Leigh Woods N Som'set 16 D2
Leighswood W Midlands 35 E6
Leighterton Glos 16 B5
Leighton N Yorks 51 B7
Leighton Powys 33 E8
Leighton Shrops 34 E2
Leighton Som'set 16 G4
Leighton Bromswold Cambs 37 H7
Leighton Buzzard Beds 28 F6
Leinthall Earls Heref'd 25 B11
Leinthall Starkes Heref'd 25 B11
Leintwardine Heref'd 25 A11
Leire Leics 35 F11
Leirinmore H'land 92 C7
Leiston Suffolk 31 B11
Leitfie Perth/Kinr 76 C5
Leith C/Edinb 69 C11
Leitholm Scot Borders 70 F6
Lelant Cornw'l 2 F4
Lelley ER Yorks 53 F8
Lem Hill Worcs 26 A4
Lemmington Hall Northum 63 B7
Lempitlaw Scot Borders 70 G6
Lenchwick Worcs 27 D7
Lendalfoot S Ayrs 66 H4
Lendrick Lodge Stirl 75 G8
Lenham Kent 20 F5
Lenham Heath Kent 20 G6
Lennel Scot Borders 71 F7
Lennoxtown E Dunb 68 C5
Lenton Lincs 36 B6
Lenton Nott'ham 36 B1
Lentran H'land 87 G8
Lenwade Norfolk 39 D6
Leny Ho. Stirl 75 G9
Lenzie E Dunb 68 C5
Leoch Angus 76 D6
Leochel-Cushnie Aberds 83 B7
Leominster Heref'd 25 C11
Leonard Stanley Glos 16 A5
Leorin Arg/Bute 64 D4
Lepe Hants 10 E3
Lephin H'land 84 D6
Lephinchapel Arg/Bute 73 D8
Lephinmore Arg/Bute 73 D8
Leppington N Yorks 52 C3
Lepton W Yorks 51 H8
Lerryn Cornw'l 4 F2
Lerwick Shetl'd 96 J6
Lesbury Northum 63 B8
Leslie Aberds 83 A7
Leslie Fife 76 G5
Lesmahagow S Lanarks 69 G7
Lesnewth Cornw'l 4 B2
Lessendrum Aberds 88 D5
Lessingham Norfolk 39 C9
Lessonhall Cumb 56 A4
Leswalt Dumf/Gal 54 C3
Letchmore Heath Herts 19 B8
Letchworth Herts 29 E9
Letcombe Bassett Oxon 17 C10
Letcombe Regis Oxon 17 C10
Letham Angus 77 C8
Letham Falk 69 B7
Letham Fife 76 F6
Letham Perth/Kinr 76 E3
Letham Grange Angus 77 C9
Lethenty Aberds 89 D8
Letheringham Suffolk 31 C9
Letheringsett Norfolk 39 B6
Lettaford Devon 5 C8
Lettan Orkney 95 D8
Letterewe H'land 86 D2
Letterfearn H'land 85 F13
Letterfinlay H'land 80 D4
Lettermorar H'land 79 C10
Lettermore Arg/Bute 78 G7
Letters H'land 86 C4
Letterston Pembs 22 D4
Lettoch H'land 82 A2
Lettoch H'land 87 H13
Letton Heref'd 25 D10
Letton Heref'd 25 A10
Letton Green Norfolk 38 E5
Letty Green Herts 29 G9
Letwell S Yorks 45 D9
Leuchars Fife 77 E7
Leuchars Ho. Moray 88 B2
Leumrabhagh W Isles 91 F8
Levan Inverc'l 73 F11
Levaneap Shetl'd 96 G6
Levedale Staffs 34 D4
Leven ER Yorks 53 E7
Leven Fife 76 G6
Levencorroch N Ayrs 66 D3
Levens Cumb 57 H6
Levens Green Herts 29 F10
Levenshulme Gtr Man 44 C2
Levenwick Shetl'd 96 L6
Leverburgh = An t-Ob W Isles 90 J5
Leverington Cambs 37 D10
Leverton Lincs 47 H8
Leverton Highgate Lincs 47 H8
Leverton Lucasgate Lincs 47 H8
Leverton Outgate Lincs 47 H8
Levington Suffolk 31 E9
Levisham N Yorks 59 G9
Levishie H'land 80 B6
Lew Oxon 27 H10
Lewannick Cornw'l 4 C3
Lewdown Devon 4 C5
Lewes E Sussex 12 E3
Leweston Pembs 22 D4
Lewisham London 19 D10
Lewiston H'land 81 A7
Lewistown Bridg 14 C5
Lewknor Oxon 18 B4
Leworthy Devon 6 F2
Leworthy Devon 6 C5
Lewtrenchard Devon 4 C5
Lexden Essex 30 F6
Ley Aberds 83 B7
Ley Cornw'l 4 E2
Leybourne Kent 20 F3
Leyfields Staffs 35 E8
Leyhill Bucks 18 A6
Leyland Lancs 50 G1
Leylodge Aberds 83 B9
Leymoor W Yorks 51 H7
Leys Aberds 89 C10
Leys Perth/Kinr 76 D5
Leys Castle H'land 87 G9
Leys of Cossans Angus 76 C6
Leysdown-on-Sea Kent 21 D7
Leysmill Angus 77 C9
Leysters Pole Heref'd 26 B2
Leyton London 19 C10
Leytonstone London 19 C10
Lezant Cornw'l 4 D4
Leziate Norfolk 38 D2
Lhanbryde Moray 88 B2
Liatrie H'land 86 H5
Libanus Powys 24 F6
Libberton S Lanarks 69 F8
Liberton C/Edinb 69 D11
Liceasto W Isles 90 H6
Lichfield Staffs 35 E7
Lickey Worcs 34 H5
Lickey End Worcs 26 A6
Lickfold W Sussex 11 B8
Liddel Orkney 95 K5
Liddesdale H'land 79 F10
Liddington Swindon 17 C9
Lidgate Suffolk 30 C4
Lidget S Yorks 45 B10
Lidget Green W Yorks 51 F7
Lidgett Notts 45 F10
Lidlington Beds 28 E6
Lidstone Oxon 27 F10
Lieurary H'land 94 D2
Liff Angus 76 D6
Lifton Devon 4 C4
Liftondown Devon 4 C4
Lighthorne Warwick 27 C10
Lightwater Surrey 18 E6
Lightwood Stoke 34 A5
Lightwood Green Ches 34 A2
Lightwood Green Wrex 33 A9
Lilbourne Northants 36 H1
Lilburn Tower Northum 62 A6
Lilleshall Telford 34 D3
Lilley Herts 29 F8
Lilley W Berks 17 D11
Lilliesleaf Scot Borders 61 A11
Lillingstone Dayrell Bucks 28 E4
Lillingstone Lovell Bucks 28 D4
Lillington Dorset 8 C5
Lillington Warwick 27 B10
Lilliput Poole 9 E9
Lilstock Som'set 7 B10
Lilyhurst Shrops 34 D3
Limbury Luton 29 F7
Limebrook Heref'd 25 B10
Limefield Gtr Man 44 A2
Limekilnburn S Lanarks 68 E6
Limekilns Fife 69 B9
Limerigg Falk 69 C7
Limerstone I/Wight 10 F3
Limington Som'set 8 B4
Limpenhoe Norfolk 39 E9
Limpley Stoke Wilts 16 E4
Limpsfield Surrey 19 F11
Limpsfield Chart Surrey 19 F11
Linby Notts 45 G9
Linchmere W Sussex 11 A7
Lincluden Dumf/Gal 60 F5
Lincoln Lincs 46 E3
Lincomb Worcs 26 B5
Lincombe Devon 5 F8
Lindal in Furness Cumb 49 B2
Lindale Cumb 49 A4
Lindean Scot Borders 70 G3
Lindfield W Sussex 12 D2
Lindford Hants 18 H5
Lindifferon Fife 76 F6
Lindley W Yorks 51 H7
Lindley Green N Yorks 51 E8
Lindores Fife 76 F5
Lindridge Worcs 26 B3
Lindsell Essex 30 F3
Lindsey Suffolk 30 D6
Linford Hants 9 D10
Linford Thurr'k 20 D3
Lingague I/Man 48 E2
Lingards Wood W Yorks 44 A4
Lingbob W Yorks 51 F6
Lingdale Redcar/Clevel'd 59 E7
Lingen Heref'd 25 B10
Lingfield Surrey 12 B2
Lingreabhagh W Isles 90 J5
Lingwood Norfolk 39 E9
Linicro H'land 85 B8
Linkenholt Hants 17 F10
Linkhill Kent 13 D7
Linkinhorne Cornw'l 4 D4
Linklater Orkney 95 K5
Linksness Orkney 95 H3
Linktown Fife 69 A11
Linley Shrops 33 F9
Linley Green Heref'd 26 C3
Linlithgow W Loth 69 C9
Linlithgow Bridge W Loth 69 C8
Linshiels Northum 62 C4
Linsiadar W Isles 90 D7
Linsidemore H'land 87 B8
Linslade Beds 28 F6
Linstead Parva Suffolk 39 H9
Linstock Cumb 61 H10
Linthwaite W Yorks 44 A5
Lintlaw Scot Borders 71 E7
Lintmill Moray 88 B5
Linton Scot Borders 70 H6
Linton Cambs 30 D2
Linton Derby 35 D8
Linton Heref'd 26 F3
Linton Kent 20 G4
Linton Northum 63 D8
Linton N Yorks 50 C5
Linton W Yorks 51 E9
Linton-on-Ouse N Yorks 51 C10
Linwood Hants 9 D10
Linwood Lincs 46 D5
Linwood Renf 68 D3
Lionacleit W Isles 84 D2
Lional W Isles 91 A10
Liphook Hants 11 A7
Liscard Mersey 42 C6
Liscombe Som'set 7 C7
Liskeard Cornw'l 4 E3
L'Islet Guernsey 11
Liss Hants 11 B6
Liss Forest Hants 11 B6
Lissett ER Yorks 53 D7
Lissington Lincs 46 D5
Lisvane Card 15 C7
Liswerry Newp 15 C9
Litcham Norfolk 38 D4
Litchborough Northants 28 C3
Litchfield Hants 17 F11
Litherland Mersey 42 C6
Litlington Cambs 29 D10
Litlington E Sussex 12 F4
Little Abington Cambs 30 D2
Little Addington Northants 28 A6
Little Alne Warwick 27 B8
Little Altcar Mersey 42 B6
Little Asby Cumb 57 F8
Little Assynt H'land 92 G4
Little Aston Staffs 35 E6
Little Atherfield I/Wight 10 G3
Little Ayre Orkney 95 J4
Little-ayre Shetl'd 96 G5
Little Ayton N Yorks 59 E6
Little Baddow Essex 30 H4
Little Badminton S Gloucs 16 C5
Little Ballinluig Perth/Kinr 76 B2
Little Bampton Cumb 61 H8
Little Bardfield Essex 30 E3
Little Barford Beds 29 C8
Little Barningham Norfolk 39 B7
Little Barrington Glos 27 G9
Little Barrow Ches 43 E7
Little Barugh N Yorks 52 B3
Little Bavington Northum 62 F5
Little Bealings Suffolk 31 D9
Little Bedwyn Wilts 17 E9
Little Bentley Essex 31 F8
Little Berkhamsted Herts 29 H9
Little Billing Northants 28 B5
Little Birch Heref'd 26 E2
Little Blakenham Suffolk 31 D8
Little Blencow Cumb 56 C6
Little Bollington Ches 43 D10
Little Bookham Surrey 19 F8
Little Bowden Leics 36 G3
Little Bradley Suffolk 30 C3
Little Brampton Shrops 33 G9
Little Brechin Angus 77 A8
Little Brickhill M/Keynes 28 E6
Little Brington Northants 28 B3
Little Bromley Essex 31 F7
Little Broughton Cumb 56 C2
Little Budworth Ches 43 F8
Little Burstead Essex 20 B3
Little Bytham Lincs 36 D6
Little Carlton Lincs 47 D7
Little Carlton Notts 45 G11
Little Casterton Rutl'd 36 E6
Little Cawthorpe Lincs 47 D7
Little Chalfont Bucks 18 B6
Little Chart Kent 20 G6
Little Chesterford Essex 30 D2
Little Cheverell Wilts 16 F6
Little Chishill Cambs 29 E11
Little Clacton Essex 31 G8
Little Clifton Cumb 56 D2
Little Colp Aberds 89 D7
Little Comberton Worcs 26 D6
Little Common E Sussex 12 F6
Little Compton Warwick 27 E9
Little Cornard Suffolk 30 E5
Little Cowarne Heref'd 26 C3
Little Coxwell Oxon 17 B9
Little Crakehall N Yorks 58 G3
Little Cressingham Norfolk 38 E4
Little Crosby Mersey 42 B6
Little Dalby Leics 36 D3
Little Dawley Telford 34 E2
Little Dens Aberds 89 D10
Little Dewchurch Heref'd 26 E2
Little Downham Cambs 37 G11
Little Driffield ER Yorks 52 D6
Little Dunham Norfolk 38 D4
Little Dunkeld Perth/Kinr 76 C3
Little Dunmow Essex 30 F3
Little Easton Essex 30 F3
Little Eaton Derby 35 A9
Little Eccleston Lancs 49 E4
Little Ellingham Norfolk 38 F6
Little End Essex 20 A2
Little Eversden Cambs 29 C10
Little Fakenham Suffolk 38 H5
Little Faringdon Oxon 17 A9
Little Fencote N Yorks 58 G3
Little Fenton N Yorks 51 F11
Little Finborough Suffolk 31 C7
Little Fransham Norfolk 38 D5
Little Gaddesden Herts 28 G6
Little Gidding Cambs 37 G7
Little Glemham Suffolk 31 C10
Little Glenshee Perth/Kinr 76 D2
Little Gransden Cambs 29 C9
Little Green Som'set 16 G4
Little Grimsby Lincs 47 C7
Little Gruinard H'land 86 C2
Little Habton N Yorks 52 B3
Little Hadham Herts 29 F11
Little Hale Lincs 37 A7
Little Hallingbury Essex 29 G11
Little Hampden Bucks 18 A5
Little Harrowden Northants 28 A5
Little Haseley Oxon 18 A3
Little Hatfield ER Yorks 53 E7
Little Hautbois Norfolk 39 C8
Little Haven Pembs 22 E3
Little Hay Staffs 35 E7
Little Hayfield Derby 44 D4
Little Haywood Staffs 34 C6
Little Heath W Midlands 35 G9
Little Hereford Heref'd 26 B2
Little Horkesley Essex 30 E6
Little Horsted E Sussex 12 E3
Little Horton W Yorks 51 F7
Little Horwood Bucks 28 E4
Little Houghton Northants 28 C5
Little Houghton S Yorks 45 B8
Little Hucklow Derby 44 E5
Little Hulton Gtr Man 43 B10
Little Humber ER Yorks 53 G7
Little Hungerford W Berks 18 D2
Little Irchester Northants 28 B6
Little Kimble Bucks 28 H5
Little Kineton Warwick 27 C10
Little Kingshill Bucks 18 B5
Little Langdale Cumb 56 F5
Little Langford Wilts 17 H7
Little Laver Essex 30 H2
Little Leigh Ches 43 E9
Little Leighs Essex 30 G4
Little Lever Gtr Man 43 B10
Little London Bucks 28 G3
Little London E Sussex 12 E4
Little London Hants 17 G10
Little London Hants 18 F3
Little London Lincs 37 C8
Little London Lincs 37 C10
Little London Norfolk 39 C7
Little London Powys 32 G6
Little Longstone Derby 44 E5
Little Lynturk Aberds 83 B7
Little Malvern Worcs 26 D4
Little Maplestead Essex 30 E5
Little Marcle Heref'd 26 E3
Little Marlow Bucks 18 C5
Little Marsden Lancs 50 F4
Little Massingham Norfolk 38 C3
Little Melton Norfolk 39 E7
Little Mill Monmouths 15 A9
Little Milton Oxon 18 A3
Little Missenden Bucks 18 B6
Little Musgrave Cumb 57 E9
Little Ness Shrops 33 D10
Little Neston Ches 42 E5
Little Newcastle Pembs 22 D4
Little Newsham Durham 58 E2
Little Oakley Essex 31 F9
Little Oakley Northants 36 G4
Little Orton Cumb 61 H9
Little Ouseburn N Yorks 51 C10
Little Paxton Cambs 29 B8
Little Petherick Cornw'l 3 B8
Little Pitlurg Moray 88 D4
Little Plumpton Lancs 49 F3
Little Plumstead Norfolk 39 D9
Little Ponton Lincs 36 B5
Little Raveley Cambs 37 H8
Little Reedness ER Yorks 52 G4
Little Ribston N Yorks 51 D9
Little Rissington Glos 27 G8
Little Ryburgh Norfolk 38 C5
Little Ryle Northum 62 B6
Little Salkeld Cumb 57 C7
Little Sampford Essex 30 E3
Little Sandhurst Brackn'l 18 E5
Little Saxham Suffolk 30 B4
Little Scatwell H'land 86 F6
Little Sessay N Yorks 51 B10
Little Shelford Cambs 29 C11
Little Singleton Lancs 49 F3
Little Skillymarno Aberds 89 C9
Little Snoring Norfolk 38 B5
Little Sodbury S Gloucs 16 C4
Little Somborne Hants 10 A2
Little Somerford Wilts 16 C6
Little Stainforth N Yorks 50 C4
Little Stainton D'lington 58 E4
Little Stanney Ches 43 E7
Little Staughton Beds 29 B8
Little Steeping Lincs 47 F8
Little Stoke Staffs 34 B5
Little Stonham Suffolk 31 B8
Little Stretton Leics 36 E2
Little Stretton Shrops 33 F10
Little Strickland Cumb 57 E7
Little Stukeley Cambs 37 H8
Little Sutton Ches 42 E6
Little Tew Oxon 27 F10
Little Thetford Cambs 37 H11
Little Thirkleby N Yorks 51 B10
Little Thurlow Suffolk 30 C3
Little Thurrock Thurr'k 20 D3
Little Torboll H'land 87 B10
Little Torrington Devon 6 E3

Little Totham *Essex* 30 G5
Little Toux *Aberds* 88 C5
Little Town *Cumb* 56 E4
Little Town *Lancs* 50 F2
Little Urswick *Cumb* 49 B2
Little Wakering *Essex* 20 C6
Little Walden *Essex* 30 D2
Little Waldingfield *Suffolk* 30 D6
Little Walsingham *Norfolk* 38 B5
Little Waltham *Essex* 30 G4
Little Warley *Essex* 20 B3
Little Weighton *ER Yorks* 52 F5
Little Weldon *Northants* 36 G5
Little Welnetham *Suffolk* 30 B5
Little Wenlock *Telford* 34 E2
Little Whittingham Green *Suffolk* 39 H8
Little Wilbraham *Cambs* 30 C2
Little Wishford *Wilts* 17 H7
Little Witley *Worcs* 26 B4
Little Wittenham *Oxon* 18 B2
Little Wolford *Warwick* 27 E9
Little Wratting *Suffolk* 30 D3
Little Wymington *Beds* 28 B6
Little Wymondley *Herts* 29 F9
Little Wyrley *Staffs* 34 E6
Little Yeldham *Essex* 30 E4
Littlebeck *N Yorks* 59 F9
Littleborough *Gtr Man* 50 H5
Littleborough *Notts* 46 D2
Littlebourne *Kent* 21 F9
Littlebredy *Dorset* 8 F4
Littlebury *Essex* 30 E2
Littlebury Green *Essex* 29 E11
Littledean *Glos* 26 G3
Littleferry *H'land* 87 B11
Littleham *Devon* 5 C11
Littleham *Devon* 6 D3
Littlehampton *W Sussex* 11 D9
Littlehempston *Devon* 5 E9
Littlehoughton *Northum* 63 B8
Littlemill *Aberds* 82 D5
Littlemill *E Ayrs* 67 E7
Littlemill *H'land* 87 F12
Littlemill *Northum* 63 B8
Littlemoor *Dorset* 8 F5
Littlemore *Oxon* 18 A2
Littleover *Derby C* 35 B9
Littleport *Cambs* 38 G1
Littlestone on Sea *Kent* 13 D9
Littlethorpe *Leics* 35 F11
Littlethorpe *N Yorks* 51 C9
Littleton *Ches* 43 F7
Littleton *Hants* 10 A3
Littleton *Perth/Kinr* 76 D5
Littleton *Som'set* 8 A3
Littleton *Surrey* 19 E7
Littleton *Surrey* 18 G6
Littleton Drew *Wilts* 16 C5
Littleton-on-Severn *S Gloucs* 16 C2
Littleton Pannell *Wilts* 17 F7
Littletown *Durham* 58 B4
Littlewick Green *Windsor* 18 D5
Littleworth *Beds* 29 D7
Littleworth *Glos* 16 A5
Littleworth *Oxon* 17 B10
Littleworth *Staffs* 34 D6
Littleworth *Worcs* 26 C5
Litton *Derby* 44 E5
Litton *N Yorks* 50 B5
Litton *Som'set* 16 F2
Litton Cheney *Dorset* 8 E4
Liurbost *W Isles* 91 E8
Liverpool *Mersey* 42 C6
Liverpool Airport *Mersey* 43 D7
Liversedge *W Yorks* 51 G8
Liverton *Devon* 5 D9
Liverton *Redcar/Clevel'd* 59 E8
Livingston *W Loth* 69 D9
Livingston Village *W Loth* 69 D9
Lixwm *Flints* 42 E4
Lizard *Cornw'l* 2 H6
Llaingoch *Angl* 40 B4
Llaithddu *Powys* 33 G6
Llan *Powys* 32 E4
Llan Ffestiniog *Gwyn* 41 F9
Llan-y-pwll *Wrex* 42 G6
Llanaber *Gwyn* 32 D2
Llanaelhaearn *Gwyn* 40 F5
Llanafan *Ceredig'n* 24 A3
Llanafan-fawr *Powys* 24 C6
Llanallgo *Angl* 40 B6
Llanandras = Presteigne *Powys* 25 B10
Llanarmon *Gwyn* 40 G6
Llanarmon Dyffryn Ceiriog *Wrex* 33 B7
Llanarmon-yn-Ial *Denbs* 42 G4
Llanarth *Ceredig'n* 23 A9
Llanarth *Monmouths* 25 G10
Llanarthne *Carms* 23 D10
Llanasa *Flints* 42 D4
Llanbabo *Angl* 40 B5
Llanbadarn Fawr *Ceredig'n* 32 G2
Llanbadarn Fynydd *Powys* 33 H7
Llanbadarn-y-Garreg *Powys* 25 D8
Llanbadoc *Monmouths* 15 B9
Llanbadrig *Angl* 40 A5
Llanbeder *Newp* 15 B9
Llanbedr *Gwyn* 32 C1
Llanbedr *Powys* 25 D8
Llanbedr *Powys* 25 F9
Llanbedr-Dyffryn-Clwyd *Denbs* 42 G4
Llanbedr-y-cennin *Conwy* 41 D9
Llanbedrgoch *Angl* 41 B7
Llanbedrog *Gwyn* 40 G5
Llanberis *Gwyn* 41 D7
Llanbethêry *V/Glam* 14 E6
Llanbister *Powys* 25 A8
Llanblethian *V/Glam* 14 D5
Llanboidy *Carms* 23 D7
Llanbradach *Caerph* 15 B7
Llanbrynmair *Powys* 32 E4
Llancarfan *V/Glam* 14 D6
Llancayo *Monmouths* 15 A9
Llancloudy *Heref'd* 25 F11
Llancynfelyn *Ceredig'n* 32 F2
Llandaff *Card* 15 D7
Llandanwg *Gwyn* 32 C1
Llandarcy *Neath P Talb* 14 B3
Llandawke *Carms* 23 E7
Llanddaniel Fab *Angl* 40 C6
Llanddarog *Carms* 23 E10
Llanddeiniol *Ceredig'n* 24 A2
Llanddeiniolen *Gwyn* 41 D7
Llandderfel *Gwyn* 32 B5
Llanddeusant *Angl* 40 B5
Llanddeusant *Carms* 24 F4
Llanddew *Powys* 25 E7
Llanddewi *Swan* 23 H9
Llanddewi-Brefi *Ceredig'n* 24 C3
Llanddewi Rhydderch *Monmouths* 25 G10
Llanddewi Velfrey *Pembs* 22 E6
Llanddewi'r Cwm *Powys* 25 D7
Llanddoged *Conwy* 41 D10
Llanddona *Angl* 41 C7
Llanddowror *Carms* 23 E7
Llanddulas *Conwy* 42 E2
Llanddwywe *Gwyn* 32 C1
Llanddyfynan *Angl* 41 C7
Llandebr Pont Steffan = Lampeter *Ceredig'n* 23 B10
Llandefaelog Fach *Powys* 25 E7
Llandefaelog-tre'r-graig *Powys* 25 F8
Llandefalle *Powys* 25 E8
Llandegai *Gwyn* 41 C7
Llandegfan *Angl* 41 C7
Llandegla *Denbs* 42 G4
Llandegley *Powys* 25 B8
Llandegveth *Monmouths* 15 B9
Llandegwning *Gwyn* 40 G4
Llandeilo *Carms* 24 F3
Llandeilo Graban *Powys* 25 D7
Llandeilo'r Fan *Powys* 24 E5
Llandeloy *Pembs* 22 D3
Llandenny *Monmouths* 15 A10
Llandevenny *Monmouths* 15 C10
Llandewednock *Cornw'l* 2 H6
Llandewi Ystradenny *Powys* 25 B8
Llandinabo *Heref'd* 26 F2
Llandinam *Powys* 32 G6
Llandissilio *Pembs* 22 D6
Llandogo *Monmouths* 15 A11
Llandough *V/Glam* 14 D5
Llandough *V/Glam* 15 D7
Llandovery = Llanymddyfri *Carms* 24 E4
Llandow *V/Glam* 14 D5
Llandre *Ceredig'n* 32 G2
Llandre *Carms* 24 D3
Llandrillo *Denbs* 32 B6
Llandrillo-yn-Rhos *Conwy* 41 B10
Llandrindod = Llandrindod Wells *Powys* 25 B7
Llandrindod Wells = Llandrindod *Powys* 25 B7
Llandrinio *Powys* 33 D8
Llandudno *Conwy* 41 B9
Llandudno Junction = Cyffordd Llandudno *Conwy* 41 C9
Llandwrog *Gwyn* 40 E6
Llandybie *Carms* 24 G3
Llandyfaelog *Carms* 23 E9
Llandyfan *Carms* 24 G3
Llandyfriog *Ceredig'n* 23 B8
Llandyfrydog *Angl* 40 B6
Llandygwydd *Ceredig'n* 23 B7
Llandynan *Denbs* 42 H4
Llandyrnog *Denbs* 42 F4
Llandysilio *Powys* 33 D8
Llandyssil *Powys* 33 F7
Llandysul *Ceredig'n* 23 B9
Llanedeyrn *Card* 15 C8
Llanedy *Carms* 23 F10
Llaneglwys *Powys* 25 E7
Llanegryn *Gwyn* 32 E1
Llanegwad *Carms* 23 D10
Llaneilian *Angl* 40 A6
Llanelian-yn-Rhos *Conwy* 41 C10
Llanelidan *Denbs* 42 G4
Llanelieu *Powys* 25 E8
Llanellen *Monmouths* 25 G10
Llanelli *Carms* 23 G10
Llanelli *Monmouths* 25 G9
Llanelltyd *Gwyn* 32 D3
Llanelly Hill *Monmouths* 25 G9
Llanelwedd *Powys* 25 C7
Llanelwy = St Asaph *Denbs* 42 E3
Llanenddwyn *Gwyn* 32 C1
Llanengan *Gwyn* 40 H4
Llanerchymedd *Angl* 40 B6
Llanerfyl *Powys* 32 E6
Llanfachraeth *Angl* 40 B5
Llanfachreth *Gwyn* 32 C3
Llanfaelog *Angl* 40 C5
Llanfaelrhys *Gwyn* 40 H4
Llanfaenor *Monmouths* 25 G11
Llanfaes *Angl* 41 C8
Llanfaes *Powys* 25 F7
Llanfaethlu *Angl* 40 B5
Llanfaglan *Gwyn* 40 D6
Llanfair *Gwyn* 32 C1
Llanfair-ar-y-bryn *Carms* 24 E5
Llanfair Caereinion *Powys* 33 E7
Llanfair Clydogau *Ceredig'n* 24 C3
Llanfair-Dyffryn-Clwyd *Denbs* 42 G4
Llanfair-Nant-Gwyn *Pembs* 22 C6
Llanfair Talhaiarn *Conwy* 42 E2
Llanfair Waterdine *Shrops* 33 H8
Llanfair-ym-Muallt = Builth Wells *Powys* 25 C7
Llanfairfechan *Conwy* 41 C8
Llanfairpwll-gwyngyll *Angl* 41 C7
Llanfairyneubwll *Angl* 40 C5
Llanfairynghornwy *Angl* 40 A5
Llanfallteg *Carms* 22 E6
Llanfaredd *Powys* 25 C7
Llanfarian *Ceredig'n* 32 H1
Llanfechain *Powys* 33 C7
Llanfechan *Powys* 24 C6
Llanfechell *Angl* 40 A5
Llanfendigaid *Gwyn* 32 E1
Llanferres *Denbs* 42 F4
Llanfflewyn *Angl* 40 B5
Llanfihangel-ar-Arth *Carms* 23 C9
Llanfihangel-Crucorney *Monmouths* 25 F10
Llanfihangel Glyn Myfyr *Conwy* 42 H2
Llanfihangel Nant Bran *Powys* 24 E6
Llanfihangel-nant-Melan *Powys* 25 C8
Llanfihangel Rhydithon *Powys* 25 B8
Llanfihangel Rogiet *Monmouths* 15 C10
Llanfihangel Tal-y-llyn *Powys* 25 F8
Llanfihangel-uwch-Gwili *Carms* 23 D9
Llanfihangel-y-Creuddyn *Ceredig'n* 32 H2
Llanfihangel-y-pennant *Gwyn* 41 F7
Llanfihangel-y-pennant *Gwyn* 32 E2
Llanfihangel-y-traethau *Gwyn* 41 G7
Llanfihangel-yn-Ngwynfa *Powys* 33 D6
Llanfihangel yn Nhowyn *Angl* 40 C5
Llanfilo *Powys* 25 E8
Llanfoist *Monmouths* 25 G9
Llanfor *Gwyn* 32 B5
Llanfrechfa *Torf* 15 B9
Llanfrothen *Gwyn* 41 F8
Llanfrynach *Powys* 25 F7
Llanfwrog *Angl* 40 B5
Llanfwrog *Denbs* 42 G4
Llanfyllin *Powys* 33 D7
Llanfynydd *Carms* 23 D10
Llanfynydd *Flints* 42 G5
Llanfyrnach *Pembs* 23 C7
Llangadfan *Powys* 32 D6
Llangadog *Carms* 24 F4
Llangadwaladr *Angl* 40 D5
Llangadwaladr *Powys* 33 B7
Llangaffo *Angl* 40 D6
Llangain *Carms* 23 E8
Llangammarch Wells *Powys* 24 D6
Llangan *V/Glam* 14 D5
Llangarron *Heref'd* 26 F2
Llangasty Talyllyn *Powys* 25 F8
Llangathen *Carms* 23 D10
Llangattock *Powys* 25 G9
Llangattock Lingoed *Monmouths* 25 F10
Llangattock nigh Usk *Monmouths* 25 H10
Llangattock-Vibon-Avel *Monmouths* 25 G11
Llangedwyn *Powys* 33 C7
Llangefni *Angl* 40 C6
Llangeinor *Bridg* 14 C5
Llangeitho *Ceredig'n* 24 C3
Llangeler *Carms* 23 C8
Llangelynin *Gwyn* 32 E1
Llangendeirne *Carms* 23 E9
Llangennech *Carms* 23 F10
Llangennith *Swan* 23 G9
Llangenny *Powys* 25 G9
Llangernyw *Conwy* 41 D10
Llangian *Gwyn* 40 H4
Llanglydwen *Carms* 22 D6
Llangoed *Angl* 41 C8
Llangoedmor *Ceredig'n* 22 B6
Llangollen *Denbs* 33 A8
Llangolman *Pembs* 22 D6
Llangorse *Powys* 25 F8
Llangovan *Monmouths* 25 H11
Llangower *Gwyn* 32 B5
Llangrannog *Ceredig'n* 23 A8
Llangristiolus *Angl* 40 C6
Llangrove *Heref'd* 26 G2
Llangua *Monmouths* 25 F10
Llangunllo *Powys* 25 A9
Llangunnor *Carms* 23 E9
Llangurig *Powys* 32 H5
Llangwm *Conwy* 32 A5
Llangwm *Monmouths* 15 A10
Llangwm *Pembs* 22 F4
Llangwnnadl *Gwyn* 40 G4
Llangwyfan *Denbs* 42 F4
Llangwyfan-isaf *Angl* 40 D5
Llangwyllog *Angl* 40 C6
Llangwyryfon *Ceredig'n* 24 A2
Llangybi *Ceredig'n* 24 C3
Llangybi *Gwyn* 40 F6
Llangybi *Monmouths* 15 B9
Llangyfelach *Swan* 14 B2
Llangynhafal *Denbs* 42 F4
Llangynidr *Powys* 25 G8
Llangynin *Carms* 23 E7
Llangynog *Carms* 23 E8
Llangynog *Powys* 33 C6
Llangynwyd *Bridg* 14 C4
Llanhamlach *Powys* 25 F7
Llanharan *Rh Cyn Taff* 14 C6
Llanharry *Rh Cyn Taff* 14 C6
Llanhennock *Monmouths* 15 B9
Llanhiledd = Llanhilleth *Bl Gwent* 15 A8
Llanhilleth = Llanhiledd *Bl Gwent* 15 A8
Llanidloes *Powys* 32 G5
Llaniestyn *Gwyn* 40 G4
Llanifyny *Powys* 32 G4
Llanigon *Powys* 25 E9
Llanilar *Ceredig'n* 24 A3
Llanilid *Rh Cyn Taff* 14 C5
Llanilltud Fawr = Llantwit Major *V/Glam* 14 E5
Llanishen *Card* 15 C7
Llanishen *Monmouths* 15 A10
Llanllawddog *Carms* 23 D9
Llanllechid *Gwyn* 41 D8
Llanllowel *Monmouths* 15 B9
Llanllugan *Powys* 33 E6
Llanllwch *Carms* 23 E8
Llanllwchaiarn *Powys* 33 F7
Llanllwni *Carms* 23 C9
Llanllyfni *Gwyn* 40 E6
Llanmadoc *Swan* 23 G9
Llanmaes *V/Glam* 14 E5
Llanmartin *Newp* 15 C9
Llanmihangel *V/Glam* 14 D5
Llanmorlais *Swan* 23 G10
Llannefydd *Conwy* 42 E2
Llannon *Carms* 23 F10
Llannor *Gwyn* 40 G5
Llanon *Ceredig'n* 24 B2
Llanover *Monmouths* 25 H10
Llanpumsaint *Carms* 23 D9
Llanreithan *Pembs* 22 D3
Llanrhaeadr *Denbs* 42 F3
Llanrhaeadr-ym-Mochnant *Powys* 33 C7
Llanrhian *Pembs* 22 C3
Llanrhidian *Swan* 23 G9
Llanrhos *Conwy* 41 B9
Llanrhyddlad *Angl* 40 B5
Llanrhystud *Ceredig'n* 24 B2
Llanrosser *Heref'd* 25 E9
Llanrothal *Heref'd* 25 G11
Llanrug *Gwyn* 41 D7
Llanrumney *Card* 15 C8
Llanrwst *Conwy* 41 D10
Llansadurnen *Carms* 23 E7
Llansadwrn *Angl* 41 C7
Llansadwrn *Carms* 24 E3
Llansaint *Carms* 23 F8
Llansamlet *Swan* 14 B2
Llansannan *Conwy* 42 F2
Llansannor *V/Glam* 14 D5
Llansantffraed *Ceredig'n* 24 B2
Llansantffraed *Powys* 25 F8
Llansantffraed Cwmdeuddwr *Powys* 24 B6
Llansantffraed-in-Elvel *Powys* 25 C7
Llansantffraid-ym-Mechain *Powys* 33 C8
Llansawel *Carms* 24 E3
Llansilin *Powys* 33 C8
Llansoy *Monmouths* 15 A10
Llanspyddid *Powys* 25 F7
Llanstadwell *Pembs* 22 F4
Llansteffan *Carms* 23 E8
Llanstephan *Powys* 25 D8
Llantarnam *Torf* 15 B9
Llanteg *Pembs* 22 E6
Llanthony *Monmouths* 25 F9
Llantilio Crossenny *Monmouths* 25 G10
Llantilio Pertholey *Monmouths* 25 G10
Llantood *Pembs* 22 B6
Llantrisant *Angl* 40 B5
Llantrisant *Monmouths* 15 B9
Llantrisant *Rh Cyn Taff* 14 C6
Llantrithyd *V/Glam* 14 D6
Llantwit Fardre *Rh Cyn Taff* 14 C6
Llantwit Major = Llanilltud Fawr *V/Glam* 14 E5
Llanuwchllyn *Gwyn* 41 G10
Llanvaches *Newp* 15 B10
Llanvair Discoed *Monmouths* 15 B10
Llanvapley *Monmouths* 25 G10
Llanvetherine *Monmouths* 25 G10
Llanveynoe *Heref'd* 25 E10
Llanvihangel Gobion *Monmouths* 25 H10
Llanvihangel-Ystern-Llewern *Monmouths* 25 G11
Llanwarne *Heref'd* 26 F2
Llanwddyn *Powys* 32 D6
Llanwenog *Ceredig'n* 23 B9
Llanwern *Newp* 15 C9
Llanwinio *Carms* 23 D7
Llanwnda *Gwyn* 40 E6
Llanwnda *Pembs* 22 C4
Llanwnnen *Ceredig'n* 23 B10
Llanwnog *Powys* 32 F6
Llanwrda *Carms* 24 E4
Llanwrin *Powys* 32 E3
Llanwrthwl *Powys* 24 B6
Llanwrtud = Llanwrtyd Wells *Powys* 24 D5
Llanwrtyd *Powys* 24 D5
Llanwrtyd Wells = Llanwrtud *Powys* 24 D5
Llanwyddelan *Powys* 33 E6
Llanyblodwel *Shrops* 33 C8
Llanybri *Carms* 23 E8
Llanybydder *Carms* 23 B10
Llanycefn *Pembs* 22 D5
Llanychaer *Pembs* 22 C4
Llanycil *Gwyn* 32 B5
Llanycrwys *Carms* 24 D3
Llanymawddwy *Gwyn* 32 D5
Llanymddyfri = Llandovery *Carms* 24 E4
Llanymynech *Powys* 33 C8
Llanynghenedl *Angl* 40 B5
Llanynys *Denbs* 42 F4
Llanyre *Powys* 25 B7
Llanystumdwy *Gwyn* 40 G6
Llanywern *Powys* 25 F8
Llawhaden *Pembs* 22 E5
Llawnt *Shrops* 33 B8
Llawr Dref *Gwyn* 40 H4
Llawryglyn *Powys* 32 F5
Llay *Wrex* 42 G6
Llechcynfarwy *Angl* 40 B5
Llecheiddior *Gwyn* 40 F6
Llechfaen *Powys* 25 F7
Llechryd *Caerph* 25 H8
Llechryd *Ceredig'n* 23 B7
Llechrydau *Powys* 33 B8
Lledrod *Ceredig'n* 24 A3
Llenmerewig *Powys* 33 F7
Llethrid *Swan* 23 G10
Llidiad Nenog *Carms* 23 C10
Llidiardau *Gwyn* 41 G10
Llidiart-y-parc *Denbs* 33 A7
Llithfaen *Gwyn* 40 F5
Llong *Flints* 42 F5
Llowes *Powys* 25 D8
Llundain-fach *Ceredig'n* 23 A10
Llwydcoed *Rh Cyn Taff* 14 A5
Llwyn *Shrops* 33 G8
Llwyn-du *Monmouths* 25 G9
Llwyn-hendy *Carms* 23 G10
Llwyn-têg *Carms* 23 F10
Llwyn-y-brain *Carms* 22 E6
Llwyn-y-groes *Ceredig'n* 23 A10
Llwyncelyn *Ceredig'n* 23 A9
Llwyndafydd *Ceredig'n* 23 A8
Llwynderw *Powys* 33 E8
Llwyndyrys *Gwyn* 40 F5
Llwyngwril *Gwyn* 32 E1
Llwynmawr *Wrex* 33 B8
Llwynypia *Rh Cyn Taff* 14 B5
Llynclys *Shrops* 33 C8
Llynfaes *Angl* 40 C6
Llys-y-frân *Pembs* 22 D5
Llysfaen *Conwy* 41 C10
Llyswen *Powys* 25 E8
Llysworney *V/Glam* 14 D5
Llywel *Powys* 24 E5
Loan *Falk* 69 C8
Loanend *Northum* 71 E8
Loanhead *Midloth* 69 D11
Loans *S Ayrs* 66 C6
Loans of Tullich *H'land* 87 D11
Lobb *Devon* 6 C3
Loch a Charnain *W Isles* 84 D3
Loch a'Ghainmhich *W Isles* 91 E7
Loch Baghasdail = Lochboisdale *W Isles* 84 G2
Loch Choire Lodge *H'land* 93 F9
Loch Euphoirt *W Isles* 84 B3
Loch Head *Dumf/Gal* 54 E6
Loch Loyal Lodge *H'land* 93 E9
Loch nam Madadh = Lochmaddy *W Isles* 84 B4
Loch Sgioport *W Isles* 84 E3
Lochailort *H'land* 79 C10
Lochaline *H'land* 79 G9
Lochanhully *H'land* 81 A11
Lochans *Dumf/Gal* 54 D3
Locharbriggs *Dumf/Gal* 60 E5
Lochassynt Lodge *H'land* 92 G4
Lochavich Ho. *Arg/Bute* 73 B8
Lochawe *Arg/Bute* 74 E4
Lochboisdale = Loch Baghasdail *W Isles* 84 G2
Lochbuie *Arg/Bute* 79 J9
Lochcarron *H'land* 85 E13
Lochdhu *H'land* 93 E13
Lochdochart House *Stirl* 75 E7
Lochdon *Arg/Bute* 79 H10
Lochdrum *H'land* 86 D5
Lochead *Arg/Bute* 72 F6
Lochearnhead *Stirl* 75 E8
Lochee *Dundee C* 76 D6
Lochend *H'land* 87 H8
Lochend *H'land* 94 D4
Locherben *Dumf/Gal* 60 D5
Lochfoot *Dumf/Gal* 60 F4
Lochgair *Arg/Bute* 73 D8
Lochgarthside *H'land* 81 B7
Lochgelly *Fife* 69 A10
Lochgilphead *Arg/Bute* 73 E7
Lochgoilhead *Arg/Bute* 74 G5
Lochhill *Moray* 88 B2
Lochindorb Lodge *H'land* 87 H12
Lochinver *H'land* 92 G3
Lochlane *Perth/Kinr* 75 E11
Lochluichart *H'land* 86 E6
Lochmaben *Dumf/Gal* 60 E6
Lochmaddy = Loch nam Madadh *W Isles* 84 B4
Lochmore Cottage *H'land* 94 F2
Lochmore Lodge *H'land* 92 F5
Lochore *Fife* 76 H4
Lochportain *W Isles* 84 A4
Lochranza *N Ayrs* 66 A2
Lochs Crofts *Moray* 88 B3
Lochside *Aberds* 77 A10
Lochside *H'land* 92 D7
Lochside *H'land* 93 F11
Lochside *H'land* 87 F11
Lochslin *H'land* 87 C11
Lochstack Lodge *H'land* 92 E5
Lochton *Aberds* 83 D9
Lochty *Angus* 77 A8
Lochty *Fife* 77 G8
Lochty *Perth/Kinr* 76 E3
Lochuisge *H'land* 79 F10
Lochurr *Dumf/Gal* 60 E3
Lochwinnoch *Renf* 68 E2
Lochwood *Dumf/Gal* 60 D6
Lochyside *H'land* 80 F3
Lockengate *Cornw'l* 3 C9
Lockerbie *Dumf/Gal* 61 E7
Lockeridge *Wilts* 17 E8
Lockerley *Hants* 10 B1
Locking *N Som'set* 15 F9
Lockinge *Oxon* 17 C11
Lockington *ER Yorks* 52 E5
Lockington *Leics* 35 C10
Lockleywood *Shrops* 34 C2
Locks Heath *Hants* 10 D4
Lockton *N Yorks* 59 G9
Lockwood *W Yorks* 51 H7
Loddington *Leics* 36 E3
Loddington *Northants* 36 H4
Loddiswell *Devon* 5 G8
Loddon *Norfolk* 39 F9
Lode *Cambs* 30 B2
Loders *Dorset* 8 E3
Lodsworth *W Sussex* 11 B8
Lofthouse *N Yorks* 51 B7
Lofthouse *W Yorks* 51 G9
Loftus *Redcar/Clevel'd* 59 E8
Logan *E Ayrs* 67 D8
Logan Mains *Dumf/Gal* 54 E3
Loganlea *W Loth* 69 D8
Loggerheads *Staffs* 34 B3
Logie *Angus* 77 A9
Logie *Fife* 77 E7
Logie *Moray* 87 F13
Logie Coldstone *Aberds* 82 C6
Logie Hill *H'land* 87 D10
Logie Newton *Aberds* 89 E6
Logie Pert *Angus* 77 A9
Logiealmond Lodge *Perth/Kinr* 76 D2
Logierait *Perth/Kinr* 76 B2
Login *Carms* 22 D6
Lolworth *Cambs* 29 B10
Lonbain *H'land* 85 C11
Londesborough *ER Yorks* 52 E4
London Colney *Herts* 19 A8
Londonderry *N Yorks* 58 H4
Londonthorpe *Lincs* 36 B5
Londubh *H'land* 91 J13
Lonemore *H'land* 87 C10
Long Ashton *N Som'set* 15 D11
Long Bennington *Lincs* 36 A4
Long Bredy *Dorset* 8 E4
Long Buckby *Northants* 28 B3
Long Clawson *Leics* 36 C3
Long Common *Hants* 10 C4
Long Compton *Staffs* 34 C4
Long Compton *Warwick* 27 E9
Long Crendon *Bucks* 28 H3
Long Crichel *Dorset* 9 C8
Long Ditton *Surrey* 19 E8
Long Drax *N Yorks* 52 G2
Long Duckmanton *Derby* 45 E8
Long Eaton *Derby* 35 B10
Long Green *Worcs* 26 E5
Long Hanborough *Oxon* 27 G11
Long Itchington *Warwick* 27 B11
Long Lawford *Warwick* 35 H10
Long Load *Som'set* 8 B3
Long Marston *Herts* 28 G5
Long Marston *N Yorks* 51 D11
Long Marston *Warwick* 27 D8
Long Marton *Cumb* 57 D8
Long Melford *Suffolk* 30 D5
Long Newnton *Glos* 16 B6
Long Newton *E Loth* 70 D4
Long Preston *N Yorks* 50 D4
Long Riston *ER Yorks* 53 E7
Long Sight *Gtr Man* 44 B3
Long Stratton *Norfolk* 39 F7
Long Street *M/Keynes* 28 D4
Long Sutton *Hants* 18 G4
Long Sutton *Lincs* 37 C10
Long Sutton *Som'set* 8 B3
Long Thurlow *Suffolk* 31 B7
Long Whatton *Leics* 35 C10
Long Wittenham *Oxon* 18 B2
Longbar *N Ayrs* 66 A6
Longbenton *Tyne/Wear* 63 G8
Longborough *Glos* 27 F8
Longbridge *Warwick* 27 B9
Longbridge *W Midlands* 34 H6
Longbridge Deverill *Wilts* 16 G5
Longburton *Dorset* 8 C5
Longcliffe *Derby* 44 G6
Longcot *Oxon* 17 B9
Longcroft *Falk* 68 C6
Longden *Shrops* 33 E10
Longdon *Staffs* 35 D6
Longdon *Worcs* 26 E5
Longdon Green *Staffs* 35 D6
Longdon on Tern *Telford* 34 D2
Longdown *Devon* 7 G7
Longdowns *Cornw'l* 2 F6
Longfield *Kent* 20 E3
Longfield *Shetl'd* 96 M5
Longford *Derby* 35 B8
Longford *Glos* 26 F5
Longford *London* 19 D7
Longford *Shrops* 34 B2
Longford *Telford* 34 D3
Longford *W Midlands* 35 G9
Longfordlane *Derby* 35 B8
Longforgan *Perth/Kinr* 76 E6
Longformacus *Scot Borders* 70 E5
Longframlington *Northum* 63 C7
Longham *Dorset* 9 E9
Longham *Norfolk* 38 D5
Longhaven *Aberds* 89 E11
Longhill *Aberds* 89 C9
Longhirst *Northum* 63 E8
Longhope *Glos* 26 G3
Longhope *Orkney* 95 J4
Longhorsley *Northum* 63 D7
Longhoughton *Northum* 63 B8
Longlane *Derby* 35 B8
Longlane *W Berks* 17 D11
Longlevens *Glos* 26 F5
Longley *W Yorks* 44 B5
Longley Green *Worcs* 26 C4
Longmanhill *Aberds* 89 B7
Longmoor Camp *Hants* 11 A6
Longmorn *Moray* 88 C2
Longnewton *Scot Borders* 70 H4
Longnewton *Stockton* 58 E4
Longney *Glos* 26 G4
Longniddry *E Loth* 70 C3
Longnor *Shrops* 33 E10
Longnor *Staffs* 44 F4
Longparish *Hants* 17 G11
Longport *Stoke* 44 H2
Longridge *Lancs* 50 F2
Longridge *Staffs* 34 D5
Longridge *W Loth* 69 D8
Longriggend *N Lanarks* 69 C7
Longsdon *Staffs* 44 G3
Longshaw *Gtr Man* 43 B8
Longside *Aberds* 89 D10
Longstanton *Cambs* 29 B10
Longstock *Hants* 17 H10
Longstone *Pembs* 22 F6
Longstowe *Cambs* 29 C10
Longthorpe *Peterbro* 37 F7
Longthwaite *Cumb* 56 D6
Longton *Lancs* 49 G4
Longton *Stoke* 34 A5
Longtown *Cumb* 61 G9
Longtown *Heref'd* 25 F10
Longview *Mersey* 43 C7
Longville in the Dale *Shrops* 33 F11
Longwick *Bucks* 28 H4
Longwitton *Northum* 62 E6
Longwood *Shrops* 34 E2
Longworth *Oxon* 17 B10
Longyester *E Loth* 70 D4
Lonmay *Aberds* 89 C10
Lonmore *H'land* 84 D7
Looe *Cornw'l* 4 F3
Loose *Kent* 20 F4
Loosley Row *Bucks* 18 A5
Lopcombe Corner *Wilts* 17 H9
Lopen *Som'set* 8 C3
Loppington *Shrops* 33 C10
Lopwell *Devon* 4 E5
Lorbottle *Northum* 62 C6
Lorbottle Hall *Northum* 62 C6
Lornty *Perth/Kinr* 76 C4
Loscoe *Derby* 45 H8
Losgaintir *W Isles* 90 H5
Lossiemouth *Moray* 88 A2
Lossit *Arg/Bute* 64 C2
Lostford *Shrops* 34 B2
Lostock Gralam *Ches* 43 E9
Lostock Green *Ches* 43 E9
Lostock Hall *Lancs* 49 G5
Lostock Junction *Gtr Man* 43 B9
Lostwithiel *Cornw'l* 4 F2
Loth *Orkney* 95 E7
Lothbeg *H'land* 93 H12
Lothersdale *N Yorks* 50 E5
Lothmore *H'land* 93 H12
Loudwater *Bucks* 18 B6
Loughborough *Leics* 35 D11
Loughor *Swan* 23 G10
Loughton *Essex* 19 B11
Loughton *M/Keynes* 28 E5
Loughton *Shrops* 34 G2
Lound *Lincs* 37 D6
Lound *Notts* 45 D10
Lound *Suffolk* 39 F11
Lount *Leics* 35 D9
Louth *Lincs* 47 D7
Love Clough *Lancs* 50 G4
Lovedean *Hants* 10 C5
Lover *Wilts* 9 B11
Loversall *S Yorks* 45 C9
Loves Green *Essex* 20 A3
Lovesome Hill *N Yorks* 58 G4
Loveston *Pembs* 22 F5
Lovington *Som'set* 8 A4
Low Ackworth *W Yorks* 51 H10
Low Barlings *Lincs* 46 E4
Low Bentham *N Yorks* 50 C2
Low Bradfield *S Yorks* 44 C6
Low Bradley *N Yorks* 50 E6
Low Braithwaite *Cumb* 56 B6
Low Brunton *Northum* 62 F5
Low Burnham *N Lincs* 45 B11
Low Burton *N Yorks* 51 A8
Low Buston *Northum* 63 C8
Low Catton *ER Yorks* 52 D3
Low Clanyard *Dumf/Gal* 54 F4
Low Coniscliffe *D'lington* 58 E3
Low Crosby *Cumb* 61 H10
Low Dalby *N Yorks* 59 H9
Low Dinsdale *D'lington* 58 E4
Low Ellington *N Yorks* 51 A8
Low Etherley *Durham* 58 D2
Low Fell *Tyne/Wear* 63 H8
Low Fulney *Lincs* 37 C8
Low Garth *N Yorks* 59 F8
Low Gate *Northum* 62 G5
Low Grantley *N Yorks* 51 B8
Low Habberley *Worcs* 34 H4
Low Ham *Som'set* 8 B3
Low Hesket *Cumb* 56 B6
Low Hesleyhurst *Northum* 62 D6
Low Hutton *N Yorks* 52 C3
Low Laithe *N Yorks* 51 C7
Low Leighton *Derby* 44 D4
Low Lorton *Cumb* 56 D3
Low Marishes *N Yorks* 52 B4
Low Marnham *Notts* 46 F2
Low Mill *N Yorks* 59 G7
Low Moor *Lancs* 50 E3
Low Moor *W Yorks* 51 G7
Low Moorsley *Tyne/Wear* 58 B4
Low Newton *Cumb* 49 A4
Low Newton-by-the-Sea *Northum* 63 A8
Low Row *Cumb* 56 C5
Low Row *Cumb* 61 G11
Low Row *N Yorks* 57 G11
Low Salchrie *Dumf/Gal* 54 C3
Low Smerby *Arg/Bute* 65 F8
Low Torry *Fife* 69 B9
Low Worsall *N Yorks* 58 F4
Low Wray *Cumb* 56 F5
Lowbridge House *Cumb* 57 F7
Lowca *Cumb* 56 D1
Lowdham *Notts* 45 H10
Lowe *Shrops* 33 B11
Lowe Hill *Staffs* 44 G3
Lower Aisholt *Som'set* 7 C11
Lower Arncott *Oxon* 28 G3
Lower Ashton *Devon* 5 C9
Lower Assendon *Oxon* 18 C4
Lower Badcall *H'land* 92 E4
Lower Bartle *Lancs* 49 F4
Lower Basildon *W Berks* 18 D3
Lower Beeding *W Sussex* 11 B11
Lower Benefield *Northants* 36 G5
Lower Boddington *Northants* 27 C11
Lower Brailes *Warwick* 27 E10
Lower Breakish *H'land* 85 F11
Lower Broadheath *Worcs* 26 C5
Lower Bullingham *Heref'd* 26 E2
Lower Cam *Glos* 16 A4
Lower Chapel *Powys* 25 E7
Lower Chute *Wilts* 17 F10
Lower Cragabus *Arg/Bute* 64 D4
Lower Crossings *Derby* 44 D4
Lower Cumberworth *W Yorks* 44 B6
Lower Cwm-twrch *Powys* 24 G4
Lower Darwen *Blackb'n* 50 G2
Lower Dean *Beds* 29 B7
Lower Diabaig *H'land* 85 B12
Lower Dicker *E Sussex* 12 E4
Lower Dinchope *Shrops* 33 G10
Lower Down *Shrops* 33 G9
Lower Drift *Cornw'l* 2 G3
Lower Dunsforth *N Yorks* 51 C10
Lower Egleton *Heref'd* 26 D3
Lower Elkstone *Staffs* 44 G4
Lower End *Beds* 28 F6
Lower Everleigh *Wilts* 17 F8
Lower Farringdon *Hants* 18 H4
Lower Foxdale *I/Man* 48 E2
Lower Frankton *Shrops* 33 B9
Lower Froyle *Hants* 18 G4
Lower Gledfield *H'land* 87 B8
Lower Green *Norfolk* 38 B5
Lower Hacheston *Suffolk* 31 C10
Lower Halistra *H'land* 84 C7
Lower Halstow *Kent* 20 E5
Lower Hardres *Kent* 21 F8
Lower Hawthwaite *Cumb* 56 H4
Lower Heath *Ches* 44 F2
Lower Hempriggs *Moray* 87 E14
Lower Hergest *Heref'd* 25 C9
Lower Heyford *Oxon* 27 F11
Lower Higham *Kent* 20 D4
Lower Holbrook *Suffolk* 31 E8
Lower Hordley *Shrops* 33 C9
Lower Horsebridge *E Sussex* 12 E4
Lower Killeyan *Arg/Bute* 64 D3
Lower Kingswood *Surrey* 19 F9
Lower Kinnerton *Ches* 42 F6
Lower Langford *N Som'set* 15 E10
Lower Largo *Fife* 77 G7
Lower Leigh *Staffs* 34 B6
Lower Lemington *Glos* 27 E9
Lower Lenie *H'land* 81 A7
Lower Lydbrook *Glos* 26 G2
Lower Lye *Heref'd* 25 B11
Lower Machen *Newp* 15 C8
Lower Maes-coed *Heref'd* 25 E10
Lower Mayland *Essex* 20 A6
Lower Midway *Derby* 35 C9
Lower Milovaig *H'land* 84 C6
Lower Moor *Worcs* 26 D6
Lower Nazeing *Essex* 29 H10
Lower Netchwood *Shrops* 34 F2
Lower Ollach *H'land* 85 E10
Lower Penarth *V/Glam* 15 D7
Lower Penn *Staffs* 34 F4
Lower Pennington *Hants* 10 E2
Lower Peover *Ches* 43 E10
Lower Pexhill *Ches* 44 E2
Lower Place *Gtr Man* 44 A3
Lower Quinton *Warwick* 27 D8
Lower Rochford *Worcs* 26 B3
Lower Seagry *Wilts* 16 C6
Lower Shelton *Beds* 28 D6
Lower Shiplake *Oxon* 18 D4
Lower Shuckburgh *Warwick* 27 B11
Lower Slaughter *Glos* 27 F8
Lower Stanton St Quintin *Wilts* 16 C6
Lower Stoke *Medway* 20 D5
Lower Stow Bedon *Norfolk* 38 F5
Lower Street *Norfolk* 39 B8
Lower Street *Norfolk* 39 D9
Lower Strensham *Worcs* 26 D6
Lower Stretton *Warrington* 43 D9
Lower Sundon *Beds* 29 F7
Lower Swanwick *Hants* 10 D3
Lower Swell *Glos* 27 F8
Lower Tean *Staffs* 34 B6
Lower Thurlton *Norfolk* 39 F10
Lower Tote *H'land* 85 B10
Lower Town *Pembs* 22 C4
Lower Tysoe *Warwick* 27 D10
Lower Upham *Hants* 10 C4
Lower Vexford *Som'set* 7 C10
Lower Weare *Som'set* 15 F10
Lower Welson *Heref'd* 25 C9
Lower Whitley *Ches* 43 E9
Lower Wield *Hants* 18 G3
Lower Winchendon *Bucks* 28 G4
Lower Withington *Ches* 44 F2
Lower Woodend *Bucks* 18 C5
Lower Woodford *Wilts* 9 A10
Lower Wyche *Worcs* 26 D4
Lowesby *Leics* 36 E3
Lowestoft *Suffolk* 39 F11
Loweswater *Cumb* 56 D3
Lowford *Hants* 10 C3
Lowgill *Cumb* 57 G8
Lowgill *Lancs* 50 C2
Lowick *Northants* 36 G5
Lowick *Northum* 71 G9
Lowick Bridge *Cumb* 56 H4
Lowick Green *Cumb* 56 H4
Lowlands *Torf* 15 B8
Lowmoor Row *Cumb* 57 D8
Lownie Moor *Angus* 77 C7
Lowsonford *Warwick* 27 B8
Lowther *Cumb* 57 D7
Lowthorpe *ER Yorks* 53 C6
Lowton *Gtr Man* 43 C9
Lowton Common *Gtr Man* 43 C9
Loxbeare *Devon* 7 E8
Loxhill *Surrey* 19 H7
Loxhore *Devon* 6 C5
Loxley *Warwick* 27 C9
Loxton *N Som'set* 15 F9
Loxwood *W Sussex* 11 A9
Lubcroy *H'land* 92 J6
Lubenham *Leics* 36 G3
Luccombe *Som'set* 7 B8
Luccombe Village *I/Wight* 10 G4
Lucker *Northum* 71 G10
Luckett *Cornw'l* 4 D4
Luckington *Wilts* 16 C5
Lucklawhill *Fife* 77 E7
Luckwell Bridge *Som'set* 7 C8
Lucton *Heref'd* 25 B11
Ludag *W Isles* 84 G2
Ludborough *Lincs* 46 C6
Ludchurch *Pembs* 22 E6
Luddenden *W Yorks* 50 G6
Luddenden Foot *W Yorks* 50 G6
Luddesdown *Kent* 20 E3
Luddington *N Lincs* 52 H4
Luddington *Warwick* 27 C8
Luddington in the Brook *Northants* 37 G7
Lude House *Perth/Kinr* 81 G10
Ludford *Lincs* 46 D6
Ludford *Shrops* 26 A2
Ludgershall *Bucks* 28 G3
Ludgershall *Wilts* 17 F9
Ludgvan *Cornw'l* 2 F4
Ludham *Norfolk* 39 D9
Ludlow *Shrops* 26 A2
Ludwell *Wilts* 9 B8
Ludworth *Durham* 58 B4
Luffincott *Devon* 6 G2
Lugar *E Ayrs* 67 D8
Lugg Green *Heref'd* 25 B11
Luggate Burn *E Loth* 70 C5
Luggiebank *N Lanarks* 68 C6
Lugton *E Ayrs* 67 A7
Lugwardine *Heref'd* 26 D2
Luib *H'land* 85 F10
Lulham *Heref'd* 25 D11
Lullenden *Surrey* 12 B3
Lullington *Derby* 35 D8
Lullington *Som'set* 16 F4
Lulsgate Bottom *N Som'set* 15 E11
Lulsley *Worcs* 26 C4
Lumb *W Yorks* 50 G6
Lumby *N Yorks* 51 F10
Lumloch *E Dunb* 68 D5
Lumphanan *Aberds* 83 C7
Lumphinnans *Fife* 69 A10
Lumsdaine *Scot Borders* 71 D7
Lumsden *Aberds* 82 A6
Lunan *Angus* 77 B9
Lunanhead *Angus* 77 B7
Luncarty *Perth/Kinr* 76 E3
Lund *ER Yorks* 52 E5
Lund *N Yorks* 52 F2
Lund *Shetl'd* 96 C7
Lunderton *Aberds* 89 D11
Lundie *Angus* 76 D5
Lundie *H'land* 80 B3
Lundin Links *Fife* 77 G7
Lunga *Arg/Bute* 72 C6
Lunna *Shetl'd* 96 G6
Lunning *Shetl'd* 96 G7
Lunnon *Swan* 23 H10
Lunsford's Cross *E Sussex* 12 E6
Lunt *Mersey* 42 B6
Luntley *Heref'd* 25 C10
Luppitt *Devon* 7 F10
Lupset *W Yorks* 51 H9
Lupton *Cumb* 50 A1
Lurgashall *W Sussex* 11 B8
Lusby *Lincs* 47 F7
Luson *Devon* 5 G7
Luss *Arg/Bute* 68 A2
Lussagiven *Arg/Bute* 72 E5
Lusta *H'land* 85 C7
Lustleigh *Devon* 5 C8
Luston *Heref'd* 25 B11
Luthermuir *Aberds* 83 G8
Luthrie *Fife* 76 F6
Luton *Devon* 5 D10
Luton *Luton* 29 F7
Luton *Medway* 20 E4
Lutterworth *Leics* 35 G11
Lutton *Devon* 5 F6
Lutton *Lincs* 37 C10
Lutton *Northants* 37 G7
Lutworthy *Devon* 7 E6
Luxborough *Som'set* 7 C8
Luxulyan *Cornw'l* 4 F1
Lybster *H'land* 94 G4
Lydbury North *Shrops* 33 G9
Lydcott *Devon* 6 C5
Lydd *Kent* 13 D9
Lydd on Sea *Kent* 13 D9
Lydden *Kent* 21 G9
Lyddington *Rutl'd* 36 F4
Lyde Green *Hants* 18 F4
Lydeard St Lawrence *Som'set* 7 C10
Lydford *Devon* 4 C6
Lydford-on-Fosse *Som'set* 8 A4
Lydgate *W Yorks* 50 G5
Lydham *Shrops* 33 F9
Lydiard Green *Wilts* 17 C7
Lydiard Millicent *Wilts* 17 C7
Lydiate *Mersey* 42 B6
Lydlinch *Dorset* 8 C6
Lydney *Glos* 16 A3
Lydstep *Pembs* 22 G5
Lye *W Midlands* 34 G5
Lye Cross *N Som'set* 15 E10
Lye Green *Bucks* 18 A6
Lye Green *E Sussex* 12 C4
Lyford *Oxon* 17 B10
Lymbridge Green *Kent* 13 B10
Lyme Regis *Dorset* 8 E2
Lyminge *Kent* 21 G8
Lymington *Hants* 10 E2
Lyminster *W Sussex* 11 D9
Lymm *Warrington* 43 D9
Lymore *Hants* 10 E1
Lympne *Kent* 13 C10
Lympsham *Som'set* 15 F9
Lympstone *Devon* 5 C10
Lynchat *H'land* 81 C9
Lyndale Ho. *H'land* 85 C8
Lyndhurst *Hants* 10 D2
Lyndon *Rutl'd* 36 E5
Lyne *Surrey* 19 E7
Lyne Down *Heref'd* 26 E3
Lyne of Gorthleck *H'land* 81 A7
Lyne of Skene *Aberds* 83 B9
Lyneal *Shrops* 33 B10
Lyneham *Oxon* 27 F9
Lyneham *Wilts* 17 D7
Lynemore *H'land* 82 A2
Lynemouth *Northum* 63 D8
Lyness *Orkney* 95 J4
Lyng *Norfolk* 39 D6
Lyng *Som'set* 8 B2
Lynmouth *Devon* 7 B6
Lynsted *Kent* 20 E6
Lynton *Devon* 6 B6
Lyon's Gate *Dorset* 8 D5
Lyonshall *Heref'd* 25 C10
Lytchett Matravers *Dorset* 9 E8
Lytchett Minster *Dorset* 9 E8
Lyth *H'land* 94 D4
Lytham *Lancs* 49 G3
Lytham St Anne's *Lancs* 49 G3
Lythe *N Yorks* 59 E9
Lythes *Orkney* 95 K5

M

Mabe Burnthouse *Cornw'l* 3 F6
Mabie *Dumf/Gal* 60 F5
Mablethorpe *Lincs* 47 D9
Macclesfield *Ches* 44 E3
Macclesfield Forest *Ches* 44 E3
Macduff *Aberds* 89 B7
Mace Green *Suffolk* 31 D8
Macharioch *Arg/Bute* 65 H8
Machen *Caerph* 15 C8
Machrihanish *Arg/Bute* 65 F7
Machynlleth *Powys* 32 E3
Machynys *Carms* 23 G10
Mackerel's Common *W Sussex* 11 B9
Mackworth *Derby* 35 B9
Macmerry *E Loth* 70 C3
Madderty *Perth/Kinr* 76 E2
Maddiston *Falk* 69 C8
Madehurst *W Sussex* 11 C8
Madeley *Staffs* 34 A3
Madeley *Telford* 34 E2
Madeley Heath *Staffs* 43 H10
Madeley Park *Staffs* 34 A3
Madingley *Cambs* 29 B10
Madley *Heref'd* 25 E11
Madresfield *Worcs* 26 D5
Madron *Cornw'l* 2 F3
Maen-y-groes *Ceredig'n* 23 A8
Maenaddwyn *Angl* 40 B6
Maenclochog *Pembs* 22 D5
Maendy *V/Glam* 14 D6
Maentwrog *Gwyn* 41 F8
Maer *Staffs* 34 B3
Maerdy *Conwy* 32 A6
Maerdy *Rh Cyn Taff* 14 B5

Maes-Treylow *Powys* 25 B9
Maesbrook *Shrops* 33 C8
Maesbury *Shrops* 33 C9
Maesbury Marsh *Shrops* 33 C9
Maesgwynne *Carms* 23 D7
Maesgwyn-Isaf *Powys* 33 B7
Maeshafn *Denbs* 42 F5
Maeslyn *Ceredig'n* 23 B8
Maesmynis *Powys* 25 D7
Maesteg *Bridg* 14 B4
Maestir *Ceredig'n* 23 B10
Maesy cwmmer *Caerph* 15 B7
Maesybont *Carms* 23 E9
Maesycrugiau *Carms* 23 B9
Maesymeillion *Ceredig'n* 23 B9
Magdalen Laver *Essex* 30 H2
Maggieknockater *Moray* 88 D3
Magham Down *E Sussex* 12 E5
Maghull *Mersey* 43 B6
Magor *Monmouths* 15 C10
Magpie Green *Suffolk* 39 H6
Maiden Bradley *Wilts* 16 H5
Maiden Law *Durham* 58 B2
Maiden Newton *Dorset* 8 E4
Maiden Wells *Pembs* 22 G4
Maidencombe *Torbay* 5 E10
Maidenhall *Suffolk* 31 D8
Maidenhead *Windsor* 18 D5
Maidens *S Ayrs* 66 F5
Maiden's Green *Brackn'l* 18 D5
Maidensgrave *Suffolk* 31 D9
Maidenwell *Cornw'l* 4 D2
Maidenwell *Lincs* 47 E7
Maidford *Northants* 28 C3
Maids Moreton *Bucks* 28 E4
Maidstone *Kent* 20 F4
Maidwell *Northants* 36 H3
Mail *Shetl'd* 96 L6
Main *Powys* 33 D7
Maindee *Newp* 15 C9
Mains of Airies *Dumf/Gal* 54 C2
Mains of Allardice *Aberds* 83 F10
Mains of Annochie *Aberds* 89 D9
Mains of Balhall *Angus* 77 A8
Mains of Ballindarg *Angus* 77 B7
Mains of Balnakettle *Aberds* 83 F8
Mains of Birness *Aberds* 89 E9
Mains of Burgie *Moray* 87 F13
Mains of Clunas *H'land* 87 G11
Mains of Crichie *Aberds* 89 D9
Mains of Dalvey *H'land* 87 H14
Mains of Dellavaird *Aberds* 83 E9
Mains of Drum *Aberds* 83 D10
Mains of Edingight *Moray* 88 C5
Mains of Fedderate *Aberds* 89 D8
Mains of Inkhorn *Aberds* 89 E9
Mains of Mayen *Moray* 88 D5
Mains of Melgund *Angus* 77 B8
Mains of Thornton *Aberds* 83 F8
Mains of Watten *H'land* 94 E4
Mainsforth *Durham* 58 C3
Mainsriddle *Dumf/Gal* 60 H5
Mainstone *Shrops* 33 G8
Maisemore *Glos* 26 F5
Malacleit *W Isles* 84 A2
Malborough *Devon* 5 H8
Malcoff *Derby* 44 D4
Maldon *Essex* 30 H5
Malham *N Yorks* 50 C5
Maligar *H'land* 85 B9
Mallaig *H'land* 79 B9
Malleny Mills *C/Edinb* 69 D10
Malling *Stirl* 75 G8
Malltraeth *Angl* 40 D6
Mallwyd *Gwyn* 32 D4
Malmesbury *Wilts* 16 C6
Malmsmead *Devon* 7 B6
Malpas *Ches* 43 H7
Malpas *Cornw'l* 3 E7
Malpas *Newp* 15 B9
Malswick *Glos* 26 F4
Maltby *Stockton* 58 E5
Maltby *S Yorks* 45 D8
Maltby le Marsh *Lincs* 47 D8
Malting Green *Essex* 30 F7
Maltman's Hill *Kent* 13 B8
Malton *N Yorks* 52 B3
Malvern Link *Worcs* 26 D4
Malvern Wells *Worcs* 26 D4
Mamble *Worcs* 26 A3
Man-moel *Caerph* 15 A7
Manaccan *Cornw'l* 3 G6
Manafon *Powys* 33 E7
Manais *W Isles* 90 J6
Manar Ho. *Aberds* 83 A9
Manaton *Devon* 5 C8
Mancetter *Warwick* 35 F9
Manchester *Gtr Man* 44 C2
Manchester Airport *Gtr Man* 44 D2
Mancot *Flints* 42 F6
Mandally *H'land* 80 C4
Manea *Cambs* 37 G10
Manfield *N Yorks* 58 E3
Mangaster *Shetl'd* 96 F5
Mangotsfield *S Gloucs* 16 D3
Mangurstadh *W Isles* 90 D5
Mankinholes *W Yorks* 50 G5
Manley *Ches* 43 E8
Mannal *Arg/Bute* 78 G2
Mannerston *W Loth* 69 C9
Manningford Bohune *Wilts* 17 F8
Manningford Bruce *Wilts* 17 F8
Manningham *W Yorks* 51 F7
Mannings Heath *W Sussex* 11 B11
Mannington *Dorset* 9 D9
Manningtree *Essex* 31 E7
Mannofield *Aberd C* 83 C11
Manor Estate *S Yorks* 45 D7
Manor Park *London* 19 C11
Manorbier *Pembs* 22 G5
Manordeilo *Carms* 24 F3
Manorhill *Scot Borders* 70 G5
Manorowen *Pembs* 22 C4
Mansel Lacy *Heref'd* 25 D11
Manselfield *Swan* 23 H10
Mansell Gamage *Heref'd* 25 D10
Mansergh *Cumb* 50 A2
Mansfield *E Ayrs* 67 E9
Mansfield *Notts* 45 F9
Mansfield Woodhouse *Notts* 45 F9
Mansriggs *Cumb* 49 A2
Manston *Dorset* 9 C7
Manston *Kent* 21 E10
Manston *W Yorks* 51 F9
Manswood *Dorset* 9 D8
Manthorpe *Lincs* 37 D6
Manthorpe *Lincs* 46 B3
Manton *N Lincs* 46 B3
Manton *Notts* 45 E9
Manton *Rutl'd* 36 E4
Manton *Wilts* 17 E8
Manuden *Essex* 29 F11
Maperton *Som'set* 8 B5
Maple Cross *Herts* 19 B7
Maplebeck *Notts* 45 F11
Mapledurham *Oxon* 18 D3
Mapledurwell *Hants* 18 F3
Maplehurst *W Sussex* 11 B10
Maplescombe *Kent* 20 E2
Mapperley *Derby* 35 A10
Mapperley Park *Nott'ham* 36 A1
Mapperton *Dorset* 8 E4
Mappleborough Green *Warwick* 27 B7
Mappleton *Derby* 44 H5
Mappleton *ER Yorks* 53 E8
Mappowder *Dorset* 8 D6
Mar Lodge *Aberds* 82 D2
Maraig *W Isles* 90 G6
Marazanvose *Cornw'l* 3 D7
Marazion *Cornw'l* 2 F4
Marbhig *W Isles* 91 F9
Marbury *Ches* 43 H8
March *Cambs* 37 F10
March *S Lanarks* 60 B5
Marcham *Oxon* 17 B11
Marchamley *Shrops* 34 C1
Marchington *Staffs* 35 B7

Marchington Woodlands *Staffs* 35 C7
Marchroes *Gwyn* 40 H5
Marchwiel *Wrex* 42 H6
Marchwood *Hants* 10 C2
Marcross *V/Glam* 14 E5
Marden *Heref'd* 26 D2
Marden *Kent* 12 B6
Marden *Tyne/Wear* 63 F9
Marden *Wilts* 17 F7
Marden Beech *Kent* 12 B6
Marden Thorn *Kent* 13 B6
Mardy *Monmouths* 25 G10
Marefield *Leics* 36 E3
Mareham le Fen *Lincs* 46 F6
Mareham on the Hill *Lincs* 46 F6
Marehay *Derby* 45 H7
Marehill *W Sussex* 11 C9
Maresfield *E Sussex* 12 D3
Marfleet *Kingston/Hull* 53 G7
Marford *Wrex* 42 G6
Margam *Neath P Talb* 14 C3
Margaret Marsh *Dorset* 9 C7
Margaret Roding *Essex* 30 G2
Margaretting *Essex* 20 A3
Margate *Kent* 21 D10
Margnaheglish *N Ayrs* 66 C3
Margrove Park *Redcar/Clevel'd* 59 E7
Marham *Norfolk* 38 D3
Marhamchurch *Cornw'l* 4 A3
Marholm *Peterbro* 37 E7
Mariandyrs *Angl* 41 B8
Marianglas *Angl* 41 B7
Mariansleigh *Devon* 7 D6
Marionburgh *Aberds* 83 C9
Marishader *H'land* 85 B9
Marjoriebanks *Dumf/Gal* 60 E6
Mark *S Ayrs* 54 B3
Mark *Som'set* 15 G9
Mark Causeway *Som'set* 15 G9
Mark Cross *E Sussex* 12 E3
Mark Cross *E Sussex* 12 C4
Markbeech *Kent* 12 B3
Markby *Lincs* 47 E8
Market Bosworth *Leics* 35 E10
Market Deeping *Lincs* 37 E7
Market Drayton *Shrops* 34 B2
Market Harborough *Leics* 36 G3
Market Lavington *Wilts* 17 F7
Market Overton *Rutl'd* 36 D4
Market Rasen *Lincs* 46 D5
Market Stainton *Lincs* 46 E6
Market Weighton *ER Yorks* 52 E4
Market Weston *Suffolk* 38 H5
Markethill *Perth/Kinr* 76 D5
Markfield *Leics* 35 D10
Markham *Caerph* 15 A7
Markham Moor *Notts* 45 E11
Markinch *Fife* 76 G5
Markington *N Yorks* 51 C8
Marks Tey *Essex* 30 F6
Marksbury *Bath/NE Som'set* 16 E3
Markyate *Herts* 29 G7
Marland *Gtr Man* 44 A2
Marlborough *Wilts* 17 E8
Marlbrook *Heref'd* 26 C2
Marlbrook *Worcs* 26 A6
Marlcliff *Warwick* 27 C7
Marldon *Devon* 5 E9
Marlesford *Suffolk* 31 C10
Marley Green *Ches* 43 H8
Marley Hill *Tyne/Wear* 63 H8
Marley Mount *Hants* 9 E11
Marlingford *Norfolk* 39 E7
Marloes *Pembs* 22 F2
Marlow *Bucks* 18 C5
Marlow *Heref'd* 33 H10
Marlow Bottom *Bucks* 18 C5
Marlpit Hill *Kent* 19 G11
Marlpool *Derby* 45 H8
Marnhull *Dorset* 9 C6
Marnoch *Aberds* 88 C5
Marnock *N Lanarks* 68 D6
Marple *Gtr Man* 44 D3
Marple Bridge *Gtr Man* 44 D3
Marr *S Yorks* 45 B9
Marrel *H'land* 93 H13
Marrick *N Yorks* 58 G1
Marrister *Shetl'd* 96 G7
Marros *Carms* 23 E7
Marsden *Tyne/Wear* 63 G9
Marsden *W Yorks* 44 A4
Marsett *N Yorks* 57 H11
Marsh *Devon* 8 D1
Marsh *W Yorks* 50 F6
Marsh Baldon *Oxon* 18 B2
Marsh Gibbon *Bucks* 28 F3
Marsh Green *Devon* 7 G9
Marsh Green *Kent* 12 B3
Marsh Green *Staffs* 44 G2
Marsh Lane *Derby* 45 E8
Marsh Street *Som'set* 7 B8
Marshall's Heath *Herts* 29 G8
Marshalsea *Dorset* 8 D2
Marshalswick *Herts* 29 H8
Marsham *Norfolk* 39 C7
Marshaw *Lancs* 50 D1
Marshborough *Kent* 21 F10
Marshbrook *Shrops* 33 G10
Marshchapel *Lincs* 47 C7
Marshfield *Newp* 15 C8
Marshfield *S Gloucs* 16 D4
Marshgate *Cornw'l* 4 B2
Marshland St James *Norfolk* 37 E11
Marshside *Mersey* 49 H3
Marshwood *Dorset* 8 E2
Marske *N Yorks* 58 F2
Marske-by-the-Sea *Redcar/Clevel'd* 59 D7
Marston *Ches* 43 E9
Marston *Heref'd* 25 C10
Marston *Lincs* 36 A4
Marston *Oxon* 28 H2
Marston *Staffs* 34 D4
Marston *Staffs* 34 C5
Marston *Warwick* 35 F8
Marston *Wilts* 16 F6
Marston Doles *Warwick* 27 C11
Marston Green *W Midlands* 35 G7
Marston Magna *Som'set* 8 B4
Marston Meysey *Wilts* 17 B8
Marston Montgomery *Derby* 35 B7
Marston Moretaine *Beds* 28 D6
Marston on Dove *Derby* 35 C8
Marston St Lawrence *Northants* 28 D2
Marston Stannett *Heref'd* 26 C2
Marston Trussell *Northants* 36 G2
Marstow *Heref'd* 26 G2
Marsworth *Bucks* 28 G6
Marthall *Ches* 44 E2
Martham *Norfolk* 39 D10
Martin *Hants* 9 C9
Martin *Kent* 21 G10
Martin *Lincs* 46 F5
Martin *Lincs* 46 G6
Martin Dales *Lincs* 46 F5
Martin Drove End *Hants* 9 B9
Martin Hussingtree *Worcs* 26 B5
Martin Mill *Kent* 21 G10
Martinhoe *Devon* 6 B5
Martinhoe Cross *Devon* 6 B5
Martinscroft *Warrington* 43 D9
Martinstown *Dorset* 8 F5
Martlesham *Suffolk* 31 D9
Martlesham Heath *Suffolk* 31 D9
Martletwy *Pembs* 22 E5
Martley *Worcs* 26 B4
Martock *Som'set* 8 C3
Marton *Ches* 44 F2
Marton *ER Yorks* 53 F8
Marton *Lincs* 46 D2
Marton *Middlesbro'* 59 E6
Marton *N Yorks* 51 C10
Marton *N Yorks* 52 A3
Marton *Shrops* 33 E8

Marton *Shrops* 33 C10
Marton *Warwick* 27 B11
Marton-le-Moor *N Yorks* 51 B9
Martyr Worthy *Hants* 10 A3
Martyr's Green *Surrey* 19 F7
Marwick *Orkney* 95 F3
Marwood *Devon* 6 C4
Mary Tavy *Devon* 4 D6
Marybank *H'land* 86 F7
Maryburgh *H'land* 87 F8
Maryhill *C/Glasg* 68 D4
Marykirk *Aberds* 83 G8
Marylebone *Gtr Man* 43 B8
Marypark *Moray* 88 E1
Maryport *Cumb* 56 C2
Maryport *Dumf/Gal* 54 F4
Maryton *Angus* 77 B9
Marywell *Aberds* 83 D7
Marywell *Aberds* 83 D11
Marywell *Angus* 77 C9
Masham *N Yorks* 51 A8
Mashbury *Essex* 30 G3
Masongill *N Yorks* 50 B2
Masonhill *S Ayrs* 67 D6
Mastin Moor *Derby* 45 E8
Mastrick *Aberd C* 83 C10
Matching *Essex* 30 G2
Matching Green *Essex* 30 G2
Matching Tye *Essex* 30 G2
Matfen *Northum* 62 F6
Matfield *Kent* 12 B5
Mathern *Monmouths* 15 B11
Mathon *Heref'd* 26 D4
Mathry *Pembs* 22 C3
Matlaske *Norfolk* 39 B7
Matlock *Derby* 44 F6
Matlock Bath *Derby* 44 G6
Matson *Glos* 26 G5
Matterdale End *Cumb* 56 D5
Mattersey *Notts* 45 D10
Mattersey Thorpe *Notts* 45 D10
Mattingley *Hants* 18 F4
Mattishall *Norfolk* 39 D6
Mattishall Burgh *Norfolk* 39 D6
Mauchline *E Ayrs* 67 D7
Maud *Aberds* 89 D9
Maugersbury *Glos* 27 F8
Maughold *I/Man* 48 C4
Mauld *H'land* 86 H7
Maulden *Beds* 29 E7
Maulds Meaburn *Cumb* 57 E8
Maunby *N Yorks* 58 H4
Maund Bryan *Heref'd* 26 C2
Maundown *Som'set* 7 D9
Mautby *Norfolk* 39 D10
Mavis Enderby *Lincs* 47 F7
Maw Green *Ches* 43 G10
Mawbray *Cumb* 56 B2
Mawdesley *Lancs* 43 A7
Mawdlam *Bridg* 14 C4
Mawgan *Cornw'l* 3 G6
Mawla *Cornw'l* 2 E6
Mawnan *Cornw'l* 3 G6
Mawnan Smith *Cornw'l* 3 G6
Mawsley *Northants* 36 H4
Maxey *Peterbro* 37 E7
Maxstoke *Warwick* 35 G8
Maxton *Scot Borders* 70 G5
Maxton *Kent* 21 G10
Maxwellheugh *Scot Borders* 70 G6
Maxwelltown *Dumf/Gal* 60 F5
Maxworthy *Cornw'l* 4 B3
May Bank *Staffs* 44 H2
Mayals *Swan* 23 G10
Maybole *S Ayrs* 66 F6
Mayfield *E Sussex* 12 D4
Mayfield *Midloth* 70 D2
Mayfield *Staffs* 44 H5
Mayfield *W Loth* 69 D8
Mayford *Surrey* 18 F6
Mayland *Essex* 20 A6
Maynard's Green *E Sussex* 12 E4
Maypole *Monmouths* 25 G11
Maypole *I/Scilly* 2 C3
Maypole Green *Essex* 30 F7
Maypole Green *Norfolk* 39 F10
Maypole Green *Suffolk* 31 B9
Maywick *Shetl'd* 96 L5
Meadle *Bucks* 28 H5
Meadowtown *Shrops* 33 E9
Meaford *Staffs* 34 B4
Meal Bank *Cumb* 57 G7
Mealabost *W Isles* 91 D9
Mealabost Bhuirgh *W Isles* 91 B9
Mealsgate *Cumb* 56 B4
Meanwood *W Yorks* 51 F8
Mearbeck *N Yorks* 50 C4
Meare *Som'set* 15 G10
Meare Green *Som'set* 8 B1
Mears Ashby *Northants* 28 B5
Measham *Leics* 35 D9
Meath Green *Surrey* 12 B1
Meathop *Cumb* 49 A4
Meaux *ER Yorks* 53 F6
Meavy *Devon* 4 E6
Medbourne *Leics* 36 F3
Medburn *Northum* 63 F7
Meddon *Devon* 6 E1
Meden Vale *Notts* 45 F9
Medlam *Lincs* 47 G7
Medmenham *Bucks* 18 C5
Medomsley *Durham* 58 A2
Medstead *Hants* 10 A5
Meer End *W Midlands* 27 A9
Meerbrook *Staffs* 44 F3
Meers Bridge *Lincs* 47 D8
Meeth *Devon* 6 F4
Meggethead *Scot Borders* 61 A7
Meidrim *Carms* 23 D7
Meifod *Denbs* 42 G3
Meifod *Powys* 33 D7
Meigle *N Ayrs* 66 C3
Meigle *Perth/Kinr* 76 C5
Meikle Earnock *S Lanarks* 68 E6
Meikle Ferry *H'land* 87 C10
Meikle Forter *Angus* 76 A4
Meikle Gluich *H'land* 87 C9
Meikle Pinkerton *E Loth* 70 C6
Meikle Strath *Aberds* 83 F8
Meikle Tarty *Aberds* 89 F9
Meikle Wartle *Aberds* 89 E7
Meikleour *Perth/Kinr* 76 D4
Meinciau *Carms* 23 E9
Meir *Stoke* 34 A5
Meir Heath *Staffs* 34 A5
Melbourn *Cambs* 29 D10
Melbourne *Derby* 35 C9
Melbourne *ER Yorks* 52 E3
Melbourne *S Lanarks* 69 F8
Melbury Abbas *Dorset* 9 B7
Melbury Bubb *Dorset* 8 D4
Melbury Osmond *Dorset* 8 D4
Melbury Sampford *Dorset* 8 D4
Melby *Shetl'd* 96 H3
Melchbourne *Beds* 29 B7
Melcombe Bingham *Dorset* 8 D6
Melcombe Regis *Dorset* 8 F5
Meldon *Devon* 6 G4
Meldon *Northum* 63 E7
Meldreth *Cambs* 29 D10
Meldrum Ho. *Aberds* 89 F8
Melfort *Arg/Bute* 73 B7
Melgarve *H'land* 81 D6
Meliden *Denbs* 42 D3
Melin-byrhedyn *Powys* 32 F4
Melin-y-coed *Conwy* 41 D10
Melin-y-ddôl *Powys* 33 E6
Melin-y-grug *Powys* 33 E6
Melin-y-Wig *Denbs* 42 H3
Melincourt *Neath P Talb* 14 A4
Melincryddan *Neath P Talb* 14 B3
Melksham *Wilts* 16 E5
Melldalloch *Arg/Bute* 73 F8
Melling *Lancs* 50 B1
Melling *Mersey* 43 B6
Melling Mount *Mersey* 43 B7
Mellis *Suffolk* 31 A8
Mellon Charles *H'land* 91 H13
Mellon Udrigle *H'land* 91 H13
Mellor *Gtr Man* 44 D3
Mellor *Lancs* 50 F2

Mellor Brook *Lancs* 50 F2
Mells *Som'set* 16 G4
Melmerby *Cumb* 57 C8
Melmerby *N Yorks* 51 B9
Melmerby *N Yorks* 58 H1
Melplash *Dorset* 8 E3
Melrose *Scot Borders* 70 G4
Melsetter *Orkney* 95 K3
Melsonby *N Yorks* 58 F2
Meltham *W Yorks* 44 A5
Melton *Suffolk* 31 C9
Melton Constable *Norfolk* 38 B6
Melton Mowbray *Leics* 36 D3
Melton Ross *N Lincs* 46 A4
Meltonby *ER Yorks* 52 D3
Melvaig *H'land* 91 J12
Melverley *Shrops* 33 D9
Melverley Green *Shrops* 33 D9
Melvich *H'land* 93 C11
Membury *Devon* 8 D1
Memsie *Aberds* 89 B9
Memus *Angus* 77 B7
Menabilly *Cornw'l* 4 F1
Menai Bridge = Porthaethwy *Angl* 41 C7
Mendham *Suffolk* 39 G8
Mendlesham *Suffolk* 31 B8
Mendlesham Green *Suffolk* 31 B7
Menheniot *Cornw'l* 4 E3
Menston *W Yorks* 51 E7
Menstrie *Clack* 75 H11
Menthorpe *N Yorks* 52 F2
Mentmore *Bucks* 28 G6
Meoble *H'land* 79 C10
Meole Brace *Shrops* 33 D10
Meols *Mersey* 42 C5
Meonstoke *Hants* 10 C5
Meopham *Kent* 20 E3
Meopham Station *Kent* 20 E3
Mepal *Cambs* 37 G10
Meppershall *Beds* 29 E8
Merbach *Heref'd* 25 D10
Mere *Ches* 43 D10
Mere *Wilts* 9 A7
Mere Brow *Lancs* 49 H4
Mere Green *W Midlands* 35 F7
Mereclough *Lancs* 50 F4
Mereside *Blackp'l* 49 F3
Mereworth *Kent* 20 F3
Mergie *Aberds* 83 E9
Meriden *W Midlands* 35 G8
Merkadale *H'land* 85 E8
Merkland *Dumf/Gal* 60 F3
Merkland Lodge *H'land* 92 G7
Merley *Poole* 9 E9
Merlin's Bridge *Pembs* 22 E4
Merrington *Shrops* 33 C10
Merrion *Pembs* 22 G4
Merriott *Som'set* 8 C3
Merrivale *Devon* 4 D6
Merrow *Surrey* 19 F7
Merrymeet *Cornw'l* 4 E3
Mersham *Kent* 13 C9
Merstham *Surrey* 19 F9
Merston *W Sussex* 11 D7
Merstone *I/Wight* 10 F4
Merther *Cornw'l* 3 E7
Merthyr *Carms* 23 D8
Merthyr Cynog *Powys* 24 E6
Merthyr-Dyfan *V/Glam* 15 E7
Merthyr Mawr *Bridg* 14 D4
Merthyr Tudful = Merthyr Tydfil *Merth Tyd* 25 H7
Merthyr Tydfil = Merthyr Tudful *Merth Tyd* 25 H7
Merthyr Vale *Merth Tyd* 14 B6
Merton *Devon* 6 E4
Merton *London* 19 D9
Merton *Norfolk* 38 F5
Merton *Oxon* 28 G2
Mervinslaw *Scot Borders* 62 B2
Meshaw *Devon* 7 E6
Messing *Essex* 30 G5
Messingham *N Lincs* 46 B2
Metfield *Suffolk* 39 G8
Metheringham *Lincs* 46 F4
Methil *Fife* 76 H6
Methlem *Gwyn* 40 G3
Methley *W Yorks* 51 G9
Methlick *Aberds* 89 E8
Methven *Perth/Kinr* 76 E3
Methwold *Norfolk* 38 F3
Methwold Hythe *Norfolk* 38 F3
Mettingham *Suffolk* 39 G9
Mevagissey *Cornw'l* 3 E8
Mewith Head *N Yorks* 50 B3
Mexborough *S Yorks* 45 B8
Mey *H'land* 94 C4
Meysey Hampton *Glos* 17 B8
Miabhag *W Isles* 90 H6
Miabhag *W Isles* 90 G5
Miabhig *W Isles* 90 D5
Michaelchurch *Heref'd* 26 F2
Michaelchurch Escley *Heref'd* 25 E10
Michaelchurch on Arrow *Powys* 25 C9
Michaelston-le-Pit *V/Glam* 15 D7
Michaelston-y-Fedw *Newp* 15 C8
Michaelston-super-Ely *Card* 15 D7
Micheldever *Hants* 10 A3
Michelmersh *Hants* 10 B2
Mickfield *Suffolk* 31 B8
Mickle Trafford *Ches* 43 F7
Micklebring *S Yorks* 45 C9
Mickleby *N Yorks* 59 E8
Mickleham *Surrey* 19 F8
Micklehurst *Gtr Man* 44 B3
Mickleover *Derby C* 35 B8
Micklethwaite *W Yorks* 51 E7
Mickleton *Durham* 57 D11
Mickleton *Glos* 27 D8
Mickletown *W Yorks* 51 G9
Mickley *N Yorks* 51 B8
Mickley Square *Northum* 62 G6
Mid Ardlaw *Aberds* 89 B9
Mid Auchinleck *Invercl* 68 C2
Mid Beltie *Aberds* 83 C8
Mid Calder *W Loth* 69 D9
Mid Cloch Forbie *Aberds* 89 C7
Mid Clyth *H'land* 94 G4
Mid Lavant *W Sussex* 11 D7
Mid Main *H'land* 86 H7
Mid Urchany *H'land* 87 G11
Mid Walls *Shetl'd* 96 H4
Mid Yell *Shetl'd* 96 D7
Midbea *Orkney* 95 D5
Middle Assendon *Oxon* 18 C4
Middle Aston *Oxon* 27 F11
Middle Barton *Oxon* 27 F11
Middle Cairncake *Aberds* 89 D8
Middle Claydon *Bucks* 28 F4
Middle Drums *Angus* 77 B8
Middle Handley *Derby* 45 E8
Middle Littleton *Worcs* 27 D7
Middle Maes-coed *Heref'd* 25 E10
Middle Mill *Pembs* 22 D3
Middle Rasen *Lincs* 46 D4
Middle Rigg *Perth/Kinr* 76 G3
Middle Tysoe *Warwick* 27 D10
Middle Wallop *Hants* 17 H9
Middle Winterslow *Wilts* 9 A11
Middle Woodford *Wilts* 17 H8
Middlebie *Dumf/Gal* 61 F8
Middleforth Green *Lancs* 49 G5
Middleham *N Yorks* 58 H2
Middlehope *Shrops* 33 G10
Middlemarsh *Dorset* 8 D5
Middlemuir *Aberds* 89 D9
Middlesbrough *Middlesbro'* 59 D6
Middleshaw *Cumb* 57 H7
Middleshaw *Dumf/Gal* 61 F7
Middlesmoor *N Yorks* 51 B6
Middlestone *Durham* 58 C3
Middlestone Moor *Durham* 58 C3
Middlestown *W Yorks* 51 H8
Middleton *Aberds* 83 B10
Middleton *Arg/Bute* 78 G2

Middleton *Cumb* 57 H8
Middleton *Derby* 44 G6
Middleton *Derby* 44 F5
Middleton *Essex* 30 E5
Middleton *Gtr Man* 44 B2
Middleton *Hants* 17 G11
Middleton *Heref'd* 26 B2
Middleton *Lancs* 49 D4
Middleton *Midloth* 70 E2
Middleton *Norfolk* 38 D2
Middleton *Northants* 36 G4
Middleton *Northum* 62 E6
Middleton *Northum* 71 H8
Middleton *N Yorks* 59 H8
Middleton *N Yorks* 51 E7
Middleton *Perth/Kinr* 76 G4
Middleton *Perth/Kinr* 76 C4
Middleton *Shrops* 33 H11
Middleton *Shrops* 33 C9
Middleton *Suffolk* 31 B11
Middleton *Warwick* 35 F7
Middleton *W Yorks* 51 G8
Middleton *W Yorks* 51 E7
Middleton Cheney *Northants* 27 D11
Middleton Green *Staffs* 34 B5
Middleton Hall *Northum* 71 H8
Middleton-in-Teesdale *Durham* 57 D11
Middleton Moor *Suffolk* 31 B11
Middleton-on-Leven *N Yorks* 58 F5
Middleton-on-Sea *W Sussex* 11 D8
Middleton on the Hill *Heref'd* 26 B2
Middleton-on-the-Wolds *ER Yorks* 52 E5
Middleton One Row *D'lington* 58 E4
Middleton Priors *Shrops* 34 F2
Middleton Quernham *N Yorks* 51 B9
Middleton St George *D'lington* 58 E4
Middleton Scriven *Shrops* 34 G2
Middleton Stoney *Oxon* 28 F2
Middleton Tyas *N Yorks* 58 F3
Middletown *Cumb* 56 F1
Middletown *Powys* 33 D9
Middlewich *Ches* 43 F9
Middlewood Green *Suffolk* 31 B7
Middlezoy *Som'set* 8 A2
Middridge *Durham* 58 D3
Midfield *H'land* 93 C8
Midge Hall *Lancs* 49 G5
Midgeholme *Cumb* 62 H2
Midgham *W Berks* 18 E2
Midgley *W Yorks* 50 G6
Midgley *W Yorks* 51 H7
Midhopestones *S Yorks* 44 C6
Midhurst *W Sussex* 11 B7
Midlem *Scot Borders* 70 H4
Midmar *Aberds* 83 C8
Midsomer Norton *Bath/NE Som'set* 16 F3
Midton *Invercl* 73 F11
Midtown *H'land* 93 C8
Midtown of Buchromb *Moray* 88 D3
Midville *Lincs* 47 G7
Midway *Ches* 44 D3
Migdale *H'land* 87 B9
Migvie *Aberds* 82 C6
Milarrochy *Stirl* 68 A3
Milborne Port *Som'set* 8 C5
Milborne St Andrew *Dorset* 9 E7
Milborne Wick *Som'set* 8 B5
Milbourne *Northum* 63 F7
Milburn *Cumb* 57 D8
Milbury Heath *S Gloucs* 16 B3
Milcombe *Oxon* 27 E11
Milden *Suffolk* 30 D6
Mildenhall *Suffolk* 30 A4
Mildenhall *Wilts* 17 E9
Mile Cross *Norfolk* 39 D8
Mile Elm *Wilts* 16 E6
Mile End *Essex* 30 F6
Mile End *Glos* 26 G2
Mile Oak *Brighton/Hove* 12 F1
Milebrook *Powys* 25 A10
Milebush *Kent* 20 G4
Mileham *Norfolk* 38 D5
Milesmark *Fife* 69 B9
Milfield *Northum* 71 G8
Milford *Derby* 45 H7
Milford *Devon* 6 D1
Milford *Powys* 33 F7
Milford *Staffs* 34 C5
Milford *Surrey* 18 G6
Milford *Wilts* 9 B10
Milford Haven = Aberdaugleddau *Pembs* 22 F4
Milford on Sea *Hants* 10 E1
Milkwall *Glos* 26 H2
Milkwell *Wilts* 9 B8
Mill Bank *W Yorks* 50 G6
Mill Common *Suffolk* 39 G10
Mill End *Bucks* 18 C4
Mill End *Herts* 29 E10
Mill Green *Essex* 20 A3
Mill Green *Norfolk* 39 G7
Mill Green *Suffolk* 30 D6
Mill Hill *London* 19 B9
Mill Lane *Hants* 18 F4
Mill of Kingoodie *Aberds* 89 F8
Mill of Muiresk *Aberds* 89 D6
Mill of Sterin *Aberds* 82 D5
Mill of Uras *Aberds* 83 E10
Mill Place *N Lincs* 46 B3
Mill Side *Cumb* 49 A4
Mill Street *Norfolk* 39 D6
Milland *W Sussex* 11 B7
Millarston *Renfrews* 68 D3
Millbank *Aberds* 89 D11
Millbeck *Cumb* 56 D4
Millbounds *Orkney* 95 E6
Millbreck *Aberds* 89 D9
Millbridge *Surrey* 18 G5
Millbrook *Beds* 29 E7
Millbrook *Cornw'l* 4 F5
Millbrook *S'thampton* 10 C2
Millburn *S Ayrs* 67 D7
Millcombe *Devon* 5 F8
Millcorner *E Sussex* 13 D7
Milldale *Staffs* 44 G5
Millden Lodge *Angus* 83 F7
Milldens *Angus* 77 B8
Millerhill *Midloth* 70 D2
Miller's Dale *Derby* 44 E5
Miller's Green *Derby* 44 G6
Millgreen *Shrops* 34 C2
Millhalf *Heref'd* 25 D9
Millhayes *Devon* 8 D1
Millhead *Lancs* 49 B4
Millheugh *S Lanarks* 68 E6
Millholme *Cumb* 57 G7
Millhouse *Arg/Bute* 73 F8
Millhouse *Cumb* 56 C5
Millhouse Green *S Yorks* 44 B6
Millhousebridge *Dumf/Gal* 61 E7
Millhouses *S Yorks* 45 D7
Milliken Park *Renfrews* 68 D3
Millin Cross *Pembs* 22 E4
Millington *ER Yorks* 52 D4
Millmeece *Staffs* 34 B4
Millom *Cumb* 49 A1
Millook *Cornw'l* 4 B2
Millpool *Cornw'l* 4 D2
Millport *N Ayrs* 73 H11
Millquarter *Dumf/Gal* 55 A9
Millthorpe *Lincs* 37 B7
Millthrop *Cumb* 57 G8
Milltimber *Aberd C* 83 C10
Milltown *Corn'wl* 4 F2
Milltown *Derby* 45 F7
Milltown *Devon* 6 C4
Milltown *Dumf/Gal* 61 F9
Milltown of Aberdalgie *Perth/Kinr* 76 E3

Milltown of Auchindoun *Moray* 88 D3
Milltown of Craigston *Aberds* 89 C7
Milltown of Edinville *Moray* 88 D2
Milltown of Kildrummy *Aberds* 82 B6
Milltown of Rothiemay *Moray* 88 D5
Milltown of Towie *Aberds* 82 B6
Milnathort *Perth/Kinr* 76 G4
Milner's Heath *Ches* 43 F7
Milngavie *E Dunb* 68 C4
Milnrow *Gtr Man* 44 A3
Milnshaw *Lancs* 50 G3
Milnthorpe *Cumb* 49 A4
Milo *Carms* 23 E10
Milson *Shrops* 26 A3
Milstead *Kent* 20 F6
Milston *Wilts* 17 G8
Milton *Angus* 76 C6
Milton *Cambs* 29 B11
Milton *Cumb* 61 G11
Milton *Derby* 35 C9
Milton *Dumf/Gal* 54 D5
Milton *Dumf/Gal* 60 E4
Milton *Dumf/Gal* 60 F3
Milton *H'land* 86 H7
Milton *H'land* 86 G7
Milton *H'land* 87 G8
Milton *H'land* 87 F10
Milton *H'land* 94 E5
Milton *H'land* 87 D10
Milton *Moray* 88 B5
Milton *Notts* 45 E11
Milton *N Som'set* 15 E9
Milton *Oxon* 27 E11
Milton *Oxon* 17 B11
Milton *Pembs* 22 F5
Milton *Perth/Kinr* 76 D2
Milton *Port'sm'th* 10 E5
Milton *Stir* 75 G8
Milton *Stoke* 44 G3
Milton *W Dunb* 68 C3
Milton Abbas *Dorset* 9 D7
Milton Abbot *Devon* 4 D5
Milton Bridge *Midloth* 69 D11
Milton Bryan *Beds* 28 E6
Milton Clevedon *Som'set* 16 H3
Milton Coldwells *Aberds* 89 E9
Milton Combe *Devon* 4 E5
Milton Damerel *Devon* 6 E2
Milton End *Glos* 17 A8
Milton Ernest *Beds* 29 C7
Milton Green *Ches* 43 G7
Milton Hill *Oxon* 17 B11
Milton Keynes *M/Keynes* 28 E5
Milton Keynes Village *M/Keynes* 28 E5
Milton Lilbourne *Wilts* 17 E8
Milton Malsor *Northants* 28 C4
Milton Morenish *Perth/Kinr* 75 D9
Milton of Auchinhove *Aberds* 83 C7
Milton of Balgonie *Fife* 76 G6
Milton of Buchanan *Stirl* 68 A3
Milton of Campfield *Aberds* 83 C8
Milton of Campsie *E Dunb* 68 C5
Milton of Corsindae *Aberds* 83 C8
Milton of Cushnie *Aberds* 83 B7
Milton of Dalcapon *Perth/Kinr* 76 B2
Milton of Edradour *Perth/Kinr* 76 B2
Milton of Gollanfield *H'land* 87 F10
Milton of Lesmore *Aberds* 82 A6
Milton of Logie *Aberds* 82 C6
Milton of Murtle *Aberd C* 83 C10
Milton of Noth *Aberds* 83 A7
Milton of Tullich *Aberds* 82 D5
Milton on Stour *Dorset* 9 B6
Milton Regis *Kent* 20 E6
Milton under Wychwood *Oxon* 27 G9
Miltonduff *Moray* 88 B1
Miltonhill *Moray* 87 E13
Miltonise *Dumf/Gal* 54 B4
Milverton *Som'set* 7 D10
Milverton *Warwick* 27 B10
Milwich *Staffs* 34 B5
Minard *Arg/Bute* 73 D8
Minchinhampton *Glos* 16 A5
Mindrum *Northum* 71 G7
Minehead *Som'set* 7 B8
Minera *Wrex* 42 G5
Minety *Wilts* 17 B7
Minffordd *Gwyn* 41 G8
Minffordd *Gwyn* 32 D3
Minffordd *Gwyn* 41 C7
Miningsby *Lincs* 47 F7
Minions *Cornw'l* 4 D3
Minishant *S Ayrs* 66 E6
Minllyn *Gwyn* 32 D4
Minnes *Aberds* 89 F9
Minngearraidh *W Isles* 84 F2
Minnigaff *Dumf/Gal* 55 C7
Minnonie *Aberds* 89 B7
Minskip *N Yorks* 51 C9
Minstead *Hants* 10 C1
Minsted *W Sussex* 11 B7
Minster *Kent* 20 D6
Minster *Kent* 21 E10
Minster Lovell *Oxon* 27 G10
Minsterley *Shrops* 33 E9
Minsterworth *Glos* 26 G4
Minterne Magna *Dorset* 8 D5
Minting *Lincs* 46 E5
Mintlaw *Aberds* 89 D10
Minto *Scot Borders* 61 A11
Minton *Shrops* 33 F10
Minwear *Pembs* 22 E5
Minworth *W Midlands* 35 F7
Mirbister *Orkney* 95 F4
Mirehouse *Cumb* 56 E1
Mireland *H'land* 94 D5
Mirfield *W Yorks* 51 H8
Miserden *Glos* 26 H6
Miskin *Rh Cyn Taff* 14 C6
Misson *Notts* 45 C10
Misterton *Leics* 36 G1
Misterton *Notts* 45 C11
Misterton *Som'set* 8 D3
Mistley *Essex* 31 E7
Mitcham *London* 19 E9
Mitchel Troy *Monmouths* 25 G11
Mitcheldean *Glos* 26 G3
Mitchell *Cornw'l* 3 D7
Mitcheltroy Common *Monmouths* 25 H11
Mitford *Northum* 63 E7
Mithian *Cornw'l* 2 D6
Mitton *Staffs* 34 D4
Mixbury *Oxon* 28 E3
Moat *Cumb* 61 F10
Moats Tye *Suffolk* 31 C7
Mobberley *Ches* 43 E10
Mobberley *Staffs* 34 A6
Moccas *Heref'd* 25 D10
Mochdre *Conwy* 41 C10
Mochdre *Powys* 33 G6
Mochrum *Dumf/Gal* 54 E6
Mockbeggar *Hants* 9 D10
Mockerkin *Cumb* 56 D2
Modbury *Devon* 5 F7
Moddershall *Staffs* 34 B5
Moelfre *Angl* 41 B7
Moelfre *Powys* 33 C7
Moffat *Dumf/Gal* 60 C6
Moggerhanger *Beds* 29 D8
Moira *Leics* 35 D9
Mol-chlach *H'land* 85 G9
Molash *Kent* 21 F7
Mold = Yr Wyddgrug *Flints* 42 F5
Moldgreen *W Yorks* 51 H7
Molehill Green *Essex* 30 F2
Molescroft *ER Yorks* 52 E6
Molesden *Northum* 63 E7
Molesworth *Cambs* 37 H6
Moll *H'land* 85 E10
Molland *Devon* 7 D7
Mollington *Ches* 42 E6
Mollington *Oxon* 27 D11
Mollinsburn *N Lanarks* 68 C6
Monachty *Ceredig'n* 24 B2

Monachylemore *Stirl* 75 F7
Monar Lodge *H'land* 86 G5
Monaughty *Powys* 25 B9
Monboddo House *Aberds* 83 F9
Mondynes *Aberds* 83 F9
Monevechadan *Arg/Bute* 74 G4
Monewden *Suffolk* 31 C9
Moneydie *Perth/Kinr* 76 E3
Moniaive *Dumf/Gal* 60 D3
Monifieth *Angus* 77 D7
Monikie *Angus* 77 D7
Monimail *Fife* 76 F5
Monington *Pembs* 22 B6
Monk Bretton *S Yorks* 45 B7
Monk Fryston *N Yorks* 51 G11
Monk Sherborne *Hants* 18 F3
Monk Soham *Suffolk* 31 B9
Monk Street *Essex* 30 F3
Monken Hadley *London* 19 B9
Monkhopton *Shrops* 34 F2
Monkland *Heref'd* 25 C11
Monknash *V/Glam* 14 D5
Monkokehampton *Devon* 6 F4
Monks Eleigh *Suffolk* 30 D6
Monk's Gate *W Sussex* 11 B11
Monks Heath *Ches* 44 E2
Monks Kirby *Warwick* 35 G10
Monks Risborough *Bucks* 18 A5
Monkseaton *Tyne/Wear* 63 F9
Monkshill *Aberds* 89 D7
Monksilver *Som'set* 7 C9
Monkspath *W Midlands* 35 H7
Monkswood *Monmouths* 15 A9
Monkton *Devon* 7 F10
Monkton *Kent* 21 E9
Monkton *Pembs* 22 F4
Monkton *S Ayrs* 67 D6
Monkton Combe *Bath/NE Som'set* 16 E4
Monkton Deverill *Wilts* 16 H5
Monkton Farleigh *Wilts* 16 E5
Monkton Heathfield *Som'set* 8 B1
Monkton Up Wimborne *Dorset* 9 C9
Monkwearmouth *Tyne/Wear* 63 H9
Monkwood *Hants* 10 A5
Monmouth = Trefynwy *Monmouths* 26 G2
Monmouth Cap *Monmouths* 25 F10
Monnington on Wye *Heref'd* 25 D10
Monreith *Dumf/Gal* 54 E6
Monreith Mains *Dumf/Gal* 54 E6
Mont Saint *Guernsey* 11
Montacute *Som'set* 8 C3
Montford *Arg/Bute* 73 G10
Montford *Shrops* 33 D10
Montford Bridge *Shrops* 33 D10
Montgarrie *Aberds* 83 B7
Montgomery = Trefaldwyn *Powys* 33 F8
Montrave *Fife* 76 G6
Montrose *Angus* 77 B10
Montsale *Essex* 21 B7
Monxton *Hants* 17 G10
Monyash *Derby* 44 F5
Monymusk *Aberds* 83 B8
Monzie *Perth/Kinr* 75 E11
Monzie Castle *Perth/Kinr* 75 E11
Moonzie *Fife* 76 F6
Moor Allerton *W Yorks* 51 F8
Moor Crichel *Dorset* 9 D8
Moor End *ER Yorks* 52 F4
Moor End *York* 52 D2
Moor Monkton *N Yorks* 51 D11
Moor of Granary *Moray* 87 F13
Moor of Ravenstone *Dumf/Gal* 54 E6
Moor Row *Cumb* 56 E2
Moor Street *Kent* 20 E5
Moorby *Lincs* 46 F6
Moordown *Bourne'm'th* 9 E9
Moore *Halton* 43 D8
Moorend *Glos* 16 A4
Moorends *S Yorks* 52 H2
Moorgate *S Yorks* 45 C8
Moorgreen *Notts* 45 H8
Moorhall *Derby* 45 E7
Moorhampton *Heref'd* 25 D10
Moorhead *W Yorks* 51 F7
Moorhouse *Cumb* 61 H9
Moorhouse *Notts* 45 F11
Moorlinch *Som'set* 15 H10
Moorsholm *Redcar/Clevel'd* 59 E7
Moorside *Gtr Man* 44 B3
Moorthorpe *W Yorks* 45 A8
Moortown *Hants* 9 D10
Moortown *I/Wight* 10 F3
Moortown *Lincs* 46 C4
Moranglea *H'land* 87 C10
Morar *H'land* 79 B9
Morborne *Cambs* 37 F7
Morchard Bishop *Devon* 7 F6
Morcombelake *Dorset* 8 E3
Morcott *Rutl'd* 36 E5
Morda *Shrops* 33 C8
Morden *Dorset* 9 E8
Morden *London* 19 E9
Mordiford *Heref'd* 26 E2
Mordon *Durham* 58 D4
More *Shrops* 33 F9
Morebath *Devon* 7 D8
Morebattle *Scot Borders* 70 H6
Morecambe *Lancs* 49 C4
Morefield *H'land* 86 B4
Moreleigh *Devon* 5 F8
Morenish *Perth/Kinr* 75 D8
Moresby Parks *Cumb* 56 E1
Morestead *Hants* 10 B4
Moreton *Dorset* 9 F7
Moreton *Essex* 30 H2
Moreton *Mersey* 42 C5
Moreton *Oxon* 18 A3
Moreton *Staffs* 34 D3
Moreton Corbet *Shrops* 34 C1
Moreton-in-Marsh *Glos* 27 E9
Moreton Jeffries *Heref'd* 26 D3
Moreton Morrell *Warwick* 27 C10
Moreton on Lugg *Heref'd* 26 D2
Moreton Pinkney *Northants* 28 D2
Moreton Say *Shrops* 34 B2
Moreton Valence *Glos* 26 H4
Moretonhampstead *Devon* 5 C8
Morfa *Carms* 23 G9
Morfa *Carms* 23 G10
Morfa Bach *Carms* 23 E8
Morfa Bychan *Gwyn* 41 G7
Morfa Dinlle *Gwyn* 40 E6
Morfa Glas *Neath P Talb* 14 A4
Morfa Nefyn *Gwyn* 40 F4
Morganstown *Card* 15 C7
Morgan's Vale *Wilts* 9 B10
Moriah *Ceredig'n* 32 H2
Morland *Cumb* 57 D7
Morley *Derby* 35 A9
Morley *Durham* 58 D2
Morley *W Yorks* 51 G8
Morley Green *Ches* 44 D2
Morley St Botolph *Norfolk* 39 F6
Morningside *C/Edinb* 69 D11
Morningside *N Lanarks* 69 E7
Morningthorpe *Norfolk* 39 F8
Morpeth *Northum* 63 E8
Morphie *Aberds* 83 F10
Morrey *Staffs* 35 D7
Morris Green *Essex* 30 E4
Morriston *Swan* 14 B2
Morston *Norfolk* 38 A6
Mortehoe *Devon* 6 B3
Mortimer *W Berks* 18 E3
Mortimer West End *Hants* 18 E3
Mortimer's Cross *Heref'd* 25 B11
Mortlake *London* 19 D9
Morton *Cumb* 56 A5
Morton *Derby* 45 F8

Morton *Lincs* 37 C6
Morton *Lincs* 46 B2
Morton *Lincs* 46 C2
Morton *Norfolk* 39 D7
Morton *Notts* 45 G11
Morton *S Gloucs* 16 B3
Morton *Shrops* 33 C8
Morton Bagot *Warwick* 27 B8
Morton-on-Swale *N Yorks* 58 G4
Morvah *Cornw'l* 2 F3
Morval *Cornw'l* 4 F3
Morvich *H'land* 80 A1
Morvich *H'land* 87 B10
Morville *Shrops* 34 F2
Morville Heath *Shrops* 34 F2
Morwenstow *Cornw'l* 6 E1
Mosborough *S Yorks* 45 D8
Moscow *E Ayrs* 67 B7
Mosedale *Cumb* 56 C5
Moseley *W Midlands* 34 F5
Moseley *W Midlands* 35 G6
Moseley *Worcs* 26 C5
Moss *Arg/Bute* 78 G2
Moss *S Yorks* 45 A9
Moss *Wrex* 42 G6
Moss Bank *Mersey* 43 C8
Moss Edge *Lancs* 49 E4
Moss End *Berks* 18 D5
Moss of Barmuckity *Moray* 88 B2
Moss Pit *Staffs* 34 C5
Moss-side *H'land* 87 F11
Moss Side *Lancs* 49 F3
Mossat *Aberds* 82 B6
Mossbank *Shetl'd* 96 F6
Mossbay *Cumb* 56 D1
Mossblown *S Ayrs* 67 D7
Mossbrow *Gtr Man* 43 D10
Mossburnford *Scot Borders* 62 B2
Mossdale *Dumf/Gal* 55 B9
Mossend *N Lanarks* 68 D6
Mosser *Cumb* 56 D3
Mossfield *H'land* 87 D9
Mossgiel *E Ayrs* 67 D7
Mosshouses *Scot Borders* 70 G4
Mossley *Ches* 44 F2
Mossley *Gtr Man* 44 B3
Mossley Hill *Mersey* 42 D6
Mosstodloch *Moray* 88 C3
Mosston *Angus* 77 C8
Mossy Lea *Lancs* 43 A8
Mosterton *Dorset* 8 D3
Moston *Gtr Man* 44 B2
Moston *Shrops* 34 C1
Moston Green *Ches* 43 F10
Mostyn *Flints* 42 D4
Mostyn Quay *Flints* 42 D4
Motcombe *Dorset* 9 B7
Mothecombe *Devon* 5 G7
Motherby *Cumb* 56 D6
Motherwell *N Lanarks* 68 E6
Mottingham *London* 19 D11
Mottisfont *Hants* 10 B2
Mottistone *I/Wight* 10 F3
Mottram in Longdendale *Gtr Man* 44 C3
Mottram St Andrew *Ches* 44 E2
Mouilpied *Guernsey* 11
Mouldsworth *Ches* 43 E8
Moulin *Perth/Kinr* 76 B2
Moulsecoomb *Brighton/Hove* 12 F2
Moulsford *Oxon* 18 C2
Moulsoe *M/Keynes* 28 D6
Moulton *Ches* 43 F9
Moulton *Lincs* 37 C9
Moulton *Northants* 28 B4
Moulton *N Yorks* 58 F3
Moulton *Suffolk* 30 B3
Moulton *V/Glam* 14 D6
Moulton Chapel *Lincs* 37 D8
Moulton Eaugate *Lincs* 37 D9
Moulton St Mary *Norfolk* 39 E9
Moulton Seas End *Lincs* 37 C9
Mounie Castle *Aberds* 83 A9
Mount *Corn'wl* 3 D6
Mount *Corn'wl* 4 E2
Mount *Kent* 21 F8
Mount Bures *Essex* 30 E6
Mount Canisp *H'land* 87 D10
Mount Hawke *Cornw'l* 2 E6
Mount Pleasant *Ches* 44 G2
Mount Pleasant *Derby* 45 H7
Mount Pleasant *Derby* 35 D8
Mount Pleasant *Flints* 42 E5
Mount Pleasant *Hants* 10 E1
Mount Pleasant *Norfolk* 38 F4
Mount Sorrel *Wilts* 9 B9
Mount Tabor *W Yorks* 51 G6
Mountain *W Yorks* 51 F6
Mountain Ash = Aberpennar *Rh Cyn Taff* 14 B6
Mountain Cross *Scot Borders* 69 F10
Mountain Water *Pembs* 22 D4
Mountbenger *Scot Borders* 70 H2
Mountfield *E Sussex* 12 D6
Mountgerald *H'land* 87 E8
Mountjoy *Cornw'l* 3 C7
Mountnessing *Essex* 20 B3
Mounton *Monmouths* 15 B11
Mountsorrel *Leics* 36 D1
Mousehole *Cornw'l* 2 G3
Mousen *Northum* 71 G10
Mouswald *Dumf/Gal* 60 F6
Mow Cop *Ches* 44 G2
Mowhaugh *Scot Borders* 62 A4
Mowsley *Leics* 36 G2
Moxley *W Midlands* 34 F5
Moy *H'land* 81 E7
Moy *H'land* 87 H10
Moy Hall *H'land* 87 H10
Moy Ho. *Moray* 87 E13
Moy Lodge *H'land* 80 E7
Moyles Court *Hants* 9 D10
Moylgrove *Pembs* 22 B6
Muasdale *Arg/Bute* 65 D7
Much Birch *Heref'd* 26 E2
Much Cowarne *Heref'd* 26 D3
Much Dewchurch *Heref'd* 25 E11
Much Hadham *Herts* 29 G11
Much Hoole *Lancs* 49 G4
Much Marcle *Heref'd* 26 E3
Much Wenlock *Shrops* 34 E2
Muchalls *Aberds* 83 D11
Muchelney *Som'set* 8 B3
Muchlarnick *Cornw'l* 4 F3
Muchrachd *H'land* 86 H5
Muckernich *H'land* 87 F8
Mucking *Thurrock* 20 C3
Muckleford *Dorset* 8 E5
Mucklestone *Staffs* 34 B3
Muckleton *Shrops* 34 C1
Muckletown *Aberds* 83 A7
Muckley Corner *Staffs* 35 E6
Muckton *Lincs* 47 D7
Mudale *H'land* 93 F8
Muddiford *Devon* 6 C4
Mudeford *Dorset* 9 E10
Mudford *Som'set* 8 C4
Mudgley *Som'set* 15 G10
Mugdock *Stirl* 68 C4
Mugeary *H'land* 85 E9
Mugginton *Derby* 35 A8
Muggleswick *Durham* 58 B1
Muie *H'land* 93 J9
Muir *Aberds* 82 E3
Muir of Fairburn *H'land* 86 F7
Muir of Fowlis *Aberds* 83 B7
Muir of Ord *H'land* 87 F8
Muir of Pert *Angus* 77 D7
Muirden *Aberds* 89 C7
Muirdrum *Angus* 77 D8
Muirhead *Angus* 76 D6
Muirhead *Fife* 76 G5
Muirhead *N Lanarks* 68 D5
Muirhead *S Ayrs* 66 C6
Muirhouselaw *Scot Borders* 70 H5
Muirhouses *Falk* 69 B9
Muirkirk *E Ayrs* 68 H4
Muirmill *Stirl* 68 B6
Muirshearlich *H'land* 80 E3
Muirskie *Aberds* 83 D10
Muirtack *Aberds* 89 E9
Muirton *H'land* 87 E10
Muirton *Perth/Kinr* 76 E4
Muirton *Perth/Kinr* 76 F3
Muirton Mains *H'land* 86 F7
Muirton of Ardblair *Perth/Kinr* 76 C4
Muirton of Ballochy *Angus* 83 G8
Muiryfold *Aberds* 89 C7
Muker *N Yorks* 57 G11
Mulbarton *Norfolk* 39 E7
Mulben *Moray* 88 C3
Mulindry *Arg/Bute* 64 C4
Mullardoch House *H'land* 86 H4
Mullion *Cornw'l* 2 H5
Mullion Cove *Cornw'l* 2 H5
Mumby *Lincs* 47 E9
Munderfield Row *Heref'd* 26 C3
Munderfield Stocks *Heref'd* 26 C3
Mundesley *Norfolk* 39 B9
Mundford *Norfolk* 38 F4
Mundham *Norfolk* 39 F9
Mundon *Essex* 20 A5
Mundurno *Aberd C* 83 B11
Munerigie *H'land* 80 C4
Muness *Shetl'd* 96 C8
Mungasdale *H'land* 86 B2
Mungrisdale *Cumb* 56 C5
Munlochy *H'land* 87 F9
Munsley *Heref'd* 26 D3
Munslow *Shrops* 33 G11
Murchington *Devon* 5 C7
Murcott *Oxon* 28 G2
Murkle *H'land* 94 D3
Murlaggan *H'land* 80 D1
Murlaggan *H'land* 80 E4
Murra *Orkney* 95 H3
Murrayfield *C/Edinb* 69 C11
Murrow *Cambs* 37 E9
Mursley *Bucks* 28 F5
Murthill *Angus* 77 B7
Murthly *Perth/Kinr* 76 D3
Murton *Cumb* 57 D9
Murton *Durham* 58 B4
Murton *Northum* 71 E8
Murton *York* 52 D2
Musbury *Devon* 8 E1
Muscoates *N Yorks* 52 A2
Musdale *Arg/Bute* 74 E2
Musselburgh *E Loth* 70 C2
Muston *Leics* 36 B4
Muston *N Yorks* 53 B6
Mustow Green *Worcs* 34 H4
Mutehill *Dumf/Gal* 55 E9
Mutford *Suffolk* 39 G10
Muthill *Perth/Kinr* 75 F11
Mutterton *Devon* 7 F9
Muxton *Telford* 34 D3
Mybster *H'land* 94 E3
Myddfai *Carms* 24 F4
Myddle *Shrops* 33 C10
Mydroilyn *Ceredig'n* 23 A9
Myerscough *Lancs* 49 F4
Mylor Bridge *Cornw'l* 3 F7
Mynachlog-ddu *Pembs* 22 C6
Myndtown *Shrops* 33 G9
Mynydd Bach *Ceredig'n* 32 H3
Mynydd-bach *Monmouths* 15 B10
Mynydd Bodafon *Angl* 40 B6
Mynydd-isa *Flints* 42 F5
Mynyddygarreg *Carms* 23 F9
Mynytho *Gwyn* 40 G5
Myrebird *Aberds* 83 D9
Myrelandhorn *H'land* 94 E4
Myreside *Perth/Kinr* 76 E5
Myrtle Hill *Carms* 24 E4
Mytchett *Surrey* 18 F5
Mytham Bridge *Derby* 44 D5
Mytholm *W Yorks* 50 G5
Mytholmroyd *W Yorks* 50 G6
Myton-on-Swale *N Yorks* 51 C10
Mytton *Shrops* 33 D10

Naast *H'land* 91 J13
Naburn *York* 52 E1
Nackington *Kent* 21 F8
Nacton *Suffolk* 31 D9
Nafferton *ER Yorks* 53 D6
Nailbridge *Glos* 26 G3
Nailsbourne *Som'set* 7 D11
Nailsea *N Som'set* 15 D10
Nailstone *Leics* 35 E10
Nailsworth *Glos* 16 B5
Nairn *H'land* 87 F11
Nalderswood *Surrey* 19 G9
Nancegollan *Cornw'l* 2 F5
Nancledra *Cornw'l* 2 F3
Nanhoron *Gwyn* 40 G4
Nannau *Gwyn* 32 C3
Nannerch *Flints* 42 F4
Nanpantan *Leics* 35 D11
Nanpean *Cornw'l* 3 D8
Nanstallon *Cornw'l* 3 C9
Nant-ddu *Powys* 24 G6
Nant-glas *Powys* 24 B6
Nant Peris *Gwyn* 41 E8
Nant Uchaf *Denbs* 42 G3
Nant-y-Bai *Carms* 24 D4
Nant-y-cafn *Neath P Talb* 14 A4
Nant-y-derry *Monmouths* 25 H10
Nant-y-ffin *Carms* 23 C10
Nant-y-moel *Bridg* 14 B5
Nant-y-pandy *Conwy* 41 C8
Nanternis *Ceredig'n* 23 A8
Nantgaredig *Carms* 23 D9
Nantgarw *Rh Cyn Taff* 15 C7
Nantglyn *Denbs* 42 F2
Nantgwyn *Powys* 32 H5
Nantlle *Gwyn* 41 E7
Nantmawr *Shrops* 33 C8
Nantmel *Powys* 25 B7
Nantmor *Gwyn* 41 F8
Nantwich *Ches* 43 G9
Nantycaws *Carms* 23 E9
Nantyffyllon *Bridg* 14 B4
Nantyglo *Bl Gwent* 25 G8
Naphill *Bucks* 18 B5
Nappa *N Yorks* 50 D4
Napton on the Hill *Warwick* 27 B11
Narberth = Arberth *Pembs* 22 E6
Narborough *Leics* 35 F11
Narborough *Norfolk* 38 D3
Nasareth *Gwyn* 40 E6
Naseby *Northants* 36 H2
Nash *Bucks* 28 E4
Nash *Heref'd* 25 B10
Nash *Newp* 15 C9
Nash *Shrops* 26 A3
Nash Lee *Bucks* 28 H5
Nassington *Northants* 37 F6
Nasty *Herts* 29 F10
Nateby *Cumb* 57 F9
Nateby *Lancs* 49 E4
Natland *Cumb* 57 H7
Naughton *Suffolk* 31 D7
Naunton *Glos* 27 F8
Naunton *Worcs* 26 E5
Naunton Beauchamp *Worcs* 26 C6
Navenby *Lincs* 46 G3
Navestock Heath *Essex* 20 B2
Navestock Side *Essex* 20 B2
Navidale *H'land* 93 H13
Nawton *N Yorks* 52 A2
Nayland *Suffolk* 30 E6
Nazeing *Essex* 29 H11
Neacroft *Hants* 9 E10
Neal's Green *Warwick* 35 G9
Neap *Shetl'd* 96 H7
Near Sawrey *Cumb* 56 G5
Neasham *D'lington* 58 E4
Neath = Castell-nedd *Neath P Talb* 14 B3
Neath Abbey *Neath P Talb* 14 B3
Neatishead *Norfolk* 39 C9
Nebo *Angl* 40 A6
Nebo *Ceredig'n* 24 B2
Nebo *Conwy* 41 E10
Nebo *Gwyn* 40 E6
Necton *Norfolk* 38 E4
Nedd *H'land* 92 F4
Nedderton *Northum* 63 E8
Nedging Tye *Suffolk* 31 D7
Needham *Norfolk* 39 G8
Needham Market *Suffolk* 31 C7
Needingworth *Cambs* 29 A10
Needwood *Staffs* 35 C7
Neen Savage *Shrops* 34 H2
Neen Sollars *Shrops* 26 A3
Neenton *Shrops* 34 G2
Nefyn *Gwyn* 40 F5
Neilston *E Renf* 68 E3
Nelly Andrews Green *Powys* 33 E8
Nelson *Caerph* 15 B7
Nelson *Lancs* 50 F4
Nelson Village *Northum* 63 F8
Nemphlar *S Lanarks* 69 F7
Nempnett Thrubwell *Bath/NE Som'set* 15 E11
Nene Terrace *Lincs* 37 E8
Nenthall *Cumb* 57 B9
Nenthead *Cumb* 57 B9
Nenthorn *Scot Borders* 70 G5
Nerabus *Arg/Bute* 64 C3
Nercwys *Flints* 42 F5
Nerston *S Lanarks* 68 E5
Nesbit *Northum* 71 G8
Ness *Ches* 42 E6
Nesscliffe *Shrops* 33 D9
Neston *Ches* 42 E5
Neston *Wilts* 16 E5
Nether Alderley *Ches* 44 E2
Nether Blainslie *Scot Borders* 70 F4
Nether Booth *Derby* 44 D5
Nether Broughton *Leics* 36 C2
Nether Burrow *Lancs* 50 B2
Nether Cerne *Dorset* 8 E5
Nether Compton *Dorset* 8 C4
Nether Crimond *Aberds* 83 A10
Nether Dalgliesh *Scot Borders* 61 C7
Nether Dallachy *Moray* 88 B3
Nether Exe *Devon* 7 F8
Nether Glasslaw *Aberds* 89 C8
Nether Handwick *Angus* 76 C6
Nether Haugh *S Yorks* 45 C8
Nether Heage *Derby* 45 G7
Nether Heyford *Northants* 28 C3
Nether Hindhope *Scot Borders* 62 B3
Nether Howecleuch *S Lanarks* 60 B6
Nether Kellet *Lancs* 49 C5
Nether Kinmundy *Aberds* 89 D10
Nether Langwith *Notts* 45 E9
Nether Leask *Aberds* 89 E10
Nether Lenshie *Aberds* 89 D6
Nether Monynut *Scot Borders* 70 D6
Nether Padley *Derby* 44 E6
Nether Park *Aberds* 89 C10
Nether Poppleton *York* 52 D1
Nether Silton *N Yorks* 58 G5
Nether Stowey *Som'set* 7 C10
Nether Urquhart *Fife* 76 G4
Nether Wallop *Hants* 17 H10
Nether Wasdale *Cumb* 56 F3
Nether Whitacre *Warwick* 35 F8
Nether Worton *Oxon* 27 E11
Netheravon *Wilts* 17 G8
Netherbrae *Aberds* 89 C7
Netherbrough *Orkney* 95 G4
Netherburn *S Lanarks* 69 F7
Netherbury *Dorset* 8 E3
Netherby *Cumb* 61 F9
Netherby *N Yorks* 51 E9
Nethercote *Warwick* 28 B2
Nethercott *Devon* 6 C3
Netherend *Glos* 16 A2
Netherfield *E Sussex* 12 D6
Netherhampton *Wilts* 9 B10
Netherlaw *Dumf/Gal* 55 E10
Netherley *Aberds* 83 D10
Netherley *Mersey* 43 D7
Nethermill *Dumf/Gal* 60 E6
Nethermuir *Aberds* 89 D9
Netherplace *E Renf* 68 E4
Netherseal *Derby* 35 D8
Netherthird *E Ayrs* 67 E8
Netherthong *W Yorks* 44 B5
Netherthorpe *S Yorks* 45 D9
Netherton *Angus* 77 B8
Netherton *Devon* 5 D9
Netherton *Hants* 17 F10
Netherton *Mersey* 43 B6
Netherton *Northum* 62 C5
Netherton *Oxon* 17 B11
Netherton *Perth/Kinr* 76 B4
Netherton *Stirl* 68 C4
Netherton *W Midlands* 34 G5
Netherton *W Yorks* 51 H8
Netherton *W Yorks* 44 A5
Netherton *Worcs* 26 D6
Nethertown *Cumb* 56 F1
Nethertown *H'land* 94 C5
Nethertown *Staffs* 35 D7
Netherwitton *Northum* 63 D7
Netherwood *E Ayrs* 68 H4
Nethy Bridge *H'land* 82 A2
Netley *Hants* 10 D3
Netley Marsh *Hants* 10 C2
Nettlebed *Oxon* 18 C4
Nettlebridge *Som'set* 16 G3
Nettlecombe *Dorset* 8 E4
Nettleden *Herts* 29 G7
Nettleham *Lincs* 46 E4
Nettlestead *Kent* 20 F3
Nettlestead Green *Kent* 20 F3
Nettlestone *I/Wight* 10 E5
Nettlesworth *Durham* 58 B3
Nettleton *Lincs* 46 B5
Nettleton *Wilts* 16 D5
Neuadd *Carms* 24 F4
Nevendon *Essex* 20 B4
Nevern *Pembs* 22 B5
New Abbey *Dumf/Gal* 60 G5
New Aberdour *Aberds* 89 B8
New Addington *London* 19 E10
New Alresford *Hants* 10 A4
New Alyth *Perth/Kinr* 76 C5
New Arley *Warwick* 35 G8
New Ash Green *Kent* 20 E3
New Barn *Kent* 20 E3
New Barnetby *N Lincs* 46 A4
New Barton *Northants* 28 B5
New Bewick *Northum* 62 A6
New-bigging *Angus* 76 C5
New Bilton *Warwick* 35 H10
New Bolingbroke *Lincs* 47 G7
New Boultham *Lincs* 46 E3
New Bradwell *M/Keynes* 28 D5
New Brancepeth *Durham* 58 B3
New Bridge *Wrex* 42 H5
New Brighton *Flints* 42 F5
New Brighton *Mersey* 42 C6
New Brinsley *Notts* 45 G8
New Broughton *Wrex* 42 G6
New Buckenham *Norfolk* 39 F6

Morton *Lincs* 37 C6
Morton *Lincs* 46 C2
Morton *Lincs* 46 F2
Morton *Norfolk* 39 D7
Morton *Notts* 45 G11
Morton *Shrops* 33 C8
Morton *S Gloucs* 16 B3
Morton Bagot *Warwick* 27 B8
Morton-on-Swale *N Yorks* 58 G4
Morvah *Cornw'l* 2 F3
Morval *Cornw'l* 4 F3
Morvich *H'land* 80 A1
Morvich *H'land* 93 J10
Morville *Shrops* 34 F2
Morville Heath *Shrops* 34 F2
Morwenstow *Cornw'l* 6 E1
Mosborough *S Yorks* 45 D8
Moscow *E Ayrs* 67 B7
Mosedale *Cumb* 56 C5
Moseley *W Midlands* 35 G6
Moseley *W Midlands* 34 F5
Moseley *Worcs* 26 C5
Moss *Arg/Bute* 78 G2
Moss *H'land* 79 E9
Moss *S Yorks* 45 A9
Moss *Wrex* 42 G6
Moss Bank *Mersey* 43 C8
Moss Edge *Lancs* 49 E4
Moss End *Brackn'l* 18 D5
Moss of Barmuckity *Moray* 88 B2
Moss Pit *Staffs* 34 C5
Moss-side *H'land* 87 F11
Moss Side *Lancs* 49 F3
Mossat *Aberds* 82 B6
Mossbank *Shetl'd* 96 F6
Mossbay *Cumb* 56 D1
Mossblown *S Ayrs* 67 D7
Mossbrow *Gtr Man* 43 D10
Mossburnford *Scot Borders* 62 B2
Mossdale *Dumf/Gal* 55 B9
Mossend *N Lanarks* 68 D6
Mosser *Cumb* 56 D3
Mossfield *H'land* 87 D9
Mossgiel *E Ayrs* 67 D7
Mosside *Angus* 77 B7
Mossley *Ches* 44 F2
Mossley *Gtr Man* 44 B3
Mossley Hill *Mersey* 43 D6
Mosstodloch *Moray* 88 C3
Mosston *Angus* 77 C8
Mossy Lea *Lancs* 43 A8
Mosterton *Dorset* 8 D3
Moston *Gtr Man* 44 B2
Moston *Shrops* 34 C1
Moston Green *Ches* 43 F10
Mostyn *Flints* 42 D4
Mostyn Quay *Flints* 42 D4
Motcombe *Dorset* 9 B7
Mothecombe *Devon* 5 G7
Motherby *Cumb* 56 D6
Motherwell *N Lanarks* 68 E6
Mottingham *London* 19 D11
Mottisfont *Hants* 10 B2
Mottistone *I/Wight* 10 F3
Mottram in Longdendale *Gtr Man* 44 C3
Mottram St Andrew *Ches* 44 E2
Mouilpied *Guernsey* 11
Mouldsworth *Ches* 43 E8
Moulin *Perth/Kinr* 76 B2
Moulsecoomb *Brighton/Hove* 12 F2
Moulsford *Oxon* 18 C2
Moulsoe *M/Keynes* 28 D6
Moulton *Ches* 43 F9
Moulton *Lincs* 37 C9
Moulton *Northants* 28 B4
Moulton *N Yorks* 58 F3
Moulton *Suffolk* 30 B3
Moulton *V/Glam* 14 D6
Moulton Chapel *Lincs* 37 D8
Moulton Eaugate *Lincs* 37 D9
Moulton St Mary *Norfolk* 39 E9
Moulton Seas End *Lincs* 37 C9
Mounie Castle *Aberds* 83 A9
Mount *Cornw'l* 3 D6
Mount *Cornw'l* 4 E2
Mount *H'land* 87 G12
Mount Bures *Essex* 30 E6
Mount Canisp *H'land* 87 D10
Mount Hawke *Cornw'l* 2 E6
Mount Pleasant *Ches* 44 G2
Mount Pleasant *Derby* 45 H7
Mount Pleasant *Derby* 35 D8
Mount Pleasant *Flints* 42 E5
Mount Pleasant *Hants* 10 E1
Mount Pleasant *W Yorks* 51 G8
Mount Sorrel *Wilts* 9 B9
Mount Tabor *W Yorks* 51 G6
Mountain *W Yorks* 51 F6
Mountain Ash = Aberpennar *Rh Cyn Taff* 14 B6
Mountain Cross *Scot Borders* 69 F10
Mountain Water *Pembs* 22 D4
Mountbenger *Scot Borders* 70 H2
Mountfield *E Sussex* 12 D6
Mountgerald *H'land* 87 E8
Mountjoy *Cornw'l* 3 C7
Mountnessing *Essex* 20 B3
Mounton *Monmouths* 15 B11
Mountsorrel *Leics* 36 D1
Mousehole *Cornw'l* 2 G3
Mousen *Northum* 71 G10
Mouswald *Dumf/Gal* 60 F6
Mow Cop *Ches* 44 G2
Mowhaugh *Scot Borders* 62 A4
Mowsley *Leics* 36 G2
Moxley *W Midlands* 34 F5
Moy *H'land* 80 E6
Moy *H'land* 87 H10
Moy Hall *H'land* 87 H10
Moy Ho. *Moray* 87 E13
Moy Lodge *H'land* 80 E6
Moyles Court *Hants* 9 D10
Moylgrove *Pembs* 22 B6
Muasdale *Arg/Bute* 65 D7
Much Birch *Heref'd* 26 E2
Much Cowarne *Heref'd* 26 D3
Much Dewchurch *Heref'd* 25 E11
Much Hadham *Herts* 29 G11
Much Hoole *Lancs* 49 G4
Much Marcle *Heref'd* 26 E3
Much Wenlock *Shrops* 34 E2
Muchalls *Aberds* 83 D11
Muchelney *Som'set* 8 B3
Muchlarnick *Cornw'l* 4 F3
Muchrachd *H'land* 86 H5
Muckernich *H'land* 87 F8
Mucking *Thurr'k* 20 C3
Muckleford *Dorset* 8 E5
Mucklestone *Staffs* 34 B3
Muckleton *Shrops* 34 C1
Muckletown *Aberds* 83 A7
Muckley Corner *Staffs* 35 E6
Muckton *Lincs* 47 D7
Mudale *H'land* 93 F8
Muddiford *Devon* 6 C4
Mudeford *Dorset* 9 E10
Mudford *Som'set* 8 C4
Mudgley *Som'set* 15 G10
Mugdock *Stirl* 68 C4
Mugeary *H'land* 85 E9
Mugginton *Derby* 35 A8
Muggleswick *Durham* 58 B1
Muie *H'land* 93 J9
Muir *Aberds* 82 E2
Muir of Fairburn *H'land* 86 F7
Muir of Fowlis *Aberds* 83 B7
Muir of Ord *H'land* 87 F8
Muir of Pert *Angus* 77 D7
Muirden *Aberds* 89 C7
Muirdrum *Angus* 77 D8
Muirhead *Angus* 76 D6
Muirhead *Fife* 76 G5
Muirhead *N Lanarks* 68 D5
Muirhead *S Ayrs* 66 C6
Muirhouselaw *Scot Borders* 70 H5
Muirhouses *Falk* 69 B9
Muirkirk *E Ayrs* 68 H5
Muirmill *Stirl* 68 B6
Muirshearlich *H'land* 80 E3
Muirskie *Aberds* 83 D10
Muirtack *Aberds* 89 E9
Muirton *H'land* 87 E10
Muirton *Perth/Kinr* 76 E4
Muirton *Perth/Kinr* 76 F2
Muirton Mains *H'land* 86 F7
Muirton of Ardblair *Perth/Kinr* 76 C4
Muirton of Ballochy *Angus* 77 A9
Muiryfold *Aberds* 89 C7
Muker *N Yorks* 57 G11
Mulbarton *Norfolk* 39 E7
Mulben *Moray* 88 C3
Mulindry *Arg/Bute* 64 C4
Mullardoch House *H'land* 86 H5
Mullion *Cornw'l* 2 H5
Mullion Cove *Cornw'l* 2 H5
Mumby *Lincs* 47 E9
Munderfield Row *Heref'd* 26 C3
Munderfield Stocks *Heref'd* 26 C3
Mundesley *Norfolk* 39 B9
Mundford *Norfolk* 38 F4
Mundham *Norfolk* 39 F9
Mundon *Essex* 20 A5
Mundurno *Aberd C* 83 B11
Munerigie *H'land* 80 C4
Muness *Shetl'd* 96 C8
Mungasdale *H'land* 86 B2
Mungrisdale *Cumb* 56 C5
Munlochy *H'land* 87 F9
Munsley *Heref'd* 26 D3
Munslow *Shrops* 33 G11
Murchington *Devon* 5 C7
Murcott *Oxon* 28 G2
Murkle *H'land* 94 D3
Murlaggan *H'land* 80 D2
Murlaggan *H'land* 80 E5
Murra *Orkney* 95 H3
Murrayfield *C/Edinb* 69 C11
Murrow *Cambs* 37 E9
Mursley *Bucks* 28 F5
Murthill *Angus* 77 B7
Murthly *Perth/Kinr* 76 D3
Murton *Cumb* 57 D9
Murton *Durham* 58 B4
Murton *Northum* 71 F8
Murton *C/York* 52 D2
Musbury *Devon* 8 E1
Muscoates *N Yorks* 52 A2
Musdale *Arg/Bute* 74 E2
Musselburgh *E Loth* 70 C2
Muston *Leics* 36 B4
Muston *N Yorks* 53 B6
Mustow Green *Worcs* 26 A5
Mutehill *Dumf/Gal* 55 E9
Mutford *Suffolk* 39 G10
Muthill *Perth/Kinr* 75 F11
Mutterton *Devon* 7 F9
Muxton *Telford* 34 D3
Mybster *H'land* 94 E3
Myddfai *Carms* 24 F4
Myddle *Shrops* 33 C10
Mydroilyn *Ceredig'n* 23 A9
Myerscough *Lancs* 49 F4
Mylor Bridge *Cornw'l* 3 F7
Mynachlog-ddu *Pembs* 22 C6
Myndtown *Shrops* 33 G9
Mynydd Bach *Ceredig'n* 32 H3
Mynydd-bach *Monmouths* 15 B10
Mynydd Bodafon *Angl* 40 B6
Mynydd-isa *Flints* 42 F5
Mynyddygarreg *Carms* 23 F9
Mynytho *Gwyn* 40 G5
Myrebird *Aberds* 83 D9
Myrelandhorn *H'land* 94 E4
Myreside *Perth/Kinr* 76 E5
Myrtle Hill *Carms* 24 E4
Mytchett *Surrey* 18 F5
Mytholm *W Yorks* 50 G5
Mytholmroyd *W Yorks* 50 G6
Myton-on-Swale *N Yorks* 51 C10
Mytton *Shrops* 33 D10

N

Na Gearrannan *W Isles* 90 C6
Naast *H'land* 91 J13
Naburn *C/York* 52 E1
Nackington *Kent* 21 F8
Nacton *Suffolk* 31 D9
Nafferton *ER Yorks* 53 D6
Nailbridge *Glos* 26 G3
Nailsbourne *Som'set* 7 D11
Nailsea *N Som'set* 15 D10
Nailstone *Leics* 35 E10
Nailsworth *Glos* 16 B5
Nairn *H'land* 87 F11
Nalderswood *Surrey* 19 G9
Nancegollan *Cornw'l* 2 F5
Nancledra *Cornw'l* 2 F3
Nanhoron *Gwyn* 40 G4
Nannau *Gwyn* 32 C3
Nannerch *Flints* 42 F4
Nanpantan *Leics* 35 D11
Nanpean *Cornw'l* 3 D8
Nanstallon *Cornw'l* 3 C9
Nant-ddu *Powys* 25 G7
Nant-glas *Powys* 24 B6
Nant Peris *Gwyn* 41 E8
Nant Uchaf *Denbs* 42 G3
Nant-y-Bai *Carms* 24 D4
Nant-y-cafn *Neath P Talb* 24 H5
Nant-y-derry *Monmouths* 25 H10
Nant-y-ffin *Carms* 23 C10
Nant-y-moel *Bridg* 14 B5
Nant-y-pandy *Conwy* 41 C8
Nanternis *Ceredig'n* 23 A8
Nantgaredig *Carms* 23 D9
Nantgarw *Rh Cyn Taff* 15 C7
Nantglyn *Denbs* 42 F3
Nantgwyn *Powys* 32 H5
Nantlle *Gwyn* 41 E7
Nantmawr *Shrops* 33 C8
Nantmel *Powys* 25 B7
Nantmor *Gwyn* 41 F8
Nantwich *Ches* 43 G9
Nantycaws *Carms* 23 E9
Nantyffyllon *Bridg* 14 B4
Nantyglo *Bl Gwent* 25 G8
Naphill *Bucks* 18 B5
Nappa *N Yorks* 50 D4
Napton on the Hill *Warwick* 27 B11
Narberth = Arberth *Pembs* 22 E6
Narborough *Leics* 35 F11
Narborough *Norfolk* 38 D3
Nasareth *Gwyn* 40 E6
Naseby *Northants* 36 H2
Nash *Bucks* 28 E4
Nash *Heref'd* 25 B10
Nash *Newp* 15 C9
Nash *Shrops* 26 A3
Nash Lee *Bucks* 28 H5
Nassington *Northants* 37 F6
Nasty *Herts* 29 F10
Nateby *Cumb* 57 F9
Nateby *Lancs* 49 E4
Natland *Cumb* 57 H7
Naughton *Suffolk* 31 D7
Naunton *Glos* 27 F8
Naunton *Worcs* 26 E5
Naunton Beauchamp *Worcs* 26 C6
Navenby *Lincs* 46 G3
Navestock Heath *Essex* 20 B2
Navestock Side *Essex* 20 B2
Navidale *H'land* 93 H13
Nawton *N Yorks* 52 A2
Nayland *Suffolk* 30 E6
Nazeing *Essex* 29 H11
Neacroft *Hants* 9 E10
Neal's Green *Warwick* 35 G9
Neap *Shetl'd* 96 H7
Near Sawrey *Cumb* 56 G5
Neasham *D'lington* 58 E4
Neath = Castell-Nedd *Neath P Talb* 14 B3
Neath Abbey *Neath P Talb* 14 B3
Neatishead *Norfolk* 39 C9
Nebo *Angl* 40 A6
Nebo *Ceredig'n* 24 B2
Nebo *Conwy* 41 E10
Nebo *Gwyn* 40 E6
Necton *Norfolk* 38 E4
Nedd *H'land* 92 F4
Nedderton *Northum* 63 E8
Nedging Tye *Suffolk* 31 D7
Needham *Norfolk* 39 G8
Needham Market *Suffolk* 31 C7
Needingworth *Cambs* 29 A10
Needwood *Staffs* 35 C7
Neen Savage *Shrops* 34 H2
Neen Sollars *Shrops* 26 A3
Neenton *Shrops* 34 G2
Nefyn *Gwyn* 40 F5
Neilston *E Renf* 68 E3
Neinthirion *Powys* 32 E5
Neithrop *Oxon* 27 D11
Nelly Andrews Green *Powys* 33 E8
Nelson *Caerph* 15 B7
Nelson *Lancs* 50 F4
Nelson Village *Northum* 63 F8
Nemphlar *S Lanarks* 69 F7
Nempnett Thrubwell *Bath/NE Som'set* 15 E11
Nene Terrace *Lincs* 37 E8
Nenthall *Cumb* 57 B9
Nenthead *Cumb* 57 B9
Nenthorn *Scot Borders* 70 G5
Nerabus *Arg/Bute* 64 C3
Nercwys *Flints* 42 F5
Nerston *S Lanarks* 68 E5
Nesbit *Northum* 71 G8
Ness *Ches* 42 E6
Nesscliffe *Shrops* 33 D9
Neston *Ches* 42 E5
Neston *Wilts* 16 E5
Nether Alderley *Ches* 44 E2
Nether Blainslie *Scot Borders* 70 F4
Nether Booth *Derby* 44 D5
Nether Broughton *Leics* 36 C2
Nether Burrow *Lancs* 50 B2
Nether Cerne *Dorset* 8 E5
Nether Compton *Dorset* 8 C4
Nether Crimond *Aberds* 89 F8
Nether Dalgliesh *Scot Borders* 61 C8
Nether Dallachy *Moray* 88 B3
Nether Exe *Devon* 7 F8
Nether Glasslaw *Aberds* 89 C8
Nether Handwick *Angus* 76 C6
Nether Haugh *S Yorks* 45 C8
Nether Heage *Derby* 45 G7
Nether Heyford *Northants* 28 C3
Nether Hindhope *Scot Borders* 62 B3
Nether Howecleuch *S Lanarks* 60 B6
Nether Kellet *Lancs* 49 C5
Nether Kinmundy *Aberds* 89 D10
Nether Langwith *Notts* 45 E9
Nether Leask *Aberds* 89 E10
Nether Lenshie *Aberds* 89 D6
Nether Monynut *Scot Borders* 70 D6
Nether Padley *Derby* 44 E6
Nether Park *Aberds* 89 C10
Nether Poppleton *C/York* 52 D1
Nether Silton *N Yorks* 58 G5
Nether Stowey *Som'set* 7 C10
Nether Urquhart *Fife* 76 G4
Nether Wallop *Hants* 17 H10
Nether Wasdale *Cumb* 56 F3
Nether Whitacre *Warwick* 35 F8
Nether Worton *Oxon* 27 E11
Netheravon *Wilts* 17 G8
Netherbrae *Aberds* 89 C7
Netherbrough *Orkney* 95 G4
Netherburn *S Lanarks* 69 F7
Netherbury *Dorset* 8 E3
Netherby *Cumb* 61 F9
Netherby *N Yorks* 51 E9
Nethercote *Warwick* 28 B2
Nethercott *Devon* 6 C3
Netherend *Glos* 16 A2
Netherfield *E Sussex* 12 E6
Netherhampton *Wilts* 9 B10
Netherlaw *Dumf/Gal* 55 E10
Netherley *Aberds* 83 D10
Netherley *Mersey* 43 D7
Nethermill *Dumf/Gal* 60 E6
Nethermuir *Aberds* 89 D9
Netherplace *E Renf* 68 E4
Netherseal *Derby* 35 D8
Netherthird *E Ayrs* 67 E8
Netherthong *W Yorks* 44 B5
Netherthorpe *S Yorks* 45 D9
Netherton *Angus* 77 B8
Netherton *Devon* 5 D9
Netherton *Hants* 17 F10
Netherton *Mersey* 42 B6
Netherton *Northum* 62 C5
Netherton *Oxon* 17 B11
Netherton *Perth/Kinr* 76 B4
Netherton *Stirl* 68 C4
Netherton *W Midlands* 34 G5
Netherton *Worcs* 26 D6
Netherton *W Yorks* 44 A5
Netherton *W Yorks* 51 H8
Nethertown *Cumb* 56 F1
Nethertown *H'land* 94 C5
Netherwitton *Northum* 63 D7
Netherwood *E Ayrs* 68 H5
Nethy Bridge *H'land* 82 A2
Netley *Hants* 10 D3
Netley Marsh *Hants* 10 C2
Netteswell *Essex* 29 G11
Nettlebed *Oxon* 18 C4
Nettlebridge *Som'set* 16 G3
Nettlecombe *Dorset* 8 E4
Nettleden *Herts* 29 G7
Nettleham *Lincs* 46 E4
Nettlestead *Kent* 20 F3
Nettlestead Green *Kent* 20 F3
Nettlestone *I/Wight* 10 E5
Nettlesworth *Durham* 58 B3
Nettleton *Lincs* 46 B5
Nettleton *Wilts* 16 D5
Neuadd *Carms* 24 F3
Nevendon *Essex* 20 B4
Nevern *Pembs* 22 B5
New Abbey *Dumf/Gal* 60 G5
New Aberdour *Aberds* 89 B8
New Addington *London* 19 E10
New Alresford *Hants* 10 A4
New Alyth *Perth/Kinr* 76 C5
New Arley *Warwick* 35 G8
New Ash Green *Kent* 20 E3
New Barn *Kent* 20 E3
New Barnetby *N Lincs* 46 A4
New Barton *Northants* 28 B5
New Bewick *Northum* 62 A6
New-bigging *Angus* 76 C5
New Bilton *Warwick* 35 H10
New Bolingbroke *Lincs* 47 G7
New Boultham *Lincs* 46 E3
New Bradwell *M/Keynes* 28 D5
New Brancepeth *Durham* 58 B3
New Bridge *Wrex* 33 A8
New Brighton *Flints* 42 F5
New Brighton *Mersey* 42 C6
New Brinsley *Notts* 45 G8
New Broughton *Wrex* 42 G6
New Buckenham *Norfolk* 39 F6
New Byth *Aberds* 89 C8
New Catton *Norfolk* 39 D8
New Cheriton *Hants* 10 B4
New Costessy *Norfolk* 39 D7
New Cowper *Cumb* 56 B3
New Cross *Ceredig'n* 32 H2
New Cross *London* 19 D10
New Cumnock *E Ayrs* 67 E9
New Deer *Aberds* 89 D8
New Delaval *Northum* 63 F8
New Duston *Northants* 28 B4
New Earswick *C/York* 52 D2
New Edlington *S Yorks* 45 C9
New Elgin *Moray* 88 B2
New Ellerby *ER Yorks* 53 F7
New Eltham *London* 19 D11
New End *Worcs* 27 C7
New Farnley *W Yorks* 51 F8
New Ferry *Mersey* 42 D6
New Fryston *W Yorks* 51 G10
New Galloway *Dumf/Gal* 55 B9
New Gilston *Fife* 77 G7
New Grimsby *I/Scilly* 2 C2
New Hainford *Norfolk* 39 D8
New Hartley *Northum* 63 F9
New Haw *Surrey* 19 E7
New Hedges *Pembs* 22 F6
New Herrington *Tyne/Wear* 58 A4
New Hinksey *Oxon* 18 A2
New Holkham *Norfolk* 38 B4
New Holland *N Lincs* 53 G6
New Houghton *Derby* 45 F8
New Houghton *Norfolk* 38 C3
New Houses *N Yorks* 50 B4
New Humberstone *Leics C* 36 E2
New Hutton *Cumb* 57 G7
New Hythe *Kent* 20 F4
New Inn *Carms* 23 C9
New Inn *Monmouths* 15 A10
New Inn *Torf* 15 B9
New Invention *Shrops* 33 H8
New Invention *W Midlands* 34 E5
New Kelso *H'land* 86 G2
New Kingston *Notts* 35 C11
New Lanark *S Lanarks* 69 F7
New Lane *Lancs* 43 A7
New Lane End *Warrington* 43 C9
New Leake *Lincs* 47 G8
New Leeds *Aberds* 89 C9
New Longton *Lancs* 49 G5
New Luce *Dumf/Gal* 54 C4
New Malden *London* 19 E9
New Marske *Redcar/Clevel'd* 59 D7
New Marton *Shrops* 33 B9
New Micklefield *W Yorks* 51 F10
New Mill *Aberds* 83 E9
New Mill *Herts* 28 G6
New Mill *Wilts* 17 E8
New Mill *W Yorks* 44 B5
New Mills *Ches* 43 D10
New Mills *Cornw'l* 3 D7
New Mills *Derby* 44 D3
New Mills *Powys* 33 E6
New Milton *Hants* 9 E11
New Moat *Pembs* 22 D5
New Ollerton *Notts* 45 F10
New Oscott *W Midlands* 35 F6
New Park *N Yorks* 51 D8
New Pitsligo *Aberds* 89 C8
New Polzeath *Cornw'l* 3 B8
New Quay = Ceinewydd *Ceredig'n* 23 A8
New Rackheath *Norfolk* 39 D8
New Radnor *Powys* 25 B9
New Rent *Cumb* 56 C6
New Ridley *Northum* 62 H6
New Road Side *N Yorks* 50 E5
New Romney *Kent* 13 D9
New Rossington *S Yorks* 45 C10
New Row *Ceredig'n* 24 A4
New Row *Lancs* 50 F2
New Row *N Yorks* 59 E7
New Sarum *Wilts* 9 A10
New Silksworth *Tyne/Wear* 58 A4
New Stevenston *N Lanarks* 68 E6
New Street *Staffs* 44 G4
New Street Lane *Shrops* 34 B2
New Swanage *Dorset* 9 F9
New Totley *S Yorks* 45 E7
New Town *E Loth* 70 C3
New Tredegar = Tredegar Newydd *Caerph* 15 A7
New Trows *S Lanarks* 69 G7
New Ulva *Arg/Bute* 72 E6
New Walsoken *Cambs* 37 E10
New Waltham *NE Lincs* 46 B6
New Whittington *Derby* 45 E7
New Wimpole *Cambs* 29 D10
New Winton *E Loth* 70 C3
New Yatt *Oxon* 27 G10
New York *Lincs* 46 G6
New York *N Yorks* 51 C7
Newall *W Yorks* 51 E7
Newark *Orkney* 95 D8
Newark *Peterbro* 37 E8
Newark-on-Trent *Notts* 45 G11
Newarthill *N Lanarks* 68 E6
Newbarns *Cumb* 49 B2
Newbattle *Midloth* 70 D2
Newbiggin *Cumb* 56 G2
Newbiggin *Cumb* 49 C2
Newbiggin *Cumb* 56 D6
Newbiggin *Cumb* 57 B7
Newbiggin *Cumb* 57 D8
Newbiggin *Durham* 57 D11
Newbiggin *N Yorks* 57 G11
Newbiggin *N Yorks* 57 H11
Newbiggin-by-the-Sea *Northum* 63 E9
Newbiggin-on-Lune *Cumb* 57 F9
Newbigging *Angus* 77 D7
Newbigging *Angus* 77 D7
Newbigging *S Lanarks* 69 F9
Newbold *Derby* 45 E7
Newbold *Leics* 35 D10
Newbold on Avon *Warwick* 35 H10
Newbold on Stour *Warwick* 27 D9
Newbold Pacey *Warwick* 27 C9
Newbold Verdon *Leics* 35 E10
Newborough *Angl* 40 D6
Newborough *Peterbro* 37 E8
Newborough *Staffs* 35 C7
Newbottle *Northants* 28 E2
Newbottle *Tyne/Wear* 58 A4
Newbourne *Suffolk* 31 D9
Newbridge *Caerph* 15 B8
Newbridge *Ceredig'n* 23 A10
Newbridge *Cornw'l* 2 F3
Newbridge *Cornw'l* 4 E4
Newbridge *Dumf/Gal* 60 F5
Newbridge *C/Edinb* 69 C10
Newbridge *Hants* 10 C1
Newbridge *I/Wight* 10 F3
Newbridge *Pembs* 22 C4
Newbridge Green *Worcs* 26 E5
Newbridge-on-Usk *Monmouths* 15 B9
Newbridge on Wye *Powys* 25 C7
Newbrough *Northum* 62 G4
Newbuildings *Devon* 7 F6
Newburgh *Aberds* 89 F9
Newburgh *Aberds* 89 C9
Newburgh *Scot Borders* 61 B9
Newburgh *Fife* 76 F5
Newburgh *Lancs* 43 A7
Newburn *Tyne/Wear* 63 G7
Newbury *W Berks* 17 E11
Newbury Park *London* 19 C11
Newby *Cumb* 57 D7
Newby *Lancs* 50 E4
Newby *N Yorks* 50 B3
Newby *N Yorks* 58 E6
Newby *N Yorks* 59 G11
Newby Bridge *Cumb* 56 H5
Newby East *Cumb* 61 H10
Newby West *Cumb* 56 A5
Newby Wiske *N Yorks* 58 H4
Newcastle *Monmouths* 25 G11
Newcastle *Shrops* 33 G8
Newcastle Emlyn = Castell Newydd Emlyn *Carms* 23 B8
Newcastle-under-Lyme *Staffs* 44 H2
Newcastle Upon Tyne *Tyne/Wear* 63 G8
Newcastleton *Scot Borders* 61 E10
Newchapel *Pembs* 23 C7
Newchapel *Powys* 32 G5
Newchapel *Staffs* 44 G2
Newchapel *Surrey* 12 B2
Newchurch *Carms* 23 D8
Newchurch *I/Wight* 10 F4
Newchurch *Kent* 13 C9
Newchurch *Lancs* 50 F4
Newchurch *Monmouths* 15 B10
Newchurch *Powys* 25 C9
Newchurch *Staffs* 35 C7
Newcott *Devon* 7 F11
Newcraighall *C/Edinb* 70 C2
Newdigate *Surrey* 19 G8
Newell Green *Brackn'l* 18 D5
Newenden *Kent* 13 D7
Newent *Glos* 26 F4
Newerne *Glos* 16 A3
Newfield *Durham* 58 C3
Newfield *H'land* 87 D10
Newford *I/Scilly* 2 C3
Newfound *Hants* 18 F2
Newgale *Pembs* 22 D3
Newgate *Norfolk* 39 A6
Newgate Street *Herts* 19 A10
Newhall *Ches* 43 H9
Newhall *Derby* 35 C8
Newhall House *H'land* 87 E9
Newhall Point *H'land* 87 E10
Newham *Northum* 71 H10
Newham Hall *Northum* 71 H10
Newhaven *Derby* 44 G5
Newhaven *C/Edinb* 69 C11
Newhaven *E Sussex* 12 F3
Newhey *Gtr Man* 44 A3
Newholm *N Yorks* 59 E9
Newhouse *N Lanarks* 68 D6
Newick *E Sussex* 12 D3
Newingreen *Kent* 13 C10
Newington *Kent* 20 E5
Newington *Kent* 21 H8
Newington *Kent* 21 E10
Newington *Notts* 45 C10
Newington *Oxon* 18 B3
Newington *Shrops* 33 G10
Newland *Glos* 26 H2
Newland *Kingston/Hull* 53 F6
Newland *N Yorks* 52 G2
Newland *Worcs* 26 D4
Newlandrig *Midloth* 70 D2
Newlands *Scot Borders* 61 D11
Newlands *H'land* 87 G10
Newlands *Moray* 88 C3
Newlands *Northum* 62 H6
Newland's Corner *Surrey* 19 G7
Newlands of Geise *H'land* 94 D2
Newlands of Tynet *Moray* 88 B3
Newlands Park *Angl* 40 B4
Newlandsmuir *S Lanarks* 68 E5
Newlot *Orkney* 95 G6
Newlyn *Cornw'l* 2 G3
Newmachar *Aberds* 83 B10
Newmains *N Lanarks* 69 E7
Newmarket *Suffolk* 30 B3
Newmarket *W Isles* 91 D9
Newmill *Scot Borders* 61 B10
Newmill *Cornw'l* 2 F3
Newmill *Moray* 88 C4
Newmill of Inshewan *Angus* 77 A7
Newmills *Monmouths* 26 H2
Newmills of Boyne *Aberds* 88 C5
Newmiln *Perth/Kinr* 76 D4
Newmilns *E Ayrs* 67 C8
Newnham *Cambs* 29 C11
Newnham *Glos* 26 G3
Newnham *Hants* 18 F4
Newnham *Herts* 29 E9
Newnham *Kent* 20 F6
Newnham *Northants* 28 C2
Newnham Bridge *Worcs* 26 B3
Newpark *Fife* 77 F7
Newport *Devon* 6 C4
Newport *ER Yorks* 52 F4
Newport *Essex* 30 E2
Newport *H'land* 94 H3
Newport *I/Wight* 10 F4
Newport *Norfolk* 39 D11
Newport *Telford* 34 D3
Newport = Casnewydd *Newp* 15 C9
Newport = Trefdraeth *Pembs* 22 C5
Newport-on-Tay *Fife* 77 E7
Newport Pagnell *M/Keynes* 28 D5
Newpound Common *W Sussex* 11 B9
Newquay *Cornw'l* 3 C7
Newsbank *Ches* 44 F2
Newseat *Aberds* 89 E7
Newseat *Aberds* 89 D10
Newsham *Northum* 63 F9
Newsham *N Yorks* 58 E2
Newsham *N Yorks* 51 A9
Newsholme *ER Yorks* 52 G3
Newsholme *Lancs* 50 D4
Newsome *W Yorks* 44 A5
Newstead *Scot Borders* 70 G4
Newstead *Notts* 45 G9
Newstead *Northum* 71 H10
Newthorpe *N Yorks* 51 F10
Newton *Arg/Bute* 73 D9
Newton *Scot Borders* 62 A2
Newton *Bridg* 14 D4
Newton *Cambs* 29 D11
Newton *Cambs* 37 D10
Newton *Card* 15 D8
Newton *Ches* 43 G8
Newton *Ches* 43 F7
Newton *Ches* 43 E8
Newton *Cumb* 49 B2
Newton *Derby* 45 G8
Newton *Dorset* 9 C6
Newton *Dumf/Gal* 61 D7
Newton *Dumf/Gal* 61 F8
Newton *Gtr Man* 44 C3
Newton *Heref'd* 25 E10
Newton *Heref'd* 26 C2
Newton *H'land* 87 E10
Newton *H'land* 92 F5
Newton *H'land* 94 F5
Newton *H'land* 87 G10
Newton *Lancs* 49 F4
Newton *Lancs* 50 D2
Newton *Lancs* 50 B1
Newton *Lincs* 36 B6
Newton *Moray* 88 B1
Newton *Norfolk* 38 D4
Newton *Notts* 36 A2
Newton *Northants* 36 G4
Newton *Northum* 62 G6
Newton *Perth/Kinr* 75 D11
Newton *S Lanarks* 68 D5
Newton *S Lanarks* 69 G8
Newton *Staffs* 34 C6
Newton *Suffolk* 30 D6
Newton *Swan* 14 C2
Newton *S Yorks* 45 B9
Newton *Warwick* 35 H11
Newton *Wilts* 9 B11
Newton *W Loth* 69 C9
Newton Abbot *Devon* 5 D9
Newton Arlosh *Cumb* 61 H7
Newton Aycliffe *Durham* 58 D3
Newton Bewley *Hartlep'l* 58 D5
Newton Blossomville *M/Keynes* 28 C6
Newton Bromswold *Northants* 28 B6
Newton Burgoland *Leics* 35 E9
Newton by Toft *Lincs* 46 D4
Newton Ferrers *Devon* 4 G6
Newton Flotman *Norfolk* 39 F8
Newton Hall *Northum* 62 G6
Newton Harcourt *Leics* 36 F2
Newton Heath *Gtr Man* 44 B2
Newton Ho. *Aberds* 83 A8
Newton Kyme *N Yorks* 51 E10
Newton-le-Willows *Mersey* 43 C8
Newton-le-Willows *N Yorks* 58 H3
Newton Longville *Bucks* 28 E5
Newton Mearns *E Renf* 68 E4
Newton Morrell *N Yorks* 58 F3
Newton Mulgrave *N Yorks* 59 E8
Newton of Ardtoe *H'land* 79 D9
Newton of Balcanquhal *Perth/Kinr* 76 F4
Newton of Falkland *Fife* 76 G5
Newton on Ayr *S Ayrs* 66 D6
Newton on Ouse *N Yorks* 51 D11
Newton-on-Rawcliffe *N Yorks* 59 G9
Newton-on-the-Moor *Northum* 63 C7
Newton on Trent *Lincs* 46 E2
Newton Park *Arg/Bute* 73 G10
Newton Poppleford *Devon* 7 H9
Newton Purcell *Oxon* 28 E3
Newton Regis *Warwick* 35 E8
Newton Reigny *Cumb* 57 C6
Newton St Cyres *Devon* 7 G7
Newton St Faith *Norfolk* 39 D8
Newton St Loe *Bath/NE Som'set* 16 E4
Newton St Petrock *Devon* 6 E3
Newton Solney *Derby* 35 C8
Newton Stacey *Hants* 17 G11
Newton Stewart *Dumf/Gal* 55 C7
Newton Tony *Wilts* 17 G9
Newton Tracey *Devon* 6 D4
Newton under Roseberry *Redcar/Clevel'd* 59 E6
Newton upon Derwent *ER Yorks* 52 E3
Newton Valence *Hants* 10 A6
Newtonairds *Dumf/Gal* 60 E4
Newtongrange *Midloth* 70 D2
Newtonhill *Aberds* 83 D11
Newtonhill *H'land* 87 G8
Newtonmill *Angus* 77 A9
Newtonmore *H'land* 81 D9
Newtown *Arg/Bute* 73 C9
Newtown *Ches* 43 E8
Newtown *Cornw'l* 2 G6
Newtown *Cumb* 56 B2
Newtown *Cumb* 61 G11
Newtown *Derby* 44 D3
Newtown *Devon* 7 D6
Newtown *Glos* 16 A3
Newtown *Glos* 26 E6
Newtown *Hants* 10 C1
Newtown *Hants* 10 B2
Newtown *Hants* 10 C5
Newtown *Hants* 17 E11
Newtown *Hants* 10 C4
Newtown *Hants* 10 D3
Newtown *Heref'd* 26 D3
Newtown *H'land* 80 C5
Newtown *I/Man* 48 E3
Newtown *I/Wight* 10 E3
Newtown *Northum* 62 C6
Newtown *Northum* 71 H9
Newtown *Northum* 71 G8
Newtown *Poole* 9 E9
Newtown *Shrops* 33 B10
Newtown *Staffs* 44 F3
Newtown *Staffs* 44 F4
Newtown *Wilts* 9 B8
Newtown = Y Drenewydd *Powys* 33 F7
Newtown Linford *Leics* 35 E11
Newtown St Boswells *Scot Borders* 70 G4
Newtown Unthank *Leics* 35 E10
Newtyle *Angus* 76 C5
Neyland *Pembs* 22 F4
Niarbyl *I/Man* 48 E2
Nibley *S Gloucs* 16 C3
Nibley Green *Glos* 16 B4
Nibon *Shetl'd* 96 F5
Nicholashayne *Devon* 7 E10
Nicholaston *Swan* 23 H10
Nidd *N Yorks* 51 C9
Nigg *Aberd C* 83 C11
Nigg *H'land* 87 D11
Nigg Ferry *H'land* 87 E10
Nightcott *Som'set* 7 D7
Nilig *Denbs* 42 G3
Nine Ashes *Essex* 20 A2
Nine Mile Burn *Midloth* 69 E10
Nine Wells *Pembs* 22 D2
Ninebanks *Northum* 57 A9
Ninfield *E Sussex* 12 E6
Ningwood *I/Wight* 10 F2
Nisbet *Scot Borders* 70 H5
Nisthouse *Orkney* 95 G4
Nisthouse *Shetl'd* 96 G7
Niton *I/Wight* 10 G4
Nitshill *C/Glasg* 68 D4
No Man's Heath *Ches* 43 H8
No Man's Heath *Warwick* 35 E8
Noak Hill *London* 20 B2
Noblethorpe *S Yorks* 44 B6
Nobottle *Northants* 28 B3
Nocton *Lincs* 46 F4
Noke *Oxon* 28 G2
Nolton *Pembs* 22 E3
Nolton Haven *Pembs* 22 E3
Nomansland *Devon* 7 E7
Nomansland *Wilts* 10 C1
Noneley *Shrops* 33 C10
Nonikiln *H'land* 87 D9
Nonington *Kent* 21 F9
Noonsbrough *Shetl'd* 96 H4
Norbreck *Blackp'l* 49 E3
Norbridge *Heref'd* 26 D4
Norbury *Ches* 43 H8
Norbury *Derby* 35 A7
Norbury *Shrops* 33 F9
Norbury *Staffs* 34 C3
Nordelph *Norfolk* 38 E1
Norden *Gtr Man* 44 A2
Norden Heath *Dorset* 9 F8
Nordley *Shrops* 34 F2
Norham *Northum* 71 F8
Norley *Ches* 43 E8
Norleywood *Hants* 10 E2
Norman Cross *Cambs* 37 F7
Normanby *N Lincs* 52 H4
Normanby *N Yorks* 52 A3
Normanby *Redcar/Clevel'd* 59 E6
Normanby-by-Spital *Lincs* 46 D4
Normanby by Stow *Lincs* 46 D2
Normanby le Wold *Lincs* 46 C5
Normandy *Surrey* 18 F6
Norman's Bay *E Sussex* 12 F5
Norman's Green *Devon* 7 F9
Normanstone *Suffolk* 39 F11
Normanton *Derby C* 35 B9
Normanton *Leics* 36 A4
Normanton *Lincs* 46 H3
Normanton *Notts* 45 G11
Normanton *Rutl'd* 36 E5
Normanton *W Yorks* 51 G9
Normanton le Heath *Leics* 35 D9
Normanton on Soar *Notts* 35 C11
Normanton-on-the-Wolds *Notts* 36 B2
Normanton on Trent *Notts* 45 F11
Normoss *Lancs* 49 F3
Norney *Surrey* 18 G6
Norrington Common *Wilts* 16 E5
Norris Green *Mersey* 43 C6
Norris Hill *Leics* 35 D9
North Anston *S Yorks* 45 D9
North Aston *Oxon* 27 F11
North Baddesley *Hants* 10 C2
North Ballachulish *H'land* 74 A3
North Barrow *Som'set* 8 B5
North Barsham *Norfolk* 38 B5
North Benfleet *Essex* 20 C4
North Bersted *W Sussex* 11 D8
North Berwick *E Loth* 70 B4
North Boarhunt *Hants* 10 C5
North Bovey *Devon* 5 C8
North Bradley *Wilts* 16 F5
North Brentor *Devon* 4 C5
North Brewham *Som'set* 16 H4
North Buckland *Devon* 6 B3
North Burlingham *Norfolk* 39 D9
North Cadbury *Som'set* 8 B5
North Cairn *Dumf/Gal* 54 B2
North Carlton *Lincs* 46 E3
North Carrine *Arg/Bute* 65 H7
North Cave *ER Yorks* 52 F4
North Cerney *Glos* 27 H7
North Charford *Wilts* 9 C10
North Charlton *Northum* 63 A7
North Cheriton *Som'set* 8 B5
North Cliff *ER Yorks* 53 E8
North Cliffe *ER Yorks* 52 F4
North Clifton *Notts* 46 E2
North Coates *Lincs* 47 B7
North Cockerington *Lincs* 47 C7
North Coker *Som'set* 8 C4
North Collafirth *Shetl'd* 96 E5
North Common *E Sussex* 12 D2
North Connel *Arg/Bute* 74 D2
North Cornelly *Bridg* 14 C4
North Cove *Suffolk* 39 G10
North Cowton *N Yorks* 58 F3
North Crawley *M/Keynes* 28 D6
North Cray *London* 19 D11
North Creake *Norfolk* 38 B4
North Curry *Som'set* 8 B2
North Dalton *ER Yorks* 52 D5
North Dawn *Orkney* 95 H5
North Deighton *N Yorks* 51 D9
North Duffield *N Yorks* 52 F2
North Elkington *Lincs* 46 C6
North Elmham *Norfolk* 38 C5
North Elmshall *W Yorks* 45 A8
North End *Bucks* 28 F5
North End *ER Yorks* 53 F8
North End *Essex* 30 G3
North End *Hants* 17 E11
North End *Lincs* 37 A8
North End *N Som'set* 15 E10
North End *Portsm'th* 10 D5
North End *Som'set* 8 B1
North End *W Sussex* 11 D10
North Erradale *H'land* 91 J12
North Fambridge *Essex* 20 B5
North Fearns *H'land* 85 E10
North Featherstone *W Yorks* 51 G10
North Ferriby *ER Yorks* 52 G5
North Frodingham *ER Yorks* 53 D7
North Gluss *Shetl'd* 96 F5
North Gorley *Hants* 9 C10
North Green *Norfolk* 39 G8
North Green *Suffolk* 31 B10
North Greetwell *Lincs* 46 E4
North Grimston *N Yorks* 52 C4
North Halley *Orkney* 95 H6
North Halling *Medway* 20 E4
North Hayling *Hants* 10 D6
North Hazelrigg *Northum* 71 G9
North Heasley *Devon* 7 C6
North Heath *W Sussex* 11 B9
North Hill *Cambs* 37 H10
North Hill *Cornw'l* 4 D3
North Hinksey *Oxon* 27 H11
North Holmwood *Surrey* 19 G8
North Howden *ER Yorks* 52 F3
North Huish *Devon* 5 F8
North Hykeham *Lincs* 46 F3
North Johnston *Pembs* 22 E4
North Kelsey *Lincs* 46 B4
North Kelsey Moor *Lincs* 46 B4
North Kessock *H'land* 87 G9
North Killingholme *N Lincs* 53 H7
North Kilvington *N Yorks* 58 H5
North Kilworth *Leics* 36 G2
North Kirkton *Aberds* 89 C11
North Kiscadale *N Ayrs* 66 D3
North Kyme *Lincs* 46 G5
North Lancing *W Sussex* 11 D10
North Lee *Bucks* 28 H5
North Leigh *Oxon* 27 G10
North Leverton with Habblesthorpe *Notts* 45 D11
North Littleton *Worcs* 27 D7
North Lopham *Norfolk* 38 G6
North Luffenham *Rutl'd* 36 E5
North Marden *W Sussex* 11 C7
North Marston *Bucks* 28 F4
North Middleton *Midloth* 70 E2
North Middleton *Northum* 62 A6
North Molton *Devon* 7 D6
North Moreton *Oxon* 18 C2
North Mundham *W Sussex* 11 D7
North Muskham *Notts* 45 G11
North Newbald *ER Yorks* 52 F5
North Newington *Oxon* 27 E11
North Newnton *Wilts* 17 F8
North Newton *Som'set* 8 A1
North Nibley *Glos* 16 B4
North Oakley *Hants* 18 F2
North Ockendon *London* 20 C2
North Ormesby *Middlesbro'* 58 D6
North Ormsby *Lincs* 46 C6
North Otterington *N Yorks* 58 H4
North Owersby *Lincs* 46 C4
North Perrott *Som'set* 8 D3
North Petherton *Som'set* 8 A1
North Petherwin *Cornw'l* 4 C3
North Pickenham *Norfolk* 38 E4
North Piddle *Worcs* 26 C6
North Poorton *Dorset* 8 E4
North Port *Arg/Bute* 74 E3
North Queensferry *Fife* 69 B10
North Radworthy *Devon* 7 C6
North Rauceby *Lincs* 46 H4
North Reston *Lincs* 47 D7
North Rigton *N Yorks* 51 E8
North Rode *Ches* 44 F2
North Roe *Shetl'd* 96 E5
North Runcton *Norfolk* 38 D2
North Sandwick *Shetl'd* 96 D7
North Scale *Cumb* 49 C1
North Scarle *Lincs* 46 F2
North Seaton *Northum* 63 E8
North Shian *Arg/Bute* 74 C2
North Shields *Tyne/Wear* 63 G9
North Shoebury *Southend* 20 C6
North Shore *Blackp'l* 49 F3
North Side *Cumb* 56 D2
North Side *Peterbro* 37 F8
North Skelton *Redcar/Clevel'd* 59 E7
North Somercotes *Lincs* 47 C8
North Stainley *N Yorks* 51 B8
North Stainmore *Cumb* 57 E10
North Stifford *Thurr'k* 20 C3
North Stoke *Bath/NE Som'set* 16 E4
North Stoke *Oxon* 18 C3
North Stoke *W Sussex* 11 C9
North Street *Hants* 10 A5
North Street *Kent* 21 F7
North Street *Medway* 20 D5
North Street *W Berks* 18 D3
North Sunderland *Northum* 71 G11
North Tamerton *Cornw'l* 6 G2
North Tawton *Devon* 6 F5
North Thoresby *Lincs* 46 C6
North Tidworth *Wilts* 17 G9
North Togston *Northum* 63 C8
North Tuddenham *Norfolk* 38 D6
North Walbottle *Tyne/Wear* 63 G7
North Walsham *Norfolk* 39 B8
North Waltham *Hants* 18 G2
North Warnborough *Hants* 18 F4
North Water Bridge *Angus* 83 G8
North Watten *H'land* 94 E4
North Weald Bassett *Essex* 19 A11
North Wheatley *Notts* 45 D11
North Whilborough *Devon* 5 E9
North Wick *Bath/NE Som'set* 16 E2
North Willingham *Lincs* 46 D5
North Wingfield *Derby* 45 F8
North Witham *Lincs* 36 C5
North Woolwich *London* 19 D11
North Wootton *Dorset* 8 C5
North Wootton *Norfolk* 38 C2
North Wootton *Som'set* 16 G2
North Wraxall *Wilts* 16 D5
North Wroughton *Swindon* 17 C8
Northacre *Norfolk* 38 F5
Northallerton *N Yorks* 58 G4
Northam *Devon* 6 D3
Northam *S'thampton* 10 C3
Northampton *Northants* 28 B4
Northaw *Herts* 19 A9
Northbeck *Lincs* 37 A6
Northborough *Peterbro* 37 E7
Northbourne *Kent* 21 F10
Northbridge Street *E Sussex* 12 D6
Northchapel *W Sussex* 11 B8
Northchurch *Herts* 28 H6
Northcott *Devon* 6 G2
Northdown *Kent* 21 D10
Northdyke *Orkney* 95 F3
Northend *Bath/NE Som'set* 16 E4
Northend *Bucks* 18 B4
Northend *Warwick* 27 C10
Northenden *Gtr Man* 44 C2
Northfield *Aberd C* 83 C11
Northfield *Scot Borders* 71 D8
Northfield *ER Yorks* 52 G6

Pilsbury Derby 44 F5
Pilsdon Dorset 8 E3
Pilsgate Peterbro 37 E6
Pilsley Derby 44 E6
Pilsley Derby 45 F8
Pilton Devon 6 C4
Pilton Northants 36 G6
Pilton Rutl'd 36 E5
Pilton Som'set 16 G2
Pilton Green Swan 23 H9
Pimperne Dorset 9 D8
Pinchbeck Lincs 37 C8
Pinchbeck Bars Lincs 37 C7
Pinchbeck West Lincs 37 C8
Pincheon Green S Yorks 52 H2
Pinehurst Swindon 17 C8
Pinfold Lancs 43 A6
Pinged Carms 23 F9
Pinhoe Devon 7 G8
Pinkneys Green Windsor 18 C5
Pinley W Midlands 35 H9
Pinmill Suffolk 31 E9
Pinminnoch S Ayrs 66 G4
Pinmore S Ayrs 66 G5
Pinmore Mains S Ayrs 66 G5
Pinner London 19 C8
Pinvin Worcs 26 D6
Pinwherry S Ayrs 66 H4
Pinxton Derby 45 G8
Pipe and Lyde Heref'd 26 D2
Pipe Gate Shrops 34 A3
Piperhill H'land 87 F11
Piper's Pool Cornw'l 4 C3
Pipewell Northants 36 G4
Pippacott Devon 6 C4
Pipton Powys 25 E8
Pirbright Surrey 18 F6
Pirnmill N Ayrs 66 B1
Pirton Herts 29 E8
Pirton Worcs 26 D5
Pisgah Ceredig'n 32 H2
Pisgah Stirl 75 G10
Pishill Oxon 18 C4
Pistyll Gwyn 40 F5
Pitagowan Perth/Kinr 81 G10
Pitblae Aberds 89 B9
Pitcairngreen Perth/Kinr 76 E3
Pitcalnie H'land 87 D11
Pitcaple Aberds 83 A9
Pitch Green Bucks 18 A4
Pitch Place Surrey 18 F6
Pitchcombe Glos 26 H5
Pitchcott Bucks 28 F4
Pitchford Shrops 33 E11
Pitcombe Som'set 8 A5
Pitcorthie Fife 77 G8
Pitcox E Loth 70 C5
Pitcur Perth/Kinr 76 D5
Pitfichie Aberds 83 B8
Pitforthie Aberds 83 F10
Pitgrudy H'land 87 B10
Pitkennedy Angus 77 B8
Pitkevy Fife 76 G5
Pitkierie Fife 77 G8
Pitlessie Fife 76 G6
Pitlochry Perth/Kinr 76 B2
Pitmachie Aberds 83 A8
Pitmain H'land 81 C9
Pitmedden Aberds 89 F8
Pitminster Som'set 7 E11
Pitmuies Angus 77 C8
Pitmunie Aberds 83 B8
Pitney Som'set 8 B3
Pitscottie Fife 77 F7
Pitsea Essex 20 C4
Pitsford Northants 28 B4
Pitsmoor S Yorks 45 D7
Pitstone Bucks 28 G6
Pitstone Green Bucks 28 G6
Pittendreich Moray 88 B1
Pittentrail H'land 93 J10
Pittenweem Fife 77 G8
Pittington Durham 58 B4
Pittodrie Aberds 83 A8
Pitton Wilts 9 A11
Pittswood Kent 20 G3
Pittulie Aberds 89 B9
Pity Me Durham 58 B3
Pityme Cornw'l 3 B8
Pityoulish H'land 81 B11
Pixey Green Suffolk 39 H8
Pixham Surrey 19 F8
Pixley Heref'd 26 E3
Place Newton N Yorks 52 B4
Plaidy Aberds 89 C7
Plains N Lanarks 68 D6
Plaish Shrops 33 F11
Plaistow W Sussex 11 A9
Plaitford Hants 10 C1
Plank Lane Gtr Man 43 C9
Plâs Carms 23 D9
Plas-canol Gwyn 32 D1
Plas Gogerddan Ceredig'n 32 G2
Plas Llwyngwern Powys 32 E3
Plas Nantyr Wrex 33 B7
Plas-yn-Cefn Denbs 42 E3
Plastow Green Hants 18 E2
Platt Kent 20 F3
Platt Bridge Gtr Man 43 B9
Platts Common S Yorks 45 B7
Plawsworth Durham 58 B3
Plaxtol Kent 20 F3
Play Hatch Oxon 18 D4
Playden E Sussex 13 D8
Playford Suffolk 31 D9
Playing Place Cornw'l 3 E7
Playley Green Glos 26 E4
Plealey Shrops 33 E10
Plean Stirl 69 B7
Pleasington Blackb'n 50 G2
Pleasley Derby 45 F9
Pleckgate Blackb'n 50 F2
Plenmeller Northum 62 G3
Pleshey Essex 30 G3
Plockton H'land 85 E13
Plocrapol W Isles 90 H6
Ploughfield Heref'd 25 D10
Plowden Shrops 33 G9
Ploxgreen Shrops 33 E9
Pluckley Kent 20 G6
Pluckley Thorne Kent 13 B8
Plumbland Cumb 56 C3
Plumley Ches 43 E10
Plumpton Cumb 57 C6
Plumpton E Sussex 12 E2
Plumpton Green E Sussex 12 E2
Plumpton Head Cumb 57 C7
Plumstead London 19 D11
Plumstead Norfolk 39 B7
Plumtree Notts 36 B2
Plungar Leics 36 B3
Plush Dorset 8 D6
Plwmp Ceredig'n 23 A8
Plymouth Plym'th 4 F5
Plympton Plym'th 4 F6
Plymstock Plym'th 4 F6
Plymtree Devon 7 F9
Pockley N Yorks 59 H7
Pocklington ER Yorks 52 E4
Pode Hole Lincs 37 C8
Podimore Som'set 8 B4
Podington Beds 28 B6
Podmore Staffs 34 B3
Point Clear Essex 31 G7
Pointon Lincs 37 B7
Pokesdown Bournem'th 9 E10
Pol a Charra W Isles 84 G2
Polbae Dumf/Gal 54 B5
Polbain H'land 92 H2
Polbathic Cornw'l 4 F4
Polbeth W Loth 69 D9
Polchar H'land 81 C10
Pole Elm Worcs 26 D5
Polebrook Northants 37 G6
Polegate E Sussex 12 F4
Poles H'land 87 B10
Polesworth Warwick 35 E8
Polgigga Cornw'l 2 G2
Polglass H'land 92 J3
Polgooth Cornw'l 3 D8
Poling W Sussex 11 D9
Polkerris Cornw'l 4 F1
Polla H'land 92 D6
Pollington ER Yorks 52 H2
Polloch H'land 79 E10
Pollok C/Glasg 68 D4
Pollokshields C/Glasg 68 D4
Polmassick Cornw'l 3 E8
Polmont Falk 69 C8
Polnessan E Ayrs 67 E7
Polnish H'land 79 C10
Polperro Cornw'l 4 F3
Polruan Cornw'l 4 F2
Polsham Som'set 15 G11
Polstead Suffolk 30 E6
Poltalloch Arg/Bute 73 D7
Poltimore Devon 7 G8
Polton Midloth 69 D11
Polwarth Scot Borders 70 E6
Polyphant Cornw'l 4 C3
Polzeath Cornw'l 3 B8
Ponders End London 19 B10
Pondersbridge Cambs 37 F8
Pondtail Hants 18 F5
Ponsanooth Cornw'l 3 F6
Ponsworthy Devon 5 D8
Pont Aber Carms 24 F4
Pont Aber-Geirw Gwyn 32 C3
Pont-ar-gothi Carms 23 D10
Pont ar Hydfer Powys 24 F5
Pont-ar-llechau Carms 24 F4
Pont Cwm Pydew Denbs 32 B6
Pont Cyfyng Conwy 41 E9
Pont Cysyllte Wrex 33 A8
Pont Dolydd Prysor Gwyn 41 G9
Pont-faen Powys 24 E6
Pont Fronwydd Gwyn 32 C4
Pont-gareg Pembs 22 B6
Pont-Henri Carms 23 F9
Pont-Llogel Powys 32 D6
Pont Pen-y-benglog Gwyn 41 D8
Pont Rhyd-goch Conwy 41 D8
Pont-Rhyd-sarn Gwyn 32 C4
Pont Rhyd-y-cyff Bridg 14 C4
Pont-rhyd-y-groes Ceredig'n 24 A4
Pont-rug Gwyn 41 D7
Pont Senni = Sennybridge Powys 24 F6
Pont-siân Ceredig'n 23 B9
Pont-y-gwaith Rh Cyn Taff 14 B6
Pont-y-pant Conwy 41 E9
Pont y Pennant Gwyn 32 C5
Pont-y-Pŵl = Pontypool Torf 15 A8
Pont yclun Rh Cyn Taff 14 C6
Pont yr Afon-Gam Gwyn 41 F9
Pont-yr-hafod Pembs 22 D4
Pontamman Carms 24 G3
Pontantwn Carms 23 E9
Pontardawe Neath P Talb 14 A3
Pontarddulais Swan 23 F10
Pontarsais Carms 23 D9
Pontblyddyn Flints 42 F5
Pontbren Araeth Carms 24 F3
Pontbren Llwyd Rh Cyn Taff 24 H6
Pontefract W Yorks 51 G10
Ponteland Northum 63 F7
Ponterwyd Ceredig'n 32 G3
Pontesbury Shrops 33 E9
Pontfadog Wrex 33 B8
Pontfaen Pembs 22 C5
Pontgarreg Ceredig'n 23 A8
Ponthir Torf 15 B9
Ponthirwaun Ceredig'n 23 B7
Pontllanfraith Caerph 15 B7
Pontlliw Swan 14 A2
Pontllyfni Gwyn 40 E6
Pontlottyn Caerph 25 H8
Pontneddfechan Powys 24 H6
Pontnewydd Torf 15 B8
Pontrhydfendigaid Ceredig'n 24 B4
Pontrhydyfen Neath P Talb 14 B3
Pontrilas Heref'd 25 F10
Pontrobert Powys 33 D7
Ponts Green E Sussex 12 E5
Pontshill Heref'd 26 F3
Pontsticill Merth Tyd 25 G7
Pontwgan Conwy 41 C9
Pontyates Carms 23 F9
Pontyberem Carms 23 E10
Pontycymer Bridg 14 B5
Pontyglasier Pembs 22 C6
Pontypool = Pont-y-Pŵl Torf 15 A8
Pontypridd Rh Cyn Taff 14 C6
Pontywaun Caerph 15 B8
Pooksgreen Hants 10 C2
Pool Cornw'l 2 E5
Pool W Yorks 51 E8
Pool o'Muckhart Clack 76 G3
Pool Quay Powys 33 D8
Poole Poole 9 E9
Poole Keynes Glos 16 B6
Poolend Staffs 44 G3
Poolewe H'land 91 J13
Pooley Bridge Cumb 56 D6
Poolfold Staffs 44 G2
Poolhill Glos 26 F4
Poolsbrook Derby 45 E8
Pootings Kent 19 G11
Pope Hill Pembs 22 E4
Popeswood Brackn'l 18 E5
Popham Hants 18 G2
Poplar London 19 C10
Popley Hants 18 F3
Porchester Notts 36 A1
Porchfield I/Wight 10 E3
Porin H'land 86 F6
Poringland Norfolk 39 E8
Porkellis Cornw'l 2 F5
Porlock Som'set 7 B7
Porlock Weir Som'set 7 B7
Port Ann Arg/Bute 73 E8
Port Appin Arg/Bute 74 C2
Port Askaig Arg/Bute 64 B5
Port Bannatyne Arg/Bute 73 G9
Port Carlisle Cumb 61 G8
Port Charlotte Arg/Bute 64 C3
Port Clarence Stockton 58 D5
Port Driseach Arg/Bute 73 F8
Port e Vullen I/Man 48 C4
Port Ellen Arg/Bute 64 D4
Port Elphinstone Aberds 83 B9
Port Erin I/Man 48 F1
Port Erroll Aberds 89 E10
Port Eynon Swan 23 H9
Port Gaverne Cornw'l 3 A9
Port Glasgow Invercl 68 C2
Port Henderson H'land 85 A12
Port Isaac Cornw'l 3 A8
Port Lamont Arg/Bute 73 F9
Port Lion Pembs 22 F4
Port Logan Dumf/Gal 54 E3
Port Mholair W Isles 91 D10
Port Mor H'land 78 D7
Port Mulgrave N Yorks 59 E8
Port Nan Giùran W Isles 91 D10
Port nan Long W Isles 84 A3
Port Nis W Isles 91 A10
Port of Menteith Stirl 75 G8
Port Quin Cornw'l 3 A8
Port Ramsay Arg/Bute 79 G11
Port St Mary I/Man 48 F2
Port Sunlight Mersey 42 D6
Port Talbot Neath P Talb 14 B3
Port Tennant Swan 14 B2
Port Wemyss Arg/Bute 64 C2
Port William Dumf/Gal 54 E6
Portachoillan Arg/Bute 72 H6
Portavadie Arg/Bute 73 G8
Portbury N Som'set 15 D11
Portchester Hants 10 D5
Portclair H'land 80 B6
Portencalzie Dumf/Gal 54 B3
Portencross N Ayrs 66 B4
Portesham Dorset 8 F5
Portessie Moray 88 B4
Portfield Gate Pembs 22 E4
Portgate Devon 4 C5
Portgordon Moray 88 B3
Portgower H'land 93 H13
Porth Cornw'l 3 C7
Porth Rh Cyn Taff 14 B6
Porth Navas Cornw'l 3 G6
Porth Tywyn = Burry Port Carms 23 F9
Porth-y-waen Shrops 33 C8
Porthaethwy = Menai Bridge Angl 41 C7
Porthallow Cornw'l 3 G6
Porthallow Cornw'l 4 F3
Porthcawl Bridg 14 D4
Porthcothan Cornw'l 3 B7
Porthcurno Cornw'l 2 G2
Porthgain Pembs 22 C3
Porthill Shrops 33 D10
Porthkerry V/Glam 14 E6
Porthleven Cornw'l 2 G5
Porthllechog Angl 40 A6
Porthmadog Gwyn 41 G7
Porthmeor Cornw'l 2 F3
Portholland Cornw'l 3 E8
Porthoustock Cornw'l 3 G7
Porthpean Cornw'l 3 D9
Porthtowan Cornw'l 2 E5
Porthyrhyd Carms 23 E10
Porthyrhyd Carms 24 E4
Portincaple Arg/Bute 73 D11
Portington ER Yorks 52 F3
Portinnisherrich Arg/Bute 73 B8
Portinscale Cumb 56 D4
Portishead N Som'set 15 D10
Portkil Arg/Bute 73 E11
Portknockie Moray 88 B4
Portlethen Aberds 83 D11
Portling Dumf/Gal 55 D11
Portloe Cornw'l 3 F8
Portmahomack H'land 87 C12
Portmeirion Gwyn 41 G7
Portmellon Cornw'l 3 E9
Portmore Hants 10 E2
Portnacroish Arg/Bute 74 C2
Portnahaven Arg/Bute 64 C2
Portnalong H'land 85 E8
Portnaluchaig H'land 79 C9
Portnancon H'land 92 C7
Portnellan Stirl 75 E7
Portobello C/Edinb 70 C2
Porton Wilts 17 H8
Portpatrick Dumf/Gal 54 D3
Portreath Cornw'l 2 E5
Portree H'land 85 D9
Portscatho Cornw'l 3 F7
Portsea Portsm'th 10 D5
Portskerra H'land 93 C11
Portskewett Monmouths 15 C11
Portslade Brighton/Hove 12 F1
Portslade-by-Sea Brighton/Hove 12 F1
Portsmouth Portsm'th 10 D5
Portsmouth W Yorks 50 G5
Portsonachan Arg/Bute 74 E3
Portsoy Aberds 88 B5
Portswood S'thampton 10 C3
Porttanachy Moray 88 B3
Portuairk H'land 78 E7
Portway Heref'd 25 E11
Portway Worcs 27 A7
Portwrinkle Cornw'l 4 F4
Poslingford Suffolk 30 D4
Postbridge Devon 5 D7
Postcombe Oxon 18 B4
Postling Kent 13 C10
Postwick Norfolk 39 E8
Potholm Dumf/Gal 61 E9
Potsgrove Beds 28 F6
Pott Row Norfolk 38 C3
Pott Shrigley Ches 44 E3
Potten End Herts 29 H7
Potter Brompton N Yorks 52 B5
Potter Heigham Norfolk 39 D10
Potter Street Essex 29 H11
Potterhanworth Lincs 46 F4
Potterhanworth Booths Lincs 46 F4
Potterne Wilts 16 F6
Potterne Wick Wilts 17 F7
Potternewton W Yorks 51 F9
Potters Bar Herts 19 A9
Potter's Cross Staffs 34 G4
Potterspury Northants 28 D4
Potterton Aberds 83 B11
Potterton W Yorks 51 F10
Potto N Yorks 58 F5
Potton Beds 29 D9
Poughill Cornw'l 6 F1
Poughill Devon 7 F7
Poulshot Wilts 16 F6
Poulton Glos 17 A8
Poulton Mersey 42 C6
Poulton-le-Fylde Lancs 49 F3
Pound Bank Worcs 26 A4
Pound Green E Sussex 12 D4
Pound Green I/Wight 10 F2
Pound Green Worcs 34 H3
Pound Hill W Sussex 12 C1
Poundfield E Sussex 12 C4
Poundland S Ayrs 66 H4
Poundon Bucks 28 F3
Poundsgate Devon 5 D8
Poundstock Cornw'l 4 B3
Powburn Northum 62 B6
Powderham Devon 5 C10
Powerstock Dorset 8 E4
Powfoot Dumf/Gal 61 G7
Powick Worcs 26 C5
Powmill Perth/Kinr 76 H3
Poxwell Dorset 8 F6
Poyle Slough 19 D7
Poynings W Sussex 12 E1
Poyntington Dorset 8 C5
Poynton Ches 44 D3
Poynton Green Telford 34 D1
Poystreet Green Suffolk 30 C6
Praa Sands Cornw'l 2 G4
Pratt's Bottom London 19 E11
Praze Cornw'l 2 F4
Praze-an-Beeble Cornw'l 2 F5
Predannack Wollas Cornw'l 2 H5
Prees Shrops 34 B1
Prees Green Shrops 34 B1
Prees Heath Shrops 34 B1
Prees Higher Heath Shrops 34 B1
Prees Lower Heath Shrops 34 B1
Preesall Lancs 49 E3
Preesgweene Shrops 33 B8
Prenderguest Scot Borders 71 E8
Prendwick Northum 62 B6
Prengwyn Ceredig'n 23 B9
Prenteg Gwyn 41 F7
Prenton Mersey 42 D6
Prescot Mersey 43 C7
Prescott Shrops 33 C10
Pressen Northum 71 G7
Prestatyn Denbs 42 D3
Prestbury Ches 44 E3
Prestbury Glos 26 F6
Presteigne = Llanandras Powys 25 B10
Presthope Shrops 34 F1
Prestleigh Som'set 16 G3
Preston Scot Borders 70 E6
Preston Brighton/Hove 12 F2
Preston Devon 5 D9
Preston Dorset 8 F6
Preston E Loth 70 C4
Preston ER Yorks 53 F7
Preston Glos 17 A7
Preston Glos 26 E3
Preston Herts 29 F8
Preston Kent 21 E7
Preston Kent 21 E9
Preston Lancs 49 G5
Preston Northum 71 H10
Preston Rutl'd 36 E4
Preston Shrops 33 D11
Preston Suffolk 30 C6
Preston Wilts 17 D7
Preston Wilts 17 D9
Preston Bagot Warwick 27 B8
Preston Bissett Bucks 28 F3
Preston Bowyer Som'set 7 D10
Preston Brockhurst Shrops 33 C11
Preston Brook Halton 43 D8
Preston Candover Hants 18 G3
Preston Capes Northants 28 C2
Preston Crowmarsh Oxon 18 B3
Preston Gubbals Shrops 33 D10
Preston on Stour Warwick 27 D9
Preston on the Hill Halton 43 D8
Preston on Wye Heref'd 25 D10
Preston Plucknett Som'set 8 C4
Preston-under-Scar N Yorks 58 G1
Preston upon the Weald Moors Telford 34 D2
Preston Wynne Heref'd 26 D2
Prestonmill Dumf/Gal 60 H5
Prestonpans E Loth 70 C2
Prestwich Gtr Man 44 B2
Prestwick Northum 63 F7
Prestwick S Ayrs 67 D6
Prestwood Bucks 18 A5
Price Town Bridg 14 B5
Prickwillow Cambs 38 G1
Priddy Som'set 15 F11
Priest Hutton Lancs 49 B5
Priest Weston Shrops 33 F8
Priesthaugh Scot Borders 61 C10
Primethorpe Leics 35 F11
Primrose Green Norfolk 39 D6
Primrose Valley N Yorks 53 B7
Primrosehill Herts 19 A7
Princes Gate Pembs 22 E6
Princes Risborough Bucks 18 A5
Princethorpe Warwick 27 A11
Princetown Caerph 25 G8
Princetown Devon 5 D6
Prion Denbs 42 F3
Prior Muir Fife 77 F8
Prior Park Northum 71 E8
Priors Frome Heref'd 26 E2
Priors Hardwick Warwick 27 C11
Priors Marston Warwick 27 C11
Priorslee Telford 34 D3
Priory Wood Heref'd 25 D9
Priston Bath/NE Som'set 16 E3
Pristow Green Norfolk 39 G7
Prittlewell Southend 20 C5
Privett Hants 10 B5
Prixford Devon 6 C4
Probus Cornw'l 3 E7
Proncy H'land 87 B10
Prospect Cumb 56 B3
Prudhoe Northum 62 G6
Ptarmigan Lodge Stirl 74 G6
Pubil Perth/Kinr 75 C7
Puckeridge Herts 29 F10
Puckington Som'set 8 C2
Pucklechurch S Gloucs 16 D3
Pucknall Hants 10 B2
Puckrup Glos 26 E5
Puddinglake Ches 43 F10
Puddington Ches 42 E6
Puddington Devon 7 E7
Puddledock Norfolk 39 F6
Puddletown Dorset 9 E6
Pudleston Heref'd 26 C2
Pudsey W Yorks 51 F8
Pulborough W Sussex 11 C9
Puleston Telford 34 C3
Pulford Ches 43 G6
Pulham Dorset 8 D6
Pulham Market Norfolk 39 G7
Pulham St Mary Norfolk 39 G8
Pulloxhill Beds 29 E7
Pumpherston W Loth 69 D9
Pumsaint Carms 24 D3
Puncheston Pembs 22 D5
Puncknowle Dorset 8 F4
Punnett's Town E Sussex 12 D5
Purbrook Hants 10 D5
Purewell Dorset 9 E10
Purfleet Thurr'k 20 D2
Puriton Som'set 15 G9
Purleigh Essex 20 A5
Purley London 19 E10
Purley W Berks 18 D3
Purlogue Shrops 33 H8
Purls Bridge Cambs 37 G10
Purse Caundle Dorset 8 C5
Purslow Shrops 33 G9
Purston Jaglin W Yorks 51 H10
Purton Glos 16 A3
Purton Glos 16 A3
Purton Wilts 17 C7
Purton Stoke Wilts 17 B7
Pury End Northants 28 D4
Pusey Oxon 17 B10
Putley Heref'd 26 E3
Putney London 19 D9
Putsborough Devon 6 B3
Puttenham Herts 28 G5
Puttenham Surrey 18 G6
Puxton N Som'set 15 E10
Pwll Carms 23 F9
Pwll-glas Denbs 42 G4
Pwll-Meyric Monmouths 15 B11
Pwll-trap Carms 23 E7
Pwll-y-glaw Neath P Talb 14 B3
Pwllcrochan Pembs 22 F4
Pwllgloyw Powys 25 E7
Pwllheli Gwyn 40 G5
Pyecombe W Sussex 12 E1
Pye Corner Newp 15 C9
Pye Green Staffs 34 D5
Pyewipe NE Lincs 46 A6
Pyle I/Wight 10 G3
Pyle = Y Pîl Bridg 14 C4
Pylle Som'set 16 H3
Pymoor Cambs 37 G10
Pyrford Surrey 19 F7
Pyrton Oxon 18 B3
Pytchley Northants 28 A5
Pyworthy Devon 6 F2

Q

Quabbs Shrops 33 G8
Quadring Lincs 37 B8
Quainton Bucks 28 G4
Quarley Hants 17 G9
Quarndon Derby 35 A9
Quarrier's Homes Invercl 68 D2
Quarrington Lincs 37 A6
Quarrington Hill Durham 58 C4
Quarry Bank W Midlands 34 G5
Quarryford E Loth 70 D4
Quarryhill H'land 87 C10
Quarrywood Moray 88 B1
Quarter S Lanarks 68 E6
Quatford Shrops 34 F3
Quatt Shrops 34 G3
Quebec Durham 58 B2
Quedgeley Glos 26 G5
Queen Adelaide Cambs 38 G1
Queen Camel Som'set 8 B4
Queen Charlton Bath/NE Som'set 16 E3
Queen Dart Devon 7 E7
Queen Oak Dorset 9 A6
Queen Street Kent 20 G3
Queen Street Wilts 17 C7
Queenborough Kent 20 D6
Queenhill Worcs 26 E5
Queen's Head Shrops 33 C9
Queen's Park Beds 29 D7
Queen's Park Northants 28 B4
Queensbury W Yorks 51 F7
Queensferry C/Edinb 69 C10
Queensferry Flints 42 F6
Queenstown Blackp'l 49 F3
Queenzieburn N Lanarks 68 C5
Quemerford Wilts 17 E7
Quendale Shetl'd 96 M5
Quendon Essex 30 E2
Queniborough Leics 36 D2
Quenington Glos 17 A8
Quernmore Lancs 49 D5
Quethiock Cornw'l 4 E4
Quholm Orkney 95 G3
Quicks Green W Berks 18 D2
Quidenham Norfolk 38 G6
Quidhampton Hants 18 F2
Quidhampton Wilts 9 A10
Quilquox Aberds 89 E9
Quina Brook Shrops 33 B11
Quindry Orkney 95 J5
Quinton Northants 28 C4
Quinton W Midlands 34 G5
Quintrell Downs Cornw'l 3 C7
Quixhill Staffs 35 A7
Quoditch Devon 6 G3
Quoig Perth/Kinr 75 E11
Quorndon Leics 36 D1
Quothquan S Lanarks 69 G8
Quoyloo Orkney 95 F3
Quoyness Orkney 95 H3
Quoys Shetl'd 96 B8
Quoys Shetl'd 96 G6

R

Raasay Ho. H'land 85 E10
Rabbit's Cross Kent 20 G4
Raby Mersey 42 E6
Rachan Mill Scot Borders 69 G10
Rachub Gwyn 41 D8
Rackenford Devon 7 E7
Rackham W Sussex 11 C9
Rackheath Norfolk 39 D8
Racks Dumf/Gal 60 F6
Rackwick Orkney 95 J3
Rackwick Orkney 95 D5
Radbourne Derby 35 B8
Radcliffe Gtr Man 43 B10
Radcliffe Northum 63 C8
Radcliffe on Trent Notts 36 B2
Radclive Bucks 28 E3
Radcot Oxon 17 B9
Raddery H'land 87 F10
Radernie Fife 77 G7
Radford Semele Warwick 27 B10
Radipole Dorset 8 F5
Radlett Herts 19 B8
Radley Oxon 18 B2
Radmanthwaite Notts 45 F9
Radmoor Shrops 34 C2
Radmore Green Ches 43 G8
Radnage Bucks 18 B4
Radstock Bath/NE Som'set 16 F3
Radstone Northants 28 D2
Radway Warwick 27 D10
Radway Green Ches 43 G10
Radwell Beds 29 C7
Radwell Herts 29 E9
Radwinter Essex 30 E3
Radyr Card 15 C7
Rafford Moray 87 F13
Ragdale Leics 36 D2
Raglan Monmouths 25 H11
Ragnall Notts 46 E2
Rahane Arg/Bute 73 E11
Rainford Mersey 43 B7
Rainford Junction Mersey 43 B7
Rainham London 20 C2
Rainham Medway 20 E5
Rainhill Mersey 43 C7
Rainhill Stoops Mersey 43 C8
Rainow Ches 44 E3
Rainton N Yorks 51 B9
Rainworth Notts 45 G9
Raisbeck Cumb 57 F8
Raise Cumb 57 B9
Rait Perth/Kinr 76 E5
Raithby Lincs 47 D7
Raithby Lincs 47 F7
Rake W Sussex 11 B7
Rakewood Gtr Man 44 A3
Ram Carms 23 B10
Ram Lane Kent 20 G6
Ramasaig H'land 84 D6
Rame Cornw'l 2 F6
Rame Cornw'l 4 G5
Rameldry Mill Bank Fife 76 G6
Ramnageo Shetl'd 96 C8
Rampisham Dorset 8 D4
Rampside Cumb 49 C2
Rampton Cambs 29 B11
Rampton Notts 45 E11
Ramsbottom Gtr Man 50 H3
Ramsbury Wilts 17 D9
Ramscraigs H'land 94 H3
Ramsdean Hants 10 B6
Ramsdell Hants 18 F2
Ramsden Oxon 27 G10
Ramsden Bellhouse Essex 20 B4
Ramsden Heath Essex 20 B4
Ramsey Cambs 37 G8
Ramsey Essex 31 E9
Ramsey I/Man 48 C4
Ramsey Forty Foot Cambs 37 G9
Ramsey Heights Cambs 37 G7
Ramsey Island Essex 30 H6
Ramsey Mereside Cambs 37 G8
Ramsey St Mary's Cambs 37 G8
Ramseycleuch Scot Borders 61 B8
Ramsgate Kent 21 E10
Ramsgill N Yorks 51 B7
Ramshorn Staffs 44 H4
Ramsnest Common Surrey 11 A8
Ranais W Isles 91 E9
Ranby Lincs 46 E6
Ranby Notts 45 D10
Rand Lincs 46 E5
Randwick Glos 26 H5
Ranfurly Renf 68 D2
Rangag H'land 94 F3
Rangemore Staffs 35 C7
Rangeworthy S Gloucs 16 C3
Rankinston E Ayrs 67 E7
Ranmoor S Yorks 45 D7
Ranmore Common Surrey 19 F8
Rannerdale Cumb 56 E3
Rannoch School Perth/Kinr 75 B8
Rannoch Station Perth/Kinr 75 B7
Ranochan H'land 79 C11
Ranskill Notts 45 D10
Ranton Staffs 34 C4
Ranworth Norfolk 39 D9
Raploch Stirl 68 A6
Rapness Orkney 95 D6
Rascal Moor ER Yorks 52 F4
Rascarrel Dumf/Gal 55 E10
Rashiereive Aberds 89 F9
Raskelf N Yorks 51 B10
Rassau Bl Gwent 25 G8
Rastrick W Yorks 51 G7
Ratagan H'land 85 G14
Ratby Leics 35 E11
Ratcliffe Culey Leics 35 F9
Ratcliffe on Soar Leics 35 C10
Ratcliffe on the Wreake Leics 36 D2
Rathen Aberds 89 B10
Rathillet Fife 76 E6
Rathmell N Yorks 50 D4
Ratho C/Edinb 69 C10
Ratho Station C/Edinb 69 C10
Rathven Moray 88 B4
Ratley Warwick 27 D10
Ratlinghope Shrops 33 F10
Rattar H'land 94 C4
Ratten Row Lancs 49 E4
Rattery Devon 5 E8
Rattlesden Suffolk 30 C6
Rattray Perth/Kinr 76 C4
Raughton Head Cumb 56 B5
Raunds Northants 28 A6
Ravenfield S Yorks 45 C8
Ravenglass Cumb 56 G2
Raveningham Norfolk 39 F9
Ravenscar N Yorks 59 F10
Ravenscraig Invercl 73 F11
Ravensdale I/Man 48 C3
Ravensden Beds 29 C7
Ravenseat N Yorks 57 F10
Ravenshead Notts 45 G9
Ravensmoor Ches 43 G9
Ravensthorpe Northants 28 A3
Ravensthorpe W Yorks 51 G8
Ravenstone Leics 35 D10
Ravenstone M/Keynes 28 C5
Ravenstonedale Cumb 57 F9
Ravenstown Cumb 49 B3
Ravenstruther S Lanarks 69 F8
Ravensworth N Yorks 58 F2
Raw N Yorks 59 F10
Rawcliffe ER Yorks 52 G2
Rawcliffe C/York 52 D1
Rawcliffe Bridge ER Yorks 52 G2
Rawdon W Yorks 51 F8
Rawmarsh S Yorks 45 C8
Rawreth Essex 20 B4
Rawridge Devon 7 F11
Rawtenstall Lancs 50 G4
Raxton Aberds 89 E8
Raydon Suffolk 31 E7
Raylees Northum 62 D5
Rayleigh Essex 20 B5
Rayne Essex 30 F4
Rayners Lane London 19 C8
Raynes Park London 19 E9
Reach Cambs 30 B2
Read Lancs 50 F3
Reading Reading 18 D4
Reading Street Kent 13 C8
Reagill Cumb 57 E8
Rearquhar H'land 87 B10
Rearsby Leics 36 D2
Reaster H'land 94 D4
Reawick Shetl'd 96 J5
Reay H'land 93 C12
Rechullin H'land 85 C13
Reculver Kent 21 E9
Red Dial Cumb 56 B4
Red Hill Worcs 26 C5
Red Houses Jersey 11
Red Lodge Suffolk 30 A3
Red Rail Heref'd 26 F2
Red Rock Gtr Man 43 B8
Red Roses Carms 23 E7
Red Row Northum 63 D8
Red Street Staffs 44 G2
Red Wharf Bay Angl 41 B7
Redberth Pembs 22 F5
Redbourn Herts 29 G8
Redbourne N Lincs 46 C3
Redbrook Glos 26 G2
Redbrook Wrex 33 A11
Redburn H'land 87 E8
Redburn H'land 87 G12
Redburn Northum 62 G3
Redcar Redcar/Clevel'd 59 D7
Redcastle Angus 77 B9
Redcastle H'land 87 G8
Redcliff Bay N Som'set 15 D10
Redding Falk 69 C8
Reddingmuirhead Falk 69 C8
Reddish Gtr Man 44 C2
Redditch Worcs 27 B7
Rede Suffolk 30 C5
Redenhall Norfolk 39 G8
Redesdale Camp Northum 62 D4
Redesmouth Northum 62 E4
Redford Aberds 83 F9
Redford Angus 77 C8
Redford Durham 58 C1
Redfordgreen Scot Borders 61 B9
Redgorton Perth/Kinr 76 E3
Redgrave Suffolk 38 H6
Redhill Aberds 89 E6
Redhill Aberds 83 C9
Redhill N Som'set 15 E11
Redhill Surrey 19 F9
Redhouse Arg/Bute 73 G7
Redhouses Arg/Bute 64 B4
Redisham Suffolk 39 G10
Redland Bristol 16 D2
Redland Orkney 95 F4
Redlingfield Suffolk 31 A8
Redlynch Som'set 8 A6
Redlynch Wilts 9 B11
Redmarley D'Abitot Glos 26 E4
Redmarshall Stockton 58 D4
Redmile Leics 36 B3
Redmire N Yorks 58 G1
Redmoor Cornw'l 4 E1
Rednal Shrops 33 C9
Redpath Scot Borders 70 G4
Redpoint H'land 85 B12
Redruth Cornw'l 2 E5
Redvales Gtr Man 44 B2
Redwick Newp 15 C10
Redwick S Gloucs 15 C11
Redworth D'lington 58 D3
Reed Herts 29 E10
Reedham Norfolk 39 E10
Reedness ER Yorks 52 G3
Reeds Beck Lincs 46 F6
Reepham Lincs 46 E4
Reepham Norfolk 39 C6
Reeth N Yorks 58 G1
Regaby I/Man 48 C4
Regoul H'land 87 F11
Reiff H'land 92 H2
Reigate Surrey 19 F9
Reighton N Yorks 53 B7
Reighton Gap N Yorks 53 B7
Reinigeadal W Isles 90 G7
Reisque Aberds 83 B10
Reiss H'land 94 E5
Rejerrah Cornw'l 3 D6
Releath Cornw'l 2 F5
Relubbus Cornw'l 2 F4
Relugas Moray 87 G12
Remenham Wokingham 18 C4
Remenham Hill Wokingham 18 C4
Remony Perth/Kinr 75 C10
Rempstone Notts 36 C1
Rendcomb Glos 27 H7
Rendham Suffolk 31 B10
Rendlesham Suffolk 31 C10
Renfrew Renf 68 D4
Renhold Beds 29 C7
Renishaw Derby 45 E8
Rennington Northum 63 B8
Renton W Dunb 68 C2
Renwick Cumb 57 B7
Repps Norfolk 39 D10
Repton Derby 35 C9
Reraig H'land 85 F13
Rescobie Angus 77 B8
Resipole H'land 79 E10
Resolis H'land 87 E9
Resolven Neath P Talb 14 A4
Reston Scot Borders 71 D7
Reswallie Angus 77 B8
Retew Cornw'l 3 D8
Retford Notts 45 D11
Rettendon Essex 20 B4
Rettendon Place Essex 20 B4
Revesby Lincs 46 F6
Revesby Bridge Lincs 47 F7
Rew Street I/Wight 10 E3
Rewe Devon 7 G8
Reydon Suffolk 39 H10
Reydon Smear Suffolk 39 H11
Reymerston Norfolk 38 E6
Reynalton Pembs 22 F5
Reynoldston Swan 23 G9
Rezare Cornw'l 4 D4
Rhaeadr Gwy = Rhayader Powys 24 B6
Rhandirmwyn Carms 24 D4
Rhayader = Rhaeadr Gwy Powys 24 B6
Rhedyn Gwyn 40 G4
Rhemore H'land 79 F8
Rhencullen I/Man 48 C3
Rhes-y-cae Flints 42 E4
Rhewl Denbs 42 F4
Rhewl Denbs 42 H4
Rhian H'land 93 H8
Rhicarn H'land 92 G3
Rhiconich H'land 92 D5
Rhicullen H'land 87 D9
Rhidorroch Ho. H'land 86 B4
Rhifail H'land 93 E10
Rhigos Rh Cyn Taff 24 H6
Rhilochan H'land 93 J10
Rhiroy H'land 86 C4
Rhisga = Risca Caerph 15 B8
Rhiw Gwyn 40 H4
Rhiwabon = Ruabon Wrex 33 A9
Rhiwbina Card 15 C7
Rhiwbryfdir Gwyn 41 F8
Rhiwderin Newp 15 C8
Rhiwlas Gwyn 41 D7
Rhiwlas Gwyn 32 B5
Rhiwlas Powys 33 B7
Rhodes Gtr Man 44 B2
Rhodes Minnis Kent 21 G8
Rhodesia Notts 45 E9
Rhodiad Pembs 22 D2
Rhondda Rh Cyn Taff 14 B5
Rhonehouse or Kelton Hill Dumf/Gal 55 D10
Rhoose = Y Rhws V/Glam 14 E6
Rhôs Carms 23 C8
Rhôs Neath P Talb 14 A3
Rhos-fawr Gwyn 40 G5
Rhos-hill Pembs 22 B6
Rhos-on-Sea Conwy 41 B10
Rhos-y-brithdir Powys 33 C7
Rhos-y-garth Ceredig'n 24 A3
Rhos-y-gwaliau Gwyn 32 B5
Rhos-y-llan Gwyn 40 G4
Rhos-y-Madoc Wrex 33 A9
Rhos-y-meirch Powys 25 B9
Rhosamman Carms 24 G4
Rhosbeirio Angl 40 A5
Rhoscefnhir Angl 41 C7
Rhoscolyn Angl 40 C4
Rhoscrowther Pembs 22 F4
Rhosesmor Flints 42 F5
Rhosgadfan Gwyn 41 E7
Rhosgoch Angl 40 B6
Rhosgoch Powys 25 D8
Rhoshirwaun Gwyn 40 H3
Rhoslan Gwyn 40 F6
Rhoslefain Gwyn 32 E1
Rhosllanerchrugog Wrex 42 H5
Rhosmaen Carms 24 F3
Rhosmeirch Angl 40 C6
Rhosneigr Angl 40 C5
Rhosnesni Wrex 42 G6
Rhosrobin Wrex 42 G6
Rhossili Swan 23 H9
Rhosson Pembs 22 D2
Rhostryfan Gwyn 40 E6
Rhostyllen Wrex 42 H6
Rhosybol Angl 40 B6
Rhu Arg/Bute 73 G7
Rhu Arg/Bute 73 E11
Rhualt Denbs 42 E3
Rhuddall Heath Ches 43 F8
Rhuddlan Ceredig'n 23 B9
Rhuddlan Denbs 42 E3
Rhue H'land 86 B3
Rhulen Powys 25 D8
Rhunahaorine Arg/Bute 65 D8
Rhuthun = Ruthin Denbs 42 G4
Rhyd Gwyn 41 F8
Rhyd Powys 32 E5
Rhyd-Ddu Gwyn 41 E7
Rhyd-moel-ddu Powys 33 H6
Rhyd-Rosser Ceredig'n 24 B2
Rhyd-uchaf Gwyn 32 B5
Rhyd-wen Gwyn 32 D3
Rhyd-y-clafdy Gwyn 40 G5
Rhyd-y-foel Conwy 42 E2
Rhyd-y-fro Neath P Talb 24 H4
Rhyd-y-gwin Swan 14 A2
Rhyd-y-meirch Monmouths 25 H10
Rhyd-y-meudwy Denbs 42 G4
Rhyd-y-pandy Swan 14 A2
Rhyd-y-sarn Gwyn 41 F8
Rhyd-yr-onen Gwyn 32 E2
Rhydaman = Ammanford Carms 24 G3
Rhydargaeau Carms 23 D9
Rhydcymerau Carms 23 C10
Rhydd Worcs 26 D5
Rhydding Neath P Talb 14 B3
Rhydfudr Ceredig'n 24 B2
Rhydlewis Ceredig'n 23 B8
Rhydlios Gwyn 40 G3
Rhydlydan Conwy 41 E10
Rhydness Powys 25 D8
Rhydowen Ceredig'n 23 B9
Rhydspence Heref'd 25 D9
Rhydtalog Flints 42 G5
Rhydwyn Angl 40 B5
Rhydycroesau Shrops 33 B8
Rhydyfelin Ceredig'n 32 H1
Rhydyfelin Rh Cyn Taff 14 C6
Rhydymain Gwyn 32 C4
Rhydymwyn Flints 42 F5
Rhyl = Y Rhyl Denbs 42 D3
Rhymney = Rhymni Caerph 25 H8
Rhymni = Rhymney Caerph 25 H8
Rhynd Fife 77 E7
Rhynd Perth/Kinr 76 E4
Rhynie Aberds 82 A6
Rhynie H'land 87 D11
Ribbesford Worcs 26 A4
Ribblehead N Yorks 50 B3
Ribbleton Lancs 50 F1
Ribchester Lancs 50 F2
Ribigill H'land 93 D8
Riby Lincs 46 B5
Riby Cross Roads Lincs 46 B5
Riccall N Yorks 52 F2
Riccarton E Ayrs 67 C7
Richards Castle Heref'd 25 B11
Richings Park Bucks 19 D7
Richmond London 19 D8
Richmond N Yorks 58 F2
Rickarton Aberds 83 E10
Rickinghall Suffolk 38 H6
Rickleton Tyne/Wear 58 A3
Rickling Essex 29 E11
Rickmansworth Herts 19 B7
Riddings Cumb 61 F10
Riddings Derby 45 G8
Riddlecombe Devon 6 E5
Riddlesden W Yorks 51 E6
Riddrie C/Glasg 68 D5
Ridge Dorset 9 F8
Ridge Hants 10 C2
Ridge Wilts 9 A8
Ridge Green Surrey 19 G10
Ridge Lane Warwick 35 F8
Ridgebourne Powys 25 B7
Ridgehill N Som'set 15 E11
Ridgeway Cross Heref'd 26 D4
Ridgewell Essex 30 D4
Ridgewood E Sussex 12 E3
Ridgmont Beds 28 E6
Riding Mill Northum 62 G6
Ridleywood Wrex 43 G7
Ridlington Norfolk 39 B9
Ridlington Rutl'd 36 E4
Ridsdale Northum 62 E5
Riechip Perth/Kinr 76 C3
Riemore Perth/Kinr 76 C3
Rienachait H'land 92 F3
Rievaulx N Yorks 59 H6
Rift House Hartlep'l 58 C5
Rigg Dumf/Gal 61 G8
Riggend N Lanarks 68 C6
Rigsby Lincs 47 E8
Rigside S Lanarks 69 G7
Riley Green Lancs 50 G2
Rileyhill Staffs 35 D7
Rilla Mill Cornw'l 4 D3
Rillington N Yorks 52 B4
Rimington Lancs 50 E4
Rimpton Som'set 8 B5
Rimswell ER Yorks 53 G9
Rinaston Pembs 22 D4
Ringasta Shetl'd 96 M5
Ringford Dumf/Gal 55 D9
Ringinglow S Yorks 44 D6
Ringland Norfolk 39 D7
Ringles Cross E Sussex 12 D3
Ringmer E Sussex 12 E3
Ringmore Devon 5 G7
Ringorm Moray 88 D2
Ring's End Cambs 37 E9
Ringsfield Suffolk 39 G10
Ringsfield Corner Suffolk 39 G10
Ringshall Herts 28 G6
Ringshall Suffolk 31 C7
Ringshall Stocks Suffolk 31 C7
Ringstead Norfolk 38 A3
Ringstead Northants 36 H5
Ringwood Hants 9 D10
Ringwould Kent 21 G10
Rinmore Aberds 82 B6

Rinnigill Orkney 95 J4
Rinsey Cornw'l 2 G4
Riof W Isles 90 D6
Ripe E Sussex 12 E4
Ripley Derby 45 G7
Ripley Hants 9 E10
Ripley N Yorks 51 C8
Ripley Surrey 19 F7
Riplingham ER Yorks 52 F5
Ripon N Yorks 51 B9
Rippingale Lincs 37 C6
Ripple Kent 21 G10
Ripple Worcs 26 E5
Ripponden W Yorks 50 H6
Rireavach H'land 86 B3
Risabus Arg/Bute 64 D4
Risbury Heref'd 26 C2
Risby Suffolk 30 B4
Risca = Rhisga Caerph 15 B8
Rise ER Yorks 53 E7
Riseden E Sussex 12 C5
Risegate Lincs 37 C8
Riseholme Lincs 46 E3
Riseley Beds 29 B7
Riseley Wokingham 18 E4
Rishangles Suffolk 31 B8
Rishton Lancs 50 F3
Rishworth W Yorks 50 H6
Rising Bridge Lancs 50 G3
Risley Derby 35 B10
Risley Warrington 43 C9
Risplith N Yorks 51 C8
Rispond H'land 92 C7
Rivar Wilts 17 E10
Rivenhall End Essex 30 G5
River Bank Cambs 30 B2
Riverhead Kent 20 F2
Rivington Lancs 43 A9
Roa Island Cumb 49 C2
Roachill Devon 7 D7
Road Green Norfolk 39 F8
Roade Northants 28 C4
Roadhead Cumb 61 F11
Roadmeetings S Lanarks 69 F7
Roadside H'land 94 D3
Roadside of Catterline Aberds 83 F10
Roadside of Kinneff Aberds 83 F10
Roadwater Som'set 7 C9
Roag H'land 85 D7
Roath Card 15 D7
Roberton Scot Borders 61 B10
Roberton S Lanarks 69 H8
Robertsbridge E Sussex 12 D6
Roberttown W Yorks 51 G7
Robeston Cross Pembs 22 F3
Robeston Wathen Pembs 22 E5
Robin Hood W Yorks 51 G9
Robin Hood's Bay N Yorks 59 F10
Roborough Devon 6 E4
Roborough Devon 4 E6
Roby Mersey 43 C7
Roby Mill Lancs 43 B8
Rocester Staffs 35 B7
Roch Pembs 22 D3
Roch Gate Pembs 22 D3
Rochdale Gtr Man 44 A2
Roche Cornw'l 3 C8
Rochester Medway 20 E4
Rochester Northum 62 D4
Rochford Essex 20 B5
Rock Cornw'l 3 B8
Rock Northum 63 A8
Rock Worcs 26 A4
Rock W Sussex 11 C10
Rock Ferry Mersey 42 D6
Rockbeare Devon 7 G9
Rockbourne Hants 9 C10
Rockcliffe Cumb 61 G9
Rockcliffe Dumf/Gal 55 D11
Rockfield H'land 87 C12
Rockfield Monmouths 25 G11
Rockford Hants 9 D10
Rockhampton S Gloucs 16 B3
Rockingham Northants 36 F4
Rockland All Saints Norfolk 38 F5
Rockland St Mary Norfolk 39 E9
Rockland St Peter Norfolk 38 F5
Rockley Wilts 17 D8
Rockwell End Bucks 18 C4
Rockwell Green Som'set 7 D10
Rodborough Glos 16 A5
Rodbourne Swindon 17 C8
Rodbourne Wilts 16 C6
Rodbourne Cheney Swindon 17 C8
Rodd Heref'd 25 B10
Roddam Northum 62 A6
Rodden Dorset 8 F5
Rode Som'set 16 F5
Rode Heath Ches 44 G2
Rodeheath Ches 44 F2
Roden Telford 34 D1
Rodhuish Som'set 7 C9
Rodington Telford 34 D1
Rodley Glos 26 G4
Rodley W Yorks 51 F8
Rodmarton Glos 16 B6
Rodmell E Sussex 12 F3
Rodmersham Kent 20 E6
Rodney Stoke Som'set 15 F10
Rodsley Derby 35 A8
Rodway Som'set 15 H8
Rodwell Dorset 8 G5
Roe Green Herts 29 E10
Roecliffe N Yorks 51 C9
Roehampton London 19 D9
Roesound Shetl'd 96 G5
Roffey W Sussex 11 A10
Rogart H'land 93 J10
Rogart Station H'land 93 J10
Rogate W Sussex 11 B7
Rogerstone Newp 15 C8
Roghadal W Isles 90 J5
Rogiet Monmouths 15 C10
Rogue's Alley Cambs 37 E9
Roke Oxon 18 B3
Roker Tyne/Wear 63 H10
Rollesby Norfolk 39 D10
Rolleston Leics 36 E3
Rolleston Notts 45 G11
Rolleston-on-Dove Staffs 35 C8
Rolston ER Yorks 53 E8
Rolvenden Kent 13 C7
Rolvenden Layne Kent 13 C7
Romaldkirk Durham 57 D11
Romanby N Yorks 58 G4
Romannobridge Scot Borders 69 F10
Romansleigh Devon 7 D6
Romford London 20 C2
Romiley Gtr Man 44 C3
Romsey Hants 10 B2
Romsey Town Cambs 29 C11
Romsley Shrops 34 G3
Romsley Worcs 34 H5
Ronague I/Man 48 E2
Rookhope Durham 57 B11
Rookley I/Wight 10 F4
Rooks Bridge Som'set 15 F9
Roos ER Yorks 53 F8
Roosebeck Cumb 49 C2
Rootham's Green Beds 29 C8
Rootpark S Lanarks 69 E8
Ropley Hants 10 A5
Ropley Dean Hants 10 A5
Ropsley Lincs 36 B5
Rora Aberds 89 C10
Rorandle Aberds 83 B8
Rorrington Shrops 33 E9
Roscroggan Cornw'l 2 E5
Rose Cornw'l 3 D6
Rose Ash Devon 7 D6
Rose Green W Sussex 11 E8
Rose Grove Lancs 50 F4
Rose Hill E Sussex 12 E3
Rose Hill Lancs 50 F4
Rose Hill Suffolk 31 D8
Roseacre Kent 20 F4
Roseacre Lancs 49 F4
Rosebank S Lanarks 69 F7
Rosebrough Northum 71 H10
Rosebush Pembs 22 D5
Rosecare Cornw'l 4 B2
Rosedale Abbey N Yorks 59 G8
Roseden Northum 62 A6
Rosefield H'land 87 F11
Rosehall H'land 92 J7
Rosehaugh Mains H'land 87 F9
Rosehearty Aberds 89 B9
Rosehill Shrops 34 B2
Roseisle Moray 88 B1
Roselands E Sussex 12 F5
Rosemarket Pembs 22 F4
Rosemarkie H'land 87 F10
Rosemary Lane Devon 7 E10
Rosemount Perth/Kinr 76 C4
Rosenannon Cornw'l 3 C8
Rosewell Midloth 69 D11
Roseworth Stockton 58 D5
Roseworthy Cornw'l 2 F5
Rosgill Cumb 57 E7
Roshven H'land 79 D10
Roskhill H'land 85 D7
Roskill House H'land 87 F9
Rosley Cumb 56 B5
Roslin Midloth 69 D11
Rosliston Derby 35 D8
Rosneath Arg/Bute 73 E11
Ross Dumf/Gal 55 E9
Ross Northum 71 G10
Ross Perth/Kinr 75 E10
Ross-on-Wye Heref'd 26 F3
Rossett Wrex 42 G6
Rossett Green N Yorks 51 D9
Rossie Ochill Perth/Kinr 76 F3
Rossie Priory Perth/Kinr 76 D5
Rossington S Yorks 45 C10
Rosskeen H'land 87 E9
Rossland Renf 68 C3
Roster H'land 94 G4
Rostherne Ches 43 D10
Rosthwaite Cumb 56 E4
Roston Derby 35 A7
Rosyth Fife 69 B10
Rothbury Northum 62 C6
Rotherby Leics 36 D2
Rotherfield E Sussex 12 D4
Rotherfield Greys Oxon 18 C4
Rotherfield Peppard Oxon 18 C4
Rotherham S Yorks 45 C8
Rothersthorpe Northants 28 C4
Rotherwick Hants 18 F4
Rothes Moray 88 D2
Rothesay Arg/Bute 73 G9
Rothiebrisbane Aberds 89 E7
Rothienorman Aberds 89 E7
Rothiesholm Orkney 95 F7
Rothley Leics 36 D1
Rothley Northum 62 E6
Rothley Shield East Northum 62 D6
Rothmaise Aberds 89 E6
Rothwell Lincs 46 C5
Rothwell Northants 36 G4
Rothwell W Yorks 51 G9
Rothwell Haigh W Yorks 51 G9
Rotsea ER Yorks 53 D6
Rottal Angus 82 G5
Rotten End Suffolk 31 B10
Rottingdean Brighton/Hove 12 F2
Rottington Cumb 56 E1
Roud I/Wight 10 F4
Rough Close Staffs 34 B5
Rough Common Kent 21 F8
Rougham Norfolk 38 C4
Rougham Suffolk 30 B6
Rougham Green Suffolk 30 B6
Roughburn H'land 80 E5
Roughlee Lancs 50 E4
Roughley W Midlands 35 F7
Roughsike Cumb 61 F11
Roughton Lincs 46 F6
Roughton Norfolk 39 B8
Roughton Shrops 34 F3
Roughton Moor Lincs 46 F6
Roundhay W Yorks 51 F9
Roundstonefoot Dumf/Gal 61 C7
Roundstreet Common W Sussex 11 B9
Roundway Wilts 17 E7
Rous Lench Worcs 27 C7
Rousdon Devon 8 E1
Routenburn N Ayrs 73 G10
Routh ER Yorks 53 E6
Row Cornw'l 4 D1
Row Cumb 56 H6
Row Heath Essex 31 G8
Rowanburn Dumf/Gal 61 F10
Rowardennan Stirl 74 H6
Rowde Wilts 16 E6
Rowen Conwy 41 C9
Rowfoot Northum 62 G2
Rowhedge Essex 31 F7
Rowhook W Sussex 11 A10
Rowington Warwick 27 B9
Rowland Derby 44 E6
Rowland's Castle Hants 10 C6
Rowlands Gill Tyne/Wear 63 H7
Rowledge Surrey 18 G5
Rowley ER Yorks 52 F5
Rowley Shrops 33 E9
Rowley Hill W Yorks 44 A5
Rowley Regis W Midlands 34 G5
Rowlstone Heref'd 25 F10
Rowly Surrey 19 G7
Rowney Green Worcs 27 A7
Rownhams Hants 10 C2
Rowrah Cumb 56 E2
Rowsham Bucks 28 G5
Rowsley Derby 44 F6
Rowstock Oxon 17 C11
Rowston Lincs 46 G4
Rowton Ches 43 F7
Rowton Shrops 33 D9
Rowton Telford 34 D2
Roxburgh Scot Borders 70 G6
Roxby N Lincs 52 H5
Roxby N Yorks 59 E8
Roxton Beds 29 C8
Roxwell Essex 30 H3
Royal Leamington Spa Warwick 27 B10
Royal Oak D'lington 58 D3
Royal Oak Lancs 43 B7
Royal Tunbridge Wells Kent 12 C4
Roybridge H'land 80 E4
Roydhouse W Yorks 44 A6
Roydon Essex 29 H11
Roydon Norfolk 38 C3
Roydon Norfolk 39 G6
Roydon Hamlet Essex 29 H11
Royston Herts 29 D10
Royston S Yorks 45 A7
Royton Gtr Man 44 B3
Rozel Jersey 11
Ruabon = Rhiwabon Wrex 33 A9
Ruaig Arg/Bute 78 G3
Ruan Lanihorne Cornw'l 3 E7
Ruan Minor Cornw'l 2 H6
Ruarach H'land 80 A1
Ruardean Glos 26 G3
Ruardean Woodside Glos 26 G3
Rubery Worcs 34 H5
Ruckcroft Cumb 57 B7
Ruckhall Common Heref'd 25 E11
Ruckinge Kent 13 C9
Ruckland Lincs 47 E7
Ruckley Shrops 33 E11
Rudbaxton Pembs 22 D4
Rudby N Yorks 58 F5
Ruddington Notts 36 B1
Rudford Glos 26 F4
Rudge Shrops 34 F4
Rudge Som'set 16 F5
Rudgeway S Glouc 16 C3
Rudgwick W Sussex 11 A9
Rudhall Heref'd 26 F3
Rudheath Ches 43 E9
Rudley Green Essex 20 A5
Rudry Caerph 15 C7
Rudston ER Yorks 53 C6
Rudyard Staffs 44 G3
Rufford Lancs 49 H4
Rufforth C/York 51 D11
Rugby Warwick 35 H11
Rugeley Staffs 34 D6
Ruglen S Ayrs 66 F5
Ruilick H'land 87 G8
Ruishton Som'set 8 B1
Ruisigearraidh W Isles 90 J4
Ruislip London 19 C7
Ruislip Common London 19 C7
Rumbling Bridge Perth/Kinr 76 H3
Rumburgh Suffolk 39 G9
Rumford Cornw'l 3 B7
Rumney Card 15 D8
Runcorn Halton 43 D8
Runcton W Sussex 11 D7
Runcton Holme Norfolk 38 E2
Rundlestone Devon 5 D6
Runfold Surrey 18 G5
Runhall Norfolk 39 E6
Runham Norfolk 39 E11
Runham Norfolk 39 D10
Runnington Som'set 7 D10
Runsell Green Essex 30 H4
Runswick Bay N Yorks 59 E9
Runwell Essex 20 B4
Ruscombe Wokingham 18 D4
Rush Green London 20 C2
Rush-head Aberds 89 D8
Rushall Heref'd 26 E3
Rushall Norfolk 39 G7
Rushall Wilts 17 F8
Rushall W Midlands 34 E6
Rushbrooke Suffolk 30 B5
Rushbury Shrops 33 F11
Rushden Herts 29 E10
Rushden Northants 28 B6
Rushenden Kent 20 D6
Rushford Norfolk 38 G5
Rushlake Green E Sussex 12 E5
Rushmere Suffolk 39 G10
Rushmere St Andrew Suffolk 31 D9
Rushmoor Surrey 18 G5
Rushmoor Wilts 9 C8
Rushock Worcs 26 A5
Rusholme Gtr Man 44 C2
Rushton Ches 43 F8
Rushton Northants 36 G4
Rushton Shrops 34 E2
Rushton Spencer Staffs 44 F3
Rushwick Worcs 26 C5
Rushyford Durham 58 D3
Ruskie Stirl 75 G9
Ruskington Lincs 46 G4
Rusland Cumb 56 H5
Rusper W Sussex 19 H9
Ruspidge Glos 26 G3
Russell's Water Oxon 18 C4
Russel's Green Suffolk 31 A9
Rusthall Kent 12 C4
Rustington W Sussex 11 D9
Ruston N Yorks 52 A5
Ruston Parva ER Yorks 53 C6
Ruswarp N Yorks 59 F9
Rutherford Scot Borders 70 G5
Rutherglen S Lanarks 68 D5
Ruthernbridge Cornw'l 3 C9
Ruthin = Rhuthun Denbs 42 G4
Ruthrieston Aberd C 83 C11
Ruthven Aberds 88 D5
Ruthven Angus 76 C5
Ruthven H'land 87 H11
Ruthven H'land 81 D9
Ruthven House Angus 76 C6
Ruthvoes Cornw'l 3 C8
Ruthwell Dumf/Gal 60 G6
Ruyton-XI-Towns Shrops 33 C9
Ryal Northum 62 F6
Ryal Fold Blackb'n 50 G2
Ryall Dorset 8 E3
Ryarsh Kent 20 F3
Rydal Cumb 56 F5
Ryde I/Wight 10 E4
Rye E Sussex 13 D8
Rye Foreign E Sussex 13 D7
Rye Harbour E Sussex 13 E8
Rye Park Herts 29 G10
Rye Street Worcs 26 E4
Ryecroft Gate Staffs 44 F3
Ryehill ER Yorks 53 G8
Ryhall Rutl'd 36 D6
Ryhill W Yorks 45 A7
Ryhope Tyne/Wear 58 A5
Rylstone N Yorks 50 D5
Ryme Intrinseca Dorset 8 C4
Ryther N Yorks 52 F1
Ryton Glos 26 E4
Ryton N Yorks 52 B3
Ryton Shrops 34 E3
Ryton Tyne/Wear 63 G7
Ryton-on-Dunsmore Warwick 27 A10

S

Sabden Lancs 50 F3
Sacombe Herts 29 G10
Sacriston Durham 58 B3
Sadberge D'lington 58 E4
Saddell Arg/Bute 65 E8
Saddington Leics 36 F2
Saddle Bow Norfolk 38 D2
Saddlescombe W Sussex 12 E1
Sadgill Cumb 57 F6
Saffron Walden Essex 30 E2
Sageston Pembs 22 F5
Saham Hills Norfolk 38 E5
Saham Toney Norfolk 38 E5
Saighdinis W Isles 84 B3
Saighton Ches 43 F7
St Abb's Scot Borders 71 D8
St Abb's Haven Scot Borders 71 D8
St Agnes Cornw'l 2 D6
St Agnes I/Scilly 2 D2
St Albans Herts 29 H8
St Allen Cornw'l 3 D7
St Andrews Fife 77 F8
St Andrew's Major V/Glam 15 D7
St Anne Alderney 11
St Annes Lancs 49 G3
St Ann's Dumf/Gal 60 D6
St Ann's Chapel Cornw'l 4 D5
St Ann's Chapel Devon 5 G7
St Anthony Cornw'l 3 G6
St Anthony's Hill E Sussex 12 F5
St Arvans Monmouths 15 B11
St Asaph = Llanelwy Denbs 42 E3
St Athan V/Glam 14 E6
St Aubin Jersey 11
St Austell Cornw'l 3 D9
St Bees Cumb 56 E1
St Blazey Cornw'l 4 F1
St Boswells Scot Borders 70 G4
St Brelade Jersey 11
St Breock Cornw'l 3 B8
St Breward Cornw'l 4 D1
St Briavels Glos 16 A2
St Bride's Pembs 22 E3
St Brides Major V/Glam 14 D4
St Bride's Netherwent Monmouths 15 C10
St Brides super Ely V/Glam 14 D6
St Brides Wentlooge Newp 15 C8
St Budeaux Plym'th 4 F5
St Buryan Cornw'l 2 G3
St Catherine Bath/NE Som'set 16 D4
St Catherine's Arg/Bute 73 C10
St Clears = Sanclêr Carms 23 E7
St Cleer Cornw'l 4 E3
St Clement Cornw'l 3 E7
St Clements Jersey 11
St Clether Cornw'l 4 C3
St Colmac Arg/Bute 73 G9
St Columb Major Cornw'l 3 C8
St Columb Minor Cornw'l 3 C7
St Columb Road Cornw'l 3 D8
St Combs Aberds 89 B10
St Cross South Elmham Suffolk 39 G8
St Cyrus Aberds 77 A10
St David's Perth/Kinr 76 E2
St David's = Tyddewi Pembs 22 D2
St Day Cornw'l 2 E6
St Dennis Cornw'l 3 D8
St Devereux Heref'd 25 E11
St Dogmaels Pembs 22 B6
St Dogwells Pembs 22 D4
St Dominick Cornw'l 4 E5
St Donat's V/Glam 14 E5
St Edith's Wilts 16 E6
St Endellion Cornw'l 3 B8
St Enoder Cornw'l 3 D7
St Erme Cornw'l 3 D7
St Erney Cornw'l 4 F4
St Erth Cornw'l 2 F4
St Ervan Cornw'l 3 B7
St Eval Cornw'l 3 C7
St Ewe Cornw'l 3 E8
St Fagans Card 15 D7
St Fergus Aberds 89 C10
St Fillans Perth/Kinr 75 E9
St Florence Pembs 22 F5
St Genny's Cornw'l 4 B2
St George Conwy 42 E2
St George's V/Glam 14 D6
St Germans Cornw'l 4 F4
St Giles Lincs 46 E3
St Giles in the Wood Devon 6 E4
St Giles on the Heath Devon 6 G2
St Harmon Powys 24 A6
St Helen Auckland Durham 58 D2
St Helena Warwick 35 E8
St Helen's E Sussex 13 E7
St Helens I/Wight 10 F5
St Helens Mersey 43 C8
St Helier London 19 E9
St Helier Jersey 11
St Hilary Cornw'l 2 F4
St Hilary V/Glam 14 D6
Saint Hill W Sussex 12 C2
St Illtyd Bl Gwent 15 A8
St Ippollitts Herts 29 F8
St Ishmael's Pembs 22 F3
St Issey Cornw'l 3 B8
St Ive Cornw'l 4 E4
St Ives Cambs 29 A10
St Ives Cornw'l 2 E4
St Ives Dorset 9 D10
St James South Elmham Suffolk 39 G9
St Jidgey Cornw'l 3 C8
St John Cornw'l 4 F5
St John's I/Man 48 D2
St John's Jersey 11
St John's Surrey 18 F6
St John's Worcs 26 C5
St John's Chapel Durham 57 C10
St John's Fen End Norfolk 37 D11
St John's Highway Norfolk 37 D11
St John's Town of Dalry Dumf/Gal 55 A9
St Judes I/Man 48 C3
St Just Cornw'l 2 F2
St Just in Roseland Cornw'l 3 F7
St Katherine's Aberds 89 E7
St Keverne Cornw'l 3 G6
St Kew Cornw'l 3 B9
St Kew Highway Cornw'l 3 B9
St Keyne Cornw'l 4 E3
St Lawrence Cornw'l 3 C9
St Lawrence Essex 20 A6
St Lawrence I/Wight 10 G4
St Leonard's Bucks 28 H6
St Leonards Dorset 9 D10
St Leonards E Sussex 13 F6
Saint Leonards S Lanarks 68 E5
St Levan Cornw'l 2 G2
St Lythans V/Glam 15 D7
St Mabyn Cornw'l 3 B9
St Madoes Perth/Kinr 76 E4
St Margaret South Elmham Suffolk 39 G9
St Margaret's Heref'd 25 E10
St Margarets Herts 29 G10
St Margaret's at Cliffe Kent 21 G10
St Margaret's Hope Orkney 95 J5
St Mark's I/Man 48 E2
St Martin Cornw'l 3 G6
St Martin Cornw'l 4 F3
St Martin's Jersey 11
St Martins Perth/Kinr 76 D4
St Martin's Shrops 33 B9
St Mary Bourne Hants 17 F11
St Mary Church V/Glam 14 D6
St Mary Cray London 19 E11
St Mary Hill V/Glam 14 D5
St Mary Hoo Medway 20 D5
St Mary in the Marsh Kent 13 D9
St Mary's Jersey 11
St Mary's Orkney 95 H5
St Mary's Bay Kent 13 D9
St Maughans Monmouths 25 G11
St Mawes Cornw'l 3 F7
St Mawgan Cornw'l 3 C7
St Mellion Cornw'l 4 E4
St Mellons Card 15 C8
St Merryn Cornw'l 3 B7
St Mewan Cornw'l 3 D8
St Michael Caerhays Cornw'l 3 E8
St Michael Penkevil Cornw'l 3 E7
St Michael South Elmham Suffolk 39 G9
St Michael's Kent 13 C7
St Michaels Worcs 26 B2
St Michael's on Wyre Lancs 49 E4
St Minver Cornw'l 3 B8
St Monans Fife 77 G8
St Neot Cornw'l 4 E2
St Neots Cambs 29 B8
St Newlyn East Cornw'l 3 D7
St Nicholas Pembs 22 C3
St Nicholas V/Glam 14 D6
St Nicholas at Wade Kent 21 E9
St Ninians Stirl 68 A6
St Osyth Essex 31 G8
St Osyth Heath Essex 31 G8
St Ouens Jersey 11
St Owens Cross Heref'd 26 F2
St Paul's Cray London 19 E11
St Paul's Walden Herts 29 F8
St Peter Port Guernsey 11
St Peter's Jersey 11
St Peter's Kent 21 E10
St Petrox Pembs 22 G4
St Pinnock Cornw'l 4 E3
St Quivox S Ayrs 67 D6
St Ruan Cornw'l 2 H6
St Sampson Guernsey 11
St Stephen Cornw'l 3 D8
St Stephen's Cornw'l 4 C4
St Stephens Cornw'l 4 F5
St Stephens Herts 29 H8
St Teath Cornw'l 4 C1
St Thomas Devon 7 G8
St Tudy Cornw'l 4 D1
St Twynnells Pembs 22 G4
St Veep Cornw'l 4 F2
St Vigeans Angus 77 C9
St Wenn Cornw'l 3 C8
St Weonards Heref'd 25 F11
Saintbury Glos 27 E8
Salcombe Devon 5 H8
Salcombe Regis Devon 7 H10
Salcott Essex 30 G6
Sale Gtr Man 43 C10
Sale Green Worcs 26 C6
Saleby Lincs 47 E8
Salehurst E Sussex 12 D6
Salem Ceredig'n 32 G2
Salem Carms 24 F3
Salen Arg/Bute 79 G8
Salen H'land 79 E9
Salesbury Lancs 50 F2
Salford Beds 28 D6
Salford Gtr Man 44 C2
Salford Oxon 27 F9
Salford Priors Warwick 27 C7
Salfords Surrey 19 G9
Salhouse Norfolk 39 D9
Saline Fife 69 A9
Salisbury Wilts 9 B10
Sallachan H'land 74 A2
Sallachy H'land 86 H2
Sallachy H'land 93 J8
Salle Norfolk 39 C7
Salmonby Lincs 47 E7
Salmond's Muir Angus 77 D8
Salperton Glos 27 F7
Salph End Beds 29 C7
Salsburgh N Lanarks 69 D7
Salt Staffs 34 C5
Salt End ER Yorks 53 G7
Saltaire W Yorks 51 F7
Saltash Cornw'l 4 F5
Saltburn H'land 87 E10
Saltburn-by-the-Sea Redcar/Clevel'd 59 D7
Saltby Leics 36 C4
Saltcoats Cumb 56 G2
Saltcoats N Ayrs 66 B5
Saltdean Brighton/Hove 12 F2
Salter Lancs 50 C2
Salterforth Lancs 50 E4
Salterswall Ches 43 F9
Saltfleet Lincs 47 C8
Saltfleetby All Saints Lincs 47 C8
Saltfleetby St Clements Lincs 47 C8
Saltfleetby St Peter Lincs 47 D8
Saltford Bath/NE Som'set 16 E3
Salthouse Norfolk 39 A6
Saltmarshe ER Yorks 52 G3
Saltney Flints 43 F6
Salton N Yorks 52 B3
Saltwick Northum 63 F7
Saltwood Kent 21 H8
Salum Arg/Bute 78 G3
Salvington W Sussex 11 D10
Salwarpe Worcs 26 B5
Salway Ash Dorset 8 E3
Sambourne Warwick 27 B7
Sambrook Telford 34 C3
Samhla W Isles 84 B2
Samlesbury Lancs 50 F1
Samlesbury Bottoms Lancs 50 G2
Sampford Arundel Som'set 7 E10
Sampford Brett Som'set 7 B9
Sampford Courtenay Devon 6 F5
Sampford Peverell Devon 7 E9
Sampford Spiney Devon 4 D6
Sampool Bridge Cumb 56 H6
Samuelston E Loth 70 C3
Sanachan H'land 85 D13
Sanaigmore Arg/Bute 64 A3
Sanclêr = St Clears Carms 23 E7
Sancreed Cornw'l 2 G3
Sancton ER Yorks 52 F5
Sand H'land 86 B2
Sand Shetl'd 96 J5
Sand Hole ER Yorks 52 F4
Sand Hutton N Yorks 52 D2
Sandaig H'land 85 H12
Sandal Magna W Yorks 51 H9
Sandale Cumb 56 B4
Sandbach Ches 43 F10
Sandbank Arg/Bute 73 E10
Sandbanks Poole 9 F9
Sandend Aberds 88 B5
Sanderstead London 19 E10
Sandfields Glos 26 F6
Sandford Cumb 57 E9
Sandford Devon 7 F7
Sandford Dorset 9 F8
Sandford I/Wight 10 F4
Sandford N Som'set 15 F10
Sandford Shrops 34 B1
Sandford S Lanarks 68 F6
Sandford on Thames Oxon 18 A2
Sandford Orcas Dorset 8 B5
Sandford St Martin Oxon 27 F11
Sandfordhill Aberds 89 D11
Sandgate Kent 21 H8
Sandgreen Dumf/Gal 55 E8
Sandhaven Aberds 89 B9
Sandhead Dumf/Gal 54 E3
Sandhills Surrey 18 H6
Sandhoe Northum 62 G5
Sandholme ER Yorks 52 F4
Sandholme Lincs 37 B9
Sandhurst Brackn'l 18 E5
Sandhurst Glos 26 F5
Sandhurst Kent 13 D6
Sandhurst Cross Kent 13 D6
Sandhutton N Yorks 51 A9
Sandiacre Derby 35 B10
Sandilands Lincs 47 D9
Sandilands S Lanarks 69 G7
Sandiway Ches 43 E9
Sandleheath Hants 9 C10
Sandling Kent 20 F4
Sandlow Green Ches 43 F10
Sandness Shetl'd 96 H3
Sandon Essex 20 A4
Sandon Herts 29 E10
Sandon Staffs 34 B5
Sandown I/Wight 10 F4
Sandplace Cornw'l 4 F3
Sandridge Herts 29 G8
Sandridge Wilts 16 E6
Sandringham Norfolk 38 C2
Sandsend N Yorks 59 E9
Sandside Ho. H'land 93 C12
Sandsound Shetl'd 96 J5
Sandtoft N Lincs 45 B11
Sandway Kent 20 F5
Sandwell W Midlands 34 G6
Sandwich Kent 21 F10
Sandwick Cumb 56 E6
Sandwick Orkney 95 K5
Sandwick Shetl'd 96 L6
Sandwith Cumb 56 E1
Sandy Beds 29 D8
Sandy Carms 23 F9
Sandy Bank Lincs 46 G6
Sandy Haven Pembs 22 F3
Sandy Lane Wilts 16 E6
Sandy Lane Wrex 33 A9
Sandycroft Flints 42 F6
Sandyford Dumf/Gal 61 D8
Sandyford Stoke 44 G2
Sandygate I/Man 48 C3
Sandyhills Dumf/Gal 55 D11
Sandylands Lancs 49 C4
Sandypark Devon 5 C8
Sandysike Cumb 61 G9
Sangobeg H'land 92 C7
Sangomore H'land 92 C7
Sanna H'land 78 E7
Sanndabhaig W Isles 91 D9
Sanndabhaig W Isles 84 D3
Sannox N Ayrs 66 B3
Sanquhar Dumf/Gal 60 C3
Santon N Lincs 46 A3
Santon Bridge Cumb 56 F3
Santon Downham Suffolk 38 G4
Sapcote Leics 35 F10
Sapey Common Heref'd 26 B4
Sapiston Suffolk 38 H5
Sapley Cambs 29 A9
Sapperton Glos 16 A6
Sapperton Lincs 36 B6
Saracen's Head Lincs 37 C9
Sarclet H'land 94 F5
Sardis Carms 23 F10
Sarn Bridg 14 C5
Sarn Powys 33 F8
Sarn Bach Gwyn 40 H5
Sarn Meyllteyrn Gwyn 40 G4
Sarnau Carms 23 E8
Sarnau Ceredig'n 23 A8
Sarnau Gwyn 32 B5
Sarnau Powys 25 E7
Sarnau Powys 33 D8
Sarnesfield Heref'd 25 C10
Saron Carms 23 E8
Saron Carms 24 G3
Saron Denbs 42 F3
Saron Gwyn 40 E6
Saron Gwyn 41 D7
Sarratt Herts 19 B7
Sarre Kent 21 E9
Sarsden Oxon 27 F9
Sarsgrum H'land 92 C6
Satley Durham 58 B2
Satron N Yorks 57 G11
Satterleigh Devon 6 D5
Satterthwaite Cumb 56 G5
Satwell Oxon 18 C4
Sauchen Aberds 83 B8
Saucher Perth/Kinr 76 D4
Sauchie Clack 69 A7
Sauchieburn Aberds 83 G8
Saughall Ches 42 E6
Saughtree Scot Borders 61 D11
Saul Glos 26 H4
Saundby Notts 45 D11
Saundersfoot Pembs 22 F6
Saunderton Bucks 18 A4
Saunton Devon 6 C3
Sausthorpe Lincs 47 F7
Saval H'land 93 J8
Savary H'land 79 G9
Savile Park W Yorks 51 G6
Sawbridge Warwick 28 B2
Sawbridgeworth Herts 29 G11
Sawdon N Yorks 59 H10
Sawley Derby 35 B10
Sawley Lancs 50 E3
Sawley N Yorks 51 C8
Sawston Cambs 29 D11
Sawtry Cambs 37 G7
Saxby Leics 36 D4
Saxby Lincs 46 D4
Saxby All Saints N Lincs 52 H5
Saxelbye Leics 36 C3
Saxham Street Suffolk 31 B7
Saxilby Lincs 46 E2
Saxlingham Norfolk 38 B6
Saxlingham Green Norfolk 39 F8
Saxlingham Nethergate Norfolk 39 F8
Saxlingham Thorpe Norfolk 39 F8
Saxmundham Suffolk 31 B10
Saxon Street Cambs 30 C3
Saxondale Notts 36 B2
Saxtead Suffolk 31 B9
Saxtead Green Suffolk 31 B9
Saxthorpe Norfolk 39 B7
Saxton N Yorks 51 F10
Sayers Common W Sussex 12 E1
Scackleton N Yorks 52 B2
Scadabhagh W Isles 90 H6
Scaftworth Notts 45 C10
Scagglethorpe N Yorks 52 B4
Scaitcliffe Lancs 50 G3
Scalasaig Arg/Bute 72 D2
Scalby ER Yorks 52 G4
Scalby N Yorks 59 G11
Scaldwell Northants 28 A4
Scale Houses Cumb 57 B7
Scaleby Cumb 61 G10
Scaleby Hill Cumb 61 G10
Scales Cumb 49 B2
Scales Cumb 56 D5
Scales Lancs 49 F4
Scalford Leics 36 C3
Scaling N Yorks 59 E8
Scaling Dam Redcar/Clevel'd 59 E8
Scallastle Arg/Bute 79 H9
Scalloway Shetl'd 96 K6
Scalpay W Isles 90 H7
Scalpay Ho. H'land 85 F11
Scalpsie Arg/Bute 73 H9
Scamadale H'land 79 B10
Scamblesby Lincs 46 E6
Scamodale H'land 79 D11
Scampston N Yorks 52 B4
Scampton Lincs 46 E3
Scapa Orkney 95 H5
Scapegoat Hill W Yorks 51 H6
Scar Orkney 95 D7
Scarborough N Yorks 59 H11
Scarcliffe Derby 45 F8
Scarcroft W Yorks 51 E9
Scarcroft Hill W Yorks 51 E9
Scardroy H'land 86 F5
Scarff Shetl'd 96 E4
Scarfskerry H'land 94 C4
Scargill Durham 58 E1
Scarinish Arg/Bute 78 G3
Scarisbrick Lancs 43 A6
Scarning Norfolk 38 D5
Scarrington Notts 36 A3
Scartho NE Lincs 46 B6
Scarwell Orkney 95 F3
Scatness Shetl'd 96 M5
Scatraig H'land 87 H10
Scawby N Lincs 46 B3
Scawsby S Yorks 45 B9
Scawton N Yorks 51 A11
Scayne's Hill W Sussex 12 D2
Scethrog Powys 25 F8
Scholar Green Ches 44 G2
Scholes W Yorks 44 B5
Scholes W Yorks 51 G7
Scholes W Yorks 51 F9
School Green Ches 43 F9
Scleddau Pembs 22 C4
Sco Ruston Norfolk 39 C8
Scofton Notts 45 D10
Scole Norfolk 39 H7
Scolpaig W Isles 84 A2
Scone Perth/Kinr 76 E4
Sconser H'land 85 E10
Scoonie Fife 76 G6
Scoor Arg/Bute 78 K7
Scopwick Lincs 46 G4
Scoraig H'land 86 B3
Scorborough ER Yorks 52 E6
Scorrier Cornw'l 2 E6
Scorton Lancs 49 E5
Scorton N Yorks 58 F3
Scotbheinn W Isles 84 C3
Scotby Cumb 61 H10
Scotch Corner N Yorks 58 F3
Scotforth Lancs 49 D4
Scothern Lincs 46 E4
Scotland Gate Northum 63 E8
Scotlandwell Perth/Kinr 76 G4
Scotsburn H'land 87 D10
Scotscalder Station H'land 94 E2
Scotscraig Fife 77 E7
Scots'Gap Northum 62 E6
Scotston Aberds 83 F9
Scotston Perth/Kinr 76 C2
Scotstoun C/Glasg 68 D4
Scotstown H'land 79 E11
Scotswood Tyne/Wear 63 G7
Scottas H'land 85 H12
Scotter Lincs 46 B2
Scotterthorpe Lincs 46 B2
Scottlethorpe Lincs 37 C6
Scotton Lincs 46 C2
Scotton N Yorks 58 G2
Scotton N Yorks 51 D9
Scottow Norfolk 39 C8
Scoughall E Loth 70 B5
Scoulag Arg/Bute 73 H10
Scoulton Norfolk 38 E5
Scourie H'land 92 E4
Scourie More H'land 92 E4
Scousburgh Shetl'd 96 M5
Scrabster H'land 94 C2
Scrafield Lincs 47 F7
Scrainwood Northum 62 C5
Scrane End Lincs 37 A9
Scraptoft Leics 36 E2
Scratby Norfolk 39 D11
Scrayingham N Yorks 52 C3
Scredington Lincs 37 A6
Scremby Lincs 47 F8
Scremerston Northum 71 F9
Screveton Notts 36 A3
Scrivelsby Lincs 46 F6
Scriven N Yorks 51 D9
Scrooby Notts 45 C10
Scropton Derby 35 B7
Scrub Hill Lincs 46 G6
Scruton N Yorks 58 G3
Sculcoates Kingston/Hull 53 F6
Sculthorpe Norfolk 38 B4
Scunthorpe N Lincs 46 A2
Scurlage Swan 23 H9
Sea Palling Norfolk 39 C10
Seaborough Dorset 8 D3
Seacombe Mersey 42 C6
Seacroft Lincs 47 F9
Seacroft W Yorks 51 F9
Seadyke Lincs 37 B9
Seafield S Ayrs 66 D6
Seafield W Loth 69 D9
Seaford E Sussex 12 G3
Seaforth Mersey 42 C6
Seagrave Leics 36 D2
Seaham Durham 58 B5
Seahouses Northum 71 G11
Seal Kent 20 F2
Sealand Flints 42 F6
Seale Surrey 18 G5
Seamer N Yorks 58 E5
Seamer N Yorks 52 A6
Seamill N Ayrs 66 B5
Searby Lincs 46 B4
Seasalter Kent 21 E7
Seascale Cumb 56 F2
Seathorne Lincs 47 F9
Seathwaite Cumb 56 G4
Seathwaite Cumb 56 E4
Seatoller Cumb 56 E4
Seaton Cornw'l 4 F4
Seaton Cumb 56 C2
Seaton Devon 8 F1
Seaton Durham 58 A4
Seaton ER Yorks 53 E7
Seaton Northum 63 F9
Seaton Rutl'd 36 F5
Seaton Burn Tyne/Wear 63 F8
Seaton Carew Hartlep'l 58 D6
Seaton Delaval Northum 63 F9
Seaton Ross ER Yorks 52 E3
Seaton Sluice Northum 63 F9
Seatown Aberds 88 B5
Seatown Dorset 8 E3
Seave Green N Yorks 59 F6
Seaview I/Wight 10 E5
Seaville Cumb 56 A3
Seavington St Mary Som'set 8 C3
Seavington St Michael Som'set 8 C3
Sebergham Cumb 56 B5
Seckington Warwick 35 E8
Second Coast H'land 86 B2
Sedbergh Cumb 57 G8
Sedbury Glos 15 B11
Sedbusk N Yorks 57 G10
Sedgeberrow Worcs 27 E7
Sedgebrook Lincs 36 B4
Sedgefield Durham 58 D4
Sedgeford Norfolk 38 B3
Sedgehill Wilts 9 B7
Sedgley W Midlands 34 F5
Sedgwick Cumb 57 H7
Sedlescombe E Sussex 13 E6
Sedlescombe Street E Sussex 13 E6
Seend Wilts 16 E6
Seend Cleeve Wilts 16 E6
Seer Green Bucks 18 B6
Seething Norfolk 39 F9
Sefton Mersey 42 B6
Seghill Northum 63 F8
Seifton Shrops 33 G10
Seighford Staffs 34 C4
Seilebost W Isles 90 H5
Seion Gwyn 41 D7
Seisdon Staffs 34 F4
Seisiadar W Isles 91 D10
Selattyn Shrops 33 B8
Selborne Hants 10 A6
Selby N Yorks 52 F2
Selham W Sussex 11 B8
Selhurst London 19 E10
Selkirk Scot Borders 70 H3
Sellack Heref'd 26 F2
Sellafield Station Cumb 56 F2
Sellafirth Shetl'd 96 D7
Sellibister Orkney 95 D8
Sellindge Kent 13 C9
Sellindge Lees Kent 13 C10
Selling Kent 21 F7
Sells Green Wilts 16 E6
Selly Oak W Midlands 34 G6
Selmeston E Sussex 12 F4
Selsdon London 19 E10
Selsey W Sussex 11 E7
Selsfield Common W Sussex 12 C2
Selsted Kent 21 G9
Selston Notts 45 G8
Selworthy Som'set 7 B8
Semblister Shetl'd 96 H5
Semer Suffolk 30 D6
Semington Wilts 16 E5
Semley Wilts 9 B7
Send Surrey 19 F7
Send Marsh Surrey 19 F7
Senghenydd Caerph 15 B7
Sennen Cornw'l 2 G2
Sennen Cove Cornw'l 2 G2
Sennybridge = Pont Senni Powys 24 F6
Serlby Notts 45 D10
Sessay N Yorks 51 B10
Setchey Norfolk 38 D2
Setley Hants 10 D2
Setter Shetl'd 96 H5
Setter Shetl'd 96 E6
Setter Shetl'd 96 J7
Settiscarth Orkney 95 G4
Settle N Yorks 50 C4
Settrington N Yorks 52 B4
Seven Kings London 19 C11
Seven Sisters Neath P Talb 24 H5
Sevenhampton Glos 27 F7
Sevenoaks Kent 20 F2
Sevenoaks Weald Kent 20 F2
Severn Beach S Gloucs 15 C11
Severn Stoke Worcs 26 D5
Severnhampton Swindon 17 B9
Sevington Kent 13 B9
Sewards End Essex 30 E2
Sewardstone Essex 19 B10
Sewardstonebury Essex 19 B10
Sewerby ER Yorks 53 C7
Seworgan Cornw'l 2 F6
Sewstern Leics 36 C4
Sezincote Glos 27 E8
Sgarasta Mhor W Isles 90 H5
Sgiogarstaigh W Isles 91 A10
Shabbington Bucks 28 H3
Shackerstone Leics 35 E9
Shackleford Surrey 18 G6
Shade W Yorks 50 G5
Shadforth Durham 58 B4
Shadingfield Suffolk 39 G10
Shadoxhurst Kent 13 C8
Shadsworth Blackb'n 50 G3
Shadwell Norfolk 38 G5
Shadwell W Yorks 51 F9
Shaftesbury Dorset 9 B7
Shafton S Yorks 45 A7
Shalbourne Wilts 17 E10
Shalcombe I/Wight 10 F2
Shalden Hants 18 G3
Shaldon Devon 5 D10
Shalfleet I/Wight 10 F3
Shalford Essex 30 F4
Shalford Surrey 19 G7
Shalford Green Essex 30 F4
Shallowford Devon 6 B6
Shalmsford Street Kent 21 F7
Shalstone Bucks 28 E3
Shamley Green Surrey 19 G7
Shandon Arg/Bute 73 E11
Shandwick H'land 87 D11
Shangton Leics 36 F3
Shankhouse Northum 63 F8
Shanklin I/Wight 10 F4
Shanquhar Aberds 88 E5
Shanzie Perth/Kinr 76 B5
Shap Cumb 57 E7
Shapwick Dorset 9 D8
Shapwick Som'set 15 H10
Shardlow Derby 35 B10

Shareshill *Staffs* 34 E5
Sharlston *W Yorks* 51 H9
Sharlston Common *W Yorks* 51 H9
Sharnbrook *Beds* 28 C6
Sharnford *Leics* 35 F10
Sharoe Green *Lancs* 49 F5
Sharow *N Yorks* 51 B9
Sharp Street *Norfolk* 39 C9
Sharpenhoe *Beds* 29 E7
Sharperton *Northum* 62 C5
Sharpness *Glos* 16 A3
Sharpthorne *W Sussex* 12 C2
Sharrington *Norfolk* 38 B6
Shatterford *Worcs* 34 G3
Shaugh Prior *Devon* 4 E6
Shavington *Ches* 43 G10
Shaw *Gtr Man* 44 B3
Shaw *W Berks* 17 E11
Shaw *Wilts* 16 E5
Shaw Green *Lancs* 49 H5
Shaw Mills *N Yorks* 51 C8
Shawbury *Shrops* 34 C1
Shawdon Hall *Northum* 62 B6
Shawell *Leics* 35 G11
Shawford *Hants* 10 B3
Shawforth *Lancs* 50 G4
Shawhead *Dumf/Gal* 60 F4
Shawhill *Dumf/Gal* 61 G8
Shawton *S Lanarks* 68 F5
Shawtonhill *S Lanarks* 68 F5
Shear Cross *Wilts* 16 G5
Shearington *Dumf/Gal* 60 G6
Shearsby *Leics* 36 F2
Shebbear *Devon* 6 F3
Shebdon *Staffs* 34 C3
Shebster *H'land* 93 C13
Sheddens *E Renf* 68 E4
Shedfield *Hants* 10 C4
Sheen *Staffs* 44 F5
Sheepscar *W Yorks* 51 F9
Sheepscombe *Glos* 26 G5
Sheepstor *Devon* 5 E6
Sheepwash *Devon* 6 F3
Sheepway *N Som'set* 15 D10
Sheepy Magna *Leics* 35 E9
Sheepy Parva *Leics* 35 E9
Sheering *Essex* 30 G2
Sheerness *Kent* 20 D6
Sheet *Hants* 11 B6
Sheffield *S Yorks* 45 D7
Sheffield Bottom *W Berks* 18 E3
Sheffield Green *E Sussex* 12 D3
Shefford *Beds* 29 E8
Shefford Woodlands *W Berks* 17 D10
Sheigra *H'land* 92 C4
Sheinton *Shrops* 34 E2
Shelderton *Shrops* 33 H10
Sheldon *Derby* 44 F5
Sheldon *Devon* 7 F10
Sheldon *W Midlands* 35 G7
Sheldwich *Kent* 21 F7
Shelf *W Yorks* 51 G7
Shelfanger *Norfolk* 39 G7
Shelfield *Warwick* 27 B8
Shelfield *W Midlands* 34 E6
Shelford *Notts* 36 A2
Shellacres *Northum* 71 F7
Shelley *Essex* 20 A2
Shelley *Suffolk* 31 E7
Shelley *W Yorks* 44 A6
Shellingford *Oxon* 17 B10
Shellow Bowells *Essex* 30 H3
Shelsley Beauchamp *Worcs* 26 B4
Shelsley Walsh *Worcs* 26 B4
Shelthorpe *Leics* 35 D11
Shelton *Beds* 29 B7
Shelton *Norfolk* 39 F8
Shelton *Notts* 36 A3
Shelton *Shrops* 33 D10
Shelton Green *Norfolk* 39 F8
Shelve *Shrops* 33 F9
Shelwick *Heref'd* 26 D2
Shenfield *Essex* 20 B3
Shenington *Oxon* 27 D10
Shenley *Herts* 19 A8
Shenley Brook End *M/Keynes* 28 E5
Shenley Church End *M/Keynes* 28 E5
Shenleybury *Herts* 19 A8
Shenmore *Heref'd* 25 E10
Shennanton *Dumf/Gal* 54 C6
Shenstone *Staffs* 35 E7
Shenstone *Worcs* 26 A5
Shenton *Leics* 35 E9
Shenval *H'land* 80 A6
Shenval *Moray* 82 A4
Shepeau Stow *Lincs* 37 D9
Shephall *Herts* 29 F9
Shepherd's Green *Oxon* 18 C4
Shepherd's Port *Norfolk* 38 B2
Shepherdswell *Kent* 21 G9
Shepley *W Yorks* 44 B5
Shepperdine *S Gloucs* 16 B3
Shepperton *Surrey* 19 E7
Shepreth *Cambs* 29 D10
Shepshed *Leics* 35 D10
Shepton Beauchamp *Som'set* 8 C3
Shepton Mallet *Som'set* 16 G3
Shepton Montague *Som'set* 8 A5
Shepway *Kent* 20 F4
Sheraton *Durham* 58 C5
Sherborne *Dorset* 8 C5
Sherborne *Glos* 27 G8
Sherborne St John *Hants* 18 F3
Sherbourne *Warwick* 27 B9
Sherburn *Durham* 58 B4
Sherburn *N Yorks* 52 B5
Sherburn Hill *Durham* 58 B4
Sherburn in Elmet *N Yorks* 51 F10
Shere *Surrey* 19 G7
Shereford *Norfolk* 38 C4
Sherfield English *Hants* 10 B1
Sherfield on Loddon *Hants* 18 F3
Sherford *Devon* 5 G8
Sheriff Hutton *N Yorks* 52 C2
Sheriffhales *Shrops* 34 D3
Sheringham *Norfolk* 39 A7
Sherington *M/Keynes* 28 D5
Shernal Green *Worcs* 26 B6
Shernborne *Norfolk* 38 B3
Sherrington *Wilts* 16 H6
Sherston *Wilts* 16 C5
Sherwood Green *Devon* 6 D4
Shettleston *C/Glasg* 68 D5
Shevington *Gtr Man* 43 B8
Shevington Moor *Gtr Man* 43 A8
Shevington Vale *Gtr Man* 43 B8
Sheviock *Cornw'l* 4 F4
Shide *I/Wight* 10 F3
Shiel Bridge *H'land* 80 B1
Shieldaig *H'land* 85 C13
Shieldaig *H'land* 85 A13
Shieldhill *Dumf/Gal* 60 E6
Shieldhill *Falk* 69 C7
Shieldhill *S Lanarks* 69 F9
Shielfoot *H'land* 79 E9
Shielhill *Angus* 77 B7
Shielhill *Invercl* 73 F11
Shifford *Oxon* 17 A10
Shifnal *Shrops* 34 E3
Shilbottle *Northum* 63 C7
Shildon *Durham* 58 D3
Shillingford *Devon* 7 D8
Shillingford *Oxon* 18 B2
Shillingford St George *Devon* 5 C10
Shillingstone *Dorset* 9 C7
Shillington *Beds* 29 E8
Shillmoor *Northum* 62 C4
Shilton *Oxon* 27 H9
Shilton *Warwick* 35 G10
Shilvington *Northum* 63 E7
Shimpling *Norfolk* 39 G7
Shimpling *Suffolk* 30 C5
Shimpling Street *Suffolk* 30 C5
Shincliffe *Durham* 58 B3
Shiney Row *Tyne/Wear* 58 A4
Shinfield *Wokingham* 18 E4
Shingham *Norfolk* 38 E3
Shingle Street *Suffolk* 31 D10
Shinner's Bridge *Devon* 5 E8
Shinness *H'land* 93 H8
Shipbourne *Kent* 20 F2
Shipdham *Norfolk* 38 E5
Shipham *Som'set* 15 F10
Shiphay *Torbay* 5 E9
Shiplake *Oxon* 18 D4
Shipley *Derby* 35 A10
Shipley *Northum* 63 B7
Shipley *Shrops* 34 F4
Shipley *W Sussex* 11 B10
Shipley *W Yorks* 51 F7
Shipley Shiels *Northum* 62 D3
Shipmeadow *Suffolk* 39 G9
Shippea Hill Station *Cambs* 38 G2
Shippon *Oxon* 17 B11
Shipston-on-Stour *Warwick* 27 D9
Shipton *Glos* 27 G7
Shipton *N Yorks* 52 D1
Shipton *Shrops* 34 F1
Shipton Bellinger *Hants* 17 G9
Shipton Gorge *Dorset* 8 E3
Shipton Green *W Sussex* 11 D7
Shipton Moyne *Glos* 16 C5
Shipton on Cherwell *Oxon* 27 G11
Shipton Solers *Glos* 27 G7
Shipton-under-Wychwood *Oxon* 27 G9
Shiptonthorpe *ER Yorks* 52 E4
Shirburn *Oxon* 18 B3
Shirdley Hill *Lancs* 42 A6
Shirebrook *Derby* 45 F9
Shiregreen *S Yorks* 45 C7
Shirehampton *Bristol* 15 D11
Shiremoor *Tyne/Wear* 63 F9
Shirenewton *Monmouths* 15 B10
Shireoaks *Notts* 45 D9
Shirkoak *Kent* 13 C8
Shirl Heath *Heref'd* 25 C11
Shirland *Derby* 45 G7
Shirley *Derby* 35 A8
Shirley *London* 19 E10
Shirley *S'thampton* 10 C3
Shirley *W Midlands* 35 H7
Shirrell Heath *Hants* 10 C4
Shirwell *Devon* 6 C4
Shirwell Cross *Devon* 6 C4
Shiskine *N Ayrs* 66 D2
Shobdon *Heref'd* 25 B11
Shobnall *Staffs* 35 C8
Shobrooke *Devon* 7 F7
Shoby *Leics* 36 D2
Shocklach *Ches* 43 H7
Shoeburyness *Southend* 20 C6
Sholden *Kent* 21 F10
Sholing *S'thampton* 10 C3
Shoot Hill *Shrops* 33 D10
Shop *Cornw'l* 6 E1
Shop *Cornw'l* 3 B7
Shop Corner *Suffolk* 31 E9
Shore Mill *H'land* 87 E10
Shoreditch *London* 19 C10
Shoreham *Kent* 20 E2
Shoreham-By-Sea *W Sussex* 11 D11
Shoresdean *Northum* 71 F8
Shoreswood *Northum* 71 F8
Shoreton *H'land* 87 E9
Shorncote *Glos* 17 B7
Shorne *Kent* 20 D3
Short Heath *W Midlands* 34 E5
Shortacombe *Devon* 4 C6
Shortgate *E Sussex* 12 E3
Shortlanesend *Cornw'l* 3 E7
Shortlees *E Ayrs* 67 C7
Shortstown *Beds* 29 D7
Shorwell *I/Wight* 10 F3
Shoscombe *Bath/NE Som'set* 16 F4
Shotatton *Shrops* 33 C9
Shotesham *Norfolk* 39 F8
Shotgate *Essex* 20 B4
Shotley *Suffolk* 31 E9
Shotley Bridge *Durham* 58 A1
Shotley Gate *Suffolk* 31 E9
Shotleyfield *Northum* 58 A1
Shottenden *Kent* 21 F7
Shottermill *Surrey* 11 A7
Shottery *Warwick* 27 C8
Shotteswell *Warwick* 27 D11
Shottisham *Suffolk* 31 D10
Shottle *Derby* 45 H7
Shottlegate *Derby* 45 H7
Shotton *Durham* 58 C5
Shotton *Flints* 42 F6
Shotton *Northum* 71 G7
Shotton Colliery *Durham* 58 B4
Shotts *N Lanarks* 69 D7
Shotwick *Ches* 42 E6
Shouldham *Norfolk* 38 E2
Shouldham Thorpe *Norfolk* 38 E2
Shoulton *Worcs* 26 C5
Shover's Green *E Sussex* 12 C5
Shrawardine *Shrops* 33 D10
Shrawley *Worcs* 26 B5
Shrewley Common *Warwick* 27 B9
Shrewsbury *Shrops* 33 D10
Shrewton *Wilts* 17 G7
Shripney *W Sussex* 11 D8
Shrivenham *Oxon* 17 C9
Shropham *Norfolk* 38 F5
Shrub End *Essex* 30 F6
Shucknall *Heref'd* 26 D2
Shudy Camps *Cambs* 30 D3
Shulishadermor *H'land* 85 D9
Shurdington *Glos* 26 G6
Shurlock Row *Windsor* 18 D5
Shurrery *H'land* 93 D13
Shurrery Lodge *H'land* 93 D13
Shurton *Som'set* 7 B11
Shustoke *Warwick* 35 F8
Shute *Devon* 8 E1
Shute *Devon* 7 F7
Shutford *Oxon* 27 D10
Shuthonger *Glos* 26 E5
Shutlanger *Northants* 28 C4
Shuttington *Warwick* 35 E8
Shuttlewood *Derby* 45 E8
Siabost bho Dheas *W Isles* 90 C7
Siabost bho Thuath *W Isles* 90 C7
Siadar *W Isles* 91 B8
Siadar Iarach *W Isles* 91 B8
Siadar Uarach *W Isles* 91 B8
Sibbaldbie *Dumf/Gal* 61 E7
Sibbertoft *Northants* 36 G2
Sibdon Carwood *Shrops* 33 G10
Sibford Ferris *Oxon* 27 E10
Sibford Gower *Oxon* 27 E10
Sible Hedingham *Essex* 30 E4
Sibsey *Lincs* 47 G7
Sibson *Cambs* 37 F6
Sibson *Leics* 35 E9
Sibthorpe *Notts* 45 H11
Sibton *Suffolk* 31 B10
Sibton Green *Suffolk* 31 A10
Sicklesmere *Suffolk* 30 B5
Sicklinghall *N Yorks* 51 E9
Sid *Devon* 7 H10
Sidbury *Devon* 7 G10
Sidbury *Shrops* 34 G2
Sidcot *N Som'set* 15 F10
Sidcup *London* 19 D11
Siddick *Cumb* 56 C2
Siddington *Ches* 44 E2
Siddington *Glos* 17 B7
Sidemoor *Worcs* 26 A6
Sidestrand *Norfolk* 39 B8
Sidford *Devon* 7 G10
Sidlesham *W Sussex* 11 E7
Sidley *E Sussex* 12 F6
Sidlow *Surrey* 19 G9
Sidmouth *Devon* 7 H10
Sigford *Devon* 5 D8
Sigglesthorne *ER Yorks* 53 E7
Sighthill *C/Edinb* 69 C10
Sigingstone *V/Glam* 14 D5
Signet *Oxon* 27 G9
Silchester *Hants* 18 E3
Sildinis *W Isles* 91 F7
Sileby *Leics* 36 D1
Silecroft *Cumb* 49 A1
Silfield *Norfolk* 39 F7
Silian *Ceredig'n* 23 A10
Silk Willoughby *Lincs* 37 A6
Silkstone *S Yorks* 44 B6
Silkstone Common *S Yorks* 44 B6
Silloth *Cumb* 56 A3
Sills *Northum* 62 C4
Sillyearn *Moray* 88 C5
Siloh *Carms* 24 E4
Silpho *N Yorks* 59 G10
Silsden *W Yorks* 50 E6
Silsoe *Beds* 29 E7
Silver End *Essex* 30 G5
Silverburn *Midloth* 69 D11
Silverdale *Lancs* 49 B4
Silverdale *Staffs* 44 H2
Silvergate *Norfolk* 39 C7
Silverhill *E Sussex* 13 E6
Silverley's Green *Suffolk* 39 H8
Silverstone *Northants* 28 D3
Silverton *Devon* 7 F8
Silvington *Shrops* 34 H2
Silwick *Shetl'd* 96 J4
Simmondley *Derby* 44 C4
Simonburn *Northum* 62 F4
Simonsbath *Som'set* 7 C6
Simonstone *Lancs* 50 F3
Simprim *Scot Borders* 71 F7
Simpson *M/Keynes* 28 E5
Simpson Cross *Pembs* 22 E3
Sinclair's Hill *Scot Borders* 71 E7
Sinclairston *E Ayrs* 67 E7
Sinderby *N Yorks* 51 A9
Sinderhope *Northum* 57 A10
Sindlesham *Wokingham* 18 E4
Singdean *Scot Borders* 61 C11
Singleborough *Bucks* 28 E4
Singleton *Lancs* 49 F3
Singleton *W Sussex* 11 C7
Singlewell *Kent* 20 D3
Sinkhurst Green *Kent* 13 B7
Sinnahard *Aberds* 82 B6
Sinnington *N Yorks* 59 H8
Sinton Green *Worcs* 26 B5
Sipson *London* 19 D7
Sirhowy *Bl Gwent* 25 G8
Sisland *Norfolk* 39 F9
Sissinghurst *Kent* 13 C6
Sisterpath *Scot Borders* 70 F6
Siston *S Gloucs* 16 D3
Sithney *Cornw'l* 2 G5
Sittingbourne *Kent* 20 E5
Six Ashes *Staffs* 34 G3
Six Hills *Leics* 36 C2
Six Mile Bottom *Cambs* 30 C2
Sixhills *Lincs* 46 D5
Sixpenny Handley *Dorset* 9 C8
Sizewell *Suffolk* 31 B11
Skail *H'land* 93 E10
Skaill *Orkney* 95 G3
Skaill *Orkney* 95 E5
Skaill *Orkney* 95 H6
Skares *E Ayrs* 67 E8
Skateraw *E Loth* 70 C6
Skaw *Shetl'd* 96 G7
Skeabost *H'land* 85 D9
Skeabrae *Orkney* 95 F3
Skeeby *N Yorks* 58 F3
Skeffington *Leics* 36 E3
Skeffling *ER Yorks* 53 H9
Skegby *Notts* 45 F8
Skegness *Lincs* 47 F9
Skelberry *Shetl'd* 96 M5
Skelbo *H'land* 87 B10
Skelbrooke *S Yorks* 45 A9
Skeldyke *Lincs* 37 B9
Skellingthorpe *Lincs* 46 E3
Skellister *Shetl'd* 96 H6
Skellow *S Yorks* 45 A9
Skelmanthorpe *W Yorks* 44 A6
Skelmersdale *Lancs* 43 B7
Skelmonae *Aberds* 89 E8
Skelmorlie *N Ayrs* 73 G10
Skelmuir *Aberds* 89 D9
Skelpick *H'land* 93 D10
Skelton *Cumb* 56 C6
Skelton *ER Yorks* 52 G3
Skelton *N Yorks* 58 F1
Skelton *Redcar/Clevel'd* 59 E7
Skelton *C/York* 52 D1
Skelton-on-Ure *N Yorks* 51 C9
Skelwick *Orkney* 95 D5
Skelwith Bridge *Cumb* 56 F5
Skendleby *Lincs* 47 F8
Skene Ho. *Aberds* 83 C9
Skenfrith *Monmouths* 25 F11
Skerne *ER Yorks* 52 D6
Skeroblingarry *Arg/Bute* 65 F8
Skerray *H'land* 93 C9
Skerton *Lancs* 49 C4
Sketchley *Leics* 35 F10
Sketty *Swan* 14 B2
Skewen *Neath P Talb* 14 B3
Skewsby *N Yorks* 52 B2
Skeyton *Norfolk* 39 C8
Skiag Bridge *H'land* 92 G5
Skibo Castle *H'land* 87 C10
Skidbrooke *Lincs* 47 C8
Skidbrooke North End *Lincs* 47 C8
Skidby *ER Yorks* 52 F6
Skilgate *Som'set* 7 D8
Skillington *Lincs* 36 C4
Skinburness *Cumb* 61 H7
Skinflats *Falk* 69 B8
Skinidin *H'land* 84 D7
Skinnet *H'land* 93 C8
Skinningrove *Redcar/Clevel'd* 59 D8
Skipness *Arg/Bute* 73 H7
Skippool *Lancs* 49 E3
Skipsea *ER Yorks* 53 D7
Skipsea Brough *ER Yorks* 53 D7
Skipton *N Yorks* 50 D5
Skipton-on-Swale *N Yorks* 51 B9
Skipwith *N Yorks* 52 F2
Skirbeck *Lincs* 37 A9
Skirbeck Quarter *Lincs* 37 A9
Skirlaugh *ER Yorks* 53 F7
Skirling *Scot Borders* 69 G9
Skirmett *Bucks* 18 C4
Skirpenbeck *ER Yorks* 52 D3
Skirwith *Cumb* 57 C8
Skirza *H'land* 94 D5
Skulamus *H'land* 85 F11
Skullomie *H'land* 93 C9
Skyborry Green *Shrops* 25 A9
Skye of Curr *H'land* 82 A1
Skyreholme *N Yorks* 51 C6
Slackhall *Derby* 44 D4
Slackhead *Moray* 88 B4
Slad *Glos* 26 H5
Slade *Devon* 6 B4
Slade *Pembs* 22 E4
Slade Green *London* 20 D2
Slaggyford *Northum* 57 A8
Slaidburn *Lancs* 50 D3
Slaithwaite *W Yorks* 44 A4
Slaley *Northum* 62 H5
Slamannan *Falk* 69 C7
Slapton *Bucks* 28 F6
Slapton *Devon* 5 G9
Slapton *Northants* 28 D3
Slatepit Dale *Derby* 45 F7
Slattocks *Gtr Man* 44 B2
Slaugham *W Sussex* 12 D1
Slaughterford *Wilts* 16 D5
Slawston *Leics* 36 F3
Sleaford *Hants* 18 H5
Sleaford *Lincs* 46 H4
Sleagill *Cumb* 57 E7
Sleapford *Telford* 34 D2
Sledge Green *Worcs* 26 E5
Sledmere *ER Yorks* 52 C5
Sleightholme *Durham* 57 E11
Sleights *N Yorks* 59 F9
Slepe *Dorset* 9 E8
Slickly *H'land* 94 D4
Sliddery *N Ayrs* 66 D2
Sligachan Hotel *H'land* 85 F9
Slimbridge *Glos* 16 A4
Slindon *Staffs* 34 B4
Slindon *W Sussex* 11 D8
Slinfold *W Sussex* 11 A10
Sling *Gwyn* 41 D8
Slingsby *N Yorks* 52 B2
Slioch *Aberds* 88 E5
Slip End *Beds* 29 G7
Slip End *Herts* 29 E9
Slipton *Northants* 36 H5
Slitting Mill *Staffs* 34 D6
Slochd *H'land* 81 A10
Slockavullin *Arg/Bute* 73 D7
Sloley *Norfolk* 39 C8
Sloothby *Lincs* 47 E8
Slough *Slough* 18 D6
Slough Green *W Sussex* 12 D1
Sluggan *H'land* 81 A10
Slumbay *H'land* 85 E13
Slyfield *Surrey* 18 F6
Slyne *Lancs* 49 C4
Smailholm *Scot Borders* 70 G5
Small Dole *W Sussex* 11 C11
Small Hythe *Kent* 13 C7
Smallbridge *Gtr Man* 50 H5
Smallburgh *Norfolk* 39 C9
Smallburn *Aberds* 89 D10
Smallburn *E Ayrs* 68 H5
Smalley *Derby* 35 A10
Smallfield *Surrey* 12 B2
Smallridge *Devon* 8 D2
Smannell *Hants* 17 G10
Smardale *Cumb* 57 F9
Smarden *Kent* 13 B7
Smarden Bell *Kent* 13 B7
Smeatharpe *Devon* 7 E10
Smeeth *Kent* 13 C9
Smeeton Westerby *Leics* 36 F2
Smercleit *W Isles* 84 G2
Smerral *H'land* 94 G3
Smethwick *W Midlands* 34 G6
Smirisary *H'land* 79 D9
Smisby *Derby* 35 D9
Smith Green *Lancs* 49 D4
Smithfield *Cumb* 61 G10
Smithincott *Devon* 7 E9
Smith's Green *Essex* 30 F2
Smithstown *H'land* 85 A12
Smithton *H'land* 87 G10
Smithy Green *Ches* 43 E10
Smockington *Leics* 35 G10
Smoogro *Orkney* 95 H4
Smyth's Green *Essex* 30 G6
Snaigow House *Perth/Kinr* 76 C3
Snailbeach *Shrops* 33 E9
Snailwell *Cambs* 30 B3
Snainton *N Yorks* 52 A5
Snaith *ER Yorks* 52 G2
Snape *N Yorks* 51 A8
Snape *Suffolk* 31 C10
Snape Green *Lancs* 43 A6
Snarestone *Leics* 35 E9
Snarford *Lincs* 46 D4
Snargate *Kent* 13 D8
Snave *Kent* 13 D9
Snead *Powys* 33 F9
Sneath Common *Norfolk* 39 G7
Sneaton *N Yorks* 59 F9
Sneatonthorpe *N Yorks* 59 F10
Snelland *Lincs* 46 D4
Snelston *Derby* 35 A7
Snettisham *Norfolk* 38 B2
Snig's End *Glos* 26 F4
Sniseabhal *W Isles* 84 E2
Snitter *Northum* 62 C6
Snitterby *Lincs* 46 C3
Snitterfield *Warwick* 27 C9
Snitton *Shrops* 34 H1
Snodhill *Heref'd* 25 D10
Snodland *Kent* 20 E3
Snowden Hill *S Yorks* 44 B6
Snowdown *Kent* 21 F9
Snowshill *Glos* 27 E7
Snydale *W Yorks* 51 H10
Soar *Angl* 40 C5
Soar *Carms* 24 F3
Soar *Devon* 5 H8
Soar-y-Mynydd *Ceredig'n* 24 C4
Soberton *Hants* 10 C5
Soberton Heath *Hants* 10 C5
Sockbridge *Cumb* 57 D7
Sockburn *D'lington* 58 F4
Soham *Cambs* 30 A2
Soham Cotes *Cambs* 38 H1
Solas *W Isles* 84 A3
Soldon Cross *Devon* 6 E2
Soldridge *Hants* 10 A5
Sole Street *Kent* 20 E3
Sole Street *Kent* 21 G7
Solihull *W Midlands* 35 H7
Sollers Dilwyn *Heref'd* 25 C11
Sollers Hope *Heref'd* 26 E3
Sollom *Lancs* 49 H4
Solva *Pembs* 22 D2
Somerby *Leics* 36 D3
Somerby *Lincs* 46 B4
Somercotes *Derby* 45 G8
Somerford *Dorset* 9 E10
Somerford Keynes *Glos* 17 B7
Somerley *W Sussex* 11 E7
Somerleyton *Suffolk* 39 F10
Somersal Herbert *Derby* 35 B7
Somersby *Lincs* 47 E7
Somersham *Cambs* 37 H9
Somersham *Suffolk* 31 D7
Somerton *Oxon* 27 F11
Somerton *Som'set* 8 B3
Sompting *W Sussex* 11 D10
Sonning *Wokingham* 18 D4
Sonning Common *Oxon* 18 C4
Sonning Eye *Oxon* 18 D4
Sontley *Wrex* 42 H6
Sopley *Hants* 9 E10
Sopwell *Herts* 29 H8
Sopworth *Wilts* 16 C5
Sorbie *Dumf/Gal* 55 E7
Sordale *H'land* 94 D3
Sorisdale *Arg/Bute* 78 E5
Sorn *E Ayrs* 68 H4
Sornhill *E Ayrs* 67 C8
Sortat *H'land* 94 D4
Sotby *Lincs* 46 E6
Sots Hole *Lincs* 46 F5
Sotterley *Suffolk* 39 G10
Soudley *Shrops* 34 C3
Soughton *Flints* 42 F5
Soulbury *Bucks* 28 F5
Soulby *Cumb* 57 E9
Souldern *Oxon* 28 E2
Souldrop *Beds* 28 B6
Sound *Ches* 43 H9
Sound *Shetl'd* 96 H5
Sound *Shetl'd* 96 J6
Sound Heath *Ches* 43 H9
Soundwell *S Gloucs* 16 D3
Sourhope *Scot Borders* 62 A4
Sourin *Orkney* 95 E5
Sourton *Devon* 6 G4
Soutergate *Cumb* 49 A2
South Acre *Norfolk* 38 D4
South Allington *Devon* 5 H8
South Alloa *Falk* 69 A7
South Ambersham *W Sussex* 11 B8
South Anston *S Yorks* 45 D9
South Ascot *Windsor* 18 E6
South Ballachulish *H'land* 74 B3
South Balloch *S Ayrs* 66 G6
South Bank *Redcar/Clevel'd* 59 D6
South Barrow *Som'set* 8 B5
South Beach *Gwyn* 40 G5
South Benfleet *Essex* 20 C4
South Bersted *W Sussex* 11 D8
South Brent *Devon* 5 E7
South Brewham *Som'set* 16 H4
South Broomhill *Northum* 63 D8
South Burlingham *Norfolk* 39 E9
South Cadbury *Som'set* 8 B5
South Cairn *Dumf/Gal* 54 C2
South Carlton *Lincs* 46 E3
South Cave *ER Yorks* 52 F5
South Cerney *Glos* 17 B7
South Chard *Som'set* 8 D2
South Charlton *Northum* 63 A7
South Cheriton *Som'set* 8 B5
South Cliffe *ER Yorks* 52 F4
South Clifton *Notts* 46 E2
South Cockerington *Lincs* 47 D7
South Cornelly *Bridg* 14 C4
South Cove *Suffolk* 39 G10
South Creagan *Arg/Bute* 74 C2
South Creake *Norfolk* 38 B4
South Croxton *Leics* 36 D2
South Croydon *London* 19 E10
South Dalton *ER Yorks* 52 E5
South Darenth *Kent* 20 E2
South Duffield *N Yorks* 52 F2
South Elkington *Lincs* 46 D6
South Elmsall *W Yorks* 45 A8
South End *Bucks* 28 F5
South End *Cumb* 49 C2
South End *N Lincs* 53 G7
South Erradale *H'land* 85 A12
South Fambridge *Essex* 20 B5
South Fawley *W Berks* 17 C10
South Ferriby *N Lincs* 52 G5
South Garth *Shetl'd* 96 D7
South Garvan *H'land* 80 F1
South Glendale *W Isles* 84 G2
South Godstone *Surrey* 19 G10
South Gorley *Hants* 9 C10
South Green *Essex* 20 B3
South Green *Kent* 20 E5
South-haa *Shetl'd* 96 E5
South Ham *Hants* 18 F3
South Hanningfield *Essex* 20 B4
South Harting *W Sussex* 11 C6
South Hatfield *Herts* 29 H9
South Hayling *Hants* 10 E6
South Hazelrigg *Northum* 71 G9
South Heath *Bucks* 18 A6
South Heighton *E Sussex* 12 F3
South Hetton *Durham* 58 B4
South Hiendley *W Yorks* 45 A7
South Hill *Cornw'l* 4 D4
South Hinksey *Oxon* 18 A2
South Hole *Devon* 6 D1
South Holme *N Yorks* 52 B2
South Holmwood *Surrey* 19 G8
South Hornchurch *London* 20 C2
South Hykeham *Lincs* 46 F3
South Hylton *Tyne/Wear* 63 H9
South Kelsey *Lincs* 46 C4
South Kessock *H'land* 87 G9
South Killingholme *N Lincs* 53 H7
South Kilvington *N Yorks* 51 A10
South Kilworth *Leics* 36 G2
South Kirkby *W Yorks* 45 A8
South Kirkton *Aberds* 83 C9
South Kiscadale *N Ayrs* 66 D3
South Kyme *Lincs* 46 H5
South Lancing *W Sussex* 11 D10
South Leigh *Oxon* 27 H10
South Leverton *Notts* 45 D11
South Littleton *Worcs* 27 D7
South Lopham *Norfolk* 38 G6
South Luffenham *Rutl'd* 36 E5
South Malling *E Sussex* 12 E3
South Marston *Swindon* 17 C8
South Middleton *Northum* 62 A5
South Milford *N Yorks* 51 F10
South Millbrex *Aberds* 89 D8
South Milton *Devon* 5 G8
South Mimms *Herts* 19 A9
South Molton *Devon* 6 D6
South Moreton *Oxon* 18 C2
South Mundham *W Sussex* 11 D7
South Muskham *Notts* 45 G11
South Newbald *ER Yorks* 52 F5
South Newington *Oxon* 27 E11
South Newton *Wilts* 9 A9
South Normanton *Derby* 45 G8
South Norwood *London* 19 E10
South Nutfield *Surrey* 19 G10
South Ockendon *Thurr'k* 20 C2
South Ormsby *Lincs* 47 E7
South Otterington *N Yorks* 58 H4
South Owersby *Lincs* 46 C4
South Oxhey *Herts* 19 B8
South Perrott *Dorset* 8 D3
South Petherton *Som'set* 8 C3
South Petherwin *Cornw'l* 4 C4
South Pickenham *Norfolk* 38 E4
South Pool *Devon* 5 G8
South Port *Arg/Bute* 74 E3
South Radworthy *Devon* 7 C6
South Rauceby *Lincs* 46 H4
South Raynham *Norfolk* 38 C4
South Reston *Lincs* 47 D8
South Runcton *Norfolk* 38 E2
South Scarle *Notts* 46 F2
South Shian *Arg/Bute* 74 C2
South Shields *Tyne/Wear* 63 G9
South Shore *Blackp'l* 49 F3
South Somercotes *Lincs* 47 C8
South Stainley *N Yorks* 51 C9
South Stainmore *Cumb* 57 E10
South Stifford *Thurr'k* 20 D3
South Stoke *Oxon* 18 C2
South Stoke *W Sussex* 11 D9
South Street *E Sussex* 12 E2
South Street *London* 19 F11
South Street *Kent* 21 E8
South Street *Kent* 21 F7
South Tawton *Devon* 6 G5
South Thoresby *Lincs* 47 E8
South Tidworth *Wilts* 17 G9
South Town *Hants* 18 H3
South View *Hants* 18 F3
South Walsham *Norfolk* 39 D9
South Warnborough *Hants* 18 G4
South Weald *Essex* 20 B2
South Weston *Oxon* 18 B4
South Wheatley *Cornw'l* 4 B3
South Wheatley *Notts* 45 D11
South Whiteness *Shetl'd* 96 J5
South Widcombe *Bath/NE Som'set* 16 F2
South Wigston *Leics* 36 F1
South Willingham *Lincs* 46 D5
South Wingfield *Derby* 45 G7
South Witham *Lincs* 36 D5
South Wonston *Hants* 17 H11
South Woodham Ferrers *Essex* 20 B5
South Wootton *Norfolk* 38 C2
South Wraxall *Wilts* 16 E5
South Zeal *Devon* 6 G5
Southall *London* 19 C8
Southam *Glos* 26 F6
Southam *Warwick* 27 B11
Southampton *S'thampton* 10 C3
Southborough *Kent* 12 B4
Southbourne *Bournem'th* 9 E10
Southbourne *W Sussex* 11 D6
Southburgh *Norfolk* 38 E5
Southburn *ER Yorks* 52 D5
Southchurch *Southend* 20 C6
Southcott *Wilts* 17 F8
Southcourt *Bucks* 28 G5
Southdean *Scot Borders* 62 C2
Southdene *Mersey* 43 C7
Southease *E Sussex* 12 F3
Southend *Arg/Bute* 65 H7
Southend *W Berks* 18 D2
Southend *Wilts* 17 D8
Southend-on-Sea *Southend* 20 C5
Southernden *Kent* 20 G5
Southerndown *V/Glam* 14 D4
Southerness *Dumf/Gal* 60 H5
Southery *Norfolk* 38 F2
Southfield *Northum* 63 F8
Southfleet *Kent* 20 D3
Southgate *Ceredig'n* 32 H1
Southgate *London* 19 B9
Southgate *Norfolk* 39 C7
Southgate *Swan* 23 H10
Southill *Beds* 29 D8
Southleigh *Devon* 7 G11
Southminster *Essex* 20 B6
Southmoor *Oxon* 17 B10
Southoe *Cambs* 29 B8
Southolt *Suffolk* 31 B8
Southorpe *Peterbro* 37 E6
Southowram *W Yorks* 51 G7
Southport *Mersey* 49 H3
Southpunds *Shetl'd* 96 L6
Southrepps *Norfolk* 39 B8
Southrey *Lincs* 46 F5
Southrop *Glos* 17 A8
Southrope *Hants* 18 G3
Southsea *Portsm'th* 10 E5
Southstoke *Bath/NE Som'set* 16 E4
Southtown *Norfolk* 39 E11
Southtown *Orkney* 95 J5
Southwaite *Cumb* 56 B6
Southwark *London* 19 D10
Southwater *W Sussex* 11 B10
Southwater Street *W Sussex* 11 B10
Southway *Som'set* 15 G11
Southwell *Dorset* 8 G5
Southwell *Notts* 45 G10
Southwick *Hants* 10 D5
Southwick *Northants* 36 F6
Southwick *Tyne/Wear* 63 H9
Southwick *Wilts* 16 F5
Southwick *W Sussex* 11 D11
Southwold *Suffolk* 39 H11
Southwood *Norfolk* 39 E9
Southwood *Som'set* 8 A4
Soval Lodge *W Isles* 91 E8
Sowber Gate *N Yorks* 58 H4
Sowerby *N Yorks* 51 A10
Sowerby *W Yorks* 50 G6
Sowerby Bridge *W Yorks* 51 G6
Sowerby Row *Cumb* 56 C5
Sowood *W Yorks* 51 H6
Sowton *Devon* 7 G8
Soyal *H'land* 87 B8
Spa Common *Norfolk* 39 B8
Spacey Houses *N Yorks* 51 D9
Spadeadam Farm *Cumb* 61 F11
Spalding *Lincs* 37 C8
Spaldington *ER Yorks* 52 F3
Spaldwick *Cambs* 29 A8
Spalford *Notts* 46 F2
Spanby *Lincs* 37 B6
Sparham *Norfolk* 39 D6
Spark Bridge *Cumb* 49 A3
Sparkford *Som'set* 8 B5
Sparkhill *W Midlands* 35 G6
Sparkwell *Devon* 5 F6
Sparrow Green *Norfolk* 38 D5
Sparrowpit *Derby* 44 D4
Sparsholt *Hants* 10 A3
Sparsholt *Oxon* 17 C10
Spartylea *Northum* 57 B10
Spaunton *N Yorks* 59 H8
Spaxton *Som'set* 7 C11
Spean Bridge *H'land* 80 E4
Spear Hill *W Sussex* 11 C10
Speen *Bucks* 18 B5
Speen *W Berks* 17 E11
Speeton *N Yorks* 53 B7
Speke *Mersey* 43 D7
Speldhurst *Kent* 12 B4
Spellbrook *Herts* 29 G11
Spelsbury *Oxon* 27 F10
Spelter *Bridg* 14 B4
Spencers Wood *Wokingham* 18 E4
Spennithorne *N Yorks* 58 H2
Spennymoor *Durham* 58 C3
Spetchley *Worcs* 26 C5
Spetisbury *Dorset* 9 D8
Spexhall *Suffolk* 39 G9
Spey Bay *Moray* 88 B3
Speybridge *H'land* 82 A2
Speyview *Moray* 88 D2
Spilsby *Lincs* 47 F8
Spindlestone *Northum* 71 G10
Spinkhill *Derby* 45 E8
Spinningdale *H'land* 87 C9
Spirthill *Wilts* 16 D6
Spital Hill *S Yorks* 45 C10
Spital in the Street *Lincs* 46 D3
Spithurst *E Sussex* 12 E3
Spittal *Dumf/Gal* 54 D6
Spittal *E Loth* 70 C3
Spittal *H'land* 94 E3
Spittal *Northum* 71 E9
Spittal *Pembs* 22 D4
Spittal *Stirl* 68 B4
Spittal of Glenmuick *Aberds* 82 E5
Spittal of Glenshee *Perth/Kinr* 82 F3
Spittalfield *Perth/Kinr* 76 C4
Spixworth *Norfolk* 39 D8
Splayne's Green *E Sussex* 12 D3
Spofforth *N Yorks* 51 D9
Spon End *W Midlands* 35 H9
Spon Green *Flints* 42 F5
Spondon *Derby C* 35 B10
Spooner Row *Norfolk* 39 F6
Sporle *Norfolk* 38 D4
Spott *E Loth* 70 C5
Spratton *Northants* 28 A4
Spreakley *Surrey* 18 G5
Spreyton *Devon* 6 G5
Spridlington *Lincs* 46 D4
Spring Vale *S Yorks* 44 B6
Spring Valley *I/Man* 48 E3
Springburn *C/Glasg* 68 D5
Springfield *Dumf/Gal* 61 G9
Springfield *Essex* 30 H4
Springfield *Fife* 76 F6
Springfield *Moray* 87 F13
Springfield *W Midlands* 35 G6
Springhill *Staffs* 34 E5
Springholm *Dumf/Gal* 55 C11
Springkell *Dumf/Gal* 61 F8
Springside *N Ayrs* 67 C6
Springthorpe *Lincs* 46 D2
Springwell *Tyne/Wear* 63 H8
Sproatley *ER Yorks* 53 F7
Sproston Green *Ches* 43 F10
Sprotbrough *S Yorks* 45 B9
Sproughton *Suffolk* 31 D8
Sprouston *Scot Borders* 70 G6
Sprowston *Norfolk* 39 D8
Sproxton *Leics* 36 C4
Sproxton *N Yorks* 52 A2
Spurstow *Ches* 43 G8
Spynie *Moray* 88 B2
Squires Gate *Blackp'l* 49 F3
Srannda *W Isles* 90 J5
Sronphadruig Lodge *Perth/Kinr* 81 F9
Stableford *Shrops* 34 F3
Stableford *Staffs* 34 B4
Stacey Bank *S Yorks* 44 C6
Stackhouse *N Yorks* 50 C4
Stackpole *Pembs* 22 G4
Staddiscombe *Devon* 4 F6
Staddlethorpe *ER Yorks* 52 G4
Stadhampton *Oxon* 18 B3
Stadhlaigearraidh *W Isles* 84 E2
Staffield *Cumb* 57 B7
Staffin *H'land* 85 B9
Stafford *Staffs* 34 C5
Stagsden *Beds* 28 D6
Stainburn *Cumb* 56 D2
Stainburn *N Yorks* 51 E8
Stainby *Lincs* 36 C5
Staincross *S Yorks* 45 A7
Staindrop *Durham* 58 D2
Staines *Surrey* 19 D7
Stainfield *Lincs* 37 C6
Stainfield *Lincs* 46 E5
Stainforth *N Yorks* 50 C4
Stainforth *S Yorks* 45 A10
Staining *Lancs* 49 F3
Stainland *W Yorks* 51 H6
Stainsacre *N Yorks* 59 F10
Stainsby *Derby* 45 F8
Stainton *Cumb* 57 H7
Stainton *Cumb* 57 D6
Stainton *Durham* 58 E1
Stainton *Middlesbro'* 58 E5
Stainton *N Yorks* 58 G2
Stainton *S Yorks* 45 C9
Stainton by Langworth *Lincs* 46 E4
Stainton le Vale *Lincs* 46 C5
Stainton with Adgarley *Cumb* 49 B2
Staintondale *N Yorks* 59 G10
Stair *Cumb* 56 D4
Stair *E Ayrs* 67 D7
Stairhaven *Dumf/Gal* 54 D5
Staithes *N Yorks* 59 E8
Stake Pool *Lancs* 49 E4
Stakeford *Northum* 63 E8
Stalbridge *Dorset* 8 C6
Stalbridge Weston *Dorset* 8 C6
Stalham *Norfolk* 39 C9
Stalham Green *Norfolk* 39 C9
Stalisfield Green *Kent* 20 F6
Stalling Busk *N Yorks* 57 H11
Stallingborough *NE Lincs* 46 A5
Stalmine *Lancs* 49 E3
Stalybridge *Gtr Man* 44 C3
Stambourne *Essex* 30 E4
Stambourne Green *Essex* 30 E4
Stamford *Lincs* 36 E6
Stamford Bridge *Ches* 43 F7
Stamford Bridge *ER Yorks* 52 D3
Stamfordham *Northum* 62 F6
Stanah *Cumb* 56 E5
Stanborough *Herts* 29 G9
Stanbridge *Beds* 28 F6
Stanbridge *Dorset* 9 D9
Stanbrook *Worcs* 26 D5
Stanbury *W Yorks* 50 F6
Stand *Gtr Man* 43 B10
Stand *N Lanarks* 68 D6
Standburn *Falk* 69 C8
Standeford *Staffs* 34 E5
Standen *Kent* 13 B7
Standford *Hants* 11 A7
Standingstone *Cumb* 56 C2
Standish *Gtr Man* 43 A8
Standlake *Oxon* 17 A10
Standon *Hants* 10 B3
Standon *Herts* 29 F10
Standon *Staffs* 34 B4
Stane *N Lanarks* 69 E7
Stanfield *Norfolk* 38 C5
Stanford *Beds* 29 D8
Stanford *Kent* 13 C10
Stanford Bishop *Heref'd* 26 C3
Stanford Bridge *Worcs* 26 B4
Stanford Dingley *W Berks* 18 D2
Stanford in the Vale *Oxon* 17 B10
Stanford le Hope *Thurr'k* 20 C3
Stanford on Avon *Northants* 36 H1
Stanford on Soar *Notts* 35 C11
Stanford on Teme *Worcs* 26 B4
Stanford Rivers *Essex* 20 A2
Stanfree *Derby* 45 E8
Stanghow *Redcar/Clevel'd* 59 E7
Stanground *Peterbro* 37 F8
Stanhoe *Norfolk* 38 B4
Stanhope *Scot Borders* 69 H10
Stanhope *Durham* 57 C11
Stanion *Northants* 36 G5
Stanley *Derby* 35 A10
Stanley *Durham* 58 A2
Stanley *Lancs* 43 B7
Stanley *Perth/Kinr* 76 D4
Stanley *Staffs* 44 G3
Stanley *W Yorks* 51 G9
Stanley Common *Derby* 35 A10
Stanley Gate *Lancs* 43 B7
Stanley Hill *Heref'd* 26 D3
Stanlow *Ches* 43 E7
Stanmer *Brighton/Hove* 12 F2
Stanmore *London* 19 B8
Stanmore *Hants* 10 B3
Stanmore *W Berks* 17 D11
Stannergate *Dundee C* 77 D7
Stanningley *W Yorks* 51 F8
Stannington *Northum* 63 F8
Stannington *S Yorks* 45 D7
Stansbatch *Heref'd* 25 B10
Stansfield *Suffolk* 30 C4
Stanstead *Suffolk* 30 D5
Stanstead Abbotts *Herts* 29 G10
Stansted *Kent* 20 E3
Stansted Airport *Essex* 30 F2
Stansted Mountfitchet *Essex* 30 F2
Stanton *Glos* 27 E7
Stanton *Monmouths* 25 F10
Stanton *Northum* 63 E7
Stanton *Staffs* 44 H5
Stanton *Suffolk* 30 A6
Stanton by Bridge *Derby* 35 C9
Stanton-by-Dale *Derby* 35 B10
Stanton Drew *Bath/NE Som'set* 16 E2
Stanton Fitzwarren *Swindon* 17 B8
Stanton Harcourt *Oxon* 27 H11
Stanton Hill *Notts* 45 F8
Stanton in Peak *Derby* 44 F6
Stanton Lacy *Shrops* 33 H10
Stanton Long *Shrops* 34 F1
Stanton-on-the-Wolds *Notts* 36 B2
Stanton Prior *Bath/NE Som'set* 16 E3
Stanton St Bernard *Wilts* 17 E7
Stanton St John *Oxon* 28 H2
Stanton St Quintin *Wilts* 16 D6
Stanton Street *Suffolk* 30 B6
Stanton under Bardon *Leics* 35 D10
Stanton upon Hine Heath *Shrops* 34 C1
Stanton Wick *Bath/NE Som'set* 16 E3
Stanwardine in the Fields *Shrops* 33 C10
Stanwardine in the Wood *Shrops* 33 C10
Stanway *Essex* 30 F6
Stanway *Glos* 27 E7
Stanway Green *Suffolk* 31 A9
Stanwell *Surrey* 19 D7
Stanwell Moor *Surrey* 19 D7
Stanwick *Northants* 28 A6
Stanwick-St-John *N Yorks* 58 E2
Stanwix *Cumb* 61 H10
Stanydale *Shetl'd* 96 H4
Staoinebrig *W Isles* 84 E2
Stape *N Yorks* 59 G8
Stapehill *Dorset* 9 D9
Stapeley *Ches* 43 H9
Stapenhill *Staffs* 35 C8
Staple *Kent* 21 F9
Staple *Som'set* 7 B10
Staple Cross *E Sussex* 13 D6
Staple Fitzpaine *Som'set* 8 C1
Staplefield *W Sussex* 12 D1
Stapleford *Cambs* 29 C11
Stapleford *Herts* 29 G10
Stapleford *Leics* 36 D4
Stapleford *Lincs* 46 G2
Stapleford *Notts* 35 B10
Stapleford *Wilts* 17 H7
Stapleford Abbotts *Essex* 20 B2
Stapleford Tawney *Essex* 20 B2
Staplegrove *Som'set* 7 D11
Staplehay *Som'set* 7 D11
Staplehurst *Kent* 13 B6
Staplers *I/Wight* 10 F4
Stapleton *Bristol* 16 D3
Stapleton *Cumb* 61 F11
Stapleton *Heref'd* 25 B10
Stapleton *Leics* 35 F10
Stapleton *N Yorks* 58 E3
Stapleton *Shrops* 33 E10
Stapleton *Som'set* 8 B3
Stapley *Som'set* 7 E10
Staploe *Beds* 29 B8
Staplow *Heref'd* 26 D3
Star *Fife* 76 G6
Star *Pembs* 23 C7
Star *Som'set* 15 F10
Stara *Orkney* 95 F3
Starbeck *N Yorks* 51 D9
Starbotton *N Yorks* 50 B5
Starcross *Devon* 5 C10
Stareton *Warwick* 27 A10
Starkholmes *Derby* 45 G7

Y

Z